FOURTH UNCLE IN THE MOUNTAIN

FOURTH UNCLE IN THE MOUNTAIN

A Memoir of a Barefoot Doctor in Vietnam

Quang Van Nguyen and *Marjorie Pivar*

ST. MARTIN'S PRESS ✠ NEW YORK

Maps copyright © 2004 by Jeffrey L. Ward.

www.stmartins.com

Library of Congress Cataloging-in-Publication Data

Van Nguyen, Quang.
    Fourth uncle in the mountain : a memoir of a barefoot doctor in Vietnam/Quang Van Nguyen and Majorie Pivar.—1st ed.
        p. cm.
    ISBN 0-312-31430-2
    EAN 978-0312-31430-9
    1. Quang, Van Nguyen. 2. Healers—Vietnam—Biography. 3. Traditional medicine—Vietnam. 4. Medicine, Magic, mystic, and spagiric—Vietnam. 5. Magic—Vietnam. 6. Buddhism—Vietnam—Customs and practices. 7. Vietnam—Social life and customs. 8. Vietnam—Religious life and customs. I. Pivar, Majorie. II. Title.

GR313.Q83Q83 2004
615.8'52'092—dc22
[B]   2003066807

10 9 8 7 6 5 4 3

To my father, Thau Van Nguyen,

To our beloved teacher,

To the spirits of the forbidden mountain

Who helped others through us

And put food into our hands

CONTENTS

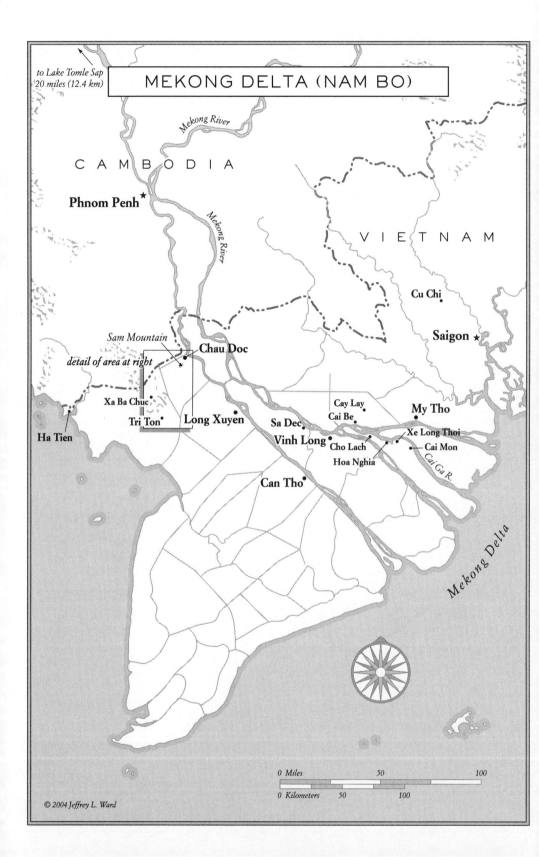

MEKONG DELTA (NAM BO)

to Lake Tomle Sap
20 miles (12.4 km)

Mekong River

C A M B O D I A

Phnom Penh ★

Mekong River

V I E T N A M

Cu Chi

Saigon ★

Sam Mountain

Chau Doc

detail of area at right

Xa Ba Chuc

Tri Ton

Long Xuyen

Sa Dec

Cay Lay

Cai Be

My Tho

Vinh Long

Xe Long Thoi

Cho Lach

Cai Mon

Hoa Nghia

Cai Ga R.

Ha Tien

Can Tho

Mekong Delta

0 Miles   50   100

0 Kilometers   50   100

© 2004 Jeffrey L. Ward

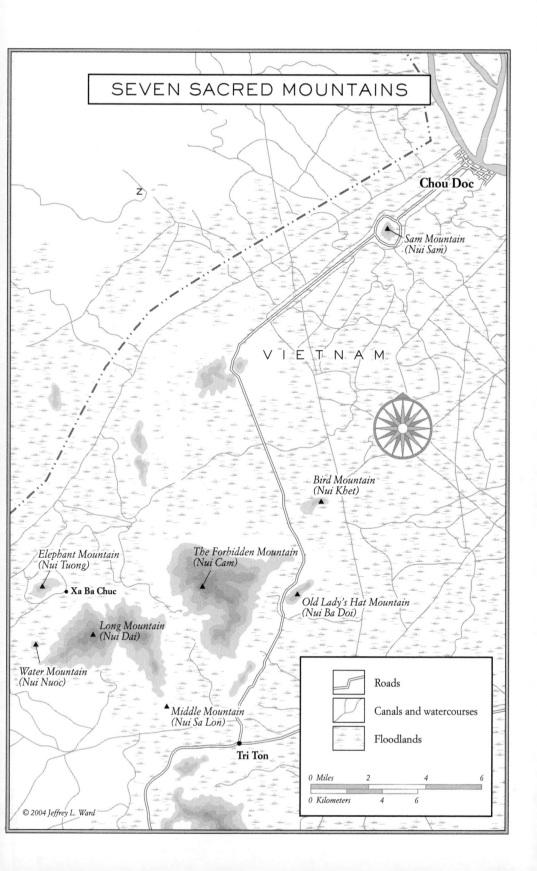

SEVEN SACRED MOUNTAINS

Chou Doc

*Sam Mountain
(Nui Sam)*

V I E T N A M

*Bird Mountain
(Nui Khet)*

*Elephant Mountain
(Nui Tuong)*

• **Xa Ba Chuc**

*The Forbidden Mountain
(Nui Cam)*

*Old Lady's Hat Mountain
(Nui Ba Doi)*

*Long Mountain
(Nui Dai)*

*Water Mountain
(Nui Nuoc)*

*Middle Mountain
(Nui Sa Lon)*

Tri Ton

	Roads
	Canals and watercourses
	Floodlands

0 Miles · 2 · 4 · 6

0 Kilometers · 4 · 6

© 2004 Jeffrey L. Ward

FOURTH UNCLE IN THE MOUNTAIN

In the realm of people, Good and Evil tumble in and out and through each other, and so weave the stories of nations. Many believe that Good will always overpower Evil, but I know that Evil has a marked advantage. Evil, according to its nature, stalks the earth like a hungry ghost and preys on us when we have lost heart, while Good sails up to heaven without leaving much of a trace at all. And so there are those among us who must consciously draw the Good back down to earth, where it may take root and grow strong in our hearts and minds, strong enough to subdue Evil.

I

MY FATHER COMES FOR ME

July 1959
Cai Mon Village, Mekong Delta, South Vietnam

One hot day in July, I looked up at the flesh-eating sun and taunted, "I can lick you with a flick of my hand. Oh, you don't believe me? Well, didn't you know that my father is the most powerful sorcerer in Vietnam? He can go to the forbidden mountain anytime he wants to. Watch out, I'm going to squash you like a lightning bug." I sucked in my breath so strong that I sucked the storm clouds closer and closer together until they banged into each other and snuffed out the fire-breather. They crashed together a second time and split themselves open like fish bellies full of roe and sprayed me with their wet bullets until they coated me in armor.

Our ducks appeared around my legs looking for worms, but I found them first and put them into my calabash gourd. I grabbed my net and my line and took off down the path to meet my friends. It was good fishing weather.

I was going to fish by the big bridge about half a mile from my house. It wasn't really bigger than any other bridge, it was just longer because it crossed over the widest river in Cai Mon. It was a kind of meeting place. In the blurry distance I thought I saw my father coming across the bridge. He didn't come to visit very often, only six or seven times a year.

I ran closer and peered at him through the raindrops. He was carrying so many packages that he could barely hold on to the handrail. Someone who didn't know who he was might have been alarmed to see an old monk balancing along a single bamboo pole in the rain with so many things in his arms, but I was never afraid for my father, even though he was older than a grandfather.

I wondered what kind of food he brought for us this time. He didn't eat much meat, but sometimes he brought sections of a roasted pig that he had received as payment for chanting at a funeral. He liked to bring me special treats we couldn't get in Cai Mon, like French butter cookies and coconut caramel and sugarcane rock candy. This time he was carrying more than usual. It was too good to be true. My mouth started watering. He called out to me, "Quang, hurry, take this before it falls into the river."

He handed me two bamboo birdcages full of birds. In his arms were three more cages. He must have just bought them from a birdcatcher at the Cai Mon bus stop.

"I didn't bring you any presents this time, because today I am taking you home with me."

"Can I go with you another time? Trung's father said that Trung and I could help him on his fishing boat this week." They fished on the Mekong and sometimes on the ocean. The best part was that on the way home Trung's father grilled up all the fish, lobsters, and shrimp we could eat.

"I don't think so, son."

We walked in single file back to the house. We always walked in single file so people going the other way could have room to pass on foot, bicycle, or motorbike. Nobody liked to step into the tall grass just in case a Communist guerrilla or a French soldier had put a land mine there overnight. I had to walk fast to keep up with my father.

A big canal ran through my aunt's backyard. We kept our boat moored to a tall willow tree that shaded the house. My favorite tree was in the front yard. It was a *trung ca* tree.

Aunt Gioi (pronounced Yoi) used the boat to stock up on provisions for her store. It would take us a long time to get to the market because she would always go on the smaller rivers, in order to avoid the big boats and ships on the Mekong River. Aunt Gioi told me that when she was a girl in Cai Mon, it was dangerous to go on the smaller rivers because of the crocodiles. She said that the oldest and wisest ones could hold on to the rushes, and whack you right out of your boat with their tails and gobble you up.

Even though Aunt Gioi had enough money to have a French-style house, she built a small thatched house with a dirt floor. You could say the dirt floor was one of the fanciest things about her house, because she had it prepared with sea salt and packed down very hard to keep the insects out. It was the color of ground coffee. Your feet would get muddy if they were wet. My aunt didn't mind me playing on the floor and getting my clothes all dirty even though she made them all and washed them herself.

Although she could have hired help, she didn't trust anyone in her house. She used to have people doing the housework and minding the store, but she was robbed many times. What they were really after were her gold teeth. All but four of my aunt's teeth were made of gold. She would take them out after meals to wash them. Every night before going to bed, she hid them carefully in case someone was looking in the window. She was afraid someone might try to sneak in while she was asleep and steal them right out of her mouth.

My aunt had no children of her own. After her husband died, she adopted a two-year-old orphan girl. When her daughter was eighteen years old, she robbed my aunt. The girl knew where my aunt kept her valuables buried under the floor. One day she came with her boyfriend, and they dug up all her money and jewelry. My aunt forgave her, but the girl kept stealing money until my aunt had to tell her to leave. That broke my aunt's heart because her daughter never came back home.

My aunt was seventy-three, but still strong like my father. Even though she was old, she still liked to look beautiful. Her husband had been a Catholic with a good job in the government. My aunt got used to being with French people and wearing French makeup. She colored her hair black and even wore a hair-piece to fill out her skimpy bun. If she ran out of makeup, she would lick red incense paper and rub it onto her cheeks and lips.

"What happened to the *trung ca* tree?" My father stopped short and was staring in disbelief at our missing tree. It was a shocking sight. Our house looked as if it was missing a vital organ. Our giant *trung ca* tree had been reduced to a stump about two feet high and four feet wide.

My aunt was always spanking me for climbing that tree, but I did it anyway. She didn't understand that tree was my mother, who would never drop me. I could climb to the top on a moonless night in the fog. I felt her strong, caressing arms against my body as I slid along her bark like a slippery eel so fast that she could never catch me. I was lucky to have a *trung ca* tree for my mother, because she was the wealthiest tree of all. She had many hidden chambers where she hung her jewels for me to eat all year round.

My *trung ca* tree was the tallest in our neighborhood. People treasured them, because they provided the thickest shade. I could sit at the top and throw stones at our neighbors' thatched roofs to warn the nestling mice that a green snake might be approaching. I could see the canals being sucked into the great dragon river and then see the water rising up again, later in the day, filled with more fish. From up there, I could see the blue smoke of the cooking fires and smell which of our neighbors were having fish for dinner and which of them were having just rice.

One evening I came home after helping our neighbors with their rice harvest and saw my tree sprawled across the yard. At first I thought it had been hit by a bomb. Sometimes the French hit our houses by mistake. They were bombing the jungle all around Cai Mon to kill the Communists who were hiding there. The Communists had already kicked the French out of the north and were trying to get us southerners to finish the job. But southerners are different; we like religion more than politics.

I screamed for Aunt Gioi, because I thought she was dead. She came running out of the kitchen clutching a handful of noodles. She looked at me and said sadly, "You climbed too high, Quang, I told you many times." It was true. She told me every day and I never listened.

I didn't cry when I saw Tien, my favorite storyteller, lying in his blood after a bomb hit his shelter. But when I saw my tree-mother's face pressed into the dust, straining to turn her head for a breath of air, the tears swarmed down my face like fire ants and bit into my sunburned cheeks.

I made contact with her contorted limbs and tried to find my place again. She couldn't hold me anymore. I turned my eyes respectfully away from her splayed limbs.

It took many days for the neighbors to cut her up and carry her away. I didn't ask where they were taking her.

"Quang, what happened to the tree?" my father repeated.

"Aunt Gioi gave it to the neighbors, because she was afraid I would fall."

My father set the finches, canaries, kingfishers, and lorikeets down under the jackfruit tree. Birdcatchers catch all kind of birds and sell them to people who roast them to eat. The rain had stopped and the mists rose up from the puddles like the spirits of fallen soldiers. My father's voice wafted through the muggy air like incense. He always chanted for the birds before letting them go. He prayed for them to find their mates again and for Buddha to keep them safe.

I interrupted, "Ba, If I go with you, when will I come back home to Cai Mon?"

My father took me by my shoulders and looked into my eyes and said, "When you were just a baby and I couldn't take care of you by myself, Aunt Gioi and I had made an agreement that you would live here with her until you were old enough to begin your education. You are nine years old now. It is time for you to begin your spiritual training and to learn about medicine. One day, you will become a healer and a medical doctor as your grandfather was. As I am. You will be able to help many people. It won't matter if you lose your house and all your money in the war. You will always be able to make a living with the tools that are inside of you, with your hands and your mind, with the plants that grow everywhere. From now on, you will live with me so I can teach you. We can always come back to visit."

He reached into one of the cages, and I heard my fluttering heart. His big hand fished around and came out with a golden canary. He drew a magic symbol in the air over the bird and whispered, "May Buddha guide you home."

My aunt came outside, and I took off like the bird. My legs carried me away like wings. I watched to see where they would bring me. Before I knew it, I was up in my neighbor's *trung ca* tree.

I looked down at Hoa's garden and fish pond. She was one of my best friends. I liked to go to her house to use her toilet. Aunt Gioi had an outhouse in the backyard. During the rainy season, my bare feet would get sucked into the slimy mud mixed with duck and chicken droppings. The smell of the mud and the outhouse used to make me feel sick. When we had guests at our house, my aunt would give them a shovel so they could go into the forest to do their business instead of visiting our outhouse. I begged my aunt to let me use the shovel, too, but she would not let me. She knew that I wouldn't bother to dig a hole every time.

Hoa had a fish pond toilet. Some people raised a kind of fish that likes to eat human waste. These fish are big and have a lot of meat. They have pink flesh like salmon but without scales, and they taste like shellfish. You have to climb up a bamboo ladder and step over a little stall onto a wooden platform that reaches out over the pond. There are two boards to place your feet while you squat and aim for the middle. The fish churn the water like angry sharks fighting to eat, but I bomb-blasted many fish right out of the water.

From up in the tree, I called out for Hoa, but my father found me first. There was a switch in his hand. Aunt Gioi had never used a switch on me. He stalked menacingly under my tree like a hungry tiger. In a calm voice, he told me that he wouldn't hit me if I came down right away. I didn't respond. This wasn't my father. It was just a crazy old man with a wet beard dressed in a patched-up old shirt wearing strange banana-leaf shoes. This wasn't my father, who could heal both the living and the dead, who spoiled me with money and presents, and who hugged me and told me stories about living in the jungle with monkeys, pythons, and tigers. This was a funny-looking person with no neck. I looked down at his turned-up face, a matted river otter. It couldn't be my father. I was overcome by a strange feeling, like the time I was bewitched by spirits one day when I was walking to my friend's house on the outskirts of our village.

For some reason, it was taking much longer to get there. I didn't understand what was happening, because I saw exactly where I was and I knew how much farther I had to go.

All the same, it seemed as if I would never get there. My legs started to ache as if I had been walking for hours. I tried to talk to some people, but they didn't see or hear me. That's when I realized the spirits were controlling my mind.

I remembered my father's words: "All you have to do to break the spell is to turn around and look between your legs in the direction you were heading." It worked. My village vanished, and I found myself at the far end of a rice paddy, headed into the jungle. I had no idea where I was, but I ran in the opposite direction until I came to a footpath and then to a house.

A man took me home in his boat. I was very lucky the ghost was invisible to me, because if it had assumed a human form and had offered me candy I wouldn't have been able to resist. Once you taste their food, you can't break the spell yourself. You would never come back unless somebody found you.

When I got home, there was already a search party out looking for me. Usually if a child was missing, people would think it was either a grenade or a ghost. In Cai Mon we had both.

When I came down from the tree, my father whipped my bottom one time. He said the next time I would get two.

It wasn't as if I'd never been caned. At school my teacher hit me a lot. I had gotten off to a bad start, and he didn't like me. During my first few weeks of school, someone stole my book bag. I was too ashamed to tell my aunt, so I carried my books to school. This was my downfall, because children in my village had to bow to every adult who said good morning to you. You had to fold your arms across your chest and bow your head. Well, there was no way I could keep up with the other kids, because every time I put my books down to bow, my papers would blow away. I was caned first thing every morning for arriving late.

One day I decided to look down at my feet the whole way to school so as not to see any adults. If they talked to me, I would pretend that I had just stepped on a thorn. This didn't work, because someone told on me and I got hit anyway.

My father's switch hurt my pride more than anything my teacher ever did to me. The sting propelled me back to the house, where I found my aunt sitting on

8

the stump of my tree, her face buried in her hands. My father told his sister not to bother packing my clothes, because we were leaving right away. She got up to hug me. I felt so sad to see her cry. My father promised his sister that he would bring me back every month to visit. Then my aunt reached into her pocket and gave me a shrew stone. I never knew she had one.

Shrew stones were the luckiest things you could find around our village. Shrews can't see well; that's why the babies form a chain behind the mother, each one holding on to the tail of the one in front. At night the mother shrew carries the stone in her mouth to light the way. I had seen the green light scooting across the floor in my aunt's house. I don't know where the shrews find the stones, because you can dig forever and never find a single rock. In the delta there is only river silt. It is very difficult to get a shrew stone away from the mother shrew. She will put it down to eat, but she is very mindful of her stone, because other shrews will sneak up and try to steal it. Some people trap the shrews to get their stones, but it only weakens the power of the stone.

I told my aunt that I wanted her to keep the stone for me, because she had the best hiding places. I wanted the stone's magic to keep her company, especially at night. In Vietnam, we have two kinds of pillows: one to rest your head and one long round one for hugging. When I was small, my aunt told me that she didn't need her hugging pillow anymore because she had me.

It took an hour to walk to the highway where the bus stopped. We could walk side by side most of the way. My father tried to cheer me up by handing me a tangerine, but I didn't take it.

From Cai Mon, it wasn't really a long way to Ben Cac, where my father lived, but it took about six hours or more, because we had to take three buses and two ferries, and then we had to walk some more.

The minivan bus pulled up, and as usual it was packed with people, animals, and things. I didn't like to ride on the bus, because it was so hot and smelly. It always took a long time to load everybody on and off while the conductor packed or unpacked the roof. The conductor told us to get on the bus even though all the seats were taken, and he made people move over to fit us in. He wasn't nice about it, either; bus drivers are really gangsters.

2

GOOD FRAGRANCE

FROM THE SACRED MOUNTAIN

While we were on the ferry, my father gave me a grapefruit. A big part of the branch was still attached to the stem. Even my father looked surprised as he handed it to me. Some people laughed, pointed at the grapefruit, and asked my father why he didn't leave the tree behind.

We got off the third bus at Cay Lay and walked down a street with many colorful shops in the Chinese neighborhood. The smell of roasting pork and frying noodles lured us toward an outdoor restaurant-bar.

"Would you like to try some Chinese food?" my father said.

Some of the other customers were dozing next to their cold drinks after a hard day's work. Outdoor restaurants and bars sometimes had hammocks for people to lie down and take a rest. The restaurant owners didn't usually mind if you slept for a while.

My father ordered me a plate of roasted pork with fried rice and salad. He ordered fish for himself. If it had been a fasting day he would have ordered tofu. In my religion there are certain days of the month when we are required to refrain from eating food made from animals and animal products. Most Buddhist people in Vietnam fast at least seven days a month, on certain days that are traditionally set aside for fasting: the first, fourteenth, fifteenth, eighteenth, twenty-third, twenty-ninth, and thirtieth day. I don't know why these are the designated fasting days.

After dinner my father sat down on one of the hammocks and kicked off his shoes. He pointed to the hammock next to his. "Let's take a rest before we walk to the house."

"I'm not tired," I answered. "Can I take a look in the shops?"

"No. Tomorrow we will come back and buy you some clothes and shoes. Come lie down. Would you like a custard apple or some chom choms? How about a mango?"

"I want some candy."

"I'll buy you some candy later. Here, take this."

He reached his arm over to the hammock next to his and dropped into it a handful of chom choms.

A chom chom is a kind of fruit that looks like a mouth-sized exploding firework. I climbed into the hammock and split open the pink, orange, and red spiky skin of a chom chom and popped the slippery white flesh into my mouth as if I weren't afraid to eat a dead, cold eyeball.

"Ba, if I am going to be like you, don't I need to learn some magic? Aunt Gioi's friend said your charms really work. She said that one time, when you stayed in Cai Mon, her son went to you every day, and you put a charm on his forehead so he could stand next to a tree and not be seen. She said the soldiers walked right past him several times when they had come to take people to the army. She said it was because of you that her son isn't fighting on either side."

My father said, "It is not easy to use magic to help people. Many people can do magic, but very few can do magic without causing more problems than they started out with. Magic is not important right now. You must learn how to help people with medicine."

"You help people with magic," I said.

"Medicine is more important."

I had finished all the chom choms and had tossed the hairy peels over the side of my hammock.

"Ba, can you buy me some candy now?"

My father felt around with his feet for the strange-looking shoes he liked to make out of banana-leaf twine, and we headed down the busy street to a bakery. He bought some mung bean, and moon pastries to take home, and some sugar-cane rock candy for me to eat along the way.

We followed the flow of outgoing traffic from the city to the villages. The dirt lane was crowded with bicycles, pedestrians, motorbikes, and larger motor-cycles. Many people wanted to talk to my father on our way to Ben Cac village. I didn't mind, because he wasn't paying attention to how much candy I was eating. Both he and Aunt Gioi didn't like me to eat too many sweets.

Even though my father's house looked identical to all the others, it was really a temple on the inside as well as a clinic. Most people kept two altars outside, one on the boundary of their land for the nature spirits, and one closer to the house for heaven and earth. My father kept a third altar for the little people we call the *cac dan*. Did you ever see a painting of the Buddha with lots of children climbing on him? Maybe you thought they were children, but they are supposed to be the *cac dan*. I will tell you more about them later.

In Vietnam, everyone, including my father, kept a family altar just inside the front door to remind you of your ancestors every time you entered your house. We believe it is our responsibility to send daily prayers to our ancestors. My father kept nine altars inside his front door. On each one was a tray of Chinese teacups, a statue or two, fresh fruit and flowers, red candles, and incense. He used up many packages of incense each day.

Whenever my father had a house, it was because some wealthy person had donated it to him. That was the customary way to keep a doctor nearby. The only people who could afford to donate a house for my father were landowners and people who worked for the French. That was only a handful of people. Most people had nothing to spare.

Housebuilding was something the villagers did for one another, because it cost too much money to pay a builder. All the materials to build the house could be found anywhere. The frame of the house was made from bamboo and other straight, slender trees, lashed together with banana-stem twine. The inner and outer walls were made of water-palm or lemongrass thatch.

That evening when we went to bed, my father told me about the master of his religion, Phat Thay Tay An, the Buddha Master of Western Peace, who founded a spiritual community in the That Son Bay Nui, the Seven Sacred Mountains at the western border of South Vietnam. My father said he was going to take me there to live when I was older.

Phat Thay Tay An, or To Thay for short (pronounced Toe Tie), was the son of a poor widow and had suffered from poor health all his life. He left his mother to study healing, meditation, and magic in South Vietnam and Cambodia. My father said that even though To Thay himself was not strong, he was able to use his healing powers to save the lives of many people during the cholera epidemic that happened in 1849, one hundred years before I was born. People started to love To Thay because he had healed so many. That is how he earned his title.

My father said that To Thay could predict the future. He told his followers that Vietnam would soon fall under foreign rule. Everyone thought he was referring to the Chinese, because China had conquered Vietnam two times in the past and had ruled for more than one thousand years. When the French became a governing force in South Vietnam 1867, eleven years after To Thay died, many people began to have faith in his divinations.

To Thay had also predicted that in a hundred years' time, the Vietnamese culture would be destroyed in a war of apocalyptic proportions. He told people that fire was going to fall from the sky and burn people alive, that the rivers would be poisoned, and that the earth would have the life burned out of it. He said we would be haunted by many tormented ghosts.

I told my father I didn't believe what the Buddha Master predicted. "The war is here now and people just hide underground in their bunkers."

My father said he hoped I was right.

Many people believed in To Thay and followed him into the wilderness of the Seven Sacred Mountains to build a new kind of spiritual community, in the hope of preserving the esoteric knowledge of Vietnam from the coming apocalypse.

In those days it was dangerous and almost impossible to reach the Seven Sacred Mountains. Each mountain was an impenetrable fortress of primordial jungle, home to elephant, python, panther, and tiger. Surrounded by crocodile-infested marshes and flood lands, the region was a no-man's land where bands of rebels and outlaws hid out, and mystics and hermits wandered.

The exodus into the Seven Sacred Mountains continued long after To Thay's death. Taoist sages, Zen Buddhist monks, and skilled Cambodian sorcerers who believed the Buddha Master's prophecy founded new villages and added their skills, wisdom, and knowledge to the community. Some of them knew how to communicate with the jungle animals, and they created a trust between the animals and the people.

This is how the Buddha Master of Western Peace created our religion. He called it *Buu Son Ky Huong*, which means "good fragrance from the sacred mountain."

In 1867, when my grandfather Ky Van Nguyen was twenty-five, he left Cai Mon for the Seven Sacred Mountains to study medicine, healing, and meditation with To Thay's followers. A few years later, he went to Nui Cam, the one mountain that was forbidden to be settled, in search of a teacher from whom he could learn more about meditation and the cultivation of power and wisdom. He lived alone on the forbidden mountain for a year before finding such a teacher. My grandfather lived in the cave with his teacher for ten years before returning home to Cai Mon, where he started a family and a medical practice. Several times during his life, my grandfather went back to the cave to study meditation with his teacher, about twenty-five years altogether.

My grandfather brought my father to do the same, and my father said he would take me. So far my father had spent about twenty years meditating with the teacher in the cave.

My grandfather, my father, and others who studied healing in the Seven Sacred Mountains were known throughout South Vietnam as *cuu dan do the*, the ones who healed people and rescued mankind. I grew up knowing that my father was important and that many people loved and needed him, but I didn't pay much attention to that. To me, he was just my father.

My father told me about his religion that first night at his house, and about the responsibility he carried for our people. He said that he was passing that responsibility on to me, and that over time I would master the skills and acquire enough power to be able to help many people, too. That night, my father told me many things about the person I would become in the future, but he didn't tell me who I really was until I was fifteen.

Now I am going to tell you a story about who I really am and who my father really was. I will start from when I was just a few months old. By the time I finish telling you all the things I learned when I was fifteen, we will end up back at my father's house, the next morning, on the day I began my education with my father.

3

THE YEAR I WAS BORN

September 1950
Cho Lach Village, Mekong Delta, South Vietnam

The early-morning sun was muted by shreds of white mist rising from the muddy, meandering waterways like cocoons of unraveling silk. Men and women in earth-tone-colored pajamas and conical sun hats rode their canoes and sampans over the rippling wakes of other boats. They stood or crouched on the stern decks of their boats, a triangular platform just wide enough for their feet, and rowed or paddled their way to market.

Some were carrying items to sell at the market, baskets of fresh fruit and vegetables from their gardens, mounds of polished rice from the mill, or buckets of this morning's catch.

Boats were jammed five rows deep at the market quay with all the coming and going. Some villagers chose to do all their buying and selling directly from their boats without bothering to wait for a spot at the pier.

At eight o'clock in the morning, just like every other morning at the Farmers' Market in Cho Lach, the French national anthem hissed and crackled over a tinny loudspeaker that was wired to the flagpole. Everyone had to stop doing business, face the flag, and stand at attention. Police in white uniforms scanned the crowd and swung their batons as a warning. If you were caught talking, you would have to pay a fine or go to jail. Either way, it meant your family would go hungry.

It was the anthem that woke me. When the song was over, everyone at the market could hear me crying from inside a covered basket that seemed to have appeared out of nowhere at the foot of the flagpole. Suddenly there was a large audience listening to me, as if my angry, trembling infant screams had been deliberately added to the tail of the anthem as an ironic commentary. The villagers remained silent a few moments longer than usual before reverting to a swarming mass of buyers and sellers that spilled out the sides of the open-air pavilion.

I continued to cry amidst the activity around me. As the morning progressed, it became obvious that my mother was not coming back for me. It wasn't unusual for babies to be abandoned at the market, because people were starving. Everybody knew that if a stranger came up to you and asked you to mind her baby while she went to the toilet, you would think twice about it.

In 1950, there was a war going on in Vietnam, the Indochina War. Even though the fighting and the famine were mostly in the north, we in the south also suffered, because rice farmers were required to give a percentage of their rice harvest to the French to feed their army and to be sold on the European market for a profit. If for some reason a farmer's rice crop failed, he or she would have to come up with his biannual quota of rice somehow or go to prison. After paying this rice tax, most families had barely enough rice to feed their children one meal a day.

Some of the villagers, mostly women and children, made their way to the flagpole, to my basket. When they lifted the lid, they were surprised to see how tiny I was. I couldn't have been more than three months old. I was lying on my back, naked, on a stained and soiled cloth. My face was all slimy with mucous, tears, and sweat.

Nobody ventured to pick me up. Perhaps they were frozen with pity, or maybe they were afraid they would get stuck with me and have to take me home.

Several of the market children wanted to carry me down to the river to cool me off, but the adults wouldn't let them. Instead, they gave them a cloth to dip into the water and bring back, so they could wash my face and drip water into my mouth. The children wriggled their way in and surrounded my basket. They tried to cheer me up, but I was far too young to respond to their playful hands and faces.

Children as young as five years old came to the market on their own, to sell whatever they could find. They were from the poorest and most desperate families. Many of them saw their siblings die of starvation, and many had fathers and mothers who were locked up in prison. Some didn't even know where their parents were. People generally regarded these children as beggars and wouldn't think of buying food from them, because they often ripped the fruit off the trees so carelessly that they would tear off the unripe fruit along with the ripe. Their leafy greens looked as if they had been yanked from the side of the road where someone might have peed on them. The market children were never allowed to sit inside the pavilion with the established vendors, so they had to look for a spot of shade under a tree.

Some of the farmers who had regular concession stands came forward and said they saw a woman who could have been my mother earlier that morning. They saw her ducking through the crowd as if she were afraid to be seen. Two friends who had walked to market together at daybreak told the group they saw a woman running like the devil toward the forest. "We just took one look at her and knew she was fleeing for her life. All we could do for her was to say a prayer."

Some others went to the flagpole to report that they had seen my parents around Cho Lach but didn't know their names or where they were from. They said my parents just showed up one day out of nowhere and kept to themselves. It was assumed that they were living somewhere in the forest. My father looked like a monk who had stopped shaving his head. People thought he must have been in trouble, because he didn't even come looking for a midwife when I was born. Everyone knew instinctively not to approach or befriend my parents. We Vietnamese have learned that butting your nose into someone else's business could mean the difference between life and death for everyone involved.

Sensing that the adults were distracted in conversation, one of the children lifted me out of my basket and snuck me down to the river accompanied by the others. The children waded between the boats and dipped my feet into the opaque, silty water, and I screamed even louder.

By then word had gotten around about the abandoned baby and the mysterious couple who were in trouble with the French. More people gathered around my basket at the flagpole. They took off their rubber flip-flops to sit on, or else took a banana leaf. They set their baskets all around mine and proceeded as they would at a village meeting.

Someone reported that a body had been found in a ditch that morning on the outskirts of one of the hamlets. It was my father, the runaway monk. He had been shot.

The children brought me back. "He won't stop screaming. He wants his mother." They put me back inside my basket just as miserable as when they took me out.

When Thau Van Nguyen (pronounced Tao Van Wing) arrived at the market with his wife Co, he was immediately informed about the troubling news and escorted to the meeting at the flagpole. Thau was a monk and doctor who carried great responsibility for his people. He had studied for twenty years in the Seven Sacred Mountains with the most learned and powerful monks and healers in all of Vietnam, and he practiced an ancient lineage of Chinese medicine. The market children knew and loved Thau, not because of his reputation, but because he was their best customer. Thau reached into his pockets for treats and distributed them to the small reaching hands that crowded around him. The villagers called him by his nickname, "Ong Sau," which means he was the fifth-born child of his parents.

Although he was a high-ranking monk, Thau didn't believe in spending his life meditating within the sanctuary of a temple. Instead, he planted himself in the villages and worked seven days a week to help anyone who came seeking him. He and his wife sat down with the others.

The villagers explained, "The soldiers killed a runaway monk this morning. The monk's wife ran away and left their baby behind."

Thau shook his head sadly. "The French are building a national army now with money from the Americans. French soldiers have been entering temples and drafting the monks. This one must have escaped. Up until now, the French have been very careful about handing out weapons to us. Even the civil and prison guards have had to make do with truncheons. The Communist revolution is spreading south. The French don't have enough men. They have no choice but to train us to fight in their army."

"But why would the soldiers go through all that trouble just to hunt down one runaway monk?" asked a villager.

"And why would they bother to go after his wife?" added another.

Thau lifted his hand to stroke his beard and think.

The old monk hadn't any children of his own. At sixty-four, he was unusually tall and strong for a Vietnamese. His gray hair and beard were long and neatly combed. He wore his hair in a topknot held in place with a stick. He had sewn so many patches onto his collarless button-down shirt that it was impossible to determine its original cloth.

Nobody spoke. Everyone was waiting for Thau to respond. He closed his eyes. He seemed to be listening to my miniature fury. When he opened his eyes again, they were filled with sadness. He said, "The soldiers who killed the runaway monk went after his wife, too. If she had not left her infant son behind, he would also have been killed."

Then, speaking to the women, he said, "What this means is that the soldiers will not only kill you if your husbands refuse the draft, but they will kill your entire family so your children won't join the other side."

My presence suddenly took on a portentous meaning.

Thau continued, "We are being led as captives into a devastating war. Each and every one of us will be forced to take sides. Neighbor will turn against neighbor, brother against brother."

Nobody dared to breathe. Vietnamese peasants must be among the toughest people on earth. We have learned to expect a life of backbreaking labor, hunger, fear, heartbreak, and brutality, but we always had our family and our neighbors to rely on.

A breeze kicked up. It grew stronger until it blew the hats off people's heads to hang by wide bands of cloth on their backs. The French flag began to snap its red, white, and blue stripes like a whip. Then the wind died out.

"What should we do about this baby?" someone asked the group. Nobody spoke up.

One of the children said, "Ong Sau, why don't you take him?"

Someone added, "You have no heir. You can teach him your skill."

Thau gathered up his beard and flicked it. He looked at his wife, Co. It would never work. She didn't like children much, and he was no more than a fugitive himself, hiding out in the jungle for days, weeks, and even months at a time.

You see, after the Buddha Master died, two of his apostles became involved in the peasant rebellions to drive out the French. Believing their leader's prophecy, they hoped that by driving out the French, they could change the outcome of the predicted apocalypse.

It wasn't long before the French sent their spies into the Seven Sacred Mountains to keep track of the "Sky Warriors." They knew that Thau was an important and well-respected member of the Buddha Master's sect, so he remained on their wanted list for decades.

The adults agreed, "Ong Sau, you have no child, no heir to pass on your knowledge. Why don't you take him?"

They took me out of my basket and put me into Co's arms. She had a beautiful face, but she didn't smile much. She didn't feel natural with me, so she handed me to her husband. That was when I stopped crying. I quieted myself down and took a good look at him.

Thau looked at me and then at his wife. Without saying anything, he put me back inside my basket, picked it up, and walked off to comb the market for a baby bottle.

This was the day Thau Van Nguyen became my father.

4

BANANA HAMMOCK

Thau had never considered having a child of his own, or a wife either for that matter, but he got both. He didn't even like to own anything except the clothes on his back and his medicine bag. He would say, "I'm like a boat. If I carry too much, I will tip over."

Thau, my new father, carried me back to his house. Some of the market children came along in the excitement, exercising their only privilege, which was to be perpetually unsupervised. My new mother lagged farther and farther behind.

The children scampered barefooted down the coral-colored clay footpath that ran next to the canal, scooting past villagers returning from market. Women, squatting at the water's edge, glanced up from their washing and noticed the odd procession.

"We have found an heir for Ong Sau!" the street children boasted.

Neighborhood people paddled leisurely by with children and empty baskets in their canoes. In those days, people grew what they needed plus a little extra to sell.

Every now and then, the market children disappeared up an especially inviting *trai sang* tree and reappeared with sticky blue hands and faces. Thau decided to stop and wait for his wife to appear round the bend.

Bicycles and an occasional moped whizzed by on either side. Small children, barely old enough to walk, assumed full responsibility for their ride. They clung to the handlebars and dug their feet into the diagonal crossbar between the cyclist's legs. One or two riders on the back fender held on to infants and other cargo.

I was still asleep in my basket. My new father took the opportunity to study my face and to say a prayer for my unfortunate parents. It was clear that Co had stopped somewhere along the way. Just ahead he heard the sounds of the market children gathering at a water cistern. It was a custom for people to keep some water in the front yard next to the path for passersby, but before you dip in, you must first call out hello.

One of them called out, "Hello, hello to the master of this house. Thank you for some water."

Up from behind a mound of cucumber vines rose a crabby old person of undeterminable gender. Bowing respectfully, another child fumbled, "Um . . . Uh . . . did you hear the good news? We have found an heir for Ong Sau."

Thau joined the children in a cup of water and then sent them on their way.

You know when you are approaching my father's house, because he burns a lot of incense. The smoke keeps the mosquitoes and the bad energy away.

When my father reached his house, there were no patients waiting in his yard. Usually there were crowds of people there all day long. He kept the clinic open seven days a week on a first-come-first-serve basis. People came to him for medical care and for help when they were in trouble with the police. My father's prayers were strong, and he knew many magic charms to make people well and to keep them safe. When he traveled to another village to check up on his patients, he would usually find a line of people outside his patients' houses, waiting to be blessed by him. For some reason, though, whenever he left for the day, no patients would show up at his house. I didn't ask him how this happened until the very end of his life.

He brought me into the tiny bedroom and set my basket down on the bed. Then he went outside to build two cooking fires out of dried coconut husks and brush. Over one, he put my glass baby bottle and nipple up to boil. He went back inside the house for his grindstone to make my rice formula. He ground some rice, measured four teaspoons of the powder into two cups of water, and cooked it on the other fire, stirring it with a wooden spoon until it turned milky. When my formula was done, he poured it into the baby bottle and left it inside a hollow coconut to stay warm.

It was time for my father's siesta. He brought the coconut into the bedroom and set it on the dirt floor next to his bed. During the heat of the day, it was much cooler to nap in a hammock, swinging up a little breeze. As usual, he tied up his banana-twine hammock so that it hung over his bed. My father swung himself to sleep above me, listening to the whistling of my little nose.

5

HOW MY PARENTS MET

My parents met under unusual circumstances.

In 1912, when she turned twelve, my mother came down with a terrible skin disease that covered her legs from the knees down. Spongy, raised sores protruded from her skin like red and white cauliflowers oozing with blood and pus. The swelling caused her so much pain that she had to keep her legs elevated on pillows at night so she could sleep. My mother came from a landowning family in Tan Thuyen, not far from Cho Lach.

Her parents summoned many doctors to the house, and they tried everything they knew to cure her, but not one of them could. One of their servants designed a special chair for my mother. It was a bamboo chair that was upholstered with cotton and silk. Underneath the chair he fastened a wheel that he had removed from a cart, and on the back of the chair he attached two handles that he had carved from wood so the servants could push her around the house and take her on outings.

My mother wasn't kind to start out with, but all her suffering made her more difficult. She felt sorry for herself and began ordering her personal servants and her parents around. Her mother and father loved her very much; she was their only child. They tried everything they could think of to please her. They bought her fancy mechanical toys and dolls made in France. They hired a music tutor to teach her to sing and play the lute, but my mother didn't try. Since her mother and her father occasionally traveled to Saigon, they were able to buy exquisite silks from Thailand and China and have them made into beautiful dresses for their daughter. Co wore dresses that were fit for a princess. Every day, the servants dressed her like royalty and took her on long outings in her wheelchair, but it seemed the more they tried to please her, the more difficult she became.

The sickness continued through her teens and twenties, and my mother gave up hope of ever marrying or having a normal life. It was worse for her parents to see her suffering in loneliness. Co had become used to her solitude. She was used to having her every request granted by her parents and her servants.

When she was twenty-eight years old, she started having recurring dreams about an old man with a long white beard. He would talk to her and say things like, "Go to the market tomorrow morning. There will be a man there who can help you. You must love him and marry him."

The old man visited her dreams about twice a month. Co finally told her mother about them. My grandmother told my mother not to pay attention to the dreams. She could not bear to have her daughter suffer any more disappointment.

That old man kept appearing in Co's dreams for months, telling her to go to the market on certain days and to look for the man who would be able to cure her of her disease.

Co became convinced that the old man was real and that what he was telling her was true. Eventually her parents believed in the dream, too. They told their daughter, "Next time that old man comes, we'll do whatever he says."

About three weeks later, the old man of her dreams returned and said, "Tomorrow, go to the Chinese apothecary. The man who can help you will be there. You must love him and marry him." Co woke up in the dark and called for her parents. The lamps were lit and her servants were summoned. Her bathwater was warmed on the fire, and she was brought outside to be bathed under the stars. Co chose one of her most beautiful silk dresses to wear.

At sunrise, Co was sitting in her boat with her wheelchair, looking very beautiful and smelling like jasmine. Her servants rowed her to the market along the canals, steering through the noisy market traffic. Co was used to being stared at, but this time they were staring because she looked so beautiful.

Her servant pushed her into the Chinese apothecary, and left her there. My father was there ordering medicine. When she saw him, she couldn't believe her eyes. He looked like a poor peasant. At forty-two years old, he had just come back from living for sixteen years on the forbidden mountain.

When my father turned around, he was startled by the sight of the beautiful young lady who appeared out of nowhere as if sitting on a throne.

Co thought, "This couldn't be the doctor I am looking for." Still, she had better make sure. She asked my father, "Are you buying medicine?" He told her that he was going home to prepare medicine for some people who were sick. Then she asked, "Would you mind stepping out of the store so we can talk in private?" My father wheeled her outside and looked for a nice shady tree. Then she lifted her dress and asked, "Do you have anything for my legs?"

My father understood her sickness. "Oh, that's easy." His confidence made Co think that she had found the man who could cure her. She told my father about the old man who visited her in her dreams. She said, "I am supposed to marry you." He told her, "Thank you very much, but I do not have time for a wife or for children. Wait here while I order your medicine." My father walked back into the store.

When he came out again, he was holding a large paper bundle of medicinal herbs. He told her how to cook the medicine and to soak her legs in it. He added, "Just open the packets and pour them into the pot. Do not touch them or they will not be strong."

When Co returned home with the medicine, she told her mother that she was relieved that the man in rags did not want to marry her. Her mother began preparing the medicine right away, but when she looked at the contents she was certain they were the same herbs that they had tried before. The bubble of their shared dream burst. Her mother could barely stop the tears that welled up in her eyes. She thought, "I should never have believed her. Now she will become more depressed than ever." Her mother cooked the medicine anyway and made sure not to touch the grasses, bark, leaves, and flower buds.

Co soaked her legs in the cooked medicine for twenty minutes. The next day her pain was gone, and she felt better. Servants were sent for more medicine. After three more treatments, Co's legs were completely healed for the first time in sixteen years. She was very happy for about three months, but then the sores came back.

This time her disease was worse. Co forgot about my father. She went to other doctors. Whenever she soaked her legs in medicine, the water became red with blood and pus. Her parents took her to Saigon in hopes of finding a good French doctor, but every doctor they consulted wanted to amputate Co's legs from the knees down. Co cried every day.

Then one night the old man returned. He said, "I told you that you have to love the man who helped you. If you don't love him and marry him, you will be sick your whole life. Go and find him." When Co told her parents about the dream, they realized that she hadn't followed the old man's advice.

The servants were sent to my father's house. When they returned, they said that his house had been burned down. Nobody knew where my father had gone, or whether the French had put him in prison or had him killed. More servants were hired to go to the prisons to inquire about him. They searched the neighboring villages and provinces, but none came back with any news.

The French had a hard time catching my father, because he was able see into the future. By the time the soldiers reached his house, he was already living in the forest in another province on a hammock that he wove out of banana-leaf twine. During the day, he filled his medicine bag with medicinal herbs he collected in the jungle, and he would go to the villages to treat the sick, get a little money, and buy some cooked food.

My father was happy to be living with the animals once again. Every night, many different kinds of animals came to sleep on or around his hammock. Snakes coiled around the ropes, poisonous and nonpoisonous alike. Monkeys and birds slept in the branches of the trees, and mice slept in my father's clothes. Frogs croaked all around the spot, and even insects like walking sticks and butterflies gathered in the trees. The animals came, because my father's essence was good.

Each morning, my father warned the animals, "Animals, you have to move. Go hide in the jungle. If you stay, hunters might find you and kill you." So the animals went away each day and returned in the evening.

That is why my mother's servants could not find him. My mother prayed to Buddha every day and every night to tell her if my father was alive. She waited many months for the old man in her dreams to come back, but he never came.

She decided to go out looking for him herself. Six servants were hired to carry her in a litter from town to town. At night they slept in the homes of many people, both rich and poor. They asked these people if they knew my father.

In one of the villages near where my father lived, there was an old man with an ax who worked in the jungle, chopping firewood. One day, Co spotted him in the marketplace selling his wood. Since he looked very much like the old man in her dreams, she asked him, "Do you know a sturdy-looking man dressed in a patched-up shirt who knows about medicine and came here from another province?" Then she told the old woodcutter about her dreams and her mission to marry that man.

The old woodcutter had seen the hammock in the jungle and a man who fit that description. He told my mother to check back in a few days. During the next days the woodcutter went to chop wood near my father's hammock. When my father passed by, he would begin a conversation, like, "Why isn't a handsome young man like you happily married?" My father told him, "I am poor; I have nothing. I must live in the forest. I would not make a good husband."

The old woodcutter made a point of having a conversation with my father every time he saw him and deliberately brought up the idea of marriage. The woodcutter reassured him, "You are young and strong. You can make a good living as a doctor. I am sure you could be loved by a wonderful woman."

My mother waited at the market every day for the old woodcutter to return. One day she spotted him arriving at the market, carrying his bundles of firewood on either end of a strong stick that he carried across his shoulders. The old woodcutter led my mother and her servants into the forest to a spot where my father often went to collect medicine. He was there.

When my father saw Co sitting in her litter, he was surprised, because he thought she had been cured. He asked if she had taken the medicine. She replied, "I'm sorry, but the old man in my dreams said I must love you and marry you and only then will I be cured." My father said nothing. My mother said, "If you don't want to marry me, I will be your servant."

My father told my mother that he needed three days to find the right medicine. She was to meet him in three days. He had to find certain plants as well as a black ox. There is a certain ox whose dung contains a strong medicine. When the time came, my father had prepared a very strong medicine for Co to soak her legs in. Afterward, he smeared the dung from the black ox onto her legs. He told her she had to keep the dung on until it was dry. In a few days she was better, but the muscles in her legs were still too weak for her to walk very far.

Co begged my father to come home with her and marry her, but my father could not imagine having a wife. He was a fugitive. Co went crying to him every day. After a while, my father couldn't stop wondering about the old man in her dreams. He thought, "Maybe it is my destiny to marry Co. Maybe this has all been arranged in heaven."

In the end he gave in.

.   .   .

Co's parents were overjoyed that their daughter's dream had come true. Co was walking for the first time in so many years and would have a normal life as the wife of a doctor. It was of no concern to them that my father was poor.

Co's parents arranged a beautiful and generous wedding to express their gratitude to Buddha for their good fortune. All their tenants and laborers were invited to bring their families for a feast. Afterward, a fancy new French-style house was built for my parents out of cement. My mother told my father that he no longer had to work, because her parents would support them for the rest of their lives. My father told her that he was given responsibility from Buddha to help people and that he had no choice but to continue his work. Since his wife didn't permit him to have a clinic at the house, my father traveled to his patients' homes. Sometimes he stayed away for days or weeks at a time.

Once when he was away, Co arranged for locks to be put on all the doors of the house, and iron grilles to be installed on all the windows. When he returned, she locked him inside and told the servants not to let him out, because the soldiers were looking for him again.

My father demanded to be let out, but the servants refused, thinking they were acting in his best interest. My father sent a letter to one of his wealthy patients who owned a car, asking him to personally deliver to him two rolls of tobacco wrapped up in paper. Two rolls were enough for ten packs of cigarettes.

My father paced his room like a caged animal for the next few days. Finally, the sound of a car brought my father to the barred window. The servants let the distinguished visitor into the house.

My father thanked his patient for coming and explained a few things to him. Then he unwrapped the tobacco and started eating it. The patient watched in disbelief as my father swallowed an entire roll. He saw my father's face begin to puff up and watched in horror as my father lay down on his bed, groaning with pain. Thirty minutes later, the skin on my father's face became swollen and raw, and eventually turned brown and blue.

My father nodded to his patient, who recognized the signal and ran out of the room shouting for help. Everyone came rushing in. The patient offered to take my father to the hospital in his car. My mother wanted to come along, but he told her to stay home and make some food to bring to the hospital.

When they got far enough away, my father put his finger down his throat and vomited up the tobacco. The patient brought my father somewhere where he could rest.

My mother arrived at the hospital with a tray of hot food. The wealthy patient was waiting there for her. He said, "Your husband was taken to another hospital, but I don't know which one." My mother had her driver take her to another hospital. After a few days, she showed up at the wealthy patient's home. He told her that he didn't know where my father was, but he did know that he wasn't coming back to live with her.

My mother searched for him constantly, because she was afraid her sickness would return. A year had passed before she found him. She begged him to come back, but he refused.

After two years had passed, my father decided to give my mother another chance. He told her that he would come back only if she went with him to the forbidden mountain. He wanted her to learn about his religion, and he especially wanted her to meet his teacher in the cave. He needed her to understand the kind of responsibility he carried.

My mother agreed to go, but she was terrified at the thought of traveling into the wilderness. She knew that my father carried with him the herbal antidotes for every kind of poisonous snake and scorpion bite, but she couldn't stop thinking about the cobras, pythons, and tigers.

My father told Co that the magic on the mountain was very good and would protect her, but secretly he was worried that the mountain might try to keep her away.

In those days there were only cattle tracks and footpaths leading from Chau Doc City through the marshes and flood lands to the mountains. There was a canal running from Chau Doc City to Nui Dai, Long Mountain. My parents went by boat almost all the way to Long Mountain and then hired a driver with a horse-drawn cart to take them the rest of the way through the marshes to the forbidden mountain.

Some people from my father's religion were building a new temple on the forbidden mountain. They were building it on the ruins of another temple that had been destroyed by the French. They reused that site because the jungle was already cleared and there was a path. When my father was living on the mountain, he was looking through the rubble of the temple ruins and found three gold statues of Buddha in perfect condition. The smallest was twelve inches high and the other two were about eighteen inches. There was also a five-inch black stone Buddha with a core of clear quartz. He went to ask his teacher what to do with the statues. His teacher told him to hide them in a certain cave and that sometime in the future he would tell my father where to take them.

Co tried to keep up with my father's long strides as they made their way up the jungle path to Chua Phat Lan temple. Co noticed that the color of the clayish earth was brighter than she had ever seen, magenta, pink, and bright yellow in some places.

The lush tropical jungle enveloped them. The perfume of the jungle flowers was new to her, and my mother began to relax. She looked around and saw trees with strange-looking fruit. A cloud of iridescent butterflies with wings larger than her hands dazzled her as they took off suddenly from a butterfly bush. My father had to keep slowing down as Co struggled up the slippery rocks covered with emerald moss and etched in golden lichen. My father strung his hammock between two trees for my mother to rest while he went to pick some fruit.

He came back with a large *mang cau* fruit for my mother to try. She had never seen one so big. They are a dark green, bumpy, pear-shaped fruit with a crooked neck. The outer skin is easy to tear. Inside, the meat is milky white with a thick creamy juice that is fragrant but not too sweet. The chewy pulp comes out in sections, each one harboring a shiny black seed. The *mang cau* satisfies hunger like a complete meal.

They still had far to go. My mother was feeling reassured and did her best to keep up with my father. When they reached the top of the first hill, the path leveled out. My mother looked around her and noticed thick vines creeping up the trees. She couldn't help feeling that any moment a python could drop onto her shoulders and squeeze her throat shut. No herbal medicine could stop an animal that size, one that could eat a medium-size cow.

Several birds swooped just over their heads, screeching and squawking at them. My mother screamed. This surprised my father. He listened for a few moments to find out what was wrong, but there didn't seem to be anything out of the ordinary, so he took my mother's hand, and they continued along the narrow path. Ten minutes later a pack of monkeys clambered down to the lower branches and began to jump up and down, screaming at them and scolding them.

My father didn't understand why the animals were behaving like this. He listened very carefully for a long time, but he didn't hear any sounds of danger. He wondered, was it his wife? Did the animals mistrust her?

My mother begged him to turn around, but he told her not to worry. "I told you. The animals here never bother people."

My mother held on to my father's shirttail. She kept her eyes looking down. They climbed over more rocks, and then my father halted abruptly. There was a huge python lying across the path. Now my mother really started crying. She wouldn't let my father go, so he just picked her up and stepped over the snake. He could not understand why the animals were acting like this.

My father put my mother down and tried to reassure her. She buried her face in his shirt, and they walked on. Then my father noticed that the jungle was strangely quiet, the way it gets when the animals are hiding from hunters. Even the cicadas and the birds were quiet.

They came to a lookout on the crest of a hill. It was a dizzying sight. Far below them houses the size of beans stood in two long rows on either side of a long dirt road that vanished over the horizon. There was nothing but water on either side of the rows of houses for many miles. The specks on the water were boats as small as grains of rice. My father took some fruit out of his medicine bag, and they rested there.

Just as they turned onto the path again they were greeted by a king cobra who was standing four feet high, swaying with its flame-colored mouth open, keeping its eyes focused on my father's eyes. My mother started crying again.

"Don't worry," my father told her calmly, "I have the antidote."

A battalion of birds poured down from the canopy and began nipping at my father's shoulders and hands. My mother was so frightened this time, my father decided to stop and wait.

He wondered, did the animals dislike my mother? Was her essence that offensive? He couldn't think of an explanation. My mother was sobbing. She said she had changed her mind and wanted to go home. Just then came a low-pitched growl, so dense that it vibrated the trunks of the trees. This time my father became really worried, because he knew my mother would not be able to scramble up a tree.

My father ordered my mother not to move. He began racing around to find a tree with branches low enough for him to boost her up. There wasn't one. Maybe he could find a tree with vines hanging down. Darting from tree to tree, my father was startled at the sight of an old man standing quietly next to a butterfly bush. He was dressed in white and was wearing a white cloth tied around his head. The old man said, "You can't go this way. The French have mined the mountain. Go through the brush that way." He extended his arm at an angle.

Suddenly everything made sense. My father thought, "Oh, so my friends were trying to warn me of the danger." He went to get my mother. When he returned with her to thank the old man, he was nowhere to be seen. That confused my father again.

They climbed uphill through the brush the way the old man had told them, and the animals didn't bother them anymore. My mother felt relieved when she caught sight of the temple roof.

Chua Phat Lon, Big Buddha Temple, was built entirely of stone. Even the roof was stone. When my parents appeared in the clearing, the monks and their families looked stunned to see them.

They asked, "How did you manage to get here in one piece? We can't get down and nobody can come up. There are mines hidden everywhere. Several visitors have been killed." My father bowed his head. "Buddha helped us," he said.

My father explained to the monk the purpose of my mother's visit, and the monks were happy to help. My father continued up the mountain to visit his teacher and to see if the statues were still in the cave. The monks kept my mother very busy at the temple during the next ten days.

She tried very hard to become humble. She worked on memorizing part of a sutra, and she chanted and prayed with the people in the temple four times a day.

Two weeks later my father returned.

"Tomorrow we will go to the cave," he announced.

My parents set off the next morning into the jungle. There was no path. No one except my father knew about the cave.

"We have to walk to the other side of the mountain," my father told my mother. "It will take about five hours."

My mother was very tired when they came to a waterfall that had a round pool beneath.

He said, "Let's relax here for a while. The cave is another two hours from here."

My father immersed himself in the cool, fresh water, enjoying himself immensely. My mother only wet her feet. Some monkeys began chattering in the trees. My father got out of the water and walked over to his medicine bag.

"I have something for you," my father called up to them. He took some red bonbon cherries out of his bag and tossed them one by one up to the monkeys.

They continued their ascent up the mountain and eventually came to a steep, rocky area. They climbed from rock to rock straight up the mountain until they came to the edge of a cliff. A narrow ledge jutted from the face of the cliff about ten feet long, just wide enough to walk on. My father told Co, "This is the only way to get there. Just lean into the wall as you go. Don't look down." My mother was trying very hard to be brave. The jungle canopy stretched beneath them like a lush green carpet. My mother took tiny steps, sliding her feet along the gravelly ledge. She knew that if she got dizzy, she could fall to her death.

"There is only one more of those, and it is shorter," my father said as they entered the jungle again.

They crossed the second ledge, and then my father said, "It's just little farther through those bushes."

My mother looked ahead and saw a sea of thorns.

"I'll never make it though that," she whimpered.

"Don't worry, just follow me," my father said, trying to reassure her, but her clothes kept getting snagged no matter how close she stayed to my father. She said the bushes were trying to hold her back.

"The cave is there." My father pointed to a tree that was growing out of a rock formation. "There is an overhang of rock just underneath the tree. The entrance to the cave is back there, behind those bushes."

"What should I do when I meet your teacher?" my mother wanted to know.

"Don't do anything."

"Should I bow and pray to Buddha?"

"No, he is not like that. He does not pray to Buddha. His masters are much older than Buddha."

You would never notice the opening of the cave unless you went behind the bushes and crawled all the way under the overhang of rock. Then you might see a diagonal slit between two big stones about two feet wide and four feet high. My father lit the candles and gave one to my mother. He took hold of her hand and led her in.

My mother could see in the candlelight that the walls of the cave were not one solid surface. They consisted of many stones and boulders leaning one against the other. She wondered what was keeping them from collapsing in on her. They were brown and moist like a cold sweat.

They had to stay low and creep from rock to rock through a long tunnel and then the cave went straight down, like a well. My mother climbed down after my father, making sure the top of his head always stayed in view. In some places, the hole became so narrow that she couldn't understand how her big-boned husband could fit through.

"I feel like a turd squeezing through in the bowels of the earth," she said.

"We are almost at the end of this downward tunnel. Just about ten minutes more, and we will reach a chamber that is light enough to see. It has an underground spring. We can bathe."

"I need to get out of here," she whispered.

Before my father had a chance to calm her down, she was on her way up the tunnel. He had to bring her home.

My father wasn't convinced that my mother understood his relationship with his teacher in the cave or his responsibility to help people, but he decided to give her another chance. He tried to make it clear to her that if she ever tried to interfere with his work again, he wouldn't hesitate to leave her and never come back.

My mother never became an easy person to live with, but she gave my father the freedom he needed.

6

MY MOTHER LEAVES

y father was sitting on the ground next to the wood stove stirring
more formula for me, this time a nighttime supply. In South Vietnam, we keep the kitchen outside, under an awning, right next to
the house. A Vietnamese wood stove is a freestanding wide-brimmed ceramic
bowl that contains the fire. You can fit only one pot or wok per stove. They are
made of baked river mud mixed with rice hulls and are shaped so that the pots
rest on three prongs, never four. We use three prongs because they stand for the
three kitchen gods who dwell at the hearth, where they can keep an eye on us.
Every year on Tet, the Vietnamese lunar new year, they ride on an orange carp
up to heaven to report our good and bad deeds to the Jade Emperor, and return
with good luck for the coming year. There is a story about how the kitchen gods
came to be.

Once long ago, there was an unhappy couple. The husband was a poor
woodcutter who drank too much and would beat his wife. One day she ran
away to another province. Being a healthy and hard-working woman, she was
able to start her life over in a new marriage.

Many years went by. One evening, when her second husband was out hunting, a beggar came to her door asking for food. She invited the beggar inside
and recognized her former husband. She wept at the sight of his filthy face and

torn clothing. She gave him food and drew water for him to bathe. Then she mended and washed his clothes.

The woman stacked a big pile of brush in the yard to make a fire for the clothes to dry quickly, but before she could light the fire, her husband, having just returned, called from inside the house, "Wife, where are you? I have been lucky today."

The woman quickly hid the naked beggar and his clothes under the brush pile an instant before her husband came outside to show her the small deer he had shot. When he noticed the pile of brush, he went straight to light it, saying, "You must have known we would eat meat tonight."

The wife expected her former husband to jump out of the fire, but he did not for fear of getting her in trouble. She could not bear for him to die on her behalf, so she flung herself into the fire to die with him. The husband was so distraught to see his wife perish that he also threw himself into the flames. The Jade Emperor was so touched by the deep love they felt that he granted them eternal life in the hearth of every home, to protect us from getting burned by fire.

My mother was still not back. In anticipation of dinner, Thau had chopped several different kinds of vegetables and left them on the chopping block. When my formula was ready, he poured it into a glass jar that he had sterilized. He meant to leave it in the warm ashes of the cooking fire before going to bed.

By the time Co returned home with her shopping basket, the sun was already sliding down the fringes of the coconut palms like a slippery egg yolk. A refreshing breeze was kicking up. The setting sun cast a sidewise glance at the house and lit up the feathery strips of thatch in lavender and brass. My new mother walked into the kitchen and set her basket down on the table. She noticed that Thau had used his machete again to chop the vegetables. This annoyed her, because he used that machete for everything. Leaning against the table, she watched my father filling the baby bottle. He started to hum absent-mindedly, which meant he didn't know what to say.

"What are you doing?" she asked.

"He really took to this rice formula. He's had three feedings already."

Co stared incredulously at her husband as if he were playing a cruel joke on her. At fifty, she had finally come to peace with the fact that they were a childless couple. Adoption had always been out of the question; it would never occur to her to raise another person's child.

Co watched her husband fidget with the bottle, trying to get it to fit into the coconut thermos. For a moment she tried to imagine the two of them living the normal life of a couple with children. She thought, "He's out of his mind." In all the time they had been married, she had never seen her husband do a single impractical thing. This scenario was so absurd to her that she couldn't even find the leverage to get angry.

My father hummed, "He's asleep on the bed. Go and have a look, I'll cook dinner."

Not knowing what else to do, my mother slipped into the house and peered into the bedroom they shared. The mosquito net had been lowered around their narrow bed. The light of the dying sun soaked the cream-colored netting with the color of hope. As if in a dream, she approached the blurred form of her baby sleeping behind the gauze veil. The sound of my soft, quick, animal-like breathing mesmerized her. She had never listened to an infant's breathing before. An overwhelming and totally unfamiliar feeling came over her. She felt she could hardly restrain herself from tossing me out the window or chucking me into the river.

She lifted the net. I was sleeping on my stomach on top of a towel. My legs were tucked under my belly in the fetal position. My fists were the size of kumquats. My mother fumbled around on the bed like a dog preparing to lie down, but there was no room. I was lying in the middle of the bed. Afraid to touch me, she laid herself down propped up on her side at the very edge of the rattan bed, stiff as a salted fish.

Although I was tiny and thin, my skin had a healthy glow. My mother watched me for a long time. The only thing she found beautiful about me were my eyelids. She remarked that they glimmered as if they were sprinkled with stardust.

"I can't sleep with that baby in my bed," she later told my father as he served the dinner to her under the awning. In Vietnam, children never sleep alone. "I can't relax around him, he is so delicate."

"Don't worry, I'll sleep with him," my father reassured her.

The sun had slipped away once more, and the dimming sky seemed to finalize their conversation. It was dawning on my mother that she would be the one to wake up nights to feed and care for me, because my father got so little sleep as it was. He woke up every night at midnight to meditate for an hour or two, and then he woke up shortly after that, at four o'clock, to set up the clinic and to chant.

Before she had a chance to express her feelings of resentment, my cries brought them both to the bedroom. It was all soft gray shadows. My father felt for my small shape inside the net. He lifted me up and tossed my soiled towel into a basket.

"Here," he whispered, "hold him while I go and get his bottle."

My father returned with my bottle. I cried until my father showed my mother how to poke my cheek with the nipple first so I could find it. He left us alone.

My parents took me to the family altar. They introduced me to their ancestors as Quang Van Nguyen (pronounced Wang Van Wing). My father lit the candles and the incense and prayed for a while. He took me from my mother and held me up toward the altar to receive a blessing from my grandfather Ky Van Nguyen. My grandfather died just four years before I was born. He was stronger than my father, because he stayed with the teacher in the cave about five years longer. He lived to be 104 years old.

It turned out that I wasn't an easy baby. My stomach was so small that I cried to be fed every three hours. My mother had never taken care of anyone in her life. My father had hoped his wife would discover some happiness as a new mother, but it turned out to be just the opposite. She resented not having the time to go out with her friends. Most of all, she suffered from waking up nights with me.

It wasn't easy to be married to my father. There were always crowds of people in and around the house, seven days a week, sick people. Sometimes they had to stay for days in the guest room, because they required round-the-clock care. Emergency cases were brought in the middle of the night, children who were having febrile seizures, people who were beaten by the soldiers. My mother would often complain that she needed some peace and quiet, and she would go home to her parents for a week or two. Now with me disturbing her sleep, it wasn't long before she decided to take me to stay with her parents.

On the day we came back, a child who had broken her leg and a toddler who had swallowed some rotten fish were brought into the clinic at the same time. My mother could not endure their screams of pain any longer. She had had enough. After six weeks of trying her best to take care of me, my mother left and never came back. She went to live as a groundskeeper at a temple in Ben Tre. She wasn't afraid that the sickness on her legs would come back again. I never saw her except during Tet, when she came back to visit.

My father did the best he could, taking care of me without my mother. He left me in the yard all day with his patients. There were always plenty of nursing mothers to give me some mother's milk. My father wasn't happy about this arrangement, because he believed it was best for me to love just one mother. Instead, I had different mothers every day.

After work, my father insisted on taking care of me himself so that I would know that he was my father. I made it difficult for him to chant or to meditate, and this put him out of sorts. Meditating was the way my father renewed his power. People couldn't help noticing how tired he looked.

One day, someone brought a man into the clinic who had been beaten by the soldiers, a schoolteacher. There was a new captain by the name of Beroux who was looking for a Vietnamese man who spoke good French to spy in the army. The schoolteacher spoke French very well. Beroux accompanied his men to the schoolteacher's house and served him a draft notice. He wanted the schoolteacher to be a driver in the convoy, and spy on the native soldiers to find out if they were secretly working for the Communists. The schoolteacher refused. Beroux gave orders for his soldiers to break his ribs. They pinned him to the ground and stomped on his rib cage until they heard a crack. The captain told the schoolteacher that they would be back in the morning to see if he had changed his mind. My father bound up the teacher's rib cage and gave him some medicine for the swelling and the pain. That night, the schoolteacher ran away.

A few weeks later, I was playing in the medicine room while my father was chopping medicine. I was able to pull myself up to standing and reach the lowest drawers of the apothecary and throw the medicine onto the floor. That morning something horrible happened. Some neighbors came rushing into the clinic.

"Ong Sau, they are making the teacher carry the head of his daughter from house to house. They caught him in Dalat and brought him home. They cut off his daughter's head and strung it on a wire like a lantern. They said they want to show us what they do to people who desert the army."

"Ong Sau, you must leave immediately; the soldiers are coming this way. They are arresting a lot of people."

My father scooped me up and went to get his medicine bag. He was going to take me to hide out with him in the jungle, but the soldiers started coming into the house. Before climbing out the window, he handed me to the neighbors and said, "Take Quang to my sister Gioi in Cai Mon."

He didn't get far. Armed soldiers engulfed him, marched him all the way to the highway, and threw him into a dull-green prison truck. There were about forty other people packed inside, including some women with babies. The doors slammed shut, and the truck took off. There were no windows, no ventilation; it was a closed metal box. The babies screamed the whole time. There was no way to see where they were being taken. By the time they arrived at the prison, many people had fainted from the heat.

If my father had been able to meditate every night as usual, I believe he would have foreseen the danger in time to get away.

7

CROCODILE PRISON

The truck finally stopped. Vietnamese guards opened the doors and banged on them with their truncheons, ordering everyone out. Those who had fainted were dragged out by their arms and dropped onto the cement of the barbed-wire-enclosed prison courtyard, where other truckloads of prisoners were already waiting. The guards made everyone stand in the hot sun for hours without offering them any water. My father looked around at the other unfortunate ones, the war resisters, the homeless, those who had stolen, those who could not pay their taxes, and those who belonged to civilian militia groups like the Hoa Hao and the Cao Dai religious sects.

Prisoners with the initials CM embroidered in red on their blue prison uniforms assisted the guards and carried rattan whips. These were the caplans, half prisoner/half guard. The prisoners called the caplans *mat cat*, which means macaque, a kind of monkey with fat cheeks that likes to snack. One by one, they escorted the new prisoners into the cement-block building. After performing the "phoenix dance" or strip search on the new prisoners, they took away their clothes and gave them light blue uniforms to wear. Then they shaved their heads and escorted them to their cells.

The prison guards accused my father of belonging to the Hoa Hao sect, whose armed members fought not only the French but the Communists as well.

Their leader, Huynh Phu So, claimed to be the reincarnation of the Buddha Master of Western Peace. He had been assassinated three years earlier by the Viet Minh.

My father was brought to a long and narrow cell that smelled like sickness and sewage, packed with twenty suffering men. The head prisoners started shouting at the caplans, bargaining with them to take my father to another cell so they could have a little more space. All the cells were just as filthy and crowded.

One of the ways to become the head prisoner of a cell was to have relatives who paid the macaques money for special treatment. The macaques often went to the prisoners' families and told them that their loved ones were getting badly beaten in prison. The macaques offered to serve as bodyguards to protect their loved ones from harm, for a fee.

Two of the prisoners in my father's cell had their heads shaved on only one side, so the guards would know they were exceptionally violent, or had tried to escape.

There was no way to keep the cell clean. The only ventilation came from one small barred window in the steel cell door. The toilet was a hole in the floor at the far end of the cell. It often overflowed onto the floor where the prisoners slept. Many men had excrement and urine on their uniforms.

There were benches along the two long walls of the cells. Only the prisoners who received protection by the macaques could sleep on a bench. Everyone else, including my father, slept on the floor on a rush mat. It was so crowded that there was not enough room for everyone to lie down at the same time unless they were lying on their sides. When one turned over, others had to turn over.

My father chanted and prayed in the cell four times a day, and he sat up and meditated every night. Once they discovered my father was a monk, one of the prisoners wanted to give my father his place on the bench, but my father refused because he did not like to have a higher status than other people. Some of the prisoners in the cell were Communists and did not respect my father for being a monk, but when the majority of prisoners wanted my father to pray out loud, they didn't make a fuss.

Once you were locked up in prison, there was no way of knowing when, if ever, you would be released. About one-third of the prisoners died in prison from disease, work-related accidents, and beatings. If one prisoner complained, ate too slowly, or lost or tore his uniform, everyone in the cell might be beaten. Sometimes prisoners killed other prisoners. In prison, killing was an ordinary thing.

During the day, the prisoners were taken to work at vanilla, pepper, and tin plantations, and also construction sites and road crews. It was back-breaking work on two meager meals a day.

Even though my father was old, he was assigned to work at a labor camp in the middle of the jungle by the Cambodian border, where the prisoners were clearing the trees and building a road.

It was a three-acre site along one of the widest parts of the Mekong River, in Chau Doc province. Even though they were in the jungle, it was almost impossible to escape, because land mines that fanned out over one hundred feet were planted along the circumference of the entire camp. The prison guards didn't bother planting any land mines along the riverbank. Nobody would even think of going near the river, because it was swarming with twenty-foot-long crocodiles. There was a fence to keep the crocodiles out of the camp, where they would enjoy an endless supply of fresh human meat. Many armed guards patrolled the area day and night. It was useless to attempt an escape, though many prisoners died trying.

My father worked alongside the younger men for many months sawing down trees and digging out roots. This was an area of the jungle infested with malarial mosquitoes. Many men came down with fevers and died. Others suffered from cholera and typhoid fever. My father tried to help the sick by giving them medicine that grew inside the camp, but he could not save many.

When the guards saw that my father knew about plants, they assigned him to cook duty, hoping he could find them some food to eat besides their daily allotment, which was far better than the food given to the prisoners. The prisoners ate "motorcycle soup," a flatulence-producing soup that was made from dried fish and fermented rice. My father was allowed to roam the camp with a knife, looking for mushrooms, fungus, roots, and other edible things. He was allowed to eat the same food the guards ate. It was then that he came up with a plan to escape.

While collecting bamboo shoots for dinner, he sometimes managed to split off a long splint of bamboo and hide it inside the bushes. Over many weeks, my father managed to store up about one hundred splints of bamboo. That would be enough.

Next he made a lot of twine. It is very easy to make strong twine if you have a banana leaf. You take the wide, hollow stalk that runs down the center of the leaf, and you can easily pull the longitudinal fibers apart. You just twist them together in a looping chain to make good twine.

Little by little, when nobody was looking, my father was able to tie the bamboo splints together into a full suit of armor. He made a wide tube for his torso and abdomen and narrower tubes for his upper arms and forearms and his legs. The leggings were very long, like stilts, with a bar inside to rest his feet on, so that he could walk right through the crocodiles on his way to the water. Then he made a tube to cover his head and neck. He didn't dare try it on; he just had to do his best to estimate the size. The pieces had to be just the right length and width, so they would fit snugly and not slip off.

My father had to figure out a path to the river that would allow him to stop every few feet to hide. He stayed up for many nights to observe the guards for clues. My father was very lucky, because he could see in the dark about as well as a cat. That was from spending so much time in the darkness when he lived in the cave. I know how well he could see, because the same thing happened to me, and I lived in the cave only four years.

I know there was a physical change in my eyes that could be noticed by a doctor, because one time when I was injured in a land mine accident and was hospitalized for two months, the doctors kept bringing other doctors to shine their flashlights into my eyes.

My father stayed awake nights to observe the guards' patrol patterns until he felt that he had figured out the safest route to the river. He prepared it inch by inch by clearing away the dried sticks and thinning out the brush.

Then one rainy night, when the rain smacked against a billion surfaces and drummed up a sound curtain, he vanished into the darkness and crept down his path, holding the armor on either side of his body like a blind. He made his way toward the river ever so slowly so as not to make jerky movements or an extra sound. He tried on the armor for the first time. Some of the pieces were too tight. He would have to go back to fix the suit and wait for another chance to try again.

During the next weeks, he cut more splints, taking care not to be seen. He also made two long walking sticks this time, to help him balance on his stilts. The only thing he hadn't quite worked out was how to lower himself into the water without attracting the attention of too many crocodiles.

Old crocodiles are very smart and, of course, large, large enough to swallow a man as big as my father. My father was hoping they would think he was a log, even though he smelled like game to them.

My father had been at the camp for more than a year, which is a long time to survive in a place like that. Prisoners and even guards were dying from disease. He had become thin and weak, but he ate many raw medicinal plants to stay strong.

He was getting nervous that his armor would be discovered. If that happened, he would certainly be shot on the spot.

He waited for a downpour or at least a new moon. He could count on the darkness, but not the rainstorm. As it turned out, the nights were dry. He decided to go without the sound blind of the falling rain.

He left his mat on the night of the new moon in the pitch blackness, stepping over many sleeping bodies as lightly as a shadow, then creeping on his belly slowly, like stars moving across the night sky, to his cache. He uncovered all the pieces, eight in all plus the walking sticks.

He inched over the trail and climbed silently over the zigzag log fence, making his way to a patch of small trees on the crocodile side.

Leaning against a tree, he assembled his armor using slow, deliberate movements. The armor fit well enough. He was able to hold on to trees and tree branches as he tested his stilts.

He had second thoughts about the stilts. Walking was too risky; the animals would recognize him as a human. As soon as he dropped into the water, they would be swarming and biting.

At the last minute, he changed his mind. He scanned the area for a long time to find the clearest way to the water, which was about fifty feet away. Setting his sticks against the tree, he leaned over toward the next tree and walked his arms down the trunk slowly, all the way down, until he was lying on the ground.

He rolled very slowly toward the deep grass where he would not be seen. He could look through the slats of bamboo in the direction he was facing. He hoped he would make it all the way to the water without bumping into a sleeping crocodile.

He did. He made it to the water without arousing the crocodiles or the soldiers, and soon he was floating like a log past the sleeping crocodiles. He floated down the Mekong River past the camp heading in the direction of his home, which was eighty miles downstream. He floated all that night until dawn, when he managed to make his way to land.

My father was afraid to be seen in his uniform because people would know he was an escaped convict. He hid in the forest during the day and walked by night toward home. Three weeks later, he showed up in Cai Mon, emaciated and weak.

8

A SHORT VISIT TO HEAVEN

Aunt Gioi took care of my father for a few weeks, until he felt strong enough to go to the forbidden mountain to regain his power. He stayed there for three months. When he returned, he set up a clinic in Ben Cac.

Shortly after that, I became very ill. It started out as chicken pox, but I was still running a high fever after two weeks.

My aunt took me to see my father at his new house. It was a long way for an old woman to take a sick baby. She had to carry me for an hour's walk to the road, then she had to take the three buses and two ferries to Cay Lay, and walk from there.

My father checked my pulse and understood my sickness. He prepared some medicine for my aunt to cook for me when we got home. We left the following morning.

The medicine was very bitter and strong. The only way Aunt Gioi could get me to swallow it was to pry my mouth open with a chopstick and pour it down my throat. She gave it to me every day for fourteen days, but my fever continued, and I had little energy to play.

Aunt Gioi brought me back to my father. He was surprised to see that I was still sick. He didn't understand. He had helped many children with a similar sickness, some of them much weaker than I was. He gave her more medicine to cook for me and told her to bring me back in two weeks.

During that time my fever continued, and I only grew weaker. The medicine didn't seem to be working. My aunt brought me back. When my father saw me the third time he became afraid. Why wasn't his medicine working? He tried to compose himself so he could read my pulse.

He took my wrist again and again. Aunt Gioi looked at him. She watched as her confident and powerful brother turned into a helpless old man. He found her eyes. "Quang is failing." It is a sign of impending death when the steady beats of the pulse are interrupted by erratic pauses and flutters.

This time I stayed at my father's house, and my aunt took care of me while my father worked. One day, when he was busy in the clinic, Aunt Gioi thought I had slipped away into death. She raced into the clinic to get my father, and they both went running through the house to me.

My father put his lips in front of my nose but could detect no breath. He put his ear to my chest and found that my heart had stopped. He breathed his breath into me and pumped my heart, but it did not work. My father let out a loud bellow of anguish. Everyone came rushing into the room. They had never seen my father upset before, but now he was beside himself, weeping and pleading to Buddha that he was sorry he had neglected me. He cried out, "Dear Buddha, his father was taken away from him, but now he has me. Please let him live." Everyone was crying.

My father carried me to the altar and prayed with me on his lap. Everyone prayed with him. After a while, some of his students went outside to build a coffin.

My father prayed with his patients and students until the small wooden coffin was brought into the room. It was made of mango wood and lined with red cloth. My father placed me inside and then went back to the clinic. Aunt Gioi and some of the others stayed with me and prayed.

My father returned a few hours later to join the others in prayer. He sat down beside me and touched my face and my chest. Suddenly he stood up. My chest was still warm. He placed his hand on my forehead and looked up to Buddha and shouted, "Dear Buddha, dear Mother and Father of Buddha, let my son come back to me! If the Buddha gives me the responsibility and power of a doctor, please give my son the power to live. If my son goes away and leaves me alone, I think I will no longer be able to help people." Then my father sent his power into my forehead.

From inside the coffin, I made a choking sound and cried out loudly three times. This startled everybody, and they ran out of the room thinking a ghost had entered my body. Only my father and Aunt Gioi remained. They waited for me to make eye contact with them. Then they saw it was me.

My father lifted me out of the box and brought me to the altar. He took a glass of water from the altar and put a prayer into it and gave me some to drink. Aunt Gioi brought me some soup, and I ate a bit. My father was worried that my heart wasn't strong enough to beat through the night, but I made it.

I became stronger every day, and Aunt Gioi brought me back to her house in Cai Mon. In a few months, I was healthy and plump. I was never sick after that. My father came to visit me every two months.

It would take hundreds of people all praying together in one breath to have power like my father.

9

THE CURSE OF
THE FORBIDDEN MOUNTAIN

June 1956
Cai Mon Village

The bombs were always fired from a distance. Sometimes the soldiers warned us beforehand, but often they did not, in hopes of catching the Communist guerrillas off guard and aboveground.

By 1954, the Communists in the north had defeated the French army and liberated themselves from French rule. North Vietnam had become a new sovereign nation, a Communist country under the leadership of Ho Chi Minh. The Communist Party was certain they could liberate the south from the French as well, but first they had to convince the southerners to join their Communist revolution. After the war, tens of thousands of Viet Minh guerrillas sneaked into the Mekong Delta and recruited southerners to join their underground liberation army, which was literally underground in a hundred miles of multilevel tunnels, too deep to be bombed. The villagers sustained the highest number of casualties from the bombing. On average, it came once every two months for about ten days at a stretch.

As a preschooler growing up in a war zone, I wasn't conscious of the terror that was going on all around me. Bombs were just another kind of weather condition. Aunt Gioi was determined to raise me as if we lived in a happy world. She made sure that I woke up every morning feeling safe, snuggled against her body. We played and giggled together before climbing out of bed. I would put my face up to hers so our noses touched, and I stared with all my might into her eyes. That would make her scream with laughter, because she said the will inside my little head had pinned the will inside her big old head. We wrestled and tickled and sang silly songs almost every morning. It didn't bother me that she didn't have her teeth in yet.

After breakfast, my aunt washed the clothes and I went fishing. My friends taught me many different ways to fish. To catch shrimp you have to swim underwater and follow them to their hole in the canal bank and then scoop them out. Fish are harder to catch by hand, because they are covered with slippery mucous. It was easy to catch snails. Just throw a branch into the water and the snails will come to eat the fungus on the branch.

I remember one morning just before my sixth birthday when the bombing started without warning. I remember that day, because turning six was an important event. It means you are old enough to start school. I was expecting my father to appear at any moment, and I went every day to the big bridge to wait for him. I was far away from our shelter when the bombing started.

Our village had an alarm system worked out. If someone knew the bombing was imminent he or she would strike two bamboo sticks together in a signal that was passed from house to house. This time the bombing came fast and heavy. My aunt stood up from her washing and screamed out my name, but I did not answer.

She went running to the places where I usually played near the house, up in trees, in the canal, in front of her store, but I was in none of the usual places. My aunt wasn't afraid of the bombs as much as she was afraid of losing me. She ran halfway to the big bridge and found me running home. Together we ran under a sky raining with bombs. They screeched like a pack of demons before they burst open, their fire and stench stinging our eyes with smoke. My aunt clutched my arm just above the elbow so tightly that I cried all the way home.

We scrambled into our bomb shelter. It was darker than shut eyes down there. My aunt slid a board over our heads to cover the hole. It had sandbags and logs piled on top. We crawled diagonally downward and entered a small burrow, so small that my head just about touched the ceiling when I was seated. My aunt had to lie curled up on her side around me. We kept a chamberpot down there and some water and dehydrated cooked rice. That's all.

We could hear the sounds of war over our heads and could feel the ground shaking when the bombs exploded. Every now and then, when the bombing had stopped, we would creep out of the shelter to get some food and quickly bathe in the canal and stretch our legs. We had no idea whether it would be day or night. Sometimes we would hear people crying, but we didn't dare stray too far from our shelter to find out who had died.

I was still too young to understand the tragedy of death. I saw many gruesome things, but I never cried. One time my aunt and I heard wailing coming from a nearby house. We followed the sound and found our neighbor dead. His head was crushed, and his eyes were popping out like a fish's. He had taken me fishing with him at the big river just the other day. I rode on the back fender of his bicycle and held our poles and bait can tightly in one hand the whole way. We went to the Mekong at high tide and caught two big monkfish. He tied the fish onto the bar of his bicycle and rode with them between his legs. I helped him build a fire in his clay oven, and he showed me how to gut and scale the fish. Those fish were almost as big as me. His wife baked the fish in a pot with coconut milk and pineapple and green onions. We brought the fish to my house to surprise Aunt Gioi.

After the bombing, people would always be crying for many days, but I never cried about people dying in the war.

The bombing was not the main danger. There was an everyday danger I wasn't at all aware of. Whenever the Communists showed up at the house, my aunt had to give them anything they wanted in the way of food and supplies from her store. Since she was an old woman and I was just a young child, they never asked us to run messages or spy for them. Eventually they tunneled to a spot that was practically underneath her store. They came out at night like mice and helped themselves. This is the principle reason why we did not have much food to eat.

Sometimes the army soldiers would show up at random times to search our house for evidence that we were helping the guerrillas. If the soldiers thought you were supporting the guerrillas, you would be arrested and tortured in prison.

Whenever the soldiers appeared at our house, my aunt invited them to stay for dinner and treated them as if they were our friends, so as not to scare me. She didn't have to worry about me talking about the guerrillas, because they came only at night, after I had gone to bed.

While the soldiers were in our house, they searched the grounds for items that might have been dropped by the guerrillas, like cigarette butts, bandages, fragments of tattered clothing, and supplies dropped in haste. Of course, my aunt spent a large part of her day searching for the exact same clues and covering them up meticulously. My aunt knew that if she appeared to be the least bit nervous, concerned, or impatient for the soldiers to leave, she would give herself away. Some of the soldiers were French, but most were Vietnamese who tried to trap my aunt in a lie. The soldiers often helped themselves to things from people's homes. If they found a radio, they would take it, because it was against the law to have one.

The soldiers sometimes stayed in our house overnight. Of course, my aunt had no idea if the Communists would suddenly appear. This made it especially difficult for her to remain calm.

If she were found to be supporting the Viet Minh, she would be arrested. It didn't matter that she was an old woman; she would be sent to prison to be tortured and then, most likely, released. This happened to so many of our neighbors, but it never happened to Aunt Gioi.

Everyone was afraid of the soldiers, but they were even more afraid of the Communists. The Viet Minh didn't have jails or prisons. They punished supporters of the French-backed regime by killing them, and sometimes they killed the entire family to make an example for the neighbors to see.

We had a lot of ghosts around, because there was so much killing. Usually if a whole family was killed inside their house, nobody else would dare to live there. We believe that a person is made up of many souls, not just one. When we die, our good souls fly away to heaven and our bad souls stay behind. It doesn't matter how kindhearted we are, or what we have done in our life, we still have both good and bad souls inside us. We believe that if a person suffers a violent death, his outrage will overcome him, and more of his souls will stay behind and become ghosts, and behave badly, making trouble for people. There are people who try to help ghosts find their way to heaven, but it is not easy.

Once my aunt took me to a place that was full of ghosts. It was an abandoned field that we always passed on our way to the highway. No one wanted to build a house or plant a garden in that field, because a lot of people had been blown up there. It was filled with traumatized souls.

My aunt made me go there with her so I would know what ghosts look like. We went at the twilight hour. I looked straight into the field, but I didn't see anything. She made me stay there for a very long time, until I saw some small white lights hovering in the air above the grass, different from fireflies, like small soap bubbles. She said that if I went up close to the bubbles and watched, I would be able to see their faces. She had seen them herself and said they were horrible. "They hold a lantern with one hand and catch insects with the other to eat," she told me.

I wouldn't go, I was too scared. War didn't scare me as much as ghosts.

By the time my father arrived, my birthday had long passed. Even so, my father, my aunt, and my uncle made a big celebration for the whole neighborhood in my honor, for turning six. Uncle Quon was the youngest of my father's siblings. He lived right next door to my aunt. My old granny lived with him, too. Uncle Quon had one son, my only cousin, just a year older than I. I didn't see my cousin much because he went to a boarding school in Saigon. We liked to build forts with Hoa, the girl next door. My cousin and I used to fight about half the time.

Ba Noi, my tiny granny, liked to stay out in the yard and sweep. She needed to hold on to a broomstick or a walking stick because her back was bent. She was so stooped over that she was almost my size. If I saw her in the kitchen eating alone I would check to see if any dead flies were floating in her soup bowl, because she wouldn't be able to see them.

I liked to help crush up her *trau* leaves and betel nuts and mix the mash with oyster-shell ashes, lime, in her special bronze mortar and pestle. This mixture is called *trau cau*. Most old women like to chew *trau cau* and rub their lips with a tobacco leaf for extra zest. My grandmother chewed on *trau cau* all day long. If you still have your molars you don't need to crush the leaves and the betel nuts in the cup first. Women start chewing *trau cau* once they are in their fifties, though I never saw my aunt chewing it. *Trau cau* is a stimulant and is addictive, but it is not bad for your health. Betel nuts have a bright red juice, like blood, and when my granny chewed *trau cau*, it looked like she was spitting blood into her spittoon. I tried some, but I didn't like it; it tasted awful, spicy and bitter.

My grandmother grew the *trau* and the *cau,* the betel nuts, in her yard, but she would buy the ashes at the market. She put them in her old *binh voi*, a special round ceramic pot that has a small hole in the top where a stick goes through that is used to spread the ashes on the leaves. We call the ashes *voi*. We also use *voi* to make cement and whitewash.

The soldiers made us whitewash all the trunks of our trees and the outer walls of our house to make it easier for them to spot the Communists sneaking around at night.

Old people usually can't keep their *binh voi* for more than twenty years because the ashes harden and gradually build up inside until they form a solid block of cement.

I once found an old *binh voi* in our canal. The hole on the top was completely sealed up. I carried it to my aunt's house because I thought that someone might have hidden their gold inside there. When my father came to visit he took the old *binh voi* home with him. I asked him why he wanted it. He told me that the cement inside an old *binh voi* like that makes very good medicine when you grind it up. It is special because it formed little by little over time inside a round, earthen container. That is more much powerful than a block of lime cement that you make in one day.

My grandmother died two years later, when I was eight. Aunt Gioi tied a white headband around my head to wear at the funeral. I remember walking beside my father and my uncles and relatives as they carried my grandmother's coffin to her gravesite. A lot of candles were burning on the top of the coffin. After my father and my uncles and relatives put my grandmother into the ground and everyone went back to my aunt's house, some neighborhood children came and took the candles away from the grave. My aunt said that was okay.

M y father had two other brothers living in Saigon, but he didn't like them much. They were both doctors, but they did not carry responsibility the way my father and my grandfather did. They were more interested in making money.

Uncle Quon was the only sibling who was willing to run the family's large coconut farm. Our ancestors had planted hundreds of coconut trees and mango, papaya, banana, orange, lemon, tangerine, grapefruit, pineapple, breadfruit, longan, chom chom, mang cau, jackfruit, durian, guava, tamarind, and many more. Many of those trees had since died, and most of the land had been sold off.

Uncle Quon dammed up a section of his canal and was planning to catch all of the fish for my birthday celebration. Some of his neighbors took turns bailing the water out. It was tiring work, because it had to be done manually by two people working together swinging a tightly woven basket. You have to be careful when the water level is low, because if you get tired and go home, someone could sneak up and steal all your fish.

Aunt Gioi and I went into the forest to look for termite mounds. A certain kind of mushroom grew on them during rainy season. We stopped by my father's oldest sister's house to invite her to my birthday party. I hardly knew her, because she always stayed at home with her husband.

It was a custom to roast a pig for special occasions, but since my father didn't like to kill animals or eat meat, he made a roast pig out of dough and stuffed it with tofu, vegetables, and mushrooms. It was as large as a real pig and had ears, feet, a tail, and a snout. He made a special sauce to baste it with, so that after cooking it in the clay oven, it looked and smelled like a roasted pig. My father once told me that the smell of meat in his house would weaken the power of his medicine and his acupuncture. If he ever did eat meat, he would fast on water to clean the meat out of his body.

My father also made a mural for me on the thatched wall of our bedroom. I helped him remove all the hairballs that Aunt Gioi had tucked into the thatch. Old women always do that. When they clean the hair from their comb, they never throw it away, they tuck it away in case of an emergency. They think the longer it's been there, the better it works for healing wounds. My granny never threw away her used tobacco leaves, either. She stuffed them into the walls along with her hair.

One time I came out of the canal with a deep gash in my thigh from a sharp piece of metal. My aunt ran into the bedroom and got four hairballs. She put two of them in a dish and burned them. She mixed the burned hair with two unburned hairballs and put the ratty, dusty mess on my cut, covered it with a banana leaf, and tied it firm with twine. She made a new a hairball dressing for me before I went to bed. By the second day, my cut was not painful. It healed quickly. I don't know why it didn't get infected, because the hairballs were dirty from being in the thatch with the insects and the lizards.

Some old women used their old tobacco leaves for bringing down a fever. You have to burn the tobacco a little bit so it isn't so strong, and then you chop it up, steep it in a cup of water, and drink it.

After we moved all the hairballs from the wall, I went outside to help my father collect things around the yard like dried grass, slivers of bamboo, feathers, eggshells, coconut husks, and seeds. When he was satisfied with what we had found, my father went back into the bedroom and painted some mountains on the wall in black ink. He made them look like they were surrounded by water. He told me they were four of the Seven Sacred Mountains, Water Mountain, Elephant Mountain, Long Mountain, and the forbidden mountain. He painted a lot of temples on Elephant Mountain and one temple on the forbidden mountain. He told me that the animals on the forbidden mountain were his friends.

He detailed the forbidden mountain with rocks, trees, bushes, and a waterfall. He glued coconut-haired monkeys and feathered birds onto the branches of the trees. A mother wolf was resting near a pile of rocks while her pups played in the foreground. On the left side, a panther was peeking through the bushes. A small herd of wild pigs with tusks and bristly tails were running down the right side of the mountain. Lower down, he pasted a tiger that he made with gold incense paper striped with black ink. He drew a cave with many tunnels, and he drew his teacher sitting in the center of the mountain.

Over the years, my father amused himself by working more on the mural. He added my grandfather Ky standing next to a tree above the entrance to the cave. He added himself as a young man with long black hair, lying down, playing with the wolf pups.

My father added me standing next to the tiger. I didn't like that. I asked my father to move me into a tree. He did as I asked, but he told me that the tiger was my friend and that I was up in the tree just for fun.

When my father was a monk living in a temple and was responsible for running funerals, he had to make a lot of things out of paper that are necessary for the ceremony. It is the custom in some Buddhist temples to send things made of paper to the spirit world by burning them. You are supposed to send a house, some clothes, and some money to the person who has just died. If the family has a lot of money, they can pay a monk to design and build a very large house, with paper furniture in every room, and lots of beautiful paper clothing and shoes. It is customary to make a house and two outfits for people who don't have money to spend on a funeral. The shirts and pants have to be at least two feet long, and everything has to be able to stand up on the table.

It is also customary to make paper clothes to send to the *cac dan*, the little people. In Vietnam we believe there are small, invisible people with really big heads. Their heads are so big and their necks are so thin that if they try to look up for too long their necks will snap in half and they will die. That is why we always put things for them down on the floor so they don't have to reach up to the table. We believe that if you don't give the little people things like food, proper clothing, and paper money, they will go looking through your stuff and get in your way, and make problems for you.

In Vietnam, we have a holiday for the little people at least four times a year, on the sixteenth day of the month. We call this day *Cac Dan*. My father celebrated *Cac Dan* every month. Sometimes he came to Cai Mon to make this holiday for me and my friends. I watched him cut dozens of little jackets, pants, and shoes out of five different colors of paper. We would go to the market and buy boxes of little meringue cookies the size of a button that were colored pink, yellow, green and white, and also some football-shaped gelatinous and colorful *banh bo* cakes.

I helped my father arrange the food and stand up the paper clothes in the front room, on a mat on the floor. Then we went out into the neighborhood to call the children to come and eat with the little people and keep them company. At the end of the party, my father made a fire, and we watched the clothing become invisible so the little people could wear it.

So far, I've mentioned five of my father's siblings, his two older sisters, and his one older and two younger brothers. He had another older brother, Bac Ba, who died at the age of forty-four. Bac Ba was the only sibling besides my father who had lived in the cave with my grandfather's teacher, but it was because of this that Bac Ba had died.

The teacher had warned my grandfather, Bac Ba, and my father that there was a powerful curse that could kill them if they ever spoke of certain things they saw on the forbidden mountain. They could speak of them among themselves, but never to someone who had not seen those things for himself. The teacher said if they told only a little, they wouldn't die, but if they told too much, there would be nothing he could do to save them.

Uncle Bac Ba's sudden death proved to my father and my grandfather how powerful that curse was. That is why I can't tell you certain things that I saw on the forbidden mountain.

My Uncle Bac Ba wanted to be a healer, so my grandfather brought him to Elephant Mountain to learn with the disciples of the Buddha master. A few years later, my grandfather took him to the cave to study meditation with his teacher. I don't know how long Bac Ba lived with the teacher, but when he returned to Cai Mon, he had a lot of healing power. He had never studied Chinese medicine like my grandfather or my father; he healed people with spiritual power.

Bac Ba eventually married a woman who belonged to the Cao Dai religion. She also worked in the healing arts. She practiced moxibustion, a Chinese technique related to acupuncture in which dried mugwort leaves are burned over the pressure points on the skin to strengthen the immune response and to restore the flows of energy in the body.

My uncle was a very kind person who helped many people, but his good intentions and pure heart didn't protect him from the curse. One night, while he was relaxing with his friends, drinking rice wine and swapping stories, he didn't realize what he was doing and told secret after secret to his friends. The next morning, Bac Ba couldn't move his legs, and by the afternoon his whole body was paralyzed. He was dead by the time my father and grandfather arrived to try to help him.

10

MY EDUCATION BEGINS

My father walked over to the bed with a lighted candle in his hand. He reached under the mosquito net and combed through my long black hair with his fingers to see which way my head was turned. It was my first day living with my father since I was a baby. His touch reminded me that I was not with Aunt Gioi on her expensive polished bed that felt so cool against my skin. I used to make faces in the black ebony wood like the man in the moon looking out of the dark cloudy sky. A termite could never bore its way into my aunt's bed, not like my father's rickety rattan bed, where the bugs could hide wherever they liked. I felt hot all night long sleeping next to my father, and his arms were too heavy when they were on me.

"Quang, it's time to wake up."

My father set the candle down in a holder, tied up the mosquito net, and pulled me to my feet. I had no choice but to follow him. I wasn't sure if I was still dreaming. Sleepy-faced, I stumbled in my father's wake, watching his hulking shadow stretch and shrink along the textured walls. Before I knew it, we were standing outside under the stars. Crickets were still trilling their night watch song. Brazen roosters were calling for the sun to return. Aunt Gioi said the roosters clear away the nightmares from the sky.

"Ba, are we going somewhere?"

"I want you to watch what I do in a day. After today, you may sleep until it is time to chant the morning sutra."

I sat down on a tree root and watched while my father built a fire. He struck a match, but it didn't light. He struck it again and again and then tried another. That box was soggy; he went back into the house and brought out a new box of matches, some candles, and some incense sticks.

"Quang, could you fill this teapot with water?"

I could see the cisterns in the semidarkness under the eaves. My father's house had an aluminum roof that caught a lot of rainwater, but it made the house very hot during the day. I patted the ground with my feet so I wouldn't trip over a tree root. His cistern came up to my armpits. I swiped the teapot about and came up with nothing every time. It was too dark to see if there was any water in there. My father called out, "There are more cisterns on the other side of the house."

After setting the water on the fire to boil, my father took the candles and incense and went to light the three altars in the yard. I could hear the distant voices of our neighbors speaking their first words of the day and see the orange flames of their cooking fires darting here and there through many layers of foliage. People with torches were already passing by the house on their way to market.

I followed my father into the house and watched him light the candles and incense on the nine altars he kept in the front of the big room, It was the only room in the house besides two small bedrooms, and was where he set up the clinic.

Two altars for my father's ancestors stood facing the open doorway. Between them was the largest of the altars. It was for Gautama, the Indian prince who attained Buddhahood. The Gautama Buddha was a wooden statue, dressed in a yellow cloth robe inside a glass case so the termites wouldn't eat him or his clothes. Four more altars representing the four directions stood beyond those three. Other Buddhas, and legendary gods and goddesses, loomed above me on all the altars.

I turned around in the direction of the doorway to look at the two altars that stood against the wall on either side of the door. Scroll paintings were attached to the thatched walls over both of them. The friendly-looking man on the right was Ong Thien. His job is to list all the good deeds you do throughout the year. To the left of the door, Ong Ac squinted accusingly at me, pointing his quill at me, letting me know that he was ready to write down every bad thing I did.

A breeze blew in through the window and the candlelight shifted, illuminating the silvery trails of incense smoke. I felt the Buddhas waking up. I saw tiny dragons the size of mice take off from the walls and fly around the room, breathing their fire and making the candles burn brighter. Snow-white cranes hovered in the air like clouds.

My father liked to glue his incense wrappers to the walls. It was a kind of patchwork wallpaper with images of dragons, flowers, birds, temples, waterfalls, and mountains.

He also used the incense wrappers to partition the room so his patients could have some privacy. He did this by stringing many rows of twine across the room and draping the wrappers on the twine by folding them in half. He made a lacquer with cassava flour boiled in water, which he brushed over the wrappers to make them stick together in one continuous sheet of paper.

A large Chinese apothecary stood against the back wall of the room. This elaborate and expensive piece of furniture had fifty slim wooden drawers labeled in Chinese and had been donated by one of my father's wealthy clients. Next to the apothecary was my father's high wooden table where he stood all day long, chopping and grinding medicine and preparing medicinal formulas for his patients. The table had a drawer in which he stuffed the money he received from people who could afford to pay. Above the table were shelves jammed with glass and ceramic jars of liquid tinctures and dried herbs. Wooden crates and cardboard boxes were stacked against the wall.

Preparing medicine was the most strenuous work he did all day, hacking through sinewy roots as dry as a bone with a machete and sawing through dozens of aged, preserved tubers as tough as leather that stick to the knife like glue. He never cut his fingernails, and sometimes they got to be over three inches long. If his nail broke off when he was making medicine, he always saved it in a drawer. I once looked in the drawer and saw a jumble of his fingernails.

Sometimes my father had to cut people's skin to drain an infection or to treat rheumatic arthritis. He would break shards from a porcelain bowl to use as a lancet and he would hide the shard between his long fingernails so the patient wouldn't become afraid.

I saw him use his fingernails to make medicine many times. Sometimes he ground them up and put them to soak in rice alcohol. He would dip his finger into the mixture and trace charms on babies' heads to help them sleep through the night. Once a woman who was midway through her pregnancy was brought to the clinic in a lot of pain. Her stomach was swollen and it was obvious the baby had died. My father burned two of his fingernails in the fire until they turned black and then ground them into a fine powder. He soaked a cup of uncooked rice in some water and then poured the starchy white water into a cup with the black nail powder. He gave it to the woman to drink. He told her the pain would get worse for about ten minutes and then it would go away. He massaged some pressure points on her hands and feet that would help her body eliminate the dead child.

The woman's pain grew worse and she started having contractions. My father pressed his thumbs on either side of her abdomen. I saw him looking up toward the ceiling while he did this, as if he were communicating with someone. Ten minutes later, the contractions stopped and the woman was not in pain any longer. My father told her, "It's done."

She asked him, "How will the baby come out?" My father didn't like to talk much. He just said, "You can go home now. It will be easy." My father gave her two packets of medicine to cook at home and drink after the miscarriage was over.

My father used both the local Vietnamese plants as well as the imported Chinese medicinal herbs. Chinese medicine works best for chronic conditions like asthma, recurring headaches, and arthritis, but for acute sicknesses like fevers, convulsions, snake bites, burns, sprains, and broken bones, Vietnamese traditional medicine works even better, and it doesn't cost anything.

My father said, "After breakfast, I am going to show you a list of ten Chinese characters that you will study during the next three days. I am also going to show you which Chinese herbs they stand for. Together they make a formula that we often use for colds."

My father used old newspaper to wrap up packets of medicine for his patients to take home. Buying paper was unheard of, because it was so expensive. The only kind of paper my father ever bought was a special kind of yellow paper that he used for writing prayers and protective charms.

"Maybe later you could help me glue together some of these newspaper scraps. I don't think I'll have enough paper for today."

My father went to the garden to look for breakfast. He brought back a papaya, a pineapple, and two bananas, sliced the fruit, and prepared a large pot of tea. He poured some for us to drink and then set the teapot aside. The kitchen table was outside under the awning, next to the cooking fire. The sky was changing color.

After he finished his breakfast, my father stood up. "You keep eating. I'm going to get the trays."

He brought over the twelve small trays, from his indoor and outdoor altars.

He put them on the table and the chopping block, and on the ground. Each tray held three or four small Chinese teacups that were still full.

I watched as my father emptied every teacup of yesterday's tea into a cooking pot. He rinsed the cups and set them back onto the same trays. Then he filled the cups with the new tea, and as he did this, he prayed. I noticed that he stopped the flow of tea three times for each cup, so it took a long time to fill all the cups. I said, "Why do you stop three times while filling each cup?" He told me it was because he put three prayers into each cup.

My father heated yesterday's tea over the fire and poured it into another teapot and placed that inside a coconut-hull thermos to keep it warm for his patients to drink. He said tea that has set on the altar for twenty-four hours holds many blessings. After restoring all the trays to their designated altars, he told me, "Come inside, it is time for the morning sutra."

My father made me sit behind him while he chanted in front of the main altar. He chanted with his prayer beads and his wood block. He touched his forehead to the floor many times as he chanted. A sutra is a long story that takes about forty minutes to sing. I couldn't understand what my father was singing about because he was singing in an old Vietnamese dialect.

At intervals that I couldn't predict, he hit a bronze bell that was shaped like a bowl, which made a clear ringing sound. He chanted to the four directions. Each time he turned, I had to scoot over behind him so I could copy everything he did. After the sutra was finished, he put the palms of his hands together and prayed out loud for peace in the world and for people to treat one another with kindness. He prayed for all people to be healed from sickness and to be relieved of suffering and heartache. He prayed for animals and people to have enough food to eat. He prayed for people who died, for their souls to find their way to heaven. The whole thing took nearly an hour.

When it was finished, we went to the river to bathe and to wash our clothes. It was already light, and there were plenty of people lined up in the yard, waiting to see my father.

11

TALKING BIRDS

My father set me up with an ink brush and bottle of ink to do my lessons outside at the kitchen table. Since we didn't have paper, he showed me how to tear green banana leaves into strips, which worked just fine. He showed me how to use the ink brush and how to draw a simple Chinese character. He made a step-by-step chart so I wouldn't forget the direction and order of the brushstrokes. He told me to write the character twenty times.

"When you have finished, come into the clinic and tell me," he said. "Then I will show you how to draw the next one."

After a while, I thought it would be a good idea to go looking for some food. The river was back in Cay Lay, about twenty minutes away. If the tide was low, I would be able to catch some crabs. Crabs are just about the easiest things to catch at low tide, because you can see their holes in the riverbank. Sometimes, if you are lucky, you will find an eel's hole, but it is almost impossible to pull those out without a strong hook and line and a lot of help, because they wrap their tails around a tree root.

I stopped to eat some guavas on the way. Sometimes you have to climb very high to get the fruit. I didn't see that a big *ran luc* snake, as thick as my arm, was coiled around a branch, and I grabbed onto it by mistake. They are difficult to see, because they can change their color to blend in with their surroundings. They like to eat birds and mice. They are not poisonous, but they can bite.

I stayed in the tree while I ate.

Some people like to eat snakes. One of our neighbors in Cai Mon discovered a python hole in the bank of his pond. Practically the whole neighborhood went to watch him catch the snake. He had placed a sturdy hook with a good-sized fish in front of the hole the night before. His children came out of the house the next morning and found the snake with his head sticking out of his hole. I got there just in time to see their father cut the head off and pull the body out of the hole. It was a twelve-foot-long male.

The father left the snake lying on the ground for the neighborhood to see. After breakfast, he took a knife and cut the snake's belly open. He scooped out the pearly balls of fat and put them into a bucket to save for medicine. If the fat was put in a bottle with rice wine, the liquid soothed burns and stopped infections.

The next night, he set the trap for the female. I saw him slit open the female's body and take out the baby snakes. Pythons aren't like other snakes, they bear live young. You had to get rid of the babies immediately, so that nobody would be tempted to sell them to an evil sorcerer who would use them to hurt people.

There was enough meat and medicine to share with the neighbors, and there was still plenty left to sell at the market. They didn't offer any meat to Aunt Gioi, because they knew she didn't eat snakes, but she did take a bottle of snake fat.

The tide was too high for catching crabs. I waded along the muddy bank past the neighbors' fishing nets. It is okay to take fruit from other people's trees, but it is forbidden to take fish out of other people's nets. The nets are set up like a box with an open lid. You have to fill the net with a lot of leafy branches. Mossy ones are best, because they attract the water insects that fish like to eat.

When the river rises higher than the top of the net, the fish will go into the net to eat the insects and smaller fish, and to hide in the branches from the bigger fish. Once they swim in, they usually make it their home. If you want to catch them, you have to wait for low tide when they cannot swim out the top. Just pull the branches out and scoop the fish out of the water with a basket.

Up ahead I saw a flock of ducks being led across the river to graze. "Oh, perfect," I thought, "a duck crossing. Maybe I can find an egg for lunch."

Diving for duck eggs in the river is fun. There are always a bunch of eggs in the mud beneath a duck crossing. Ducks don't usually lay eggs while they are swimming, but it happens sometimes. You have to feel around for them.

I was determined to find an egg, because I knew my father would like it. I dove for a long time, hoping that I would be lucky.

I found one! By the time I got back with my egg, my father was very angry.

"You may not go anywhere until you have finished your calligraphy. You have nine more characters to learn today."

"I am sorry. I thought I had plenty of time."

I held out the egg. I hadn't noticed yet that it was mottled.

"I'll give it to someone," my father said, accepting the rotten egg. "Thank you."

My father didn't like to eat old eggs. Neither did I. The only people who actually like to eat them are people who drink a lot of liquor. They boil them first and when they crack them open, a strong smell comes out, and the eggs are all gray and black with fungus. You can wash away the taste with a swig of alcohol, but the smell lasts a long time.

"Go back and finish your work," my father said sternly.

My father wasn't a very good cook, because he didn't have time. This is how he made rice: He took some newspaper scraps and put them into the woodstove. Then he took a handful of wood charcoal and put it on top of the paper and then lit it. He measured out four cups of rice and eight cups of water and set the pot on the stove. According to his plan, the paper would light the charcoal, and the charcoal would burn out just when the rice was ready. More often than not, the rice on the bottom would be scorched, and the rice on the top would be uncooked. He would make a quick vegetable stir-fry with the same vegetables that grew in the yard every time and he stir-fried an egg with onions. It really wasn't good.

We didn't always eat lunch or dinner together. He took only a short break for meals, and I was usually out playing somewhere. Sometimes I'd come back home hungry for lunch, and I'd find the rice was perfectly cooked, and there would be spring rolls and a lot of different dishes. Then I knew that one of his patients had brought food for him, women who liked my father very much. Sometimes they told me to call them "mother," which confused me. I couldn't keep track of the ones who wanted to me to call them mother, so I called every woman I saw in our kitchen "mother."

.   .   .

I had to chant with my father two times a day, but even after a few months of practice, I wasn't very good at chanting. Sometimes I crawled away when my father was facing away from the doorway. I knew he would never interrupt the sutra to go looking for me.

I met a boy my age named Chi. His father trained birds to talk, and then he sold them at market for a lot of money. I knew my father wouldn't like that, so I never spoke about it. Chi took me to his house to see the birds. They could speak very clearly, just like a person. They could sing parts of songs and recite poems. One bird sang a lullaby that Aunt Gioi used to sing.

You have to start with a baby bird, one that just hatched from the egg. The best birds to train are the *con sao,* the *con cuong,* and the crow. Chi and I climbed a lot of trees looking for nests. Sometimes my father would come out looking for me and find us up in a tree, but he never knew that we were stealing baby birds out of their nests.

You have to keep the baby crows in total darkness, as if they were back inside their eggs. If they see the sun, they will never talk. Chi's father kept them in a hole in the ground, and he only opened the hole at night to feed them. You have to repeat what you want the bird to say over the hole, so the bird can hear you. You have to repeat it many times a day, and also at night when you feed it. It takes about twenty days for a baby crow to sing its song or speak its poem to try to get your attention. Chi's father kept the smaller baby birds, the *con sao* and *con cuong,* in cages inside the house. Those didn't need to be kept in total darkness.

There is one more thing you have to do, which is the secret. You must take a bamboo knife and scrape the top layer of skin off the birds' tongues. I think it hurts the bird a lot, because their tongue bleeds a little bit. If you don't scrape off the hard outer skin four times, they will still speak but it won't sound exactly like a person.

My father had a boat someone had given him but he never used. He kept it turned over upside down to keep out the rain. That was where I went when I was feeling sorry about making my father have to go out looking for me. I had dug a little hole under there to keep my marbles. Not that he would mind me playing marbles; it's just that if he knew, he would be able to find me faster.

HAMMOCK MAGIC

Could it be? A whale in my fishing net? I'll swim underneath to get a good look at it. I scrambled onto the bed and ducked beneath the bulging banana-twine net. I could smell his scent through the water, like tree resin. The net was straining; it could give way any second. I reached my feet upward to restrain the beast. I gave my father's buttocks a gentle shove. His massive bulk swung back and forth, nearly grazing my body.

Siesta was the only time my father was not busy. He liked to relax with me and tell me stories and try to teach me about Buddha and right and wrong.

"Ba, can you tell me a monster story today?"

I caught his body in my legs like a helpless tangled old catfish. He reached down, caught both my feet, and hoisted me up into the hammock. He felt like a gorilla. My father rarely laughed out loud, because he had too much responsibility, but when I tried to tickle him, he howled like a wolf.

"A monster story. Let me see."

"Tell me the one about the time when the monster tried to eat you and your friends."

"I was going to tell you 'The Gold and the Poison Snake.'"

I got down off the hammock and sat down on a trunk that I had recently noticed under a pile of clothes and boxes. I could tell that it was going to be another monk story. I gazed out the window, trying to look as bored as possible.

"Just a minute," my father exclaimed. "Where did I put those things?" (It wasn't until I started spending siestas with my father that I realized he had been doing magic right in front of my eyes my whole life, only I hadn't noticed.)

He reached up and began feeling around for something in the thin air. I sprang on top of his stomach and began frisking him all over.

"I remember leaving it here, so that I didn't have to get up and look for it. Let's see . . . maybe over here. No . . ."

He peeked into an imaginary sack, and then he began searching through imaginary drawers, tossing all kinds of invisible stuff out.

I grabbed at his raised arms as he unscrewed an invisible jar, and I patted and peered into his long sleeves. I clutched his wrists and kept my eyes glued to his hands.

"Oh, here it was all the time." Just as he uttered those words, there was a heap of *trai man* cherries in his open hand. *Trai man* cherries did not grow anywhere near our province, but only in the southwest. They keep you busy for a long time, because you have to roll them between your hands until they get all soft or else they will taste too sour.

I cupped my hands, and he tried to fit all the cherries into them.

I asked him how he got the cherries and he answered, "My friends help me."

"What friends?"

"From an invisible world."

"You mean a ghost . . . a dead person?"

"No, a ghost could never do that."

"Well, then who?"

"Spirits from the forbidden mountain."

"Ba, I think I am ready to learn magic."

"I told you before, magic is not important. What is important is to learn medicine and meditation."

"But will you teach me one day . . . to do what you can do?"

"You must first learn what is important."

The more I thought about it, my father's magic was not all that impressive. All he could conjure up was fruit. If I asked for orange taffy or coconut cake, he would say, "Here's some money. Go and buy some at the store."

I wanted to do more important magic than that. I knew that if I listened to this monk story, chances were good that tomorrow he would tell me a scary one.

My father began, "There was once a man who meditated every day, and he became very wise. He was so wise that he began to see things before they happened.

"One day he went for a walk along a village road with some of his students. One of the students went to the side of the road to pick some fruit, and he saw something golden that was hidden in the bushes. It was a pile of gold coins.

"The student ran to get the others and he showed them the pile of gold.

" 'What gold?' said the teacher. 'I see only a poisonous snake.'

"The students looked again, and they saw a pile of gold.

" 'Let us go,' said their teacher, 'and leave the dangerous animal alone.'

"The students looked very confused. They couldn't understand why their teacher did not see the money.

"Three farmers had been standing on the other side of the bushes, and they had overheard the monks talking. They were peeking through the bushes, waiting for the monks to leave. Then they found the gold. Oh, they were so happy.

"The first farmer said, 'I'll go to my house and get some wine so we can give thanks to Buddha for giving us this fortune.' But what he was really thinking was that he would poison the wine so his friends would die and he could have all the gold.

"While the first farmer was gone, the other two farmers decided that they would each have more gold if they killed their friend when he came back.

"The first farmer was back in no time with some poisoned wine. He poured out three cups and he invited his friends to drink, but instead, they took out their knives and stabbed their friend to death.

"Afterward, the two remaining farmers lifted their cups of wine and thanked Buddha for making them wealthy. They both drank poisoned wine and died."

"Ba," I said, "do you think that snake was really a monster that could appear as a pile of gold to trick people and kill them?"

The next day I asked again for a scary story about ghosts.

"Tell me the one about Aunt Gioi's neighbors, the ones who ran away with their ducks and almost got eaten by the two monsters."

"Very well," my father said. I leapt into the hammock.

"I knew you were going to finish all your work today, so I brought you a special treat, only I seem to have misplaced it."

I held on to his arms again, not letting his hands out of my sight for a single split second as he waved them about.

"Oh, here they are."

There in his hand was cluster of tan, smooth-skinned longans still on the branch. Today there are longans in every yard, but back then you would never see a longan tree. The meat of a longan tastes very similar to a lichee, juicy and refreshing, with a kind of delicate perfume flavor.

THE GHOST THAT TRICKED THE TWO MONSTERS

There was a young couple from Cai Mon who went to work at the Cu Chi rubber plantation. Both husband and wife were from poor families. They thought they could work for a few years and be able to save enough money to buy land and build a house so they could start a family. The young wife was already pregnant.

When they arrived at the rubber plantation, they found out that they weren't allowed to leave, not even to go home on holidays to visit their parents. The supervisors beat the laborers if they showed up late or if they didn't work fast enough. After several months had passed, the husband and wife found out that they were not going to be able to save any money at all, and even if they did, they wouldn't be allowed to leave. They were trapped.

Many had tried to escape the rubber plantation before, and most of them had been caught and brought back and punished severely.

The husband and wife made up their minds to run away anyway. They ran through the night and didn't stop to sleep, because they knew the supervisors would come looking for them in their jeeps the next morning. All they had with them were two ducks, a male and a female, that they had stolen from the plantation.

They decided to go to Elephant Mountain to live in the spiritual community, but they would have to get there on foot. The couple survived on food in the forest, and occasionally there was an egg to eat.

When they thought they had gotten far enough away from the plantation, they began to go to the houses of the landowners and ask if they could do a day's work for a meal and a place to sleep, but they had no luck. It was only the poor villagers like themselves who offered them a meal and shelter for the night.

One evening, they became very tired and were relieved to see an old farmhouse in the distance. By the time they arrived at the front door, they were feeling so tired they could have fallen asleep standing on their feet.

Two old men appeared at the door and invited them into the house. The two weren't dressed like farmers; their clothing was clean and freshly pressed. They didn't look like old farmers because both old men had perfect, very white teeth.

The two old men showed the couple to a bed in the back room and said they would not be disturbed. They requested that the ducks stay outside in the pen for the night.

The husband and wife were both grateful and comforted. However, at the same time, they both had a feeling that something was not right. Instead of sleeping, they kept quiet and listened to the night sounds.

All of a sudden the ducks started screaming. The couple jumped out of bed and ran to the front of the house and looked out the window, just as the moon peeked out from behind the clouds.

The two men were sitting side by side on the front doorstep. The ducks were in their laps, and they were eating them. Blood was dripping from their mouths as they spoke.

"Let's eat them now before they wake up."

"Why not save them for breakfast?"

"I think they are awake. We better go get them now before they run away."

"NO! I want to relax and enjoy my meal. Let them run for a while and tire themselves out. We'll catch them later."

The couple climbed out of the window and started running until they could run no farther. They arrived at a place where there were many tombs and graves. There was no way they could outrun the monsters.

Just then they saw a small rundown thatched house on the far side of the burial ground. They ran up to the door and called out for help.

When another old man appeared at the door, the husband whispered to his wife to run, but she had faith that this old man was not a monster.

They told the old man why they were running. He said, "It is good that you came to my house. You are safe with me."

The husband didn't believe the man, and he tried again to convince his wife to flee, but she said she could not run anymore.

The man told them, "Quick, hide behind that wooden beam. They will be here any minute."

The husband told his wife, "See? He is not human. How would he know that?"

They had no choice but to hide, because the two monsters barged into the house that very instant and demanded, "Tell us. Did you see anyone passing this way?"

The man told them that he hadn't seen a soul, and the monsters left. The man told the couple that they could spend the night in his house, but that they were not to leave that hiding place.

It wasn't very easy to sleep sitting behind a wooden post, but they managed to lean on one another until morning. When they woke up, the house was gone and they were propped against a tombstone in the burial ground.

I patted my father's arm and remarked knowingly, "Ghosts and monsters can cast spells on people, and make them see things that are really not there." I leaned into my father's face, and taking hold of his beard I whispered, "But only monsters can actually eat people."

"That's right," my father said. "And only ghosts can hide things from monsters."

"Yeah," I said.

I3

LEMON TEMPLE

knew my father was working very hard. His legs became covered with bruises from standing on his feet all day making medicine. More times than not, there would be no dinner for me, not even rice, because my father didn't have time to cook. I used to go into the clinic where he was still working and tell him I was hungry. He would grab some money out of the drawer and tell me to go down the street and buy something. I usually bought noodle soup and a sweet rice cake.

Each morning, my father prepared a list of Chinese characters for me to learn, but I rarely got it all done. I would go off with my friends to play marbles or go fishing or hunting for birds. There were a lot of children who didn't go to school because they didn't pass their fifth-grade exam. Vietnamese public schools are very demanding and strict. Exams are given at the end of fifth grade. They are so difficult that only one student in twenty can pass. If you don't pass, you are permitted to take the exam again only once. If you fail again you can't go to public school anymore.

My father had to leave the clinic many times to go out looking for me. He would tell me, "I don't have time for this, and neither do you. Learning the Chinese names for the medicinal herbs is just the beginning. You will need to be able to read Chinese books."

He started whipping my bottom as punishment, but that didn't seem to stop me.

In December my father stopped work for three weeks in preparation for Tet. Tet is the most important holiday of the year, because it is when the spirits of our ancestors come back and visit us. It is also the time when the kitchen gods fly up to heaven on a golden carp and report whether we have been good or not. We pray that the kitchen gods will come back from heaven with blessings for a healthy and prosperous year to come.

Everybody in Vietnam is busy for most of the month of December in preparation for Tet. The house and the garden must be thoroughly clean and beautiful. Everyone must have new clothes to wear, and there must be lots of special food to present to our ancestors.

My aunt and I had always traveled to my father's house to celebrate Tet. He would first come home to Cai Mon to pray at his parents' graves. Then he would take Aunt Gioi and me back to wherever he was living. We would be the only family members at my father's Tet celebration besides Co, who always showed up. Even though I called her mother, I didn't really know her.

This was the first time I helped my father prepare the special food for Tet. We made two kinds of edible rice paper, sweet rice paper for cookies, and regular rice paper for spring rolls. We also made candied ginger, coconut, pumpkin, and bitter melon. I went with my father and some of his students to a farm where he bought two trees of tangerines. You walk through the orchard and pick however many trees you want, and of course you can choose the biggest ones. Then you pick all the tangerines off those trees and carry them home.

It didn't matter that my father bought so many tangerines, because they can last a long time if you store them in such a way that they are not touching, and the air can get underneath them. The outside will dry and become dark and hard, but the inside will be juicy and fresh.

I enjoyed making the rice paper and candy. My father cooked a huge pot of sweet rice, and when it was done, he pounded it into a dough with coconut milk and palm syrup. He broke off lichee-size chunks of dough, rolled them into balls, and then flattened them into round, paper-thin sheets with a rolling pin. My job was to place the rice paper on coconut-leaf mats to dry in the sun. Regular rice paper is made the same way, except you do not add the other ingredients into the dough.

If you want to make candied ginger, you have to prick the roots all over with a needle and boil them in water with a little alum for two minutes so they won't taste too spicy. Then you slice the roots and cook some sugar over a low fire until it turns to liquid, about one pound of sugar to one pound of sliced roots. You keep cooking until all the sugar has soaked into the roots. Cook the coconut, dried pumpkin, and bitter melon the same way. My father made so much food because he invited a lot of people to celebrate with our family, people who didn't have a family, and also his friends and students. By the end of the third week in December, we went to Cai Mon to fetch my aunt. Vietnam follows the lunar calendar, just as China does, which means that each month begins on the day of the new moon. The full moon occurs on the fifteenth and sixteenth day of the month. Holidays often occur during the full moon. Tet is celebrated at the new moon on January first of our lunar calendar and rarely coincides with the January first that is celebrated throughout most of the world. Tet can fall up to twenty days earlier or later than the New Year holiday in the west.

On the eve of Tet, we made a special soup for the ancestors, with sweet rice, white beans, potatoes, coconut milk, and sugar. My father put some soup in forty small bowls and placed them on his altars. Then he went into the clinic to meditate. On the eve of Tet, you are supposed to be sorry for all the bad things you did during the year and pray for a happy new year. Then at midnight you light fireworks. My father always bought a lot of fireworks, and I used to take some and hide them for another day.

After the fireworks, my father always went back to pray and meditate while the rest of us ate food and had fun.

We woke up early the next morning to cook a lot more food, because by nine o'clock on the morning of January first, the table must be prepared with food for the ancestors to enjoy.

I told my father I hoped he lived for one hundred years, and he told me he hoped I worked hard at my studies this year. Then we sat down to enjoy the food with our ancestors.

By February 1960, after I had been living with my father for seven months, he told me, "I am sorry I don't have enough time to teach you very much. I have made arrangements for you to live with a relative of mine in Cho Lach. He is a monk and knows *Han Viet* character writing. He has agreed to take you into his home as his student."

Han Viet is the old-style Vietnamese writing that uses Chinese characters to signify Vietnamese words. A person who knows *Han Viet* can look at a book written in Chinese and understand it in Vietnamese. *Han Viet* began to be phased out over three hundred years ago when a French Jesuit missionary named Alexandre de Rhodes introduced *quoc ngu*, our modern Latin-based phonetic alphabet.

I begged my father to let me stay and study with him. I promised that I wouldn't run away anymore. He hugged me and looked into my eyes and said, "I am not angry with you, I just don't have enough time."

My relative was a mean and ugly man in his sixties who lived with his sad-looking wife in a one-room house in a lemon orchard. The orchard didn't belong to my relative; it belonged to his neighbor. In the center of the lemon orchard was an eight-sided temple his neighbor owned. She ran the temple and was in charge of the monks who lived there. There were no other houses nearby.

My relative was not associated with that temple. He worked independently. People hired him to chant at their funerals. His wife wove hammocks for a living.

As soon as my father left, my new teacher put me to work making banana-leaf strips. He told me to make one hundred.

"Show me how much you know," he ordered.

As soon as my lesson was over, I went behind a tree and cried. I was crying for my aunt. I wanted to go home to her.

I wept until bedtime. There was only enough space in the house for the altar, a table, two chairs, and one rattan bed. I watched as my relative's wife strung a hammock over the bed for me. I couldn't wait to curl up into my hammock and comfort myself. Then I watched in utter horror as my relative's wife climbed into the hammock to sleep. I wanted to kick her all night long for making me sleep next to that ugly face with its rotten teeth and putrid breath. I cried softly to the sounds of my relative hacking up phlegm and spitting over the side of the bed.

My relative made me start working at sunrise every morning. I had to stack my strips of calligraphy in bunches of ten and tie them up in twine. Then I was to place them neatly inside a basket to be checked by my relative. After he checked it, he never threw it away into the forest. *Han Viet* is considered to be holy. The only thing you can do with it is to throw it into the river or burn it. There was no river near my relative's house, so we had to burn it.

My relative sometimes had to go away to chant at a funeral. That was the only thing I had to look forward to. Whenever he was gone, his wife let me go off to play in the orchard. Later, my relative would return with baskets of food that were his payment for conducting the funeral. My relative would appear carrying half a pig's head. It was the first time I ate pig's head meat. I could eat as much as I wanted, because it wouldn't keep. He also brought home fruit, cookies, and cake.

My father and my aunt came to visit me every two weeks or so. I cried to them and begged them to take me back, but my father told me this was the best way for me to learn. Each time he came, my father brought medicine for my relative's cough.

My relative had a *cay man* tree in his yard. *Cay man* fruits are red and round like apples and taste sweet but a little sour. We had picked all the *cay man* fruits off the tree except for the ones at the very top. The branches of the tree were too slender for me to climb.

One of the times my father came to visit me, we rested together on a hammock that was tied to that tree. I had been craving a *cay man* fruit for days, and I asked my father if he could give me one to eat. He reached up and got one right out of the air.

By 1960, the Indochina War of independence for North Vietnam had been over for six years, but war against the spreading Communist revolution was heavy in the south. Each outbreak of violence meant my relative had more funerals than he could handle. Sometimes he had to schedule as many as four funerals a day.

I started helping the monks who tended the orchard. Lemons are not easy to pick because the branches have tiny needle-sharp thorns. We picked the lemons when they were still green, and I suppose in America those are called limes, but to us they are green lemons. Even though I came home with thorns in my feet every day, I still loved to work in the orchard.

The name of the temple was Long Hung Tu, which means Pleasant Dragon Temple. The monks went into the temple to chant four times a day. One day I followed them into the temple and met the owner. She was a beautiful woman with kind eyes, but the monks were always complaining that she worked them too hard.

I worked and chanted at the temple whenever I could. I would do anything, even chant, to get away from my relative's house.

My relative was very strict, and he hit me often. He made me memorize a twenty-page classic book written in *Han Viet* about ethics called the *Tam Tu Kinh*. I had to write it from memory. One time when I didn't remember a passage, he struck me on the side of my head so hard that the ink bottle went flying, and I couldn't see. He yelled for me to pick up my brush and my bottle, but all I saw was darkness. I crawled around on the ground feeling for the bottle and the brush. He yelled at me for getting ink on my hands. Then he pulled me up and hit me some more.

My vision came back after about twenty minutes. Sometimes my relative's wife would try to protect me, and he would hit us both.

I found a way to spend more time with the master of the temple. I had discovered that my relative rarely checked my calligraphy before burning it, so when he was away for the day, I prepared my bundles of writing, but instead of writing on every page, I only wrote on the leaf at the top of the bundle. The rest were blank. I placed the bundles neatly in the basket and left to spend the day at the temple.

The next time my father and aunt came to visit me, I begged my father for permission to sleep at the temple with the monks. I took them to meet the master. My father thanked her for inviting me to live at the temple and gave his permission.

I was much happier after that. By mid-May, my relative had still not recovered from his cough. The next time my father and aunt came to see me, my father realized he was sick with tuberculosis and that he should have known sooner. I ran through the lemon orchard to the temple to say good-bye to the kind master of the temple.

14

ROBBERS

We walked slowly because of my aunt. I let her hold my hand.

"Can I go back home with you?" I asked her privately. She just squeezed my hand.

We were walking on a long dirt path to the highway. A lot of people were out working in their gardens. In those days, people kept lawns and planted their fruit trees far apart. People gave cuttings to their neighbors, so everyone had a large variety of bushes and fruit trees and vegetables and flowering plants, which attracted the insects and butterflies and birds. Today, people cram their land with as many longan trees as possible to sell the fruits to the canning factories. The trees are so crowded together that grass cannot grow for lack of light, and the soil is bare. The gardens are no longer beckoning.

We stepped onto the highway, which was very hard and hot to walk on. We had no choice because there were rice fields on either side, and the rice plants were growing right up against the asphalt. The farmers were busy spreading their freshly harvested rice along both sides of the highway to dry in the sun, like two long golden carpets. The rice took up half the lane in either direction. Nobody minded; we just stayed toward the middle and tried to avoid the oncoming pedestrians, water buffalos and cows, bicycles, pedicabs, motorbikes, and an occasional car or truck. Everyone respects rice.

The bus came bundling down the center of highway, and everyone parted to let it stop in the middle of the road. I took my father's arm and said, "Ba, can I go to my aunt's house?"

He thought for about a minute and replied, "Good idea."

It took me a moment to believe my ears. I leapt onto the bus like a fighting fish.

My father told me he was very busy because he was building a rice silo in his yard for the neighborhood in case of a failed harvest. The yard was in an uproar with all the building materials and neighborhood people helping.

My father first had the idea of building a rice silo just after the time he escaped from his wife's house by eating a lot of tobacco. He had no medicine, because he had left it at her house. He found an abandoned house, and he started to clean it out. The garden was overgrown with thorny vines, and the house was leaning over. People warned my father not to live there, because the house had brought bad luck to everyone who ever lived there.

My father didn't care, because he knew how clear away the negative memories. We believe that the ridgepole of a house can bring bad luck if an animal had been killed and its blood had been spilled on that tree. Before moving in, people usually perform a ceremony to release the traumatized spirits of any slain birds or animals from the ridgepole.

My father cleaned and fixed up the house and the garden until the feeling became good. Then he sent word to his former patients that he was seeing patients again. The only problem was that he had no medicine and no money.

At first he had to collect money from his patients and tell them to come back in two days for their medicine. He would take their money to the Chinese herb store and buy just enough for them. After a while, the store owner allowed him to take crates of dried herbs home on credit.

My father didn't have any jars or drawers to keep the medicine easy to reach, so he had to keep the crates around his worktable.

There was one kind of medicine that my father used in almost every formula. It is called Tien Ho. It is a sliced dark yellow root that is used to strengthen the lung energy. He kept the box of Tien Ho on a shelf above his worktable so he could reach up and grab some easily. One morning, he was out of Tien Ho and had to go to the Chinese herb store to buy a new box. When he came back, he had to work very fast in order to take care of everyone.

My father reached up to grab some Tien Ho and his hand came out of the box holding a wad of crumpled-up paper. "Oh," he thought, "someone cheated me." He tossed the paper back into the box because a lot of medicine was caught in between the creases.

All day long he was reaching into the box and throwing back wads of paper. He was getting annoyed, because he was busy and didn't have time to fish all the paper out of the box. At one point he was so angry that he tried to tear it in half. To his surprise, he saw a bundle of money that had been wrapped in the paper. There were about twenty bundles of money in the box. It was a fortune.

My father didn't know what to do with the money. The first thing he did was to go back to the Chinese store and ask the owner if he had lost anything. The owner said he had not. The second thing he did was to pray and meditate. That was when he had the idea to use the money to build a rice silo.

My aunt decided that it was too late to go all the way to Cai Mon, so we all got off the bus near my father's house to spend the night.

There was no one around in my father's yard; everyone had gone home for supper. I could see that they had been weaving mats and spreading them with cow dung. Dung-smeared mats were drying everywhere, on the bushes, against the trees, flat on the ground. The manure was used to seal the mats from moisture. Sun-baked cow dung is odorless and dries harder than clay.

All the mats had to be ready by the time the rice arrived, and the construction of the silo could not be started without the rice. The first mats would be stood up on their sides, overlapping to form a standing ring about four feet high and forty feet around. Then the people would carry the rice from the boat using a shoulder stick, a *don ganh,* that has a large basket on either end.

When the first ring is filled halfway up, the second ring of mats is placed on top of the rice. That ring would be filled, then another and another until all the rice was contained. The silos usually stood about ten feet high. There was a ladder for people to climb up to get some. If they had money they could leave it in a special box that was kept inside the house. Most people only took rice when they needed it, although there were always people who hoarded. They had to bring the rice to the mill before it could be used. Only unhulled rice was stored in the silo. Polished rice wouldn't last more than two or three months in a silo without getting moldy and infested with bugs.

"It's a madhouse here every day," my father told my aunt. "With my patients and the neighborhood all in one yard, I'd never know what Quang was up to."

We entered the house, and my aunt and my father stopped to light incense at the family altar. I decided to pray, too. The candles and incense on family altars are usually placed on top of a high out-of-the-way place like a large wardrobe.

My father lit two red candles and we each took a golden incense stick out of the box and held it up toward heaven to be blessed. I looked up at the altar and spotted a pineapple. "Maybe we'll eat that tomorrow morning for breakfast," I prayed.

That was enough praying for me. Kids aren't really expected to pray at the family altar. My father and my aunt knelt on the floor. They bowed and prayed for their parents and grandparents. I walked past the wardrobe toward the kitchen doorway to see if there was any food out there, but I didn't get very far. I froze in my tracks just on the other side of the wardrobe.

There were three bodies lying on the floor. I tried to scream but couldn't. I backed up toward my father and touched his back. He stopped praying and crawled around the wardrobe like a big fat spider.

They were robbers. The things they had stolen were still in their arms. They had been digging up the floor. They took a Chinese porcelain vase, a gold-plated statue of Buddha, a statue of the Jade Emperor, and a white marble statue of Quan The Am Bo Tat, the goddess of mercy.

"A two-step snake," I reasoned. The venom of a two-step snake is so potent that it will fell its victim in the time it takes to walk two steps. I had heard stories about two-step snakes in the north that protected people's houses like watchdogs, but I'd never seen one. I said, "Ba, maybe a two-step snake is protecting the house."

My father and my aunt had said nothing. They were just staring at the men. One was more of a teenager; the other two were older.

Just then one of the men made a sound. It was like crying. He mumbled something that sounded like, "Don't kill me, I beg you."

Without opening his eyes, another one muttered, "I can't move, I'm paralyzed. Forgive us, master, my children are hungry."

I realized what was going on. My father had put a spell on the house.

The three robbers were crying that they were sorry. When my father approached them, they started to scream, "Please, don't hurt us."

My father spoke to them. He said, "I do not blame you."

He told them not to be afraid, that he would not harm them. He touched them one by one. They softened, and they could move again.

He told them, "I want you to keep the things you have taken. I am giving them to you."

The robbers felt ashamed, and they cried more. My father put his hand on my shoulder and led me outside. After the robbers left, I said to my father, "You put a spell on the house, didn't you?"

He replied, "No."

"It was some kind of magic, wasn't it?" I insisted.

"Some kind of magic, yes." He started stroking his beard. I didn't like it when my father looked confused.

He said, "I think it was the power around the altar. I think the power stopped the thieves."

My aunt and I gave each other a questioning look.

"Your money is safe, then?" my aunt asked.

"Yes, quite safe," my father said.

I thought about the wooden trunk that my father kept in the bedroom. It was reinforced with bands of black wrought iron. I ran into the bedroom to see if it had been tampered with. I didn't think the thieves had noticed it at all. I started wondering about what kinds of valuable things were locked up in there.

15

SUMMER IN CAI MON

That spring and summer I spent a lot of time with Uncle Quon, whom I called Chu Tam or "Eighth Uncle." In Vietnam you never call someone by his name unless he is younger than you. I would never have known the given names of my aunts and uncles if I hadn't seen letters addressed to them. Uncle Quon was actually the seventh-born child of my grandparents, but in Vietnam, we always call the firstborn "number two" to fool the evil eye.

My friends called me Trung Hai, second brother. I called my friend Hoa Chi Muoi, tenth sister, and I called her mother Co Tu, fourth aunt. My father was called Ong Sau, sixth grandfather, and he called Aunt Gioi Chi Nam, fifth sister. Younger people addressed Aunt Gioi as Ba Nam, fifth grandmother. The number in your nickname never changes, but whether someone calls you "sister" or "aunt" or "grandmother" depends on their age relative to yours. Numbers for nicknames go from two to ten, *hai, ba, tu, nam, sau, bay, tam, chin, muoi.* You may be confused later in the story, because some of my teachers and friends have the same nicknames, and I don't know their real names.

Uncle Quon was frightening to look at if you weren't used to seeing him. He was bigger than my father. His large muscular body and his face had been slashed by pirates so many times that he looked like he needed a good ironing to smooth out his skin again. Uncle Quon was a master martial artist. He never hired any guards to come with him when he delivered a shipment of coconuts to Saigon. He wasn't afraid. He had fought off as many as five pirates at a time.

His first wife left him; I don't know why. Nobody liked his second wife, not even Aunt Gioi. People said she was stingy. They blamed her for not letting her husband hire a bodyguard. I didn't care about that. Aunt Hue was very kind to me. She had no children of her own.

Uncle Quon told me, "One day when you are older, I'll take you along with me on my boat. You could be my lookout."

"For pirates?" I asked.

"Yep."

"Why can't I go now?" I asked.

"I have to teach you how to fight first," he said.

That summer my uncle started teaching me martial arts. The first thing he did was dig a hole and put me inside.

"Now jump out of that hole without using your hands," he instructed.

I was into the hole up to my knees; there was no way I could possibly jump out without using my hands.

"It is impossible," I said.

"In time you'll see what's possible. That is your summer project," my uncle told me.

I was happy to be home in time for Cai Mon's *Cung Than* festival, the annual celebration for the guardian spirit of our village. All the villages in Vietnam have their own guardian spirits, recognized by the king long ago. Every village keeps an altar for its guardian spirit inside a special building, called the *dinh*, or "spirit house." The original certificate from the king is kept in the spirit house behind the inner wall. Nobody is allowed inside the spirit house except the keeper of the *dinh*, the village chief, and the members of the village council. Both my father and my grandfather had served on the Cai Mon village council.

The spirit house is the largest and most important building in the village. It has an enormous, heavy, tiled roof with corners curving upward. The massive roof is supported on heavy wooden pillars. One or more sides of the spirit house do not have walls, so people can see inside.

Every village has its own day of the year for celebrating *Cung Than*, which means "spirit house day." Rain or shine, *Cung Than* must be commemorated. Nobody would dare to stay home, for fear of offending the guardian spirit. Everyone in the village participates by contributing to a feast with roast pork and sweet rice and cookies. The members of the village council wear their long blue silk brocade shirts and hats. Musicians play many different kinds of drums, flutes, horns, and stringed instruments that are either bowed or strummed and plucked. People sing the old songs.

I liked to look inside the spirit house, at the racks of golden lances running along the outer wall of the inner chamber. The weapons were there to protect the guardian spirit inside in inner chamber, sixteen bladed spears with red-painted wooden handles, eight on either side of the door. There were eight different kinds of blades. My favorite was the blade that was shaped like a writhing serpent. It had a cutting edge in both directions.

The kids would say that if any unauthorized person was able to get past those spears and open the inner chamber door, the guardian spirit would strike them dead.

I once asked my father if that was true, and he told me it wasn't. He said the inner chamber was where the king's certificate was kept inside a tube-shaped steel container. The steel container was kept inside a carved wooden chest. My father saw the king's certificate. He said it was made of thick yellow and gold paper four feet long and two feet wide. The king's royal seal was stamped in red ink.

One afternoon I was playing in the orchard where it was cool and shady. There were orange, lemon, and tangerine trees planted between the coconut trees, and also flowering bushes and sugar cane. I was pretending to be fighting off pirates with a long bamboo pole, like the one my uncle used. The pirates snuck up on me from all sides, and I had to knock their spears out of their hands, sweep them off their feet, and push them off the boat. I had to duck under the strings that my uncle tied from tree to tree, so the yellow ants could go on all the citrus trees. You need yellow ants on your citrus trees because they make the fruit juicy. If you have black ants, or no ants at all, the fruit will come out dry. Yellow ants always attack you when you climb their trees, so you have to take ashes in your pocket to sprinkle and rub on all the branches you go on, so they won't follow you.

In the distance, I heard the sound of someone scything grass. I peered through a patch of sugarcane to see who it was. It was my aunt.

She was clearing a spot in the long grass around a stone about two feet high. I realized it was a grave. After trimming the grass, she set a vase of flowers and a dish of tangerines by the headstone and lit some incense and held it up against the sky. Then she knelt and bowed to the ground, disappearing from sight.

When she was gone I went to read the stone.

KY VAN NGUYEN
1842–1946

If my grandfather had been buried in a sandalwood coffin, I could have dug it up and opened it and seen his face, exactly as he looked the day he died. Sandalwood coffins preserve the body, but after a few seconds in the open air, the body falls into a pile of dust.

When someone dies in my culture, the family consults with a professional person called an Ong Thay who knows how to determine the best possible date and time of the funeral, the appropriate spot where the person should be buried, and the direction their grave should face. An Ong Thay makes calculations that are based on Chinese astrology and the law of the five elements. He factors in many details, including date and hour of birth, date and hour of death, and, if the deceased has children, the birthdays of each of the children. In my grandfather's case, there were six surviving children to take into consideration. The Ong Thay told my aunt and her siblings that they would have to hold off the burial for ten days to insure that none of the remaining children would suffer from bad luck. My father, Aunt Gioi, and their brothers and sisters wanted to build a beautiful mausoleum for their father, but the geomancer concluded that my grandfather should be buried in a simple earth mound.

One day in August, I was up in the cabin of my uncle's boat when I spotted my father coming down the lane in the rain. He had a large soggy package in one hand and a bunch of poultry hanging upside down in the other.

"Yum, chicken!"

I climbed down to the deck and jumped ashore. I hardly ever had the opportunity to eat chicken. Aunt Gioi kept chickens and ducks, but she would never kill one just to eat it. She saved them for holidays and for when the soldiers came for dinner. I loved roast chicken, especially the crackly skin and the fatty tail.

Summer was almost over; my father was probably going to take me back to live with him. I would tell him that Uncle Quon needed me more to help him run the farm when he got old.

When I was close enough to see his face, I stopped. He wasn't very happy. And those weren't chickens; they were hawks. Their legs were tied together like the handle of a dust broom. My father was angry. He reached the house before I did.

"How can anyone treat animals like this, just because they don't understand their language?" he muttered.

The hawks had become wounded in their struggle to get loose. Some had cuts and abrasions on their legs and others had dislocated wings. I followed my father around to the kitchen where he set the soggy package and the birds down on Aunt Gioi's table. He spoke to them gently and told them that first he was going to help them heal, and then he was going to set them free. The birds did not try to fight or bite him. My father unbound the five of them one by one and carefully adjusted their wings by gently stretching them open. He applied salve to their wounds and wrapped them with strips of cloth.

"That cloth might stay on long enough to do some good," he said.

He shook his wrist and down came his prayer beads. He always took them whenever he left his house. The beads were made out of miniature coconuts with a hole bored through the middle, eighteen of them, on a plastic string.

After chanting and before letting them go, he traced a magic charm over each of the birds to protect them from the birdcatchers.

I said, "Ba, Uncle Quon needs me to help him on the farm and especially on his boat. He is training me to fight."

My father said, "I brought you something good to eat. Open the package."

There was a small watermelon, a cellophane package of French cookies, a tin of chocolates, and a big fat monkfish that was already dead.

"Look at this marvelous fish your father brought for supper," my aunt said as she stepped out of the house. She started right in sharpening her knife on the stone.

Underneath the table, a small white hen lay with her brood of chicks. My aunt had put them there to protect the chicks from snakes. The small white chickens are very special. People use them to make medicine.

"Go and pick some greens, Quang. And get some scallions and red peppers and four or five limes and a green papaya and some cilantro."

I started for the garden, but when I heard my father and my aunt start talking, I came back and stood where they wouldn't notice me.

"Has there been much trouble here?"

"Things are still very bad. Quon is keeping an eye on Quang. There are other children his age who are working as spies for the Viet Minh."

"I have just returned from Elephant Mountain. I am trying to arrange for Quang to become an apprentice to the village chief. Ong Tam is a dear friend of mine. He told me he would take Quang to live with him in Buu Minh Doung Temple as soon as he turns eleven." I had just turned ten on the thirtieth of June, a birthdate that my father had chosen for me.

"Then he can go to school here in Cai Mon for one more year," my aunt said.

"No. I've arranged for him to attend a school on Elephant Mountain. He can study *Han Viet* there. The headmaster of the school has accepted Quang as a boarder and has agreed to give him private lessons after school. Quang will meet many of my friends in Xa Ba Chuc who are looking forward to making him feel as though he has come home to family. The old-timers are sure to tell him stories about his grandfather. He'll have a chance to get to know the village before he starts living in the temple."

My aunt said, "There is more fighting there than here, with the Ho Chi Minh Trail just five miles away. Please don't send him so far away from his family. He is just a boy."

"He'll be safe. Trust me. Everyone there will keep an eye on him."

My aunt left the kitchen. My father was standing alone, staring down at the bloody monkfish.

My father got me up when the first roosters crowed. It was raining lightly. Even a light rain sounds loud in Cai Mon. I could smell that Aunt Gioi had cooked us some shrimp and noodle soup. She came to the bedroom and sat down on the bed next to me and my father. She was wearing her special silk pajamas with flowers. Her thinning black hair was loose, and it hung down like a girl's.

"Remember to pray to your grandparents," she told me.

"I will, Aunt."

"And promise you won't climb so high."

"I promise," I lied.

She cried and hugged me. I was careful not to cry, or else I wouldn't be brave enough to fight pirates with my uncle.

Aunt Gioi served us the food in the bedroom. The three of us sat cross-legged on her shiny big bed.

When we were ready to leave, she gave us each a lighted torch. She knew exactly how thick to wrap the dried banana leaves so the torch would burn the whole way to Highway 1, but these would never make it that far in the rain. I ran ahead to the big bridge. The bullfrogs hushed. I stood balancing on the single pole, waiting for my father to catch up. I watched as the fishing trawlers slid past one another as silently as ghosts in the torchlight. There would be no river on Elephant Mountain. I could hear the invisible water slapping against their slimy wooden sides. The distorted image of my torch bobbed over the dark ripples. I stared at the water and saw the scattered dabs of orange light take the shape of a barbecued tofu pig. The pig started waving to me as it was being carried away by robbers. The robbers started shooting at me.

"Quang, throw your light in the water and hide. Quickly!"

I looked back and didn't see my father's light.

"They're coming this way."

I threw my torch into the water, scrambled off the bridge, and dove into the cold, wet rushes, lying facedown.

"No! Farther! Run farther from the path."

I could hear footsteps thumping. I listened to them growing louder and louder. Someone was coming toward me. I scooted like an armored scorpion, scraping my belly along the muddy ground under the grasses.

Suddenly I felt a bare foot kick my thigh, and I heard a thud. Someone had hit the ground right next to me. Two others galloped over me, and I heard two quiet splashes into the river and then a third. The ground started rumbling ominously. I scooted farther away from the riverbank. I closed my eyes and tried to disappear. My heart was beating fast, like a small animal's.

Moments later, there were many hard boots, squeaking leather, rattling metal, voices yelling, "Shoot, they're getting away!"

CRACK, CRACK, CRACK!

I could hear the scratching of gritty leather shoes scrambling over the pole.

We waited for a long time before coming out.

My father told me that the people who jumped in the river were Communists. He said the entrance to their tunnel was under the water.

"You did well, son," my father said.

"Will my aunt die when I am away?" I asked my father.

"No. Not a chance," my father said.

I believed him.

16

ELEPHANT MOUNTAIN

We took the local minivan to the Vinh Long bus depot, which was really just a big dirt lot with a lot of buses and people. We stepped off the van into a throng of men who were shouting at my father, who told them we were going to Can Tho. Some of those men shut their mouths and walked away, leaving a smaller group of about eight shouting men who started closing in on us. Sometimes bus drivers try to grab you and drag you to their bus, and sometimes they fight over you. As I said before, most bus drivers are really gangsters from the Binh Xuyen, the bus mafia. They didn't try to pull my father because he was an old man and deserved respect. Instead they called out, "Can Tho, this way," and "Express bus to Can Tho," and "Air conditioning, new bus, express to Can Tho, over here."

Before I was born, the French allied themselves with the Binh Xuyen and supplied them with arms to hunt down Communists. That is how they got to be very powerful outlaws. The police looked the other way while the Binh Xuyen also pirated the rivers and highways. In return, the bandits shared their profits with the police.

My father stood there calmly and quietly as they shouted at him. I wondered why we weren't getting on a bus. Maybe he was having second thoughts about taking me so far away from home.

These buses were different from the ones that went from village to village. These were larger, with about forty seats, but sometimes the owners added more. The front of the bus looked like the cab of a truck. Some bus drivers owned their own bus and ran it like a family business, with family members working as drivers, ticket takers, cashiers, and baggage men. Their children rode the buses all day long. Sometimes they actually lived on the bus.

We eventually got onto a bus that was owned by a woman named Huu Phuoc. She wasn't on the bus, because she owned about thirty buses. You could tell which were her buses, because she had her name painted on all of them.

As soon as our driver pulled onto the two-lane highway, he aimed the bus straight down the middle, and pressed his foot on the gas pedal. He was cruising at top speed halfway into the oncoming traffic lane. A bandit driver will expect all the oncoming traffic to veer to the side to let him pass, as if there were a special lane for bandits, which apparently there was. The crew often let other bandits come aboard the bus to get money from the passengers. There is nothing you can do about it except not make them mad.

In those days, there were no bridges strong enough to hold up a bus, so buses were ferried across the rivers. My father didn't like to be stuck on the bus waiting for the biggest ferries to arrive while plenty of smaller ferries would be coming and going, so we went only as far as the first river, before Can Tho.

My father bought me a soda at one of the café bars near the ferryboat crossing. I went to use the public fish pond toilet. All the ferryboat stations have them. While I was waiting on line, the man who was up on the platform started yelling. He stood up before his pants were all the way up. Some people on the line said that he had dropped something into the water. It turned out that he had dropped a money belt filled with gold rings. Someone went to wake up one of the men who was asleep in a hammock at the bar. He was the one who dove in to find lost money and jewelry. Our ferry arrived before I had the chance to watch.

From Can Tho we took a bus to a small ferry crossing in Long Xuyen, and from Long Xuyen we took a bus through the flood lands to Tri Ton, which was very close to Elephant Mountain.

It is always swampy around the mountains, but during the rainy season the lands become flooded when a huge lake in Cambodia overflows. We call it *Bien Ho*, "Ocean Lake." In Cambodia it is called the *Tomle Sap*. The waters don't recede until October or November, so the people who live there have only one rice harvest per year. That is why they are so poor.

I looked out the window of the bus and saw that the only solid land in sight was the highway itself and the far-distant mountains. The sun was floating down toward their jagged peaks. The endless flat silvery water began to stir and shimmer with colors like a hundred rivers of fire. I started counting the mountains in the distance.

"Ba, there are more than seven mountains. I think there are some new ones."

My father laughed, "There are many mountains, maybe twenty, or more."

"Then why do you say 'Seven Mountains'?"

"Seven of them are special. They are protected by good magic."

Tiny boats like specks of rice dotted the horizon. The bus sped by children of all ages who were playing on either side of the cracked and pitted asphalt highway. It was the only place they could play outdoors. Houses on stilts ran along either side of the highway, set back from the road. Some people were arriving home in their boats, some wading through the water to take down the laundry. During flood time, people have to put their chickens in cages above the water. Ducks huddle on the front porch and waddle into the house. The water is full of fish from the Ocean Lake and the rivers, all running together. When the waters recede, sometimes the fish get caught in puddles and the people catch them easily, but most of the fish can follow the water back to the river that goes to Nui Dai, Long Mountain.

I had never seen houses like those. They were completely open in the front, with bamboo curtains that most people kept rolled up. I was able look inside almost every house as the bus bumped slowly by. I saw a group of children sitting on the bed playing a game while their father lay sleeping. Teenage boys stretched and yawned in their hammocks like young lions. An old grandmother pushed a baby who was crying in a hammock, a woman sat alone on the edge of her bed, kids were jumping from the veranda into the water, a family sat in a circle on the floor eating dinner. I wondered where they found wood for their fires.

I looked into house after house as the light dimmed to twilight. I could no longer see the people inside the houses clearly; soft shapes were huddled in the shadows, and hammocks were swinging.

Look there," my father said as we drew closer to Tri Ton. Two silvery-green mountains stood against the lavender sky, one long and the other tall.

"Is that big one Elephant Mountain?" I asked.

"No, the big one is the forbidden mountain."

I thought of the mountain he had painted for me on my bedroom wall. The shape looked familiar, but the feeling of the mountain was not at all the same as the one on my wall. This one looked sharp and menacing.

"That other one is Long Mountain. Elephant Mountain is just on the other side of Long Mountain. We can't see it because it is so small."

"You never told me Elephant Mountain is small," I said disapprovingly.

In Tri Ton, we changed to a minivan. By 1960 there were two paved roads from Tri Ton to Elephant Mountain. Fighting had broken out earlier that day along the main road and part of it had been bombed. Our driver had no other choice than to take the secondary road. Although it was paved, it was crumbling at the edges, and chunks of it had fallen into the marsh. I kept my eyes glued on the road, terrified that our bus could tumble into a crocodile swamp at any moment. My father assured me that there weren't any more crocodiles in the swamps; they had retreated to the rivers.

Our minivan passed the forbidden mountain on our right and then followed the road around the base of Long Mountain on the left.

My father touched my arm and said, "There's Elephant Mountain. See the shape of an elephant's head, the ears, the forehead, and the trunk?"

It did look like that, exactly.

When my grandfather Ky Van Nguyen came to Elephant Mountain in 1867, the settlements were small, the jungle was undisturbed, and the elephants and other animals were plentiful. Collectively, the settlements were called *Xa Ba Chuc,* which means "village of eternal healing."

"I was just about your age when my father first brought me to Elephant Mountain," my father said. "It was about forty years after the Buddha Master had died. Land was free for the taking in western Nam Bo in those days, and when people learned about the new communities springing up on Elephant Mountain, they started coming here to live.

"A lot of them ate meat, and because they did not join our religion, they did not pay attention to the agreement between the animals and the people. There was nothing anybody could do to stop them from killing the animals."

It was difficult to hear every word of my father's story, because the minivan was crashing through potholes in the road and we were bouncing in our seats. He continued, "The first time I was here I didn't know about the agreement between the animals and the people.

"I met some kids who were going out to hunt deer. We found the trail that the deer herd used, and we made a noose, and tied it to the branch of a very strong tree. One kid hid in the tree, and I hid with the others behind a rock to wait for the herd. When the deer approached, we chased them from behind, and the kid in the tree let down the noose. We caught a deer on our first try.

"I took a stick and tried to hit the deer in the head, but I missed. The stick bounced off a rock and hit me in the head so hard that I was seeing double. I told my friends to let the deer go. But they didn't. When I went back to the temple, the master was very angry with me."

I n Vietnam we refer to the Mekong Delta as Nam Bo. Bac Bo is North Vietnam and Trung Bo is Central Vietnam. Until recently, Vietnamese people were a minority in the western part of Nam Bo. All of Nam Bo once belonged to the Khmer people of Cambodia. Besides the Khmer, there were some ethnic Chinese and Chams living there.

The Chams were originally from Indonesia. They sailed to Trung Bo sometime in the second century and built the beautiful Kingdom of Champa by the sea. The ruins of their ornate Hindu temples still stand in Da Nang.

Originally the Vietnamese lived to the north of the Chams and the Khmer people lived to the south of the Chams, in the Mekong Delta. Their kingdom, Kambjua, was very large. It extended from Thailand to the South China Sea. The Kambujan monks built the most beautiful Buddhist temple in the world, Angkor Wat. "Cambodia" is the modern name for Kambuja.

Kambuja and Champa were often at war with one another, and the Vietnamese took advantage of this. Vietnam attacked Champa during one of those wars in 1471 and drove most of the population away, and in 1720 we finished the job. The Chams fled into Kambuja. The Vietnamese Nguyen lords continued pushing southward and eventually annexed the entire Mekong Delta. The Khmer, who didn't believe in the ownership of land, were driven farther west. The Khmer still harbor resentment toward the Vietnamese for taking possession of the land. As a result, violence sometimes erupts, even in the Village of Eternal Healing.

Many of the Chinese people in western Nam Bo are the descendents of a large army of pirates under the notorious Ch'eng Ch'eng-Kung. They fled to the Mekong Delta in 1679 and were caught by the army of one of the Nguyen overlords, who then offered them asylum if they agreed to settle in the wilderness of western Nam Bo and be loyal. The Nguyen lords gave land to many outlaws and dispossessed people and asked in return that they serve as soldiers when needed to secure the region for Nguyen dynasty.

When I came to Xa Ba Chuc in 1960, the population was about 18,000, including 3,000 from my religion.

Elephant Mountain stood before us like a giant baby elephant taking a bath in the swamp waters. Our van began its ascent up the elephant's back, and all at once we were submerged inside a tropical forest with many layers of sounds. A denser, cooler, fresh, and fragrant air enveloped us.

All the people in my new school were from my religion, which meant they all wore black pajamas and had never cut their hair. I had no idea which ones were the boys and which ones were the girls, and the kids weren't too sure what I was. The building looked very much like my old school in Cai Mon, painted cement with a Chinese tile roof. The schoolyard was planted with shady trees and the ground was trampled bare. The entire school compound was enclosed behind a wrought-iron fence with a locking gate.

I was happy to be in school again with other kids, but I didn't like living with the headmaster. He gave me extra lessons every day after school and beat me just as much as my relative had. His wife was a good cook, and she gave me a lot of food to eat. I learned how to play *da cau* with the kids at school. You make a stack of pieces of cardboard, about four or five inches across, and you make a small hole through the center. Then you stick five or six chicken feathers through the hole to keep the layers together. You have to keep it in the air using your feet. You can play alone or with a group.

In my religion, men, women, children, and grandparents chanted every day at different times. The mothers chanted in the morning at five, the children after school at about one o'clock, the grandparents at five o'clock and the fathers at seven. After they finished chanting, the children helped their parents work. Besides farming and growing rice, people in the village went out to the marsh to collect rushes, which they dried in the sun and then pounded flat to use for weaving mats. Almost everyone in the village could weave. I found it very amusing to sit with the villagers under a shady tree and listen to their conversations while they were weaving, because they didn't even look at their hands.

Sometimes people went into the jungle to look for four different kinds of trees, *hau phaf, cay o duoc, cay quynh doung*, and *cay tram huong*, for making incense. *Cay tram huong* is the most special; the wood is black. To make incense, you pound the wood into powder, and then you glue the powder to a bamboo stick using resin made from the *cay o duoc* tree. The incense from Xa Ba Chuc was very special. When my father came to bring me home to celebrate Tet, he brought home a big package of incense.

17

THE TIGER

M y father came back to Elephant Mountain in June and brought me home to Cai Mon for the summer. Uncle Quon trained me all summer in the martial arts. By September I had turned eleven. My father took me back to Elephant Mountain to his friend's temple in Xa Ba Chuc.

Tall, thick hedges enclosed the small courtyard. We entered through a wrought-iron archway that was engulfed by flowering vines. Iron letters ran along the top, in yellow, Buu Minh Doung, or Treasure of a Peaceful Sunrise. I was too young to appreciate the name, and I wasn't interested in praying or chanting.

There was nothing much in the courtyard except a few cement benches, some shrubs, and a birdbath that was filled with water. The temple was a square cement building with a tile roof that was overgrown with moss. My father disappeared inside.

I peered inside the dimly lit room. There was a long table where my father was sitting, talking to a man in a black hat, black shirt, and black pants. A woman, also in black, brought them a tray of tea and oranges.

"Quang," my father called, "come and meet Ong Tam. He and your grandfather were friends."

Once my eyes adjusted to the dark I saw that there were people praying in the room, kneeling and prostrating themselves before the altars. There were no statues of Buddha or any other god or goddess, just pictures of monks.

I sat down in the chair next to my father. Ong Tam's wife and son came over and sat down, too. Their son was twenty-three years old. He could hear, but he could not speak.

Ong Tam was not only the master of the temple, but was also the village chief, the *ong ganh*, which means "the one who carries the group." In my religion, the village chief must be wise and powerful, because he holds responsibility for the safety of each one of his people. He must also protect our souls after we die. The village chief makes a special head scarf for us to wear when we die. He decorates it with many magic symbols and blessings to help our souls in the next world.

I slept on a bench next to the wall. Ong Tam's son woke me every morning at four o'clock. It was my job to fetch water from the well and fill the cisterns and the bathing stalls. I always had to put in more water than we needed, just in case we had visitors spending the night.

At five o'clock, I chanted the morning sutra with Ong Tam. He held the book for me to read along, but it was written in *Han Viet* characters. I didn't understand much of what he was saying even though the sutra was in Vietnamese.

We had rice and tea for breakfast, and then I went to school until one o'clock. It was the same school I attended the year before.

After school, I had to come straight back to the temple to chant again, and after that, I had to clean the eighteen altars. I wasn't allowed to go outside and play with my friends from school. Families came every day to the temple, to clean and fix the building, work in the garden, and prepare food for visitors and for poor people in the neighborhood. Even though there was always a lot of activity at the temple, I felt homesick for my father and Aunt Gioi.

I started going out to find my friends after school. I went off with them to play in the forest. We saw a pangolin, which is an anteater with leathery scales. Pangolins hide the ants they catch underneath their scales, to save for later. When they see people, they roll up into a ball. My friends rolled a pangolin down a hill just for fun.

One of my friends was in charge of bringing his family's water buffalo home for the night. He used to let me ride on his water buffalo's back while he led the buffalo by a rope tied to its nose ring. When I went to my friends' houses, I always checked their yards to see if they had any caged birds. If they did, I would try to set them free when no one was looking. Some birds would screech when I touched their cages, but others were quiet when I opened the doors. They would always fly to the top of a tree and thank me before flying away. Most caged birds knew how to survive in the wild, because most had been trapped as adult birds.

Ong Tam didn't hit me, but he was very angry with me for disappearing after school almost every day. He would make me stay by the altar and try to sing the sutra. Mostly I cried.

When my father came to bring me home for Tet, Ong Tam told him that I was too young to live away from my family.

M y father didn't hit me; he didn't even become angry with me. He just put his hand on my shoulder and said, "Let's go home."

"Am I going to live with you?"

"I am living in a temple in Cai Be now. There is a good Chinese school there, but you can't start until you turn twelve. You will have to finish out this school year in your old school in Cai Mon."

My spirit leapt up to the top of the elephant's head and slid down its trunk.

"Then, come September, you can attend the Chinese school and live with me."

We walked to the market square and got onto a bus. I climbed aboard our bus and scrambled into a seat by the window as usual. When my father boarded the bus, he made me change my seat.

"Sit there." My father pointed to the aisle seat in another row, three seats in from the window.

I thought he was punishing me for getting into trouble with the temple master. I argued, "Ba, what difference does it make where I sit? I like the fresh air." That was something my father would say.

My father walked down the aisle of the bus and back again. "Sit here," he repeated.

I sat in the seat he chose, and he sat next to me. The bus was only half full when it departed for the highway. There were plenty of empty window seats.

"Sit still and stop bouncing," my father scolded. He was acting strangely, which made me even more antsy.

We had just left Tri Ton when a bomb struck our bus like a bolt of lightning. A solid wall of acrid smoke and debris lifted me out of my seat and threw me against the windows. I landed in my father's lap, which was covered in blood. My face was wet with my father's blood. The bus tipped over and crashed on its side, and slid along the pavement in slow motion. The sound of metal grinding against the asphalt filled my stomach. I was choking, and my eyes burned. People were choking and screaming.

Some of the passengers tried to climb out the windows but they were jagged with broken glass. Rescue workers came to get us out. I wasn't hurt, but my father's legs had been cut by glass. The medic cleaned his wounds. He was lucky, because there was no shrapnel in his wounds.

The bomb had ripped a big gaping hole in the side of the bus. The seat I had originally chosen was blown away. The people sitting in that row were dead, and some others were badly hurt.

I tried to sit by the window on the next bus. Again my father didn't let me. This time I argued with him. I told him that what just happened would never happen again, but he wouldn't listen. He made me sit on the aisle again. There were hardly any passengers on that bus.

This time the bus ran over a land mine. The seat above the tire was blown straight through the roof. That would have been my seat.

We made it to Long Xuyen on the third try without any trouble and then to Can Tho. In Can Tho we got onto a Huu Phuoc bus. As soon as the driver saw us boarding his bus, he stood up and bowed to my father and to me.

"This is my son, Quang," my father told him.

After we sat down I whispered, "Do you know him?"

"Yes," my father answered. "He is my new student."

It was comforting to know that the bus driver wasn't a gangster.

While we were waiting in the Can Tho terminal yard for the bus to fill up with passengers, our driver turned around and told the middle-aged man sitting in front of us to open his window. The driver said, "Are you blind? Don't you see there is a master sitting behind you who doesn't want to smell your stench? Open your window so that he can breathe."

The passenger was angry with the driver and refused to open his window.

The driver climbed out of the bus, broke the passenger's window from the outside with his fist, and pulled the man out of the window and hit him.

I looked questioningly at my father.

"His name is Chu Kim, but everyone calls him the Tiger," my father winked.

During the ride, my father told me the story of how he met the Tiger. The bus wove all over the highway speeding past everything in sight. Every now and then we heard the screeching of brakes.

I liked to go to a certain Chinese herbal medicine store in Cai Be. One day, the owner of the store asked me if I would treat a friend of his who was very sick. I told him I would.

"His friend was brought into the shop and I checked him. I wrote out a prescription, and the pharmacist did all the work, chopping and grinding the herbs. His friend paid him for the medicine and the owner gave me a percentage.

"The next time I went there, the owner told me that his friend was much better and that he had lined up eight more patients for me to see in his shop. Again, I just made the diagnosis; I didn't have to prepare the medicine."

I said, "That way sounds so much easier, but what does this have to do with our bus driver?"

"Hold on. I am coming to that part."

Just then the bus pulled into a rest stop. We got off the bus to use the toilet and to buy some food. Gangsters always stop at rest stops that are run by other gangsters.

When all the passengers had boarded again, two gangsters climbed aboard and started handing out brown paper packages wrapped up with twine. They told us to put them under our seats and leave them there. Everyone did this without question, knowing that if they didn't, they would get kicked off the bus or worse.

The bus zoomed out of the rest stop at top speed, forcing all other traffic to veer aside. I looked out the window at a water buffalo relaxing in water up to his chin.

"Ba, finish the story." My heels kept bumping the brown paper box under my seat.

"Where was I?"

"The Tiger. The driver of this bus," I reminded him.

"Oh yes. I was seeing patients in that herbal shop. I liked it very much until I realized that the owner was really trying to learn my formulas without asking me."

"So what did you do?"

"I stopped seeing patients in his shop."

"Was he angry with you?"

"Not at all. He knew he wasn't doing right. A short time later he asked me if

I wanted to live in the Chinese temple in Cai Be and open a clinic there for the community. He said the temple had been abandoned."

"Ba." I kicked at the brown paper package. "I thought you were going to tell me about the bus driver."

"He will be in the story soon. Would you like something refreshing?"

He reached into the air in front of him and two tangerines appeared in his hand.

"That temple is centuries old, Quang. It is one of the oldest temples in South Vietnam. It was built for a Chinese goddess called Chua Ba Thien Hau.

"You wouldn't believe how run-down it had become. That Chinese school I was telling you about is right next door, but nobody was taking care of the temple. The only one who ever went in there was an old woman who came every day to dust. That temple has thirteen altars; all the statues and artwork are still there, but everything was covered with cobwebs and dust. The old woman was too blind to see that she was only polishing dust. And the temple was infested with mosquitoes.

"I agreed to live in the temple, mainly because of the Chinese school, but I didn't know they wanted me to clean it up by myself. I was covered in bites for a week. It took days and days just to clean out the dust. When it was clean, I lit incense and people started coming in to pray.

More and more people came to pray and chant and to study meditation with me, and I opened the clinic.

"One day I was getting ready to eat some dinner, and I heard a pack of motorcycles descending on he temple grounds. I looked up, and to my surprise I saw the Tiger standing in the doorway with his henchmen. I recognized him right away."

"It was our driver!"

"Yes. He is a notorious gangster. He is feared by every business owner."

I craned my neck to get a look at our driver, the Tiger. His partner was leaning forward like a backseat driver. The pair of them were swearing and gesturing to the other drivers.

My father continued, "I was sitting on the floor with my pot and bowl, eating old food that smelled of mildew. It was the only food I had. The Tiger stood there staring at me. I couldn't tell what it was he wanted.

"I said to him, 'You look like a hard worker; come and eat some food.' I waved my hand for the Tiger to come and sit down with me.

"His bodyguards thought I was being disrespectful to their leader, and they reached for their weapons, but the Tiger held up his hand to stop them.

"I motioned again for the Tiger to join me. I filled another bowl and held it out to him. Again the bodyguards got ready to attack me, because I had offered the food with only one hand."

"You shouldn't have done that, Ba, they could have all ganged up on you."

"You are right. I could have shown him more respect, but I used only one hand to show him that I wasn't afraid."

"Oh, that's good," I said.

"The Tiger was confused, but eventually he sat down and accepted the food. It smelled pretty bad. He watched me eat. Then he took a bite."

"He did?"

"Yes. He took a bite and then spit it out. This time his men were furious at me for insulting their boss but I said to him, 'Go on, eat, it won't hurt you.' "

"Did he eat?"

"No. He got up and walked out, because he wasn't able to eat the food without looking like a coward."

The bus stopped again and some new gangsters climbed aboard. This time they were selling bottles of medicine. Everyone had to buy a bottle.

Off we zoomed again.

"Is that all?"

"No. I heard the motorcycles again the very next day just as I was sitting down to eat my dinner. I was eating the same food; it was even more spoiled than the day before. I invited the Tiger to join me again and this time he ate all the food in his bowl. His guards were amazed, because their boss never listened to anyone.

"From that day on, the Tiger came every evening to pray and chant the sutra. He has joined my study group that meets every night after the sutra. He is now my student."

When we arrived at the Vinh Long bus depot, the Tiger wouldn't let us off the bus. He insisted on sending one of his men to drive us home. His bagman went to look for another gang member who had a motorcycle.

I wedged myself between the gangster and my father, and we roared like a hurricane, splashing through puddles and flying over potholes all the way to my aunt's house.

18

PIRATES

We arrived all splattered with mud. I ran into the house to find Aunt Gioi and noticed that she had set her cooking pots out on the floor, which meant it was time to change the roof. My father invited the gangster to spend the night. In the morning, he drove my father to the Chinese temple in Cai Be.

A few days later, the neighborhood people started arriving with their ladders to take down the old roof. My aunt and I went to market by boat to bring back lots of fish and vegetables, cakes and cookies, and three cases of rice wine to feed the work crew. My aunt would be shopping and cooking nonstop for a week.

Taking down the old leaves made a huge mess inside and outside the house. The moldy dust of the crumbling leaves got into everything, and the whole house had to be cleaned from top to bottom.

Water palm leaves are nice because they have a six-foot spine. First you remove the leaf segments from the spine. Then you drape them along the spine and sew them tight. This makes a kind of curtain rod. The rods are then hoisted up to the bamboo frame and tied on; the closer the rods, the longer the new roof will last. New thatch stays green and smells fresh for a few weeks, until the sun toasts it a warm straw color.

When the roof was finished, the neighbors reattached the metal gutters that collected rainwater into our cisterns for drinking. Most people could not afford gutters, so they filled their cisterns with the water from the canal. Canal water was considered clean enough to drink, even during the summer rainy season when soil and debris were constantly being washed into the waterways. People would swish an alum stone, or a bunch of branches from the *cay oro* tree for a few seconds in their cisterns to make the sediment sink to the bottom. Nobody ever got sick from the canal water.

My Uncle Quon was supposed to register me at my old school, but he never did it. He decided to keep me home with him, so he could teach me how to run the family farm. Aunt Gioi yelled at him to get me into school, but he didn't listen to her.

I went to live at Uncle Quon's house. It was the first time I stayed in another house in Cai Mon. Uncle Quon's wife, Hue, didn't allow me to visit Aunt Gioi, because they didn't like each other, so I had to do it behind Hue's back. Aunt Gioi insisted that I come back to live with her, but I didn't listen.

Our coconut trees yielded one thousand ripe coconuts every two months. Uncle Quon and Hue cut down the coconuts themselves with a sharp hooked knife attached to an extended bamboo pole up to fifty feet long. You need strong arms to do that.

Coconuts grow in clusters, like grapes, so you only have to make one cut and you get ten to fifteen coconuts. I carried the coconuts to the house using the Vietnamese traditional *don ganh*, or shoulder pole.

My uncle hired men to climb up and clean the trees, which can be very tall, up to eighty feet. You have to check the coconuts to see if mice or squirrels have bored holes in them for a nest. The men who climbed the trees tried to knock the squirrels and mice out of the trees. My uncle was training his new puppy, Lucky, to wait down below and catch the animals in case they survived the fall. Lucky was a medium-sized dog with a silky yellow coat and two white paws. He was very clever. I liked him more than any other dog.

My uncle told me that some people used opium to train monkeys to climb the trees and clean out the squirrels and mice. They put opium in the monkey's food and bring the monkeys into the trees and show them what to do. The only way the monkeys can get more opium is to find mice and squirrels in the trees. My uncle told me he would never do that to an animal.

Uncle Quon could hull a green coconut in one minute. He embedded the handle of a knife into the ground so that the blade stood up firmly. He jammed the newly harvested coconut onto the blade up to the brown inner nut, and then twisted it until the green hull cracked open. The hulls were sold for landfill.

As soon as the cargo ship was loaded with one thousand hulled coconuts, my uncle would deliver them to Saigon. It was a seven-day trip there and back. He sold his coconuts to a factory in Saigon, where they ground up the coconut meat, heated it up, and then squeezed out the coconut milk into cans. He said he was going to take me with him on the next trip, which was coming up soon.

My uncle trained me in martial arts three times a day. He wanted me to lift two big, empty fish sauce jugs with my fingertips squeezing around the lip of the jugs. The jugs kept slipping, but after many days I could lift them off the ground a little. When I could finally lift them easily, he started filling the jugs with sand, and I had to start over. He also dug a deeper hole for me to stand in and jump out. When I could make it out of the hole, he tied sandbags to my waist. He also taught me how to punch and kick, and made a rice sack full of sand for me to hit.

My uncle showed me the place in his boat where he wanted me to hide when the pirates were attacking, an empty space under the deck, between the engine and the rudder.

"I thought I was going to help you fight," I said.

"Not until you are sixteen," he winked.

I was still eleven years old.

I went on four trips to Saigon with my uncle before I went to live with my father again. The boat was fifty feet long and fifteen feet wide. It was made entirely out of wood. When it was loaded down with coconuts, it rode dangerously low in the water. The cargo was held in the front three-quarters of the boat, with a little space to stand in the bow. The coconuts were covered by a flat wooden board that you could walk on.

A gasoline engine powered the boat. Its huge rudder was connected to a long tiller that wended its way past the cooking area and climbed up the wall of the lower cabin to the crow's nest, where the captain sits and steers the boat. I spent most of the time in the crow's nest keeping my uncle company. He would tell me stories about the different ways the pirates had attacked his boat.

Sometimes he asked me to steer the boat while he went to pee, but I didn't have the strength to keep the boat on course. Once it started to veer to the left, and then the current pushed it into a sharp turn. The boat leaned over so far that it practically capsized. My uncle was frantic. We had to bail the water out for many hours. In a strong wind, it was impossible even for my uncle to steer the boat, so when the weather turned bad, we had to moor the boat to a tree.

The motor wasn't strong enough to move the boat from a standstill. You had to set the boat in motion first by rowing the huge oars in the bow and stern. The boat had a pole brake, a strong bamboo stick called the *cay sao cam* that could be lowered into the mud if the stopping place was shallow enough. Otherwise you had to throw the anchor overboard. The *cay sao cam* was also used to push the boat into deeper water. If you were not careful with the *cay sao cam*, you could damage other boats or break houses along the riverbank.

My uncle hid his fighting stick under the floorboards of the cabin. It was made of strong *tram dong* wood that does not bend. He could reach his stick easily from inside or outside the cabin.

Behind the cabin was a thatched awning under which we had our cooking fire and woodpile. My hiding place was underneath the woodpile. Our toilet was a small stall that jutted out over the water, behind the boat.

We set out sailing northward and then eastward, in the direction of the South China Sea. By the second day, the river water had turned so salty that we couldn't drink it. We didn't have to go all the way to the ocean because there was an inland route northward all the way to Saigon. My uncle liked to steer the ship straight down the center of the river. The Mekong was so wide in some places that you could barely see the shore. In the evening we dropped anchor close to the riverbank. We could have fished straight from the river like many people did, but my uncle didn't have the patience. Instead, he brought salted fish along, and he cut it up to make a stew. We picked water hyacinth leaves that floated on the river and put them into the stew or ate them raw as salad. Sometimes my uncle would steer the boat under a *trai ban* tree so I could stand on top of the cabin and pick the tangy, sour fruit to eat raw, or to use for sour soup. When the river was low I would have to use a stick to knock the fruit down. *Ngo ban*, cork trees, grew in abundance along the banks. Sometimes we cut some down to bring home with us. We jumped off the side of the boat every evening after supper to bathe before retiring to the cabin to sleep.

On my first voyage to Saigon with my uncle, we had just finished eating our first supper together on the boat and I climbed up to the crow's nest to look out for the pirates.

"Relax," my uncle called up to me. "They have no reason to attack until we've sold our cargo. They've already seen us and have an idea of when we will be returning with an empty hold and a sack of money."

"What if we always stay close to the other boats?"

"It doesn't make a difference; they'll attack us anyway," my uncle said definitively.

The harbor in Saigon was packed with cargo boats that looked exactly like ours but with many different kinds of cargo, bananas, durian, oranges, lemons, sugarcane, and rice. We had to wedge ourselves in, put down our anchor, and wait for our turn to move closer.

We were about twenty rows back. My uncle said it would take two to three days before all the boats ahead of us unloaded their cargo.

Besides keeping my uncle company, my usefulness became apparent at this stage of the trip because my uncle needed me to mind the ship while he went ashore. People on the other boats didn't mind if you hopped onto their boats on your way to and from shore. It was the only way.

My uncle would sometimes be gone for hours, but when he came back, he would give me cakes and candy. One time, I had to move the boat, otherwise someone else would cut in front of us. I tried to lift the anchor, but it was too heavy. Someone from another boat came and helped me.

Sometimes my uncle let me go ashore, though he didn't give me any money to spend. I just looked around the harbor and didn't go far. That was all I saw of Saigon.

When we finally reached the docks, it was Saturday and the truckers didn't come. My uncle moored our boat to the pilings, and told me to mind the boat. I was bored and fell asleep. When I woke up I found that the water level had gone down so much that the front of the boat was hanging in midair and the boat was tilted. I couldn't untie the ropes, but again, someone came to help me.

Two days later, my uncle sold our coconuts to the truckers, who unloaded them into their trucks and handed my uncle two big canvas sacks filled with money, tied shut with a bit of banana-stem twine. I was surprised that my uncle didn't bother to hide them; he just threw them into the cabin, and we shoved off for home.

It was raining all the next day. My uncle said the weather would clear the following day, the day we'd most likely be attacked.

It's not easy to dodge the pirates when they are coming after you," my uncle said. "They time it just right, so you can't steer away or outrun them." From up in the crow's nest you could see for miles. I combed the greenery for signs of the pirates.

We were approaching a deserted stretch of the Mekong between two small villages. There were no buildings in sight, just a few boats here and there on the river.

My uncle pointed. "They are somewhere out there hiding in the rushes."

"Do you see them?"

"Any minute now," he said.

I started to feel afraid. Just then my uncle spotted them. He pointed to three distant specks pulling out from the rushes.

"Three canoes. Probably five or six men."

The canoes were far enough away to meet us anywhere on the river. As we continued upstream, I could make out five heads.

"Time to hide," he said.

My uncle didn't seem to be afraid. He sat up in the crow's nest and whistled. I jumped down and shoved aside some wood and kicked at the three boards that covered my hiding place. Lifting them off, I hopped in. I left one of them off so I could peek out. I couldn't see much, just the rear of the deck from the toilet to the cabin.

My uncle cut the engine and called, "Remember, stay hidden, no matter what."

I heard the sound of fingernails clawing and knees scrambling up the back of the boat. A large hand reached up and grabbed ahold of the toilet platform. I ducked just before the pirate pulled himself up. I could hear that he was hacking the stern oar right out of the oarlock with his machete.

I wondered if they would kill us if they could. I thought about how angry my father would be if I got myself killed when I was supposed to be in school.

"Kill him!" I heard the pirates yell.

I found out what happened later. My uncle was standing in the middle of the wooden platform with the two sacks of money at his feet and his *tram dong* fighting stick in his hands. There were five of them.

I had heard my uncle yell, "If you want it, come and get it." There were heavy footsteps reverberating from the hollow wooden platform, running, faltering, struggling, thumping, and jumping. The pirates did nothing but swear at my uncle as they fought, but he didn't say anything else. It sounded like they were all in the front of the boat. I had wanted to climb out and peek through the cabin, but I held myself back. I heard several screams and groans, and splashing and swimming.

. . .

Quang, I need you to steer the boat." The boat was drifting backward in the current. I jumped out of the hole and climbed up to the crow's nest. Blood was running down my uncle's neck and bare torso. He had a few nicks on his face as well.

I took the tiller and tried to hold it steady. My uncle went down to the cabin to get his medicine kit and began applying a thick brown paste to his wounds to stop the bleeding.

He told me later that one of the pirates had a stick with a knife lashed onto the end. That one cut his neck from behind and also got him in the face. Another pirate cut him under his arm with a machete. My uncle was able to push all five of them overboard without hurting them. He was proud of that.

"I am glad that is over," I said.

"You never know," he said. "There could be more attacks before we reach home."

On the next voyage, the pirates had guns. That time my uncle pretended he was scared. He started crying and shaking and he begged, "Please don't hurt me, I'll give you anything you want."

The pirates said, "Give us your money and your boat."

"The money is over there," my uncle said pointing and walking over to where I was hiding. In half a blink, he grabbed three chunks of wood from the woodpile and chucked it so fast, their guns went flying out of their hands. Then he grabbed his stick and pushed them all overboard. It was over in about three minutes.

Aunt Gioi was very angry with my uncle for taking me away from her and for bringing me on his boat. When my father came to visit, she told him that my uncle didn't send me to school and that he was exposing me to danger.

19

DISCIPLINE BRINGS
GOOD FORTUNE TEMPLE

t was September 1962, and I was twelve. My father hired a taxi boat to take us up the Mekong River to the port town of Cai Be. Our boatman stood in the stern and rowed. My father told me about my new school. He said all the teachers and students were ethnic Chinese, and all the classes were taught in Chinese. "You start tomorrow morning at eight o'clock."

Long ago, Chinese merchants settled Cai Be for business reasons because of its ideal location at the intersection of two rivers. Cai Be is also right in the center of Nam Bo.

Our boat turned a bend, and then the river spread open like a lake. Our boatman struggled slightly with the pull of the current as we made our way across the widest part. We were crossing the spot where the two rivers collided. The face of the river was unbroken, but if you looked closely, you would see circles of varying sizes on the surface, as if they were lightly traced with your finger. These delicate-looking rings are deceiving. They are treacherous whirlpools that suck people down to the very bottom of the churning water and spin their wits out.

I hunted for whirlpools as we crossed the meeting of the waters. Looking ahead, I could see the stretch of wood pilings, and the people swarming like ants. Our boatman pulled up behind the other moored boats in the port. We would have to boat-hop to get to the pier.

I got out of the boat first, and climbed over most of the boats far ahead of my father. Just as I was stepping onto a canoe, I spotted a small whirlpool the size of an umbrella in the space between the two boats. I decided to put my foot into it and see if it would pull on me. Holding on to the canoe, I lowered my leg into the whirlpool. I didn't feel anything, so I lowered my leg a little farther. I wanted to feel the suction of the whirlpool. I braced myself in the canoe and lowered my leg up to my thigh, but the canoe started to tilt over. My leg was too far in the water for me to right the boat.

The next thing I knew, someone grabbed me by my shirt and pulled me back onto the canoe, a man in a conical hat. I looked around me, at the boats, the docks, the quay. The silence was jarring; everyone was looking at me. My father caught up with me on the pier, I'd never seen him look that angry. His lips were tight over his teeth. "If you had slipped, you could have died," he said.

We wended our way through the fishermen, merchants, and shoppers, past the fish market and the Cai Be market square, to an unusually wide and straight dirt road. My father motioned with his arm and said, "The temple is halfway up this road, on the right."

Many of the houses we passed were made of cement and tile and had spacious, well-tended gardens.

"People have nice houses here," I commented.

"That building is the Chinese school." My father pointed to a single story, off-white, L-shaped building. The Chinese temple stood beside the school, taller, boxlike, and watermelon-pink built by the Chinese ancestors of Cai Be.

Two bronze dragons, undulating from head to tail, gripped the apex of the temple roof with their scaled talons. Between them stood a fireball, a bronze hoop with flames shooting upward. People say that long ago the Jade Emperor gave the fireball to the dragons to lure them out of the sea, where they were making a nuisance of themselves by racing around and making a lot of waves. They even got into the rivers, and were so frisky that they made the rivers overflow. People complained to the Jade Emperor and asked him to get the dragons to calm down.

The Jade Emperor tried to calm them down and failed, so he thought of a way to get them out of the water. He presented them with a magic fireball that couldn't get wet. The dragons couldn't resist the fireballs. Over time, the fireballs calmed the dragons down, and eventually the dragons started to meditate and become wise. Now dragons are a model of self mastery, inner wisdom, and spiritual protection.

As we drew closer, I saw a group of kids playing in the courtyard in front of the temple. "The Chinese kids love to play basketball," my father said. "Go and try. It looks like a fun game."

My father continued through a tall wooden fence, and disappeared through the large red double doors of the temple. He had put up the fence because the basketball kept hitting and rattling the temple doors. Twenty minutes later, the smell of incense filled the courtyard; it smelled like home.

The temple was a refreshing watermelon-pink color, but on the inside, it was dark and dank. The inner walls were made of bare cement that was crumbling in a lot of places. It was kind of spooky inside, with shadowy shapes of many deities and demons on thirteen altars around the room. There weren't any windows to look out of. All the windows were high up, under the eaves, and were covered with decorative iron grills.

I was just working up the nerve to join the basketball game when my father came outside and said, "Come inside the temple now. A woman is here to cut your hair."

I watched in disbelief as my waist-length hair dropped piece by piece onto the dirty cement floor. My father had never let Aunt Gioi take a scissors to my head. He would remind her that he wanted me to follow the customs of the Buddha Master's religion in the Seven Mountains. "Now you look like the other boys," he said.

My father and I slept on a table against the back wall of the temple. The next morning, my father woke me at six-thirty and told me it was time to chant the morning sutra. He had already made breakfast, blessed all the tea, and lit the candles and incense on all the altars.

After breakfast, my father took me next door to the school and started talking to one of the teachers in Chinese. I had never heard him speaking Chinese before. The teacher led me to my classroom. The boys and girls were wearing uniforms, green skirts or shorts, and a white, short-sleeved, button-down shirt. "Don't worry about the uniform," the teacher told me in Vietnamese, "your father will have some made for you." After that, I didn't understand a thing anyone said.

School was over at three o'clock in the afternoon. During the first week, my father let me play basketball and hang out with the kids after school, but after that, he told me I had to clean two altars a day, chant the evening sutra with him, and start my homework by eight o'clock.

Cleaning the altars was a serious business. I had to climb up and stand on them in order to reach everything, and there was a lot of stuff on every altar. Some of the statues were more breakable than others. Some statues were cast in bronze or porcelain, some were carved from sandalwood, ebony, jade, or cinnabar. Many were cast in plaster, painted in bright colors, and lacquered.

A lot of the gods and goddesses had oil-painting backdrops that had to be dusted. Some wore halos made of gold and silver foil fringe. The ones with halos had electric blinking lights that made their halos glow pink, turquoise, yellow, and green. Dusting the lights and the wires took the longest.

Chua Ba Thien Hau, the temple's patron goddess, was a life-size standing statue made of porcelain. Her embroidered silk gown and robe were encrusted with rhinestones. She wore an elaborate headdress with jewels and streamers that made her much taller. People in the community chipped in their money each year to make Chua Ba Thien Hau a new outfit. Families always fought over whose turn it was to take the old outfit home, to keep for good luck.

Not only did the goddess Chuan De have eighteen arms to dust, but she also had two extra faces. She was holding many things: a sword, a bottle, a magic symbol, a pomegranate, a vase, a red feather, some metal tools, a knife, and a lot of other stuff that I didn't recognize. I had to pick through all the fruit and flowers by her feet and take out all the wilted and rotten ones.

I was extra careful dusting off the Jade Emperor, Ngoc Hoang, because he is the king of all the gods, even of Buddha. One of his reincarnations, Ong Cac De, stood next to him with one foot on a turtle's back and the other on a snake, two animals that don't move at the same speed. I expected to come back one day and find him doing a split. One of Buddha's reincarnations was also there, Dai Minh Vuong, riding on a phoenix.

I was a little brusque with Thanh Hoang, the immense, lacquered demon ruler of hell. He stood there grinning as he was crushing two men to death under his mighty feet. The men always looked up at me without any expression at all, but their blood was trickling out of the corners of their mouths and down their chins.

Best of all, I liked the shiny lacquered-plaster sea goddess, Thien Hau, riding on a cloud. Her shiny black hair was blowing behind her as she flew, looking to rescue people who were drowning at sea.

My father's clinic was on the right when you entered the temple through the big red doors. Most of his patients stopped to light incense and pray before taking a seat on the bench. Some people just came in to pray and to leave food on the altars. Sometimes they brought roasted pigs to be blessed by my father, for a special event they were having at home. On holidays the temple would be full of pigs, all lined up for my father to bless, and a lot of beer.

Each evening at seven o'clock, my father's students would come to chant the sutra with him. Afterward they would eat the food that was left on the altars, and drink tea while my father taught them about Buddhist and Taoist teachings, meditation, and herbal medicine. About twenty students came every night and stayed until ten or eleven o'clock. I didn't listen much to what my father taught his students, but one time I heard him say, "People who pray and meditate every day help others without even knowing it. Their spirits grow big like trees; their branches extend over their neighbors, family and friends."

There was one couple from Saigon who came to study with my father about once or twice a month. It was three-hour bus trip for them to come to Cai Be. On school holidays I often went to their house, where they lived with their four children. I enjoyed joining their family outings to the zoo, to the museums, to cafes, and to parties, where I saw a magician friend of theirs performing magic tricks. I was fascinated by the art of sleight of hand. Their magician friend lived down the street from their house and I went to visit him every time I went to Saigon. He could tell that I loved sleight of hand as much as he did. He taught me some of his best tricks, which involved a lot of physical coordination. I practiced them a lot.

Every evening at about a quarter to seven, the Tiger and some of his men came to the Chinese temple to chant the sutra and to participate in the study group. One time when he was getting off his motorcycle, he noticed my father talking outside with two elderly Chinese men, patrons of the temple. The Tiger overheard the two men complaining to my father about the iron grillwork fence that enclosed the courtyard, which was rusted and broken. They were annoyed with my father for not having fixed it by now.

The next day a truck came zooming down the street at full speed, causing all the street traffic to scatter. The truck headed straight for the temple and rammed the fence down. When the two patrons heard it was the Tiger's men who did it, they quickly paid for a new one.

Word started getting around that the Tiger was my father's friend. Any friend of the Tiger was to be feared. Whenever I went into a store, the owners would offer me things for free. We could ride any bus for free, too, and none of the bandits ever held us up or bothered us.

Sometimes we rode on the Tiger's bus, but that didn't stop him from terrorizing other people. One time a bus driver from another bus company cut in front of him. The Tiger chased down the other bus and crowded it off the road. Then he got out and beat up the other driver. The police arrived on the scene and hauled the Tiger off to jail.

"He'll be out by tomorrow morning," my father told me. "His boss, Huu Phuoc, always bails him out."

It was fun living in the Chinese community. I was learning Chinese quickly, because I had no choice. Outside of school, my Chinese friends preferred to speak Vietnamese.

My friends were from families that worked in commerce and had money to spend at the market. None of them ever had to find their own food every day as I did in Cai Mon. Sometimes I took my friends into the forest to pick a lot of fruit to impress their parents. I also took them to the river to catch shrimp and crabs. A few girls used to hang out with us, too.

My father was happy about my learning Chinese so well, because he said it was the key to my education in Chinese medicine.

I had never been to a school before at which the students weren't afraid of the teachers. My friends liked to play tricks on the women teachers. Previously, I had showed my friends how to get sap from a *sa ke* tree. Children from poor families take this sap and spread it over the branches of a tree. When birds land there, they get stuck in the sap and cannot fly away. The children remove the birds and bring them home to eat.

My friends put the sap on the back of our teacher's eraser. She didn't notice, so after she erased the board, she couldn't remove her fingers from the eraser. She had to dismiss us while she went to look for oil to get her fingers unstuck.

On the way to school one day, we were caught in a downpour, and many of us got our clothes soaked. My friends noticed one of the female teachers crossing the schoolyard to the bathing house that my father and I used. She was carrying an extra set of dry clothes on a wooden hangar, which she hung on the inside of the bathhouse door. My friend grabbed the hangar and pulled her dry clothes over the top of the door. We quickly stuffed them into our bookbags and took them into the school and put her clothes in the room of an unmarried male teacher.

The teacher in the shower called for help but no one heard her, because she was outside. She finally gave up and put her wet clothes back on and stormed around the school looking for her clothes. When she found them in the teacher's room, she thought that he had taken them. He tried to convince her that he hadn't, but she wasn't so sure.

My father taught me on the weekends. He started teaching me how to do pulse diagnosis.

I sat down at my father's little square table where his patients sat to have their pulses read, and he sat opposite me. On the table was a flat rectangular pillow for resting your hand, and a notebook where my father kept his patient records.

My father began, "By reading the pulses, we can understand how well the internal organs are functioning."

I looked questioningly at him.

He continued, "Like the heart, the stomach, the liver, the kidneys, and so on, we can feel if the organs are weak or congested or inflamed, or if they are working just fine."

"Oh," I said.

"We can also feel how well the blood is circulating in the body."

"Okay," I said.

"So," my father continued, "once we have an idea about what is going on inside the body, we can make medicine to help the body to function better. There are herbs that cleanse, herbs that soothe, herbs that warm, and herbs that cool. There are herbs that nourish the body and make more blood. You can prepare formulas that include all these properties. The trick is to understand what each patient needs. Two people can have the same symptoms, but most likely they will need a different kind of medicine."

"Let's begin," my father said as he put his left hand, palm up, on the red pillow.

"Now take your index finger and trace a line along the bone of my thumb like this." My father held my right index finger and guided it along his thumb.

"Continue over the heel of my hand, still following the bone, and stop just as your finger drops down onto my wrist, right here."

I noticed that my finger stopped between the first two creases at the base of his hand.

"This is the first position. Can you feel a pulse?"

I could.

"Another way to find the first position is to take hold of my index finger and lift it off the pillow like this. The point is just inside this hollow here, where the hand hinges.

"This pulse is for the heart and the valves of the heart. It is also for checking the membrane that surrounds the heart."

He put my third finger and then my fourth finger down side by side below the heart point, with a little space in between. He said the second pulse was for the liver, gallbladder, and diaphragm. The third pulse was for the kidney, colon, uterus, and prostate. I didn't know a lot of those organs, but my father told me never mind. The important thing for now was to find those three pulse positions on either hand. I told him it would be a lot easier if there was just one organ for each pulse. He said that there were pulses within pulses.

"Can you feel a pulse under each finger?" my father asked.

I told him that I did.

He put his other hand on the pillow and told me to place my three fingers on the three pulse positions. He explained, "The pulses on the right hand are for different organs. The first pulse is for the lungs and diaphragm, the second pulse is for the spleen and stomach, and the third is for the kidney, small intestine, uterus, and prostate."

He said, "I want you to practice finding the six pulse positions on different people. Once you can find them on different people, I want you to notice if the pulses strike high, toward the surface of the skin, or if they strike deep below the surface, or if they strike in the middle. I also want you to notice if the pulse beats are steady or if they beat unevenly."

About two weeks later, my father made me feel the pulses of one of his patients, a woman. He asked me, "Which pulses are high, which are low, and which are in the middle?"

I wasn't sure.

Then he said, "Can you feel the fluttering quality of this woman's pulses?"

I wasn't sure again.

Later he told me that if a woman's pulses felt fluttery, it meant she was pregnant. That is the first thing you have to know before you make medicine for a woman. Sometimes she won't know she is pregnant, and other times she doesn't want you to know. But the doctor has to know, because some kinds of herbs are not safe to use when a woman is pregnant.

A few weeks later he asked me, "Can you describe the shape of this man's pulses?"

I didn't know.

"I mean, are the pulses round at the top or flat? Do they leap up and strike your finger, or do they feel as if they are spreading out sideways?"

I put all my concentration into the tips of my fingers, but I could not tell.

He told me that it wasn't enough to know if the pulses were high or deep or even. There were such other qualities as floating, slippery, rough, surging, tight, stringlike, hollow, soggy, scattered, hidden, and knotted.

"Each of the qualities reflects the condition of an organ or organ system," my father told me. "It will help you to understand more about the person. Eventually you will be determining the qualities of each pulse point at four depths. Then you will have a highly accurate diagnosis."

My father put me to work filling prescriptions after school and on weekends. It wasn't long before I knew the ingredients of about fifty formulas. My father would write only the first two ingredients on a piece of paper, and I knew the rest. The first two ingredients are actually the name of the formula.

Each formula had between ten to fifteen different herbs. My father would write down the quantities of each ingredient in *chi,* a Chinese measurement that is more or less the weight of a grape. Ten *chi* equal one *luong.* My father never used a scale, he just knew by the feel in his hand, but I had to weigh everything on the scale. It took a long time.

My father came in and checked everything before he wrapped it up.

"You are learning very well," he would praise me proudly.

My father didn't let me spend any more summers with Uncle Quon in Cai Mon. Instead I had to prepare formulas all day long in the clinic.

I wanted my father to be proud of me. Sometimes I did special things for him in the temple. Once I took a little money without asking and went to the store and bought electrical wire and some beautiful small colored lights. Over the weekend, while my father was busy with his patients, I added a lot of new lights to the altars, so that almost every altar was illuminated in beautiful flashing colors. Luckily, I finished my lighting project just in time for the Sunday-night sutra. Everyone noticed how beautiful the temple looked; I had more than doubled the light display.

During the sutra someone suddenly stood up and shouted, "Something is burning!"

I smelled burning rubber and saw black smoke rising from the wires, but there weren't any flames yet. The Tiger was the fastest. He ran to the socket and pulled out the cords. Everyone went outside and resumed the sutra.

My father didn't even give me a disapproving look, but I still felt bad. I wanted to make up for it, so I took a little more money and went to the market to buy some gold paint.

The Chinese blessings that were painted onto the pillars in metallic gold paint were fading. There were other gold-painted ornaments that had lost their luster, the intricately carved panels over each doorway and the carved floral decorations on the altars.

Once again I worked while my father was busy, so he hardly noticed. It took me all day Saturday to paint over all the gold. Once again, my father's students came that night to worship and study. They stared at the new paint but said nothing. Even my father looked at it but didn't say a word.

Sunday morning the Tiger came to the temple with a lot of sandpaper and began sanding the paint off the detailed woodwork.

"You used the wrong paint," the Tiger explained. "It is a nice bright color, but it is too thick and is not shiny enough. Don't worry, I can get some gold paint."

My father's students worked for many weeks to sand off the wrong paint. Again, I didn't get in trouble at all.

When I was fourteen, I started getting into trouble again. I didn't show up home after school. Instead, I went out with my friends. I had become popular because I often performed magic tricks at the school parties. I had been practicing a lot and had perfected about fifteen illusions that I had learned from the magician in Saigon. I don't know why I disrespected my father so much; I liked to work in the clinic. Sometimes my friends would decide to go camping. I didn't run home every time to tell him where I was going. We would bring a lot of food and would all sleep together on a plastic tablecloth covered by a mosquito net. Boys and girls slept next to each other, but we never thought of one another in a romantic way.

My father was too busy to stay mad at me for long. He was very eager to teach me about pulse diagnosis, the immune system, anatomy and physiology, and preparing herbal formulas. I disappointed and frustrated him with my irresponsible behavior.

After the new year, he told me, "I have withdrawn you from your school.

Today I am taking you to live in a temple in Cho Lach where you will learn some discipline."

We walked in silence up to the gates of Ky Vien Tu, Discipline Brings Good Fortune Temple. It felt strange not to be going to school that morning. I had gotten used to my school and I looked forward to speaking Chinese every day. I stepped on the octagonal cement tiles of the courtyard and felt dizzy, as if they were floating upon water and could easily drift apart.

Ahead of us stood a birdbath and around it many potted *cay kien*, bonsai trees. I looked but couldn't believe my eyes. I had never seen miniature mango, coconut, and orange trees before. The mango tree was no taller than I. When spring came, I was amazed to see it had small plum-sized mangos growing on it. The coconut tree had coconuts the size of oranges, and the oranges were the size of cherries. Among them was a living tree sculpture of a dragon.

To the left of the chapel, under a trellis of flowering vines, was a long wooden table. Several monks with shaven heads and yellow robes over one shoulder were sitting quietly, as if they were expecting us. We sat down with them at the table. They all looked the same, except one of them was wearing a darker color robe and a tall pointed hat of the same color.

The monks poured some tea but said nothing. We drank our tea in silence. A few short backfiring bangs went off in the background, followed by the loud chugging of an old power generator. My father turned to me and said, "I'll be here to teach you every Wednesday and Saturday." Then, without even speaking to the monks, he stood up and walked out of the courtyard.

Two of the younger monks nodded for me to follow them in the direction of the choppy, buzzing sound to a low, long cement building behind the chapel, where the monks slept. They gestured for me to wait there, and they walked away. I stood next to rows and rows of clothesline draped with yellow cloth, woolen caps, and maroon drawstring underwear and the gasoline generator which was driving a water pump on top of a large round water tank.

There are many different schools of Buddhism in Vietnam. Some are stricter than others. In my religion, monks are permitted to marry and to live with their families at the temple. They may also own a business, so they can earn money. I had the feeling there were no women or children here.

The younger monks returned and waited with me until an older monk came outside with a razor and a chair. It was hard to tell one from another, because they all had the same expression. The older one grabbed hold of my hair and pulled it backward and down. He started scraping my scalp with a razor. My head was jerked at an awkward angle and the razor hurt. I tried to loosen his hold by leaning backward and I fell out of my chair. No one laughed.

Afterward, he told me to clean up my hair. My hair lay on the mossy tiles, dark strands of my memories, my dreams, my past. Aunt Gioi used to say the smell of my hair helped her fall back to sleep. I looked down at the pile and thought, "It looks as though I did fall between the cement tiles after all."

I picked up my hair the best I could and placed it on a pile of dead leaves and brush.

They stripped me and wound a long yellow cloth around my waist and over my shoulder. It wasn't tied on; it just hung. Now I was the same, too.

I slept in a room on a reed mat with five other monks. In the darkness I heard a drum. It was coming closer. Now it was outside our window. Time to get up. How do I put that cloth on in the dark?

I followed the single file of monks into the chapel and we knelt on the cement floor in straight yellow rows like kernels of corn. We recited sutras until the floor lightened with the sunrise. Nobody smiled. When it was over, everyone stood up and filed out in silence, except me.

I stood in the octagonal chapel alone in a market square of deities. Light trickled in through the narrow slits in wooden shutters and illuminated the streaming incense smoke.

I heard the shuffling sound of footsteps entering the chapel. I ducked behind a statue of Ameda, the brightly painted, laughing Buddha. These monks didn't like to talk, so I wasn't expecting to hear my name.

"Quang."

I didn't move, confident I could not be seen. To my relief, they didn't come looking for me.

I patted Ameda's huge belly, which looked round and blubbery, like a heap of rice noodles. I reached up and felt his fat, pendulous stone earlobes. I wanted to climb onto his lap.

Visitors started coming into the temple to pray. They brought fruit, rice cakes, noodles, tofu, and cookies and set them down on the altars before lighting incense to pray. I knelt on the floor and pretended to be praying so they wouldn't bother me.

Most of the monks at Ky Vien Tu left the temple every morning in their bare feet, holding a begging bowl, to walk the streets and pray for people. Luckily, I didn't have to go with them. I stayed behind and learned how to do all the different jobs, scything the grass, working in the garden, sweeping and washing the floors, cleaning the bathing stalls and outhouse, cooking, and washing clothes. The monks would bring their bowls to the kitchen when they returned, and the food would be used to make lunch. At every meal, we had to sit at the table and pray over our food for two hours. If anyone was caught taking a taste, he would be punished.

The monks at the temple used peanut plants for growing mushrooms. Sometimes I had to go around asking the local farmers if I could bring their harvested peanut plants to the temple. I had to put them into a pile and cover them with coconut leaves. Two months later, mushrooms would be growing all over the decomposed peanut plants. The mushrooms would keep sprouting up for about three months. I also went to the rice farmers to ask for the rice hay. A larger and tastier kind of mushroom grows on rice hay.

We made our own soap by burning dried coconut leaves and putting the ashes into a big ceramic vat. We filled the vat with water, stirred up the ashes, and then covered it. By the next day, the ashes would have settled to the bottom, and there would be a clear yellow liquid on the top that we scooped out and used to wash everything. Once all the soap is used up, you can fill the vat with water one more time.

Banana peels make an even stronger soap. We always threw them onto a pile in the garden to dry in the sun for a few weeks before we burned them into ashes for making soap.

If I was caught not doing my job, or if I wasn't working hard enough, the older monks would take me into the chapel and make me stand before one of the altars holding my arms straight out on either side until an incense stick had burned all the way down. Every time there was no one looking, I would break off a piece at the bottom and stick it back into the sand.

My father came to the temple to teach me two days a week, but after a few weeks he arranged for me to study at the home of a retired Chinese master of herbal medicine who lived near the temple with his wife.

I called him *Thay,* which means master. I went to his house every weekday morning. In addition to studying with him, I was expected to help around the house, because they were an elderly couple living alone. I collected wood, hauled water, and weeded and watered their garden. My father came to the temple every weekend to quiz me on what I had learned.

My teacher was considered to be one of the best herbal doctors in South Vietnam. He lived in a beautiful cement house with shiny cement floors. When

Thay got older, his patients stopped getting better. My father told me it could happen to any doctor, and it doesn't mean he was doing anything wrong.

Thay taught me the forbidden combinations of medicinal herbs, and how to use certain poisonous plants in formulas. There are hundreds of ways harmless plants turn into poison when combined with other plants. There are also many poisonous herbs and mushrooms that are required in some formulas, but have to be rendered harmless first. Thay told me I couldn't afford to make even a single mistake. One oversight could paralyze a person, put him into a coma, or even kill him.

Thay and his wife were both very nice to me and invited me to stay for lunch every day. It was a luxury not to have to pray for two hours before eating. Mrs. Thay often forgot where she put things.

One time I snuck into the kitchen, and when Mrs. Thay wasn't looking, I poured a lot of vinegar into the soup she was cooking. At lunch, Master Thay apologized to me and said that his wife must have lost track of how much vinegar she had used to flavor the soup.

I felt a little bad for getting Mrs. Thay into trouble, so next time I did something that could not be blamed on anyone.

My teacher and his wife did not have an underground bomb shelter in their house or out in their yard. A lot of people built a bunker around their bed by filling many tall baskets with sand and standing them all around the bed. When the shooting or bombing started, you had to go under your bed.

Their bed was in the front room of the house, so I passed by it constantly. I had the idea to grab some sand from the baskets and then throw it up in the air over my teacher's head, so that it sprinkled down on him like rain. I would stand with my back toward him so he couldn't see my arms, and I would toss the sand up when he wasn't looking. He dusted off his head and shoulders and had a baffled look on his face. I pretended that sand was falling on me, too, and I acted just as surprised as he.

At lunch, the old man asked his wife, "Wife, did you notice any sand falling down inside the house?"

The wife looked at her husband and asked, "Sand? Are you sure?"

Master Thay said, "It's the strangest thing."

I did it again all the next day, and I threw it over the wife, too. By lunchtime, they seemed to be really spooked. Master Thay got up from the table and walked out to the street just as Mrs. Thay and I started to eat our lunch. A little while later, he came back with three armed soldiers.

The soldiers searched the house like they were looking for Communists.

Then they went outside in the garden and started shooting around the bushes. After that, there was no more sand falling inside the house. The teacher said the ghosts must have been afraid of the gunfire.

When I was younger, boys my age were always playing pranks on me. I was an easy target because I wasn't very savvy, perhaps because I was brought up by people who were old. When I went to the Chinese school I tried hard to fit in. I wasn't outgoing enough to lead any pranks, but I joined in wholeheartedly. I probably thought it was quite an achievement when I eventually planned and executed my own pranks. It was a way of asserting myself and proving to myself that I could be popular. I started playing more pranks back at Discipline Brings Good Fortune Temple and I never got caught.

20

BONES OF HAPPINESS

t was the middle of June 1965. My fifteenth birthday was coming up. I had been living at Ky Vien Tu for almost six months. My father came for me one morning unexpectedly. He hadn't come to see me in three months. He found me in back of the chapel, watering my mushroom beds with a square metal can. I noticed he was carrying something in his pocket, and I thought he had brought me a birthday present.

"Ba," I said, pointing to his pocket, "did you bring that for my birthday?"

"What, this?" he said, pointing to his hip. "No, son, I am sorry. I have been traveling. Would you like a dragon's head fruit?"

"Okay." Even fruit sounded special.

I saw him do the magic clearly, now that I knew what he was doing. He reached up into the air with both hands, and then I saw the smooth-skinned magenta fruit in his hand.

"Thank you, Ba."

My father took out his knife and cut the dragon's head fruit into wedges. Dragon's head fruit grows on a narrow, flat cactus vine. You usually find it winding around trees. The fruit looks like a dragon because it has flaps of skin that hang down like scales. Inside, it is white with tiny black seeds. It is as refreshing as a watermelon, sweet, and a bit tart.

We sat in the garden on a bench. The morning sun was still low in the sky. My father placed his hand on the thing that was in his pocket.

"I found this on the forbidden mountain about fifty years ago. I just went back to get it."

He reached his hand under his shirt and took out a Buddha, black like crude iron.

"This Buddha is very old," he said. "It has a special power. The core is filled with crystal."

My father let me hold it. It was much heavier than it looked. It was about five inches high and three inches wide, an awkward size to be carrying around under your shirt.

I turned it upside down to see the crystal, but I saw that my father had sealed it up with cement.

"I found this Buddha and three others in the ruins of a temple on the forbidden mountain."

"Why did you seal the bottom?"

"I didn't want anyone to know how special this Buddha is."

"You could have left it on the temple altar. Nobody would steal it."

"I don't live in the temple anymore."

"You don't?"

"I've been staying in Cay Lay with one of my students, the owner of the Van Tho Duong Chinese herb store. I am seeing patients in the back room of his shop."

"Why can't we live in Cai Be near my friends?"

"I am getting too well known. The new president is making a lot of trouble for Buddhists."

"But who will take care of the altars?"

"The Tiger."

"The Tiger?" I repeated.

"Yes, come on, let's go. I'll buy you some clothes."

We weren't far from the Cho Lach marketplace, the place where my father and I first met. I didn't know anything about that yet, but I was to find out soon enough.

After shopping, we went to a rice shop for lunch.

"Would you like to eat some shrimp or fish or pork?"

"Pork."

At Ky Vien Tu, no animal food was ever served, not even fish sauce. What I missed most was fish sauce. My Chinese herbal medicine teacher didn't use it, but most Vietnamese use fish sauce for every meal.

Fish sauce was invented by a man who put a lot of fish into a barrel and topped it off with a lot of salt. After a few months, the fish disappeared and turned into fish sauce and bones.

When you see a dead pig or a dog, cat, or chicken floating down the river, all bloated with water, you can't cook it, but it is good for making sauce. You put the animal inside a wooden barrel with a lot of sea salt on top, about three kilos of salt to five kilos of meat. For the first two months it is so smelly that you can't go anywhere near it, but after four months, it turns clear and has a very good smell and taste. Only the bones are left.

The house where my father was now staying was right near the main intersection in Cay Lay. It was a three-story cement building with a patio and flower garden in the back. The ground floor was a Chinese medicine store, and the upper two floors were the living quarters for the family.

We entered through the store. My father introduced me to his student, a man in his fifties of Chinese descent.

It wasn't the first time I had entered such a large house with staircases. Some of my friends from the Chinese school lived in houses just as big.

"Mrs. Lee is not at home," my father said. "She is looking forward to meeting you."

My father turned to go up the staircase. "Mr. Lee built a meditation room on the third floor. That is where I sleep."

I followed my father up the second flight of stairs and into a room that was painted turquoise blue. There was a low altar made of dark varnished wood, like a table that ran along the opposite wall. On the altar were three golden statues of Buddha, sitting side by side. If they could have stood up they would have been half my size. I couldn't take my eyes off them. They each had a different face, different hair, and different robes, but each was equally moving.

"That gold paint is really good," I said.

"That is not paint. They are solid gold."

I had never seen that much gold before. "Your friend is the richest man in Cay Lay, isn't he?"

"These are the other three statues I found in the temple ruins on the forbidden mountain. I brought them here while you were at Ky Vien Tu. They are probably Cambodian."

"These gold statues are yours?"

"One day they will be yours," my father said.

The schools were closed for the summer break and I went to see my friends in Cai Be whenever I could. It wasn't that far away. American soldiers started appearing around Cay Lay. They always had a Vietnamese soldier along to translate for them. The merchants and shopkeepers were pleased to see Americans because they were good for business. They always had money in their pockets, and they loved to eat.

My friends told me about an American soldier who wanted to marry a girl from Cay Lay. After school, my schoolmates and I used go looking for Americans out of curiosity. One of my friends took cigarettes from his family store to sell to the Americans, and another took rice liquor, but the Vietnamese soldier just shooed us away.

I felt very small next to the Americans. I liked looking at their features and the different colors of their eyes, skin, and hair. I thought they looked nice.

Even though I had promised my father that I would help him at the clinic every day, I seldom showed up more than three times a week. Some weekends I would stay overnight at my friends' houses, or go traveling with them without telling my father where I was going.

When he found out that my friends were trying to sell things to the Americans, he became angrier than ever before. When I returned to the clinic one morning after being gone all weekend, he yelled, "I don't know what to do with you. You are not like me at all. I found you in the street."

There was no one there but us. I sat down on a crate and said I was sorry. I searched my father's face. It made sense. He was too old to be my father. I wasn't crushed. I never doubted his love for me. I slept against him every night. I breathed in his breath and his smell all my life.

After saying that he found me in the street, he calmed down and put his hand on my shoulder. We went outside for a walk, and he told me about the day he took me home from the market in Cho Lach.

. . .

t was August. I had lost my chance to stay in Cay Lay with my friends. My father decided to take me back to Elephant Mountain to continue my education as a doctor. I was sad to leave the best friends I ever had.

Before setting out on the long trip, we went to Cai Mon to visit Aunt Gioi.

I was fifteen, but my aunt was still a head taller at eighty. There was something changed about Aunt Gioi. She was starting to look frail. She had stopped dying her hair and using makeup. I held on to both her hands as if she was going to fade away altogether.

My father disappeared behind the house. When I saw him again, he was carrying a shovel and an empty woven sack and was headed into the coconut trees. I wondered what he was up to.

I followed him. He didn't talk to me, but he didn't tell me to go away, either. My father never spoke much, except when he was teaching. He said that if he were to chatter all day long, he would spend his power for nothing.

He crossed the small pole bridge and stopped by a row of banana trees that were growing on the other side of the canal. He began parting the grass as if he were looking for something. I thought, "Oh, he's got more gold buried around here."

He was mumbling to himself as he searched. Whatever treasure he buried, it must have been a long time ago, because there were tall bushes and mature bamboo growing on some of the places he looked.

I heard the whimpering sound of a dog and looked up to see Lucky at the other side of the canal.

I crossed the small bridge to play with Lucky for a while. When I came back to check on my father, he was digging. He had dug several holes and had left piles of earth here and there. This was taking far too long. I went off with Lucky again.

When I returned, I found my father on his hands and knees sifting through the soil. Next to him, on top of the sack, was a pile of small bones.

This was no treasure, it was a dead dog or something. Maybe he had buried a dog over the treasure so that if someone dug there they would think it was a dog's grave and nothing more. It seemed as if my father was painstakingly searching for every little bone. I wondered why he was being so meticulous about finding a bunch of old dog bones.

Then I noticed a jawbone in the pile. It had blunt teeth.

I had a creepy feeling, as if the bones were from a human. I wanted to cry out, "Just what do you think you are doing?" but I knew better.

My father put all the mottled pieces of bone into the straw sack and stood up to leave.

"That's it? No gold?" Then I thought, "This must be some kind of magic. Why else would he be making all this fuss?"

When we reached the house my father started piling up brush to make a fire. When the flames were high, he threw the bones into the fire.

I asked, "Ba, are you making a magic spell to make me good?"

He said, "You are very good and curious."

I stood and watched the flames licking at the darkening sky.

My father told me to go back to the house to get some dinner. I came back much later and found my father sitting next to the fire. I sat down beside him.

He said softly, "When I die, I want you to put the ashes of these bones inside my coffin."

I whispered, "Whose bones are they?"

"My wife."

Now I was thoroughly confused. I knew that Co was still alive, because I had seen her last New Year. Even if she had recently died, there would still be some meat on her bones.

"Lan and I were to be married when we were seventeen. I loved her very much. One month before our wedding date, she got sick and died suddenly. I went crazy with grief. I went to Ky Vien Tu temple and began my spiritual practice. I immersed myself in the Buddhist doctrines, I went out every day with my begging bowl and asked the villagers for mercy. After four years, my master began sending me out to chant at funerals. I understood the people's grief and I shared my broken heart with them, and they felt better. Before long, I had many requests to chant at funerals.

"I cried for Lan at every funeral, but it gave me no relief. I had the idea to become a doctor to save people's lives.

"I went to talk with my father, who was a powerful doctor, more powerful than I am now, and told him I wanted to become like him."

I sat looking into the fire in silence. I had never heard my father speak about his problems before. At one point he told me to go inside to bed.

My father kept the fire going through the night. When I woke up the next day, he was asleep on his hammock in the front room. After lunch, he called me to the altar. He took down a small wooden box and said, "This box contains the ashes of my first wife, Lan. When I die, put this box into my coffin with me." He placed the little box into my hands. I saw that he had carved it himself. We believe that once we die, our bones are where our spirits reside when they come back to visit this world.

21

SPIES

Our driver stopped the minibus between Tri Ton and Xa Ba Chuc because he saw some Viet Cong running into the forest up ahead. Concerned that they might have mined the road, he pulled the minibus over to wait for an army jeep to drive by. By 1965, Ho Chi Minh's Communist revolutionary army had successfully recruited tens of thousands of South Vietnamese. This new southern Communist revolutionary army was called the Viet Cong.

The minibus started heating up like a tin can. My father and I climbed out of the bus and sat under a tree. While we waited, he told me about Tam Buu Tu, the Three Treasures Temple, where I was going to live. I knew which temple it was; I had passed by Tam Buu Tu countless times on my way to school. I saw crowds of people visiting Tam Buu Tu. My father said Tam Buu Tu is where all the belongings of the Buddha Master of Western Peace are kept.

Tam Buu Tu was built in 1882 by the Buddha Master's second apostle, Ngo Tu Loi, who was also known by his nickname, Nam Thiep (pronounced Nam Tip), "master of trances." Nam Thiep named the temple "Three Treasures" to represent the Buddha Master, his teachings, and the community of people who live and study together.

Nam Thiep renamed my religion because *Buu Son Ky Huong*, "good fragrance from the sacred mountain," is a long and mysterious name. He called it *Hieu Nghia*, which means "filial piety and returning kindness."

Nam Thiep was the second of the Buddha Master's disciples to lead a series of peasant rebellions against the French. Armed with nothing but spears and farm tools, Nam Thiep and his men ambushed the French soldiers all across the Mekong Delta. Both he and Tran Van Thanh hoped that by chasing out the French, they could prevent the devastating war that had been predicted by To Thay. It wasn't long until the French considered Nam Thiep to be one of their most dangerous enemies.

When he turned fifty, Nam Thiep renounced violence, took the name Bon Su, "teacher of the original teachings," and built Tam Buu Tu. He was a wise and powerful *ong ganh*, village chief, who protected his people with magic. As *ong ganh*, he did not permit his people to fight, even during a time when a battalion of French soldiers attacked them repeatedly.

When Nam Thiep suddenly disappeared from the rebellion, the French commander used spies to find out where he had gone. The spies eventually informed the commander that Nam Thiep had become Bon Su, the *ong ganh* of Tam Buu Tu temple on Elephant Mountain. The commander thought the temple was just a front. He believed Nam Thiep was training a rebel army on Elephant Mountain.

Bon Su's followers had all renounced violence. Many of the men who had previously fought alongside Nam Thiep were injured, sick, or maimed.

Bon Su knew ahead of time when the French soldiers were going to attack the village. When the attackers arrived, there was no one to be seen. All five hundred people were hiding in the jungle in caves. Hiding was not easy, because there was no source of water near the caves, and not much food. The villagers were poor and some, especially the grandmothers and grandfathers, were sick.

The soldiers ambushed the village again and again, but Bon Su always knew the day it would happen, and he was always able to hide with his people in the jungle.

The spies told the French commander that the village was preparing to have a big celebration for an important holiday on January 15. The commander decided to try something different, so he gave the order to use many cannons to rain bombs on the temple.

Again, Bon Su knew the general's plan, and this time, the village chief also changed his plan. He decided not to cancel the holiday celebration and to use his power to protect his people. On the morning of the celebration, Bon Su announced to the villagers that the village was going to be bombed. He told everyone to stay inside the temple and continue to observe the holiday. He told them, "I guarantee that you will be safe as long as you remain inside the temple. No matter how many bombs hit the temple, do not leave."

While the people set out the holiday feast and lit the candles and incense, Bon Su remained in the Buddha Master's throne cabinet and meditated.

The bombing started while the villagers were chanting the sutra. Bon Su did not move or respond in any way, and the villagers remembered what he told them, not to go outside. No one really understood how bombs worked; they thought the master of the French was a powerful sorcerer.

Bombs started hitting the temple one after the other, and everyone stayed inside. About forty or fifty hit the temple directly. The heavy wooden beams that supported the roof came crashing down, but no one was hurt.

Two people panicked and ran outside. They were the only ones who were killed.

When the bombing stopped, Bon Su told everyone to go quickly to the caves to hide, because the soldiers were on their way to the village. When the villagers went outside, they saw that many houses in the village had been hit.

The soldiers didn't understand why only two dead bodies were found outside the temple. The French commander was very angry about the failed attempt to kill Nam Thiep and his followers.

The villagers waited a few days before coming out of hiding. Many of them didn't know if their houses were still standing. They had a lot of work ahead of them.

A lot of people came to help in the rebuilding of the homes and the temple. They came from all over Nam Bo. The French commander told his spies to pose as religious pilgrims and to go help rebuild the temple. They didn't fool Bon Su; he knew they were really spies.

Many months later, when the reconstruction of Tam Buu Tu was almost completed, the spies left to tell their master that there was to be a big celebration at the temple in honor of its completion.

This time the commander told his spies to attend the celebration, because he needed them to be there to identify Nam Thiep. Otherwise he would have no way of making sure he was killed. The commander planned to use his army to storm the temple and shoot everyone. He told his spies that they would be greatly rewarded for their role in eliminating the leader of the sky warriors.

Once again, Bon Su knew that the temple was going to be attacked. On the day before the raid, he ordered the village to be evacuated. There were many more people than usual, because hundreds had come to Elephant Mountain especially for the inauguration of the new temple. People were worried that the caves would not hold everyone.

The two spies pretended to leave with the others to go to the caves, but instead they remained behind and hid in the village. They planned to follow Bon Su and notify the soldiers of the whereabouts of his hideout.

To their surprise, Bon Su did not follow the others into the jungle. He remained in the village. The spies stayed up all night making sure he did not slip away in the dark. On the morning of the attack, they found Bon Su still in the community building, next door to the temple. Later that morning, they saw him walk into the temple.

The spies were very proud to tell the soldiers that Bon Su was helplessly alone inside the temple. He would be an easy target.

One hundred armed soldiers surrounded and stormed the temple. When they got inside, they couldn't find him anywhere. They ransacked the temple, toppling altars and ripping down banners. All they found was one of the old grandfathers who had been too sick to flee. He was a pathetic sight; he looked like a leper. His nose and hands had been eaten away, but even worse, his stench filled the air like a rotting corpse's. The soldiers left the temple in disgust. The spies felt ashamed for letting Nam Thiep get away.

After all the soldiers were gone, the spies saw Bon Su walk out of the temple and go back into the community building. It was too late to call the soldiers.

They snuck into the temple to see if they could find his hiding place. When they looked around, they noticed the leper gone.

The French commander was very angry with the two spies, but they told him not to worry because they had decided to kill the village chief themselves. The commander praised them for their good idea. He gave them a pistol and a few bullets.

On their way back to the Xa Ba Chuc, the two spies discussed when and how they would kill Bon Su. While they were trying to come up with a plan, they both realized that Bon Su was probably aware of their plan and was prepared to evade their attack. They also realized that Bon Su had used magic to disguise himself as a leper and that he had stayed behind to protect his people from being found.

As they drew closer to Xa Ba Chuc they were overcome for respect for Bon Su. When they arrived in the village, they went straight to Bon Su and begged for his forgiveness. They told him that from now on they would protect the village. The village chief believed them.

Bon Su knew that the two spies were planning to kill their French commander. He went to them and told them that he forbade them to commit an assassination. He said that we must never murder a powerful leader, no matter how evil he may be. He said that such people emerge for a reason, one that we may never understand, but interfering with karma will not change its course. The only way to change karma is to practice peace, healing, and forgiveness.

The former spies did not listen to Bon Su. Their guilt and their anger overpowered their reason. They thought they were doing the right thing, because they would be protecting the village chief and the villagers.

When the spies learned that their French master was going on a trip into Cambodia, they devised a plan to ambush the military procession where the dirt road passed by a thick stretch of jungle.

Dressed like rice farmers, wearing conical leaf hats, they walked along the road carrying baskets heaped with wild greens on shoulder poles. They had moved some big stones in the road so that the coaches would have to stop.

Then, as just they had hoped, the convoy reached the roadblock and the drivers reined the horses to a halt. Before any of the soldiers had climbed down to roll away the rocks, the two spies walked up to the window of the coach where the French master always sat and fired several bullets at his face. Blood spurted, and the two ran off into the jungle and got away.

When they returned to the temple, they found Bon Su was expecting them. He was very angry. He said, "I told you not to kill the master of the French."

Before the spies could explain their actions Bon Su said, "He is not hurt; I had to protect him."

The two looked in bewilderment at one another. They had seen the blood.

"You didn't shoot him; you killed a different man," Bon Su told them.

They told Bon Su they were certain they had killed him. They shot him at close range, and they saw him slump over.

Then Bon Su said, "I protected him by making him sit in a different seat. You killed a subordinate officer, which is very bad, but not as bad as killing the leader."

22

TATTOO

The minibus dropped us off at the Xa Ba Chuc market square. The jungle air wrapped around me and welcomed me back. There was a hum, a melody and a fragrance. I remembered the sounds had ears, and would hush in an instant at the firing of a gun.

Most of the concession stands were already closed down. I asked my father if we could eat at a restaurant, but he said we would make it to the temple in time to eat dinner. We walked along the shady dirt road that wound its way through the village, past shops and houses and my old school.

My father and I were both surprised to see that the lawn in front of the temple looked more like a bus yard than a temple. It was rutted and trampled practically bare.

"It appears the number of visitors has been steadily increasing," my father said hopefully.

We came to the row of star trees that started to the right of the village road and continued all the way to the temple doors. Star trees are good for flagpoles and ridgepoles because they grow very tall and straight; they grow up to the stars. People were strolling along the path in both directions; some were sitting on wooden benches. I could see that many were not dressed as if they were from my religion.

The star trees led us to two buildings standing side by side, the temple on the right and the community building on the left. Two sheltered walkways connected them and opened onto a stone patio in between where the drinking water was kept in fifteen wide-mouthed ceramic cisterns, eight lined up along the eaves of the temple and seven along the eaves of the community building to catch the rainwater. There was also a well in the front of the community building.

The temple was the taller of the two buildings. Its roof was made of *co tanh*, a special kind of leaf that looks like lemongrass, only longer. The roof of the community building was made of ordinary water-palm leaf.

The walls of both buildings were of old, rough pine. The cement floor in both buildings was brand new. There were no ornaments or statues inside or out. My religion is very simple.

We crossed the stone patio, entered the community building under the awning of the walkway, and found ourselves in the anteroom facing a large altar. On either side stood three large tables of people eating dinner, the elders who lived and worked at the temple as well as elders from the village. Not all of them were dressed in black. Among them was the master of Tam Buu Tu, a man about the same age as my father and a distant relative of Bon Su. My father introduced me to Ong Bay, and his wife was Ba Bay. Ong Bay invited us to sit down at his table. I wasn't really supposed to sit at the same table with the elders, so I kept my chair at an awkward angle and slightly behind my father.

Ba Bay told me that she and her family had been looking forward to meeting me for a long time. She wanted me to think of her as my mother on Elephant Mountain and to please come to her if I needed help or advice, or if I wasn't feeling well.

After dinner my father led me through a doorway to the left of the altar and into a corridor with two doors on either side. He showed me to my room, which was the second door on the right, next to the masters' room. The two rooms across the hall were where the three temple scribes slept. All of the dormitories were off the hallway between the anteroom and the large community room. The community room was where the visitors ate and slept on four long wooden beds, twenty people to a bed. If more than eighty people planned to sleep at the temple, they would be given a rush mat to sleep on the floor. Most days there were about forty or fifty visitors, but on holidays there could be as many as three or four hundred.

Next my father took me into the temple and showed me where the belongings of To Thay, the Buddha Master of Western Peace, were kept beside the main altar. That was when I saw the most important relic of all, the *ngoi long den,* To Thay's throne.

The *ngoi long den* stood under a red silk fringed and embroidered canopy. In Vietnam, a throne is not a chair, it is a box, a comfortable little room in which the master reclines on pillows. It looks like a stage with a red silk curtain. To Thay's throne was made entirely of fragrant sandalwood. Leafy vines, magic symbols, and different kinds of fruits and flowers were carved on every surface. The top of the throne was shaped like the dome of a mountain. At its base, a red silk banner presented a flaming fireball and an embroidered phoenix flying toward it from either side.

The interior of the throne was so plush and inviting that I could hardly restrain myself from leaping inside and rolling around on the fancy woolen carpet and the pile of colorful shining silk pillow.

"To Thay had a nice throne," I said to my father.

My father said, "This throne did not belong to To Thay. It is just a copy. To Thay's throne was stolen about one hundred years ago."

"Who stole it?" I asked.

"The French soldiers," my father said. "But these over here were his."

On a table next to the throne were some of To Thay's possessions, two ceramic candlesticks, a mother-of-pearl inlaid writing desk and chest of drawers, a Chinese teapot and teacups, a quilted silk blanket, some carved wooden boxes, and four embroidered wall hangings. The thing I liked the most was his black ebony table that was really a tree trunk standing on its roots. The roots had all been sanded and polished and the whole table was the same shiny black color. It looked wild, like it could scuttle out the door at any moment.

My father went to the altar, took an incense stick, and held it high above his head. I did the same. We blessed our incense, and then we lit it and knelt and bowed many times, saying our prayers, holding the burning incense in our hands. Then we put our incense in the holder.

"Let's go to your room. I want to give you something," my father said.

All the dormitory rooms had locks. My father closed the door behind us and sat down on the wide wooden bed.

"There hasn't been much fighting on Elephant Mountain. Most of it is taking place on Long Mountain, which is the next mountain over. The top of Long Mountain has been taken by the Viet Cong, and the lower part by the army. It is likely that the war will spread to Elephant Mountain."

People of my religion were lucky, because many of the members of the Viet Cong believed in the Buddha Master of Western Peace so they tried not to interfere with our lives.

"Where should I go when the bombing starts, where are the bunkers?" I asked.

"There are no bunkers around Tam Buu Tu because this part of the mountain is solid rock. You will have to run away from danger, up to the caves. Just follow everyone."

"Okay," I said.

"I want you to have money with you at all times in case you get lost. At least you will have money to buy food. Even if you end up in Cambodia, you can still use this money."

My father stood up and reached into his pocket. I could see the shape of the black stone Buddha in his other pocket. He paused a moment, took his empty hand out of his pocket, and sat back down on the bed.

He said, "You will find out soon enough that there are many sorcerers here in Xa Ba Chuc. Quang, I forbid you to spend this money to learn sorcery . . . or martial arts. The important thing is to learn character writing, herbal formulas, and acupuncture."

"But you do sorcery."

His eyes flashed. "What I do is different. It is nothing like sorcery. You could never learn that here."

Someone sounded the call for the seven o'clock sutra. My father stood up and reached into his pocket and took out a wad of soft, worn out bills. He counted out five hundred *dong*, which was probably equivalent to about fifty dollars, and handed it to me. "Keep this money with you at all times. You can spend some of it on food and supplies for school."

My father stayed at the temple for a few days, visiting his friends. He slept in my room with me. He found out that Ong Tam, the village chief whom I had lived with at Buu Minh Doung temple, had cancer of the lower lip. Skin cancer is not unusual in such a sunny country. Ong Tam had been receiving radiation and chemotherapy treatments at a hospital in Chau Doc, but the doctors told him he hadn't come for help in time and his cancer had spread. My father decided to stay in Xa Ba Chuc to take care of Ong Tam and other people who were sick. He set up his clinic in the anteroom. There wasn't much room, so he kept his medicine on the altar.

. . .

was expected to help out at the temple. The easiest job was sitting at the table where visitors signed their names in a book. One of my jobs was to draw water from the well to use in the kitchen and the bathing stalls. The well was very deep and the water was a long way down. By the end of winter, you couldn't see any water even if you leaned over the hole and stuck your head in. I had blisters on my hands the first day I drew water. My arms were aching, but I didn't really mind. There was usually a line at the well because the village people were welcome to use the water, too.

The kitchen was inside the community building, but the larger cooking stoves for cooking the huge vats of rice were outside. Anyone was welcome to come to Tam Buu Tu to eat lunch and dinner; you didn't have to belong to the *Hieu Nghia* religion. Everyone who came to eat automatically pitched in with the cooking and cleaning. There were always a lot of people working in the kitchen and the washing station.

My favorite job was serving tea and sweet rice cakes in the community room at night after the seven o'clock sutra. There wasn't much to do at night except sit around and tell stories. Curfew was between nine and ten o'clock, depending on how many visitors were spending the night. We had to tie up the mosquito nets over the long beds for the visitors. The people on the floor had to sleep without a net. On holidays, when a lot of visitors came, I had to work nonstop from five o'clock in the morning until curfew.

I discovered that I preferred sitting with the old men and listening to their stories than hanging out with kids my own age. The old-timers usually sat at the tables in the anteroom because those tables had chairs. Sometimes they discussed politics and the war, but all anybody had to go on was rumors. Nobody had a radio; they had all been confiscated by the soldiers. The old-timers often talked about the old days when my grandfather lived in Xa Ba Chuc. They also liked to talk about sorcery.

My three teachers all lived within one mile of the temple. All of them were from my religion. The oldest of the three was Ong Muoi.

Ong Muoi taught *Han Viet* character writing in a one-room schoolhouse not far from Tam Buu Temple on the lane that led down to the rice fields. Ong Muoi was very old, and he lived alone in the back room of the schoolhouse. His face was wrinkled, and he had so few long gray hairs on his head that he was not able to contain them in any way, so they hung down in front of his ears and sometimes in his face. Ong Muoi was hard of hearing, but if he thought that you were talking during class he would climb out of his hammock and beat you all over with a stick.

The first time I went to my plant teacher's house he told me to sit down while he drank some tea and ate some cookies. He didn't offer me any cookies or tea. Teachers are very strict in my country; they are never relaxed, and they never laugh with the students.

I called my teacher Thay Hai, which means "second-born teacher." He and his wife lived with their two grown sons and their sons' families. My teacher's grandchildren went to school and his sons and daughters-in-law worked in the rice fields. He treated patients in the house, and his wife cooked all day long for everyone. Sometimes I would join their large family for meals.

My acupuncture teacher was also called Thay Hai. He was about ten years younger than my plant medicine teacher. He lived in a nice wooden house with a thatched roof with his wife their two young daughters, and his wife's parents.

The first day I went to my acupuncture teacher's house he told me to go to the market and buy some fruit and cookies and red candles and incense. When I came back, he lit the candles and incense and arranged them on a table with the fruit and cookies, three glasses of water, and a pot of tea. He poured the tea into two cups while praying out loud for me to be a good student and to be kind and to help people. Then he told me to pray. While I was praying he left the table. When I stopped praying he called out to me to keep praying until he returned.

He came back and sat down at the table with some books and some paper, and asked me my birthday so he could figure out which days of the month I should come for my classes. Looking at my class schedule, I saw that my first class was a month away and that there was no regular pattern. Some weeks I had to come every day, and other weeks just one day. Some days were half-days and some were all day.

As I stood up to leave I saw a jar containing some long needles, about one foot long, soaking in a clear liquid.

"What do you use those long ones for?" I asked as respectfully as possible.

"They work well for certain kinds of persistent headaches," Thay Hai the acupuncturist replied. He touched his finger to the center of his forehead and said, "You insert it here, aiming upwards, and then you push along the bone. It will bend at the hairline and continue under the scalp until it reaches the crown point, here." He tapped the top of my head about two inches forward of my hair whorl. It was a sensitive spot.

"Does the needle ever break when it starts bending?"

"No. Hardly ever," he answered.

My father and I were invited to a party at someone's house in the neighborhood to commemorate the anniversary of their ancestor's death. The way we celebrate our ancestors' memory is to throw a feast for as many neighbors as we can afford to feed.

The house was about halfway to the market square on the village road. We arrived just as everyone was sitting down to eat in the front yard, about fifty people, helping themselves to the many different fish and vegetable dishes on every table. Our host greeted us at the front gate and escorted us to our places. She seated my father first, at the grandfathers' table, and she brought me to the older kids' table. I wasn't happy; I would much rather sit with the old men and listen to their stories.

Seated at my table were boys and girls of different ages. About half of them were wearing black, which meant they were from my religion. The food looked delicious. I helped myself to every platter. Some of the kids were looking at me, but I kept my eyes on my food because I didn't feel like meeting anybody.

Not long afterward, while I was enjoying my food, it seemed as if a lot of people had stopped eating and had started talking. Some babies began to cry, and the voices grew louder over the babies'. A couple of kids at my table were arguing, and soon they were practically shouting. While I was looking at my food I saw a hair in my food, and that made me angry. The kids started hitting each other, and their parents came over to break it up.

I reached for a stargooseberry pickle when the kid next to me grabbed the bowl and threw it down on the ground; the wet yellow-green pickles rolled in the dirt. I punched that kid in the stomach. Pretty soon everyone at my table was fighting.

I looked around. I saw that some of the old men were shouting and shaking their fists and that some of the grandmothers were scowling and pointing at one another.

My father looked calm; he motioned for me to come. I stood up just as my table got flipped over and all the delicious food that I had wanted to eat was strewn on the ground.

My father asked me, "Do you see what's happening here?"

"Ghosts?"

"Not ghosts. This is the work of sorcery."

"Is there a sorcerer here?"

"No, he's gone now."

Eventually the fighting died down and people started leaving. Our hosts encouraged everyone to forget what had just happened and to stay, but everyone left except my father and the old men. I wanted to stay and sit with them, but my father told me to go back to the temple.

M y father never stayed in the temple after the evening sutra because he didn't like to chat. He usually went straight to bed so he could wake up later and meditate.

I ladled the tea into many teapots and then carried them out to the long tables in the community room. Other volunteers brought out the teacups and sweet rice cakes. When I was finished serving the visitors I went to the kitchen to get more tea for the tables in the anteroom where the old-timers sat every night.

An animated conversation was going on at the table where the old-timers usually sat. That table was unusually crowded. I recognized some of the same old men who were at the ancestor's cursed party. I set my two steaming teapots on the altar and stood in a spot where they wouldn't be able to see me.

"But Tattoo doesn't live here anymore," someone said. "He opened a martial arts school in Chau Doc City. You know he's an undefeated champion."

"Yes, yes, I know, but he still lives here," someone said in a hoarse voice that sounded like Bald Ong Chin. "He lives in that shack beyond the marsh."

"Where? I never saw a house back there," said a younger voice.

"You take the second cattle track and go past the potato fields," replied the hoarse voice. "It's on the left, set back a ways. I saw him there just last week when I was getting firewood. He has a lot of kids now. He could never afford a house in Chau Doc."

"Well, then, maybe it was Tattoo."

"Tattoo? It couldn't have been Tattoo," said a different voice. "Ong Sau would have blocked it."

"Of course he could have blocked it," said the hoarse voice again. "But he didn't want to. He wanted to teach his kid a lesson. He told me that."

Another voice burst forth. It sounded like Ong Tu the carpenter. "He told you that, did he? But did he know how much I wanted to strangle you?"

There was laughter. I waited for a few more moments before I arrived at their table with the tea. The conversation ended abruptly.

I returned to the community room and began clearing the long tables. I loaded the teapots, teacups, and empty platters onto a tray and carried it outside to the washing station. The temple scribes were busy tying up the four huge mosquito nets. Someone sounded the curfew bell. I went to my room and, as usual, found my father already asleep. I lay down next to him. I couldn't help wondering about this man Tattoo who ran a martial arts school and practiced sorcery.

23

GRENADE

I kept my money rolled up inside the waist of my pants because I was afraid
it would fall out of my shirt pockets. On the mornings that I had plant medicine class, I would stop at the bakery and buy half a baguette and a bowl of
hot, sweetened soy milk. It took me a long time to take my money out of my
pants and put back the change. Sometimes I would arrive late to class.

My plant medicine teacher was very old-fashioned. When I arrived, he
expected me to light a fire in the kitchen and make some warm water to wash his
feet and some hot water for tea. I had never washed anyone's feet before, not
even my own. I got used to washing my teacher's feet, but I could never get used
to scooping up his poop. He had an outhouse, but on the days I was there he
relieved himself outside in the garden behind the house. He made me clean it
up with two banana leaves. And then, after I was starting to get accustomed to
doing it, he began pooping a little here and a little there just to get me to do
more work. It was not uncommon for a teacher to treat his student like that.

For each lesson, my teacher had me write down the names and medicinal uses
of three or four different plants. Then he would take me outside to find them.

He would show me all the ways to identify each plant, where it liked to grow,
the shape of the leaves, whether the edges were smooth or jagged, the number
of veins in the leaf, the pattern of the leaves on the branch, if it had thorns, how

the roots looked, and things like that. Then he would pluck off a piece and tell me to eat it. Sometimes I would chew up a leaf and it didn't taste like anything, but other times I would chew a plant that looked delicious, but it would taste so bitter that I had to spit it out. I only did that once because my plant teacher got so angry he hit me on the head. He said people who work with plant medicine never behave like that. Sometimes I pretended to chew it, but I really hid it in my cheek and spit it out when he wasn't looking.

One time I had such a bad taste in my mouth I picked what I thought was a wild green bean and was just about to eat it.

"Stop, stop! Oh no, it's too late. You've got the fungus all over your hand and wrist."

I looked at my hand and saw some light-yellow powder.

"Oh, it's nothing," I said, and I brushed it off.

"Now you've gone and spread it. We'll have to find some water to wash it off."

Not only was the *mat meo* bean poisonous, but the fuzz on the outside of the pod contained a fungus that was powerfully itchy.

Even though there was a river not far from where we were, it was too far up Long Mountain, where the Viet Cong had their base. My teacher didn't want to take a chance of possibly stepping on a land mine or springing a booby trap. We had to go all the way back to the village for water. In just a few minutes, fierce itches were jabbing at me and making my body jerk. Luckily, as soon as I rinsed off the fungus powder, the itching stopped.

Both the soldiers and the Communists had planted a lot of land mines, but it was the Viet Cong who set all kinds of booby traps. They buried live machine gun bullets under the ground cover. If you stepped on them, they would explode and blow off part of your foot. They also set up hunting traps aimed at people. These were coconut-size balls of dried clay that were studded with razor-sharp bamboo spikes. These lethal weapons were set in the treetops, attached to a trip wire. If one of those balls were to swing down and hit you, the spikes could break through your chest and pierce your heart or lungs. The guerrillas also concealed dugout pits in the ground that were filled with those sharp bamboo spikes. The tips of the spikes were sometimes dipped into excrement or rotten flesh, so the wounds would become infected on the inside.

I saw a lot of people being carried down Long Mountain on stretchers, old people, young people, and a lot of soldiers. People who were wounded in a land mine accident were usually taken to the hospital in Chau Doc City. Viet Cong guerrillas who were injured like that couldn't come out in the open for help. They had their own doctors.

The fighting finally did arrive in Xa Ba Chuc four months after my father and I arrived. One day I counted twenty-three tanks rolling toward Elephant Mountain. Those tanks plowed straight through the rice fields and tore them up. That made people madder than ever. I saw a lot of Americans together with our soldiers. They drove their tanks around all night, shooting into the marsh and the jungle, while the airplanes dropped lights in parachutes that floated slowly down in and lit up the sky.

People tried to get the parachutes because they are good for making mosquito nets. The floating lights left a lot of white powder on the ground.

There weren't many battles on Elephant Mountain. They happened every two or three months and lasted for several days. It wasn't that bad.

One evening when I was bringing water to the kitchen, I heard a round of gunfire going off in front of the temple. I ran to the courtyard and saw a line of soldiers shooting at one of the star trees. When I got a little closer I saw they were shooting at a white napkin that was nailed to the tree.

I ran over to Bald Ong Chin and asked, "Why are they shooting at that napkin?"

"Chinh Co, the sorcerer, claims he has a charm that can withstand bullets," he answered.

A lot of people had gathered. Bald Ong Chin pushed me through the crowd so I could get a closer look.

I saw that there were bullet holes in the tree all around the cloth, but not one bullet went through the cloth.

"Which one is Chinh Co?" I asked.

Bald Ong Chin pointed to a man with short graying hair, dressed in black pants and a dirty white shirt.

The soldiers kept firing until they were convinced they couldn't hit the cloth. Then Chinh Co stepped out of the crowd and walked in front of the soldiers and told them to shoot him.

No one did. They were afraid.

He said, "Give me a gun and I will do it myself."

He walked up to one of the soldiers and stood there until the soldier gave him a handgun.

Chinh Co said, "Are you sure it's loaded?"

The soldier said yes, but Chinh Co shot the tree just to make sure. Then he held his left hand in front of the barrel of the gun. People started shouting for him to stop. He fired the gun. Everyone was quiet. Chinh Co held up his hand and showed us both sides. There was no wound. I couldn't believe my eyes. Everyone started talking at once.

Chinh Co yelled to the soldiers over all the chatter, "Now shoot me. Don't worry."

Everyone hushed up again to see what the soldiers would do. Chinh Co coaxed them and kept assuring them that not one bullet would touch him.

Just two soldiers believed him. They raised their rifles and aimed for his legs and fired. They missed him.

"Aim for my heart," he insisted.

They aimed for his heart and missed him again. Then all of them started firing on him like he was a demon. He couldn't die.

I went to get a closer look at Chinh Co. I saw that he had a dark mole under his left eye and that three long hairs grew out of it. He looked like a nice person.

At tea the old men told some stories about Chinh Co. They said that everyone hated him because he never helped anyone except the soldiers. Someone said, "Next time let's throw a grenade." After that everyone started calling him Grenade.

E very fourth class, my plant teacher Thay Hai gave me a test on about fifteen plants. During the morning, we would go outside and I would have to find all the plants and pick them. Then, after lunch, my teacher would blindfold me and make me taste each one and tell him which was which. He let me take a drink of water in between. Then I had to write down the medicinal uses of each one. I usually got about four or five wrong each time, and my teacher hit me for every wrong answer. If his wife was there, she would come in and make him stop.

About once a month, he tested me on forty plants. I would pray a lot the night before for his wife to be home. If she wasn't, I usually came home with plenty of bruises.

My father had given me a special liniment to use in case I got bumps and bruises. I didn't think much of it when he told me, "Here, take this in case you get hurt," but I was beginning to think he knew exactly what I would be using it for.

. . .

I managed not to get hit much in Ong Muoi's class. We spent a lot of time copying characters off the blackboard into our notepads. While we were practicing our calligraphy, Ong Muoi would usually rest in his hammock and fan himself. Next to his hammock was a small table where he set his daily pot of tree-bark medicine that he prepared every day for his persistent cough.

There were about thirty students in the class, all boys. Every day he would choose one of us to wash his shoes and clothes. First we had to bring his clean shoes up to the front of the class where he would be waiting, seated on his hammock with his feet on the floor. Then we had to lift his legs up to take off his dirty shoes. We had to lift them again to put the clean ones on. There was a pond outside where we washed everything, and then we hung it on a line to dry. Later in the day he would make that same person eat the leftover food from his dish, which was even more disgusting than lifting up his old, flabby legs.

I hadn't really made friends with any of the kids. One morning before class started, one of the kids gave me a section of a branch. It was moist and pinkish. He told me that was filled with a sweet sap and you were supposed to suck on it like sugarcane. He said it came from a special bush that grows only in the Seven Mountains.

I knew it was a trick and that it had been soaked in red-hot chili peppers.

Everyone in the class was watching me as I thanked the boy and accepted the treat. I glanced around the room and, seeing that Ong Muoi had stepped out, I walked over to his medicine pot.

The room went silent.

"Oh, no," someone said, "he's dropped it in."

"It'll kill the old lizard."

"He'll have a heart attack."

I turned around and gave my classmates an evil grin.

Just then the sound of Ong Muoi's cough sent me scurrying to my seat.

All during class everyone kept their eyes on old Ong Muoi, wondering when he was going to take a swig of medicine. When he finally did drink, he didn't choke, but everyone figured it was because the branch hadn't soaked long enough. So they kept waiting for Ong Muoi to choke and have a heart attack and die. By lunchtime, they realized that I had tricked them.

I didn't really care about making new friends; the only thing I cared about was finding Tattoo.

. . .

arrived at the temple just when they were serving dinner. I carried my bowl outside and saw that my father was resting in his hammock. I wended my way past volunteers who were crouching in front of basins of soapy water and stacks of dirty pots, pans, cooking utensils, platters, bowls, chopsticks, and teacups, and sat on the ground next to him.

He didn't talk for a long time. Then he asked, "How are your classes going?"

"Fine," I said.

"Thay Hai your plant medicine teacher came to the temple this morning and had tea with me. He told me that you sometimes arrive late for class."

"I'm sorry," I said.

My father asked me when I was going to begin my acupuncture class, and I told him next Tuesday.

"Oh, good," he said. "Thay Hai is a decent acupuncturist, but he doesn't like to teach pulse."

My father sat upright in his hammock and said, "Here, check my pulse."

It had been a long time since I had practiced pulses. He laid his left hand on his thigh, facing up. I had to stand next to his hammock. I placed my index finger on the line of his wrist, on the thumb side, and then placed my third beside it and then my fourth.

"Lay your fingers down flatter," he said.

My father's pulse did not feel like the pulse of a seventy-nine-year-old man. An older person has a pulse that hits high, toward the surface of the skin, and slow. My father's pulse was still in the middle. It felt full and resonant.

"Quang, I would like you to stop by the clinic every other day. It doesn't have to be for long. I want to teach you more about pulse diagnosis. Also, I would like you to review the formulas."

I knew I had to be very careful with my father. I didn't want to get in trouble with him anymore.

24

FUZZY BEAN FUNGUS

I had discovered a poison bean vine growing not far from the schoolhouse, and I had an idea for a prank. I placed a large green leaf directly underneath the fuzzy beans. Then I took a long stick and tapped the beans until the pale-yellow fungus powder fell down onto my large leaf. Very carefully, so as not to let a speck of fungus fall on my skin, I curved my large leaf into a funnel and tapped it, transferring the powder onto a single spot in the middle of another large leaf which I folded again and again, and put into my pocket.

I arrived at school an hour early. Ong Muoi was out collecting his daily supply of bark medicine. I found an old bucket and dunked it into the pond. It was less than one quarter full. Then I took an old rag down from the clothesline and carried the bucket into the classroom.

I took the leaf out of my pocket, unfolded it very carefully, and then dropped it into the bucket. The yellow fungus floated on top. I dipped the rag into the water and then wiped down the four long tables and all the benches. I was careful not to wipe any fuzzy bean fungus onto my area.

I was about to return to the pond to wash off my hands, but I saw Ong Muoi coming up the path from the forest. I slipped out the side door and hid the bucket and rag in the bushes. Then I ran back to the temple.

Breakfast was just ending. I headed straight to the dishwashing station, crouched right down alongside the volunteers, and thrust my arms into a basin of soapy water.

"Oh no," said a person who sounded like a girl. "Let me roll up your sleeves for you."

She was directly in front of me on the other side of the basin. A few strands of her hair had come loose from her ponytail, and were stuck to the corner of her mouth. I held out my hands and looked at her face as she rolled up one soggy sleeve and then the other. Her eyes were a beautiful golden-brown color, like palm syrup. She smiled and wiped the hairs away from her mouth with the back of her hand. I fumbled with a few dishes and then got up to look for some food to eat.

That girl took me by surprise. Some of my friends at the Chinese school were girls, but they never made me feel like this one did.

I helped myself to a bowl of sliced melon and pineapple, and walked over to the front courtyard, hoping to avoid my father, but there he was, sitting under a star tree. I wanted to turn around and go somewhere else, but it was too late.

"Good morning, son. I didn't see you at chanting this morning." He didn't appear to be angry.

"Well, I went out for a walk . . . I felt like being alone."

"I know how you feel," he said, understandingly.

"Well, I'm off to my class," I said. I walked off, leaving my bowl of uneaten fruit sitting on the bench.

"Stop by the clinic when you have a chance," my father called.

When I got to class, everyone was standing by their seats, getting ready to bow to the teacher. If I had gotten there one second later, Ong Muoi would have made me stand in front of the class holding my hands out so he could thwack my palms with his switch.

We bowed respectfully to our teacher and sat down in our places, waiting in silence for the classroom monitors to hand out our notepads, brushes, and ink bottles. Ong Muoi was getting his shoes changed, and then he started writing the new characters on the blackboard.

I pretended to be staring off into space, but really I was looking at the table for specks of the pale yellow powder. But the color of the wood made the fungus impossible to see.

I opened my pad carefully so as not to brush against an infected area of the table. From the corners of my eyes, I watched my unsuspecting schoolmates fiddling with their ink brushes, pantomiming messages, and gesturing behind the teacher's back. I watched as one by one they began unscrewing their ink bottles and twirled the hairs of their brushes, getting ready to dip them carefully, without dripping any ink.

I noticed that Kam was wearing shorts, which was not really allowed. I saw him drop his left hand to the seat of his pants and give his bottom a scratch. I sensed some casual scratching, but nothing out of the ordinary. Maybe the fungus had sunk to the bottom of the pail and it didn't get onto the rag. Maybe I shouldn't have put so much water in.

Pretending to stretch, I slid my forearms along the table straight out in front of me, into the danger zone, to test it out on myself.

Tien suddenly clasped his forearm arm and began to scratch it furiously, making his ink brush spatter ink all over his neighbor's work. The neighbor, Chi, protested.

Ong Muoi spun around just in time to see Kam jump out of his seat clutching his rump. Everyone in the class started to laugh.

"Silence! Young man, come here at once!"

Kam went to the front of the room and held his hands out to the teacher, but just as Ong Muoi snapped his stick, Kam's hands were back on his rump.

The class exploded in laughter.

"Silence!" Ong Muoi croaked, tapping his stick on the blackboard stand.

Then, as if on cue, one after another of the students jumped out of his seat and started scratching vigorously.

"Sit down this instant!" Ong Muoi shouted incredulously. "Have you all gone mad?"

Ong Muoi charged at the students in the first row, swatting his stick at everything that moved.

Realizing that I ought to be reacting, too, I jumped out of my seat and started scratching like a monkey, but soon I was scratching for real.

The shrieks of laughter were overcome by shrieks of panic.

"We're under attack by fire ants!" someone yelled as he raced out of the schoolhouse. In just a matter of minutes everyone was in the pond except Ong Muoi, who was still standing in the classroom, staring unbelievingly at all the shirts and pants and paintbrushes and inkwells that had been flung about the room.

Ong Muoi sent everyone home to chant the sutra in case ghosts had been involved. It was still early when I set out to find Tattoo and ask him if he would accept me as his student. I had planned it so that I would be back for lunch. There was a rumbling sound in the distance. I couldn't tell whether it was thunder or war.

25

CHICKEN LEGS

P eople said the soldiers weren't able to kill the Viet Cong with missiles because they went into the caves. I heard that during Tet, the Communists played one kind of music on the top of Long Mountain, and the soldiers played another kind at the bottom, and here on Elephant Mountain, it sounded like one strange music.

The sound of thunder grew louder than the distant bombing. A short way past the schoolhouse, the lane narrowed into a path that wound its way down the mountain, through a patch of forest, and into the wetlands, where all the rice farmers in Xa Ba Chuc grew their rice. It was very convenient to grow rice there because the fields flooded naturally. Rice plants need to grow underwater for the first two months, and then in regular soil for the last month. Rice farmers can control the amount of water in their rice paddies, by surrounding them in a wall of earth so water can either be added or removed with buckets and a lot of manpower.

The marsh was ahead in the distance, diagonally to the left of where I entered the rice field. I would have to zigzag my way across, walking carefully along the walls of the paddies. Some of the edges had eroded and were only a few inches across. Blue-gray clouds came rolling over the top of Long Mountain and filled the sky with rain. The rich, chocolate-colored earth became slick and slippery.

I reached the marsh and continued walking along the walls of the rice paddy, looking for the cattle tracks. The raindrops became full and heavy. They felt as if they were hitting me on purpose. It wasn't very easy to see through the sheets of rain. I spotted the first cattle track, a thin muddy path through the tall lime-green marsh grass. Three paddies later, I came upon the second cattle path.

I hoped I wouldn't step on a snake in the marsh. I reminded myself that if I should feel even the slightest sting to check my feet for a snake bite. Sometimes people don't realize when a poisonous snake has just bitten them. They start to feel drowsy and go home for a nap and never wake up.

I followed several paths leading off to the left, but I didn't see anything but potato patches. The third time I turned off the cattle track, I came to a large peanut patch. I was about to turn back before I spotted a small house at the far end of the field.

My father told me that all sorcerers were poor, so I wasn't surprised when I saw the house. It was so shabby that I could see right through it to the other side, even in the rain. I could hear the voices of young children coming from inside.

I called out hello and walked into the clearing of their yard. A man's voice answered me, but it was not coming from inside the house. Tattoo was practicing martial arts with a long stick, out in the rain. He moved with the focus and determination of someone who was fighting for his life. His bare torso was covered with green and black markings like a crocodile. There was something else odd about him, but I couldn't tell what it was.

When Tattoo was finished, he motioned for me to come over to him. At close range, I could see that his tattoos were all magic charms. They looked similar to the ones I saw my father draw on yellow paper for people to take home, mostly loops and circles. I bowed and introduced myself and asked if I could be his student. Tattoo didn't answer, but he invited me into his house. The rain was leaking through the roof in many places and the floor was all muddy. His wife and four small, muddy children came over to meet me.

It was then that I noticed what was wrong. Tattoo wasn't wet. His shoulder-length graying hair, tied neatly at the nape of his neck, was dry. I remembered the old men talking about a charm that some sorcerers use to keep dry in the rain. My uncle would never work out in the rain. He said it's not good to sweat in the rain because the pores are open and the rain saturates the skin. The next day, you will probably have stiff, painful muscles and a cold.

Tattoo said that he couldn't accept me as a student until he consulted an oracle. He sent me to buy a butchered chicken, a pound of raw pork, a small bottle of rice liquor, and some cookies. That meant I had to go all the way back up the mountain, past the schoolhouse and the temple, to the market square. It would take me about an hour and a half. It meant I wouldn't be back for lunch.

Luckily the rain was tapering off. I bounded through the peanut patch, splashed through the puddles on the cattle track, and ran lightly on the edges of the paddies. I ran up the winding forest path to the lane, past the schoolhouse, and onto the village road. I snuck past Tam Buu Tu and walked briskly all the way to the market square, praying my father wouldn't see me.

It cost me forty *dong* for the chicken, twenty for the pork, eight for the alcohol, and five for the cookies. I kept dropping the separate bundles, so I went back into the butcher shop and asked the woman to tie them together. I kept praying until I reached the schoolhouse and then I ran gleefully the rest of the way back to Tattoo's house.

Tattoo's wife put the chicken into a pot of boiling water. She put some rice up to boil, sliced the pork, and sauteed it in a wok with bamboo shoots and bitter greens. Tattoo poured the rice liquor into small cups and put them on the table next to the cookies. He lit two candles and several sticks of incense and placed them beside the cookies and liquor. He sat down at the table and began to pray. I didn't know what to do, so I asked his wife if I could help her with lunch. She sent me out into the forest to look for mushrooms.

When I came back, Tattoo was still sitting at the table and his wife was setting out the food. She brought the chicken in on a wooden board and placed it in front of her husband. The head and feet were still on the chicken. Tattoo told me to sit down at the table with him and pray. I prayed for the intelligence and strength to make me a good student. I knew to pray a long time.

"Now I am going to find out if you will be a loyal student," Tattoo said.

He stood up and pulled the board with the chicken closer. He took hold of the chicken's legs and brought them close to his face. He was looking at the fine lines on the legs and feet to see if they were clearly defined. He continued searching for imperfections. After a few moments, he looked up and said, "Good."

I couldn't help but smile, I was bursting with excitement, but Tattoo wasn't smiling. He looked intently at me and said, "Do you swear you will never turn against me?"

"I would never do that," I said.

"Swear," he said, "you have to swear."

I swore never to turn against him without even wondering what that meant.

Tattoo's words filled my ears. "I will teach you to fight, and when you are ready, I will show you how to protect yourself with sorcery."

I nodded calmly, but inside I was jumping for joy. Tattoo called his wife and children to the table for lunch. They seemed to be just as excited as I was to have pork and chicken for lunch. I ate some rice and vegetables, but I didn't eat any chicken or pork because in my religion, we don't eat any kind of flesh except fish.

Before leaving, I told Tattoo that I didn't know when I could come for my training because I had a lot of lessons and I had to work at the temple. He said he was usually away in Chau Doc City from Tuesday through Friday, so I should come during the weekend or on a Monday. He told me to be sure to bring a pound of pork and eight ounces of rice liquor every time as payment.

I found a dry goods store just past the schoolhouse lane where I could buy pork and liquor on my way to Tattoo's house. That way I could get there in half the time. Even though I had started studying acupuncture, I was still able to go to Tattoo's house more than once a week.

Tattoo was tough on me. He made me do a heavy workout to build my strength and endurance. He drilled me on my kicks, punches, and blocks, and he sparred with me. I asked him to teach me how to fight with a stick. His style was different from my uncle's, but I liked it.

There was a windup grandfather clock in the temple that chimed the hours. I could hear it from my bedroom inside the community building. A safe time for me to practice martial arts was three o'clock in the morning. My father didn't usually come back to sleep in the room after he finished meditating at one or two o'clock in the morning. He slept the rest of the night in the temple.

During the next few months, I made an effort to study hard with all my teachers and to help my father more in the clinic. I didn't want my father to be concerned about me at all.

When Ong Muoi told our class that we were going to be studying medicinal plants in the forest, I had an idea of a way to impress my classmates. On the morning of our forest outing, I woke up before daybreak, grabbed a knife, and headed over to the schoolhouse just as sky was just changing from black to gray.

There was a particular tree I was looking for. It grew next to the pond, at the foot of the forest path. It was a sapling, about six feet tall. I got to work with my knife and severed the roots one by one. It was very hard work. My hands and arms were aching, but I knew they were strong enough to do the job because of my martial arts training. I reached under the root ball, and felt around for every root. I kept finding more. Wow, that tree had a lot of roots. I cut them all except for two small ones. I patted the dirt back down tightly around the root ball and straightened out the moss until the tree looked normal. I went back to the temple to bathe and eat breakfast.

Our first assignment at school that morning was to copy a list of *Han Viet* characters into our notepads. I recognized them all; they were the names of medicinal plants. Ong Muoi announced that anyone who was finished with his calligraphy could wait outside.

I was the first one out. I waited until a few more students came outside and then I started talking about studying martial arts with a powerful teacher. I told them I could pull a tree out of the ground. My classmates all looked at me like I was an idiot. They ignored me the rest of the time.

Ong Muoi led the class around the pond toward the path. I moved toward the back of the line, away from the teacher. I told some other kids. "I am studying martial arts. Do you want to see how I can pull a small tree out of the ground?" A boy named Phong said, "Sure. If you ever did that, I'd be your slave."

I said, "Are you sure?" He said, "Yeah." I said, "Are you sure you're sure?" He said, "Yeah."

When we reached the tree, I said, "All right slave, watch this."

I started punching and kicking an invisible enemy with all my might to warm up. Then I grabbed the tree with one hand, tightened my face, and made a grunting sound. I pretended to strain as I lifted the tree and broke the two remaining roots. The tree came up high enough for me to throw it to the ground. Its roots quivered.

I could hear Ong Muoi yelling in the background for everyone to get out of his way. When he reached the tree, he demanded to know what had happened.

Phong said, "Quang knows martial arts, sir. He just pulled that tree out of the ground."

Nobody spoke, not even Ong Muoi.

During the walk, a lot of the boys wanted to know about my teacher. I suddenly had a lot of friends. They all wanted to learn, too, but they didn't have money. Only Kam became Tattoo's student. He didn't tell his parents either. I was glad that I had at least one friend to practice with.

Tattoo was grateful to me for finding him a new student because it meant his family would have meat on the table, but as time went on, I began to think Tattoo was not a kind person and that he really didn't care about me or Kam. He yelled at me a lot and sometimes he hit me very hard. When Kam didn't have money to bring him some pork, Tattoo refused to teach him anymore. I continued as his student for many more months. I was waiting for him to teach me my first charm.

My acupuncture class was the most boring of all, because I had to sit by myself and copy the meridian lines and all the points into my notebook. The younger Thay Hai had a naked cloth man that he had made himself and stuffed with kapok. Using black ink, he traced fourteen of the meridian lines, and marked the points with dots. The meridian lines are streams of energy that flow along the surface of the skin and deep into the organs of the body. The naked cloth man also had red blood vessels and green nerves, things an acupuncturist would wish to avoid. And he had a lot of organs, a heart, a pair of lungs, a stomach, a pancreas and spleen, a liver, a gallbladder, a small intestine, a large intestine, a bladder, a pair of kidneys, two ovaries, and two testicles.

Thay Hai wouldn't let me go home until I had memorized at least ten points each time. He would say, "Three-Mile Point," and I would have to know that it was the thirty-sixth point along the Stomach Meridian and that it was located two inches below the outside edge of the knee. "Welcome Fragrance" was the twentieth point along the Large Intestine Meridian, and it was halfway between the wing of the nostril and the line where the cheek begins.

If my teacher had more than three patients at a time when I was there, he had the fourth one lie down right on the table where I was studying. I would watch him stick needles into their face and hands and feet, and then he would leave for about twenty minutes.

I had seen people with needles stuck into them before, since my father sometimes treated his patients with acupuncture. He didn't use steel needles, he made his own needles out of shards of flint.

Thay Hai told me he wouldn't allow me to do any needling until I could draw the entire cotton man by heart and locate all the points, blood vessels, and nerves on a person's body. I also had to know about many kinds of acute and chronic sicknesses, and how to treat them. Even though it was very boring, I worked very hard so I wouldn't get into trouble with my father.

26

MY FATHER SPEAKS WITH GHOSTS

One afternoon, when I was walking home from my plant medicine class, I saw my father coming down the road toward the market carrying his medicine bag. He said he was going to the forbidden mountain, but he didn't know for how long. He gave me another five hundred dong.

I went over to Kam's house to practice martial arts. I had been teaching him the stick form since he was no longer studying with Tattoo. We usually went into the sugarcane fields where no one could see us. I didn't tell Kam that Tattoo was going to start me on sorcery. I had to keep it a secret. I didn't want to ruin my only chance of finding out how sorcery worked. Even though my father had warned me not to learn it, I was convinced that he was worrying for nothing. I would never use sorcery to harm anyone. I was fascinated by the art of magic, I had to understand the mechanism of how it worked.

Kam and I sparred for a long time, and then we cooled off in the neighbor's pond. Kam told me his family was going to volunteer at the temple that afternoon to help prepare dinner. I told him I'd see him later.

I had discovered a very nice place to take a nap. It was where the scribes took their siesta, behind To Thay's throne. The scribes all grew up in the village. They were selected to be scribes because they did calligraphy very well. They were my best friends at the temple. Anh Thiep (pronounced Anh Tip), with the chipped front tooth, was the funniest; he liked to tell stories about all the strange people who visited the temple. He was the youngest scribe, just two years older than me. Anh Muoi was the oldest, in his late twenties. He was mute like the village chief's son, and very handsome. People said he was the best poet in Xa Ba Chuc. Ang The, almost twenty, liked to talk about politics and the future of Vietnam. His mother was Cambodian, and he had long wavy hair that went into ringlets. Anh The (pronounced Anh Tey) cared a lot about people. He sometimes stayed in a bad mood for days.

I walked into the temple and helped myself to some mung bean cakes and banana cookies from the altars, and then I slipped out of sight, behind To Thay's throne. Nobody ever went back there during the day except the scribes and me. (I think it was where my father slept each night, after he finished meditating.)

People who came to visit the temple often asked to have their names and the names of their loved ones written in *Han Viet* calligraphy inside a special book. If they had a little money to make a contribution to the temple, they could ask for a prayer to be written in calligraphy next to their names. All the names and prayers were read aloud during certain holidays, and then burned. The ashes are to be kept in the temple forever inside large ceramic urns. The urns are kept behind To Thay's throne.

I leaned against one of the urns and enjoyed my snack. There were fourteen urns so far. Then I stretched out on the cool, smooth concrete and fell asleep.

I was beginning to notice that a lot of the volunteers working in the community kitchen were girls. When Kam arrived for dinner that evening, he and I tried to get the girls' attention by doing martial arts by the door, but the cooks started yelling at us that we were in the way. They said, "Why don't you make your-selves useful? We could use some help."

There were about twenty volunteers inside chopping vegetables. Others were lighting the cooking fires. The girls were standing beneath the black sooty woks and pans. They were talking as they chopped lemongrass.

One of the cooks said, "Boys, take this bushel of lemongrass and chop it very small for dipping sauce."

Lemongrass dipping sauce is about the most sensational and aromatic condiment there is, but it takes so much work it is almost not worth it. The lemongrass must be chopped as finely as grains of salt. Then you add water, salt, lime juice, palm syrup, and chili pepper.

At first the girls didn't notice we were there. We tried to listen to what they were saying, but they stopped as soon as they saw us. Then they started giggling and looking over at us. Kam told me girls always giggled around boys. I didn't remember my girlfriends in Cai Be giggling like that.

I hadn't realized it at first, but the girl who had rolled up my sleeves was there, too. I asked Kam if he knew her, and he told me her name was Lieu and that she and her little brother had come to to Xa Ba Chuc live with their relatives. Kam thought her parents might be dead.

Someone had donated a large set of fancy stainless-steel knives with black wooden handles to the temple. Our cooks took great pride in them. You almost never see knives like those.

The cook gave us each a knife and we each grabbed a handful of lemongrass and started chopping. I was surprised how difficult it was, considering how good our knives were. I wondered if they had been sharpened lately.

The next afternoon, I went to the market and bought a grindstone, found a screwdriver and some screws, and attached it to my bed.

Long after curfew, I snuck past all the people sleeping in the community room, crept into the kitchen, collected all the knives, and brought them back to my room. I didn't start sharpening them until the following morning while everyone was in the temple, chanting the morning sutra. I had to work quickly, but I sharpened them all and got them back into the kitchen before the sutra was over.

That day, I went into the kitchen to volunteer for lunch. One of the cooks sent me to the well to wash the carrots, mushrooms, and scallions for the soup. When I returned, I heard someone say, "What's wrong with this knife, it doesn't cut right."

Another one said, "Mine too, it's really bad."

One of the head cooks came over and tried the knives. She said, "What the devil?"

She looked closely at the knife ran her fingers along the blade. She exclaimed, "This knife is no good."

She handed out different knives to use, but they didn't cut, either. Some of the girls were there, too. They grumbled and complained about their knives the whole time.

People eventually found out that I was responsible. I got yelled at, and the girls found out about it. I stayed away from girls after that.

.   .   .

A few days later, I noticed a crowd of patients waiting in the anteroom, old people with coughs and arthritis, a mother holding a feverish child, a man whose eyes were covered in a white film, children with swollen bellies, a little girl with skin lesions, and some who didn't look sick. I told them that my father was away, but then I saw him walk through the door with a handful each of *ngai vang* and *ngai den* leaves. When he saw me, he motioned for me to come and help.

I followed him to a boy with tear-stained cheeks who was sitting on a chair. He had fallen out of a tree and had dislocated his shoulder. My father handed me the leaves and told me to grind them in the mortar with vinegar. Then my father went to find some cloth for a bandage.

When everything was ready, my father told me to watch closely. He spoke gently to the boy, promising that he wouldn't touch his sore shoulder. He gently squeezed the boy's index and third finger with one hand, and with the other, he held the pressure points on the boy's elbow. He asked the boy if that hurt, and before the boy was finished answering, he pushed the boy's humerus gently upward into the socket.

He tore the cloth into a square for a plaster and some long strips to bind it. In no time he spread the herbs and vinegar mixture onto the square cloth, applied it to the boy's shoulder, and bandaged it neatly. He told the boy's mother the medicine would reduce the swelling and draw the tissues back together. He told her to come back tomorrow for a new dressing if the pain stopped, otherwise to leave it on for another day.

To my surprise, my father called in two new patients instead of one. He said to me, "I want you to take this woman's pulse and write down what you feel. Include her name and age and if you think she is pregnant." He handed me his small red pillow and a notepad and pencil. "Sit over there." He motioned to a table the corner room.

I took the pillow and asked the woman to follow me to the table. I felt very nervous. I asked her to tell me her name and age, and I wrote it down. She was thirty-four. She said she had a bad cold. I asked for how long, and she said two days. She said she had started sneezing after she had the sensation that something went into her nose and made it itch. The next day, however, she had a fever with chills and a dry cough and sore throat. I placed the pillow in front of her and asked her to lay the back of her left hand down on the pillow.

My father had taught me that when a healthy person has a new cold, all the pulses strike high. That means the body's immune system is strong and is fighting the cold. A healthy person will recover from a cold in two or three days if she drinks medicine to clear the cold out.

I felt the pulses on her left hand. I was still very much a beginner, I palpated at only one depth. I could identify only the most basic qualities of the pulse beat.

I wrote my observations down on the notepad using Chinese characters, that my patient's heart pulse was hitting high, her liver/diaphragm pulse was low, and her kidney/colon/uterus pulse was deep and weak.

I checked her right hand and wrote down that her lung pulse was weak, her spleen/stomach pulse was weak, and the kidney/small intestine/abdomen pulse was also weak. I noted that my patient did not have a fluttery pulse, which meant she was not pregnant.

I knew that my patient would not recover from her cold very fast, because her body was not functioning well. I knew without asking that she had a gassy stomach, sluggish bowels, painful menstrual periods, and lower back pain, and that she suffered from fatigue. I had learned that it would be difficult for her lungs to decongest until her digestion improved because gas in the gut causes heat to radiate upward and creates a drying effect on the lung tissue, making the mucous thick and sticky.

I wrote in the notepad that my patient needed herbs to improve digestion, loosen the bowel, warm and moisten the lungs, open the sinuses, and improve the circulation in the lower abdomen.

I asked my patient to wait a minute while I went outside, picked a *vay cam* vine, and stripped the leaves off. I came back and wrapped the vine around my patient's wrist two times and tied it. I don't know why, but that vine always stops chills. It doesn't take away the fever, it just makes the person more comfortable.

I told the woman that my father would check her next.

My father taught me that the two most important things are the digestion and the circulation. If a person has a healthy appetite and can absorb the nutrients well through the small intestine, that is good, but it is not enough. The blood circulation and the nervous system must also be functioning well to transport those nutrients to the muscles and organs, and to eliminate the metabolic waste.

I checked other patients for my father. At the end of the day, when all the patients had been seen, we sat down together at one of the tables. My father opened his book and began comparing my notes to his. While we were going over my observations, a husband and wife approached my father. They were not from my religion.

They asked my father for help. They said there was a ghost in their house that was bothering their children and scaring the neighbors. They told my father they had hired two exorcists to come and get rid of her, but she was only getting stronger.

They said they had bought the house from a man who didn't mention anything about a ghost, but the neighbors told them afterward that the ghost was the man's daughter. They explained, "The man's daughter was married and was expecting her first child. One day the Communists and the soldiers started shooting near the house and a stray bullet killed her."

I knew that pregnant women and mothers of young children can become the most frightening ghosts of all, because they will drive themselves mad trying to find their children. No matter how much the family loved their daughter, they wouldn't be able to bear living with her ghost. A ghost is only a fragment of a person.

The wife continued, "This ghost wanders around the house all night long with a lamp. I think she is looking for her baby, because she comes to the children's bedside often. We have all seen her face in the lamplight, her skin is green, and her expression is evil."

The husband said, "She shakes the children's bed until they wake up and see her. The children say the ghost opens her mouth and screams, but no sound comes out. Our three children have been sleeping at the neighbor's, but now the ghost has followed them there."

The couple said they had tried setting out meat for the ghost to eat to keep her happy so she wouldn't bother the children, but it didn't work.

The neighbors chipped in some money to hire an exorcist, but it didn't work, so they had to hire another. The first exorcist asked them to steam a pig's head until it was cooked, and to put it on the table with some food and alcohol. After dark, the exorcist took a long knife and started talking to the ghost. He stuck the knife into the pig's head and said he would do the same to her if she didn't leave the house. She didn't.

The second exorcist told them to buy a live chicken along with the pig's head. When he arrived at the house, the second exorcist took the chicken outside, slaughtered it, and wrung its blood into a bowl. After nightfall, he dumped a pile of hot coals near the children's bed. He walked back and forth over the red-hot coals and threatened to throw the ghost down on the coals and hold her there until she burned. He posted charms on the walls of the house, and he stuck the knife into the pig's head to scare her. Finally, he brought the bowl of chicken blood into the house and placed it on a table. The bowl started to move by itself. The exorcist said the ghost was drinking the blood. All the neighbors came rushing in to see. When it had finally stopped moving, the exorcist said the ghost had gone.

"But now she is back, and she is worse than ever," the wife told my father.

"Would you be able to get rid of her?"

My father hesitated before saying yes. The couple assumed he didn't think he could do it. They were quiet, and then they went home.

A short time later, a different couple came to ask my father for help with their fifteen-year-old son. They said he was possessed. He would do bizarre things all night long and then sleep all day. He climbed straight up the walls and sat on the roof. They once found him outside in the dark eating a live chicken. During these episodes he didn't seem to recognize his parents or acknowledge when they spoke to him. He never remembered any of it the next day. He would be so tired from the night before that all he did was sleep.

The boy's parents said they had hired two exorcists, but both of them became afraid when their son climbed upon the altar and wouldn't move.

My father agreed to help them. I went with him to the boy's house that very night. The parents asked my father if they should buy a pig's head or a chicken or the usual things that exorcists used for removing ghosts, but my father said he didn't use anything except his prayer beads. We arrived at the house just as it was getting dark. When the boy saw my father, he panicked and ran outside. The parents went outside to look for him. When they finally found him, they could barely force him back inside the house.

My father looked into the boy's eyes and said, "I have come to talk to you. I am asking you to leave and to give me back this boy. I help people, so I ask you to do the same. I try to do good. Please hear me. Go to the forbidden mountain and pray. Leave these people alone. It will be good for you in the future."

He told the ghost, "Let's work together. If you go to the forbidden mountain, I will pray for you to come back in the next life."

The boy cried out, and then he fell. He called for his parents. They came to him and cried. He didn't understand what was happening. My father told them everything was all right now, and we left.

When the first couple heard that my father had helped the boy, they came back to the temple and apologized to my father for not believing in him. I went with my father again to the other house. All he did was stand in the house and talk to the ghost.

Later I asked him, "How did you make the ghosts listen to you? You didn't do anything except talk."

My father said, "They respect me."

27

"OC OC MET POP . . ."

Tattoo's peanut patch had been destroyed. Half the plants were lying sideways and the rest were dug under. I went over to get a closer look. Pig tracks. The peanuts were still on the plants. The pigs had rooted up the entire field. Pigs will only do that if they want to punish the owner of the field. Usually they eat a little here and there, and people don't bother with them. I figured Tattoo had done something to make them really mad, otherwise they wouldn't have methodically destroyed every single plant.

"Did you bring the two hundred?" was the first thing Tattoo asked me when I showed up at his house that day.

"Yes," I said as I unrolled the top of my pants and got it out. Tattoo took the money, counted it, and put it into his pocket.

"By the way, how old are you?" he asked.

"Sixteen," I said truthfully.

Tattoo's wife was getting ready to practice her stick form. I had never seen a woman fight before. I watched her move with her stick, thrusting it into the stomach of her invisible opponent and sweeping him off his feet. She moved differently than a man, but just as fast and smooth. Tattoo said, "My wife may not be as strong as me, but she can trick me."

Tattoo pointed to a small green charm on his right breast. "I am going to teach you this one today." It was a long vertical line with a wavy line looping back and forth many times over it, and a horizontal line beneath. There were two small Chinese characters on either side of the vertical line. I could read them; they meant "spirit" and "charm."

I took a closer look at his other tattoos. Some had Chinese characters on them and others didn't. I asked him why that was so. He told me, "The others are Cambodian spells." I followed him into the house.

We sat down together at the table, and he drew the same design with circles and loops on a piece of paper.

He explained, "Every charm has a visual symbol as well as an incantation. You need to use both, or the spell won't work."

He wrote the incantation on the paper below the charm.

Oc oc met pop
tet oc net met
pot tet net met
oc net met pop

"What does it mean?" I asked.

"Nothing. It means this charm and nothing else, though I suppose it might have meant something long ago, in an ancient language."

He explained how to practice the charm. Then he said that if I studied every night, I could learn a new charm every month. The most challenging thing, he said, was to remember which incantation went with which charm.

I tucked the paper into the waist of my pants and walked home carefully so as not to slip into any puddles.

The temple was swamped with visitors. I noticed that my father had more than the usual number of patents waiting in the anteroom, so I decided to help him.

When I got there he was preparing some medicine to put into a girl's eyes. He told me to look at her eyes. I had seen it before, a white film like rice paper covering her eyes. We call it *keo may*. First the eye gets itchy. After a while, you can't see far. Then you begin seeing double. The film grows thicker until the person becomes blind.

My father said the medicine would loosen the film and make it easier to remove. But he said the medicine stings so badly that the person will suffer just as much with the medicine as without. All the medicine did was detach the film from the eye a little bit so it didn't bleed as much when you ripped it loose.

"The eye will still bleed," he said, "but not as much."

I felt sorry for the girl. She couldn't help crying. The medicine had to stay on for five minutes or more. She was so brave to let my father cut the film with a knife and tear it off her eye. She didn't even struggle when he ripped the film off her eye, that was how much she wanted her sight back. Sometimes the film keeps growing back and you have to repeat the procedure every few months. Some people wait too long, and the film becomes too thick to remove. Those people lose their sight permanently.

I worked with my father, reading pulses and preparing medicine, until he closed the clinic. We ate our dinner together in the anteroom and discussed our findings and recommended treatments.

That night, as usual, my father woke up at midnight and went into the temple to meditate. I stayed in bed for a few minutes after he left, my hand resting on the piece of paper tucked into the waist of my pants, the paper Tattoo had given me.

I went outside as if I were going to the outhouse, but I ducked inside a bathing stall and shut the door behind me. I lit a stick of incense and stuck the end into the ground. Then I sat down in front of it, took my paper out, and put it on my lap.

I began tracing the magic symbol in the air in front of the glowing ember with my two fingers as Tattoo had shown me. I traced it over and over as I chanted the magic incantation, a long vertical line with seven lines looping through it, a horizontal line along the bottom, and a Chinese character on either side. Tattoo told me not to stop tracing and chanting until the incense stick had burned out.

> *Oc oc met pop*
> *tet oc net met*
> *pot tet net met*
> *oc net met pop*

I traced and traced until my arm was aching, but I didn't dare pause even for a second.

Tattoo told me that if I did this every night without skipping a single night for twenty-eight nights, I would begin to see the magic charm standing in the air and glowing on its own. Once you see that, he said, you are almost finished. Not too long after that, maybe after four or five more nights, the glowing symbol will suddenly expand in size until it is enormous. Tattoo said that once that happens, the symbol has been programmed inside my brain.

The spell I was learning was for making people get a stomach ache. It wasn't the kind of charm I was hoping for, but I didn't dare mention this to Tattoo. Tattoo said that every charm has more than one use, but since I was only a beginner, I could only use it to make people sick.

M y acupuncture teacher was ready to let me treat patients, but not with acupuncture. I had learned all the points and how deep to needle them, but I hadn't started putting needles into people's bodies.

He said he was going to let me lance carbuncles, bleed varicose veins, and remove parasite eggs from underneath children's skin first. He said that I needed to get used to hurting people.

People usually get boils and carbuncles in their armpits and groins. If you don't clean them out, the infection can spread and the person can get sick with fever. If you catch a boil or a carbuncle soon enough, you can put medicine on it and it will go away. If not, you have to wait for it to grow into a painful lump so that it can be lanced. You have to wait until it is red before you cut it open. I had to watch my teacher do it many times. I wasn't nervous to try it for the first time.

Thay Hai kept his needles soaking in rice liquor. He poured some over my hands to sterilize them, and he handed me one of those three-sided lances that were bent at an angle. He told me to cut the boils once in the middle as if I were cutting into a piece of ginger root.

The first person I cut was a thirty-year old woman who had two carbuncles on her groin. I cut into the first red bump, and the pus started overflowing. It had a bad smell. I used the silky fluff that grows on kapok trees to wipe it. I dipped the ball of kapok in the clear yellow sap of a tree called the *cay my dau u*, which kills germs very well, and swabbed the lesion. The fruit of that tree is called *trai dau u*. We use the seeds of the fruit for medicine, too.

You take the seed and roast it in a pan until it turns black. It smells very good, like incense. Then you rub the seed on a rusty knife. The knife will get coated with a sticky black substance. Put that sticky substance on impetigo and other infections, and the skin will heal very fast. My aunt used to make *dau u* medicine and keep it in her store for anyone to use if they needed it.

People also ground the seeds and expressed the oil to burn in lamps. The grounds can be glued to a bamboo stick and used for a candle.

My teacher also taught me how to treat varicose veins. Women are more prone to varicose veins than men, especially if the woman feels tired all the time and her legs feel weak. If a woman starts seeing small blue veins appearing on her legs, she should go to the doctor for medicine to improve her circulation. If she neglects to do this, then after childbirth she will be likely to develop varicose veins in the future. The veins usually show up on the backs of the knees and make the whole knee joint hurt. They protrude and look ugly and green. The blood inside is thick and sludgy. Varicose veins can return to normal if you clean out the congealed blood out once a week for nine weeks.

The first time I did this on a forty-year-old woman, I stuck in the three-sided needle and brown blood shot out about three feet. It almost went into my mouth. It didn't hurt her very much. I had to cut the vein in two places and squeeze out the blood clot in between.

The next time she came back the vein was smaller, but the blood still came out brown. By the ninth time, her blood came out nice and red, and the vein was normal again.

The only people I minded cutting were the children. We have a kind of disease that small children get from parasites that live in chicken droppings called *tam tit*. Their bellies become distended, and the small veins and capillaries on their abdomen look black. The blood vessels on their arms also look black. The hepatic artery becomes swollen and can be seen easily under the skin because it turns bright blue. If the children don't get treatment they will die.

The way we treated this disease was to cut out the eggs of the parasite, which are deposited on the palm of the hand at the base of the third finger. The skin will be puffy there. When you cut the skin you will see that the blood comes out all sticky with little round greenish balls like tiny fish eggs. You have to cut both palms. You need both parents to hold the child, otherwise they would never let you cut them. It takes a month before the abdomen goes back to normal.

I t happened just as Tattoo said. After practicing for three weeks or so, the orange, glowing ember of the incense stick started growing and twisting around like a vine until my magic symbol appeared before my eyes on its own like a firebrand. A few nights later it shot out in all directions until it seemed to be the size of an elephant.

It was time to try it out.

The next day after the evening sutra, I sat down at a table in the community room with the scribes. They had always been nice to me, but that didn't stop my curiosity. I noticed their teapot was almost empty. I said I would get them some more tea.

I went into the kitchen and filled the teapot with more tea and looked around to make sure no one was watching me. I focused my mind and uttered the spell while I traced the symbol over the pot.

I came back to the table with the charmed tea and sat down. I filled my cup with the cursed tea. The only one to take more tea was Anh Thiep, which was lucky for me because he would probably laugh about it later. I decided it would be better if we could laugh about it together, so I drank my cup, too.

After a few minutes, we both grabbed our stomachs and ran outside to the outhouse. I sat down expecting to have violent diarrhea, but nothing came out. I stayed in the outhouse for a long time until the curse wore off, then I felt fine again. I felt more than fine, I felt powerful.

28

GUARDIAN SPIRIT

One day at my plant medicine teacher's house, Lieu and her relatives came running into the house carrying Lieu's younger brother, who had been bitten by a snake. His body was limp, and his jaws were locked shut. His face was white but his mouth and lips looked gray. Frothy mucous was oozing out of his mouth.

Thay Hai knew immediately by looking at the bite that it was a *ho mang*, a cobra. A cobra's venom is very strong; it could kill an eight-year-old boy in one hour. Thay Hai went immediately to get the medicine. He pried the boy's mouth open and made him swallow it. He also put two acupuncture needles into the boy's neck just behind the angles of the jaw.

I have never seen someone die from a cobra bite, but I have heard that their skin turns green and blood comes out of the pores at the base of the skull.

Lieu's aunt had tried to kill the cobra, but it was very large. She had struck it with her hoe, but she wasn't sure it if had died. Thay Hai said it would be better if they could find the snake and bring it in. Lieu said she would find it. I ran with her to her aunt's garden, which was about half a mile away.

People say that a cobra will take revenge on you if you try to kill it. It will hunt you down later. Even if you manage to kill it, its spirit will make sure the head of the snake will show up under your foot somewhere or drop on you. If the fangs were to break your skin, it would be the same as if it bit you.

I picked up a long bamboo pole and started parting the bushes, looking for a gray-green snake with three green rings around the neck. Lieu saw an old rice sack lying on the ground and went to get it so we could put the snake in there. She reached down to pick up the sack and saw something moving. She screamed and I grabbed a hoe and chopped the snake's head off.

I handed the body to Lieu and she put it in the sack. I held the head carefully and we ran back to Thay Hai's house. I was thinking the snake's spirit would try to make me trip and land on its fangs, but I wasn't afraid, because Thay Hai had the antidote. I also reminded myself that if the snake bit me, all I had to do was walk backward three steps and reach behind myself and grab the first thing that I touched, grass, sticks, rocks or dirt, anything. I would put whatever I grabbed into my mouth to mix with my saliva, and then apply it to the snakebite. I wouldn't even need medicine. That magic only works in Vietnam. Everyone knows about it, but it is not easy to do because your first reaction to getting bitten is to run away from the snake. The magic only works if you walk backward.

When we got back to my teacher's house, Lieu's brother's eyes were open and the color had returned to his face, but his jaw was still stiff and he couldn't talk. Thay Hai cut the snake's body and squeezed some blood into the medicine. He applied the red mixture to the snakebite, and then put some of it into the boy's mouth. Thay Hai prepared a soup with the body of the snake and some other medicinal herbs for the boy to eat later, when he could chew.

"He will be fine," Thay Hai assured the relatives. "This soup will give him diarrhea for the rest of the day. It will clean the rest of the poison out of his system."

After that, Lieu and I became friends.

I made sure to get to the schoolhouse early to try out a new spell. Tattoo told me that once a magic charm has been programmed into your brain, you have to use it at least once a month, or else you will lose it and have to start over again. Ong Muoi was still in his private room. I had to time it right this time; yesterday the spell had worn off by the time everyone arrived.

I had prepared a little paper packet of incense ashes. I took the packet out of my pocket and opened it. The timing would be difficult. My classmates were arriving; I could hear their voices drawing closer to the building.

Before anyone could see me, I traced the charm over the ashes with my index and third fingers, and chanted

An ma
ni bac yi
hawng hawng hawng ta ha

I blew the ashes over the tables and benches. My classmates were talking just outside the doorway. I wasn't finished yet. I backed into the doorway and closed my eyes until I saw the charm clearly in my mind. Then I brought my fingers up to my forehead and imagined I was plucking the charm out of my brain. I released it into the air, and it hovered there, glowing like an ember. I made it grow in size until it covered the entire room. I traced over it with my two fingers, a face with a tall hat, in the middle of a sideways rectangle with looping corners that ended in squiggle. When I finished tracing, I blew on it.

"Move," someone said, shoving me aside.

It was a sleeping charm.

I went over to my place and sat down. The classroom filled up slowly.

Ong Muoi came into the room. I had never seen him looking so pleased.

He waited until we took our places and bowed. Then he walked up to the first row, put his hands on the table, leaned over, and said, "As you know, we will be having our annual end-of-the-year party in two weeks."

We were accustomed to having parties at school. Ong Muoi held four parties every year; it was part of his curriculum to teach us how to cook. We would bring pots, pans, platters, and cooking utensils from home and spend all morning cooking for the parties.

He continued, "This year I've decided to hold a cooking contest. I will divide the class into four teams. Each team will make three dishes. During the party, a panel of judges will choose the winning team. Everyone on the winning team will be able to come with me on a field trip."

While he was talking, I started to yawn, and my head felt heavy. I had to prop it up by putting my elbows on my desk.

"We will decide on the teams during break. Quang! Sit up straight."

Ong Muoi gave the class permission to talk quietly while he wrote the day's assignment on the blackboard. It was my turn to pass out the ink bottles. I could barely stand up, my legs felt heavy. I slogged my way over to the supply closet and almost let all the bottles slide off the tray when I lifted it. I went from place to place handing out the bottles. A lot of kids asked me to be on their team. I put away the tray and made it back to my seat.

Ong Muoi had covered the entire blackboard with *Han Viet* characters.

"Copy this poem into your notebooks and write the translation on the opposite page," he said.

I looked up at the blackboard and started copying the passage into my notebook, but after a while I found myself staring into space. I tried to write, but I kept forgetting what I had just seen. Before I knew what was happening, Ong Muoi was rapping my head with his stick. "Pay attention!" he insisted.

Yawns were going around the room. More of the students were staring off into space. I put my head down on the desk. I heard Ong Muoi yelling, "Focus on your work," and "Wake up this instant." I heard the sound of his stick snapping on other heads.

Ong Muoi walked over to his hammock and lay down. He told us class was dismissed and an instant later he started snoring.

Nobody got up. I went to sleep under the table. When I woke up, I wasn't tired anymore. I saw that Ong Muoi was still asleep. Five other kids, including Kam, were sleeping on the floor, but the rest of the class had gone home. I woke up Kam and we went out to practice martial arts. He asked me, "What happened? Do you think someone put a curse on us?"

I said, "I don't know, it sure seemed like it."

Sometimes I helped the master of Tam Buu Tu, Ong Bay, and his wife, Ba Bay, in their rice field. I actually spent more time catching crabs than tending to the plants, but they didn't mind because the crabs sometimes damage the roots of the rice.

What I yearned to do most was climb the rocks on top of Elephant Mountain, along the elephant's back. I had never climbed on rocks before. My plant medicine teacher sometimes took me to the top of the mountain to collect certain medicinal plants. He showed me where the caves were, where people from my religion hid out from the French a long time ago. I didn't want to go into the caves, I preferred climbing on the rocks. I liked to look down the other side of the mountain, at the rice fields and water below, to remind myself how high up I was.

The head of the elephant was a flat, square, rocky peak several miles from Tam Buu Tu. One day I set out walking along the ridge toward the elephant's head.

It took me three hours to reach the foot of the peak. I was hoping to climb to the top, but a helicopter appeared in the sky above me and landed there first. I changed my mind. I found a path leading down from the ridge and decided to see where it led. Partway down I met an old monk in an orange robe who was carrying a shoulder pole with two big rocks in each basket. He introduced himself as Ong Nam. He told me the American and Vietnamese soldiers were setting up an army base on the elephant's head.

The path took us to the rear courtyard of a stone temple where Ong Nam lived. A small eight-sided pagoda stood in the center of the courtyard. Ong Nam said his master's body was in there. He said his master had started building the stone temple many years ago and that he had decided to carry on in his master's place. He'd been climbing the mountain every day for over twenty years to get more stones to build the temple. The temple was called An Son Tu, which means "peaceful mountain temple." I looked up and saw the elephant's head towering directly above the stone temple.

I accompanied Ong Nam up and down the mountain, and I carried some rocks for him. He invited me to stay for dinner. Three nuns lived at An Son Tu with Ong Nam. They cooked and served us our food.

After dinner Ong Nam asked someone from the neighborhood to drive me home on his Honda. It took about half an hour to get back to Tam Buu Tu. I liked Ong Nam very much and I think he liked me, too. Neither of us knew at the time that we were destined to meet.

That night, during tea, I joined the old-timers at their table just as Ong Sau the weaver was telling the others how he had ruined his brother's wedding by throwing hot peppers in the cooking fire. He said all the guests ran away because they thought the army was spraying tear gas. I missed the part about what made him do such a thing to his own brother.

Ong Tu the carpenter told about the time a six-toed cat jumped over the body of his dead uncle, who'd been dead for three days. He said the corpse sat upright and got off the table and started walking toward him and his wife. They hid under the bed, but the zombie was still coming toward them. Ong Tu said that if the zombie had touched them they would have died. It tried to touch them, but when it tried to bend, it tipped over because it was too stiff. When the zombie hit the ground the evil spirits got knocked out of the corpse. Ong Tu said after that happened, people started killing all the six-toed cats they could find in Xa Ba Chuc. He said that is why we usually put a sword or a banana across the chest of a dead person before they are buried, so evil spirits won't go inside the body.

Bald Ong Chin remembered the time when a pack of thieves robbed house after house in Xa Ba Chuc by burning opium mixed with *ca duoc* flowers under the windows and blowing the smoke into the houses while the families slept. Bald Ong Chin said he knew how to make the smoke a different way, without opium, and that he would show me how to make it some time.

My favorite story was one that every person from my religion knew. Bald Ong Chin told it to me and I didn't let on that I already knew it.

TUAN QUAN, THE GUARDIAN SPIRIT
OF THE SEVEN SACRED MOUNTAINS

Tuan Quan, the guardian spirit of the Seven Sacred Mountains, used to walk among us. He was seen several times during the founding of Xa Ba Chuc, when the original houses were connected by footpaths through the jungle. The spirit was last sighted at the time Bon Su was the *ong ganh* of Xa Ba Chuc, when my grandfather Ky was living with his teacher in the forbidden mountain. In those beginning days, new people like my grandfather showed up all the time, and were taken in by the settler and given food and shelter.

One evening a newcomer showed up at the home of a young couple. When the wife came to the door, she was surprised to see how old the traveler was. She didn't hesitate to invite him to spend the night. After having supper together, they insisted the old man sleep in their bed and they arranged to sleep on a mat in the next room.

When the wife woke up before daybreak the next morning to start the fire, she noticed the bed was empty, and assumed their guest was outside using the outhouse. The couple were concerned when their guest didn't return.

Later that morning, the wife went into the bedroom to tie up the mosquito net. She called to her husband to come quickly. The bed smelled like a wild animal and it was covered with tiger hair.

The husband and wife collected the hair and went straightaway to Bon Su, and explained about the tall old stranger. The village chief didn't seem surprised. He said, "It must have been Tuan Quan, the guardian spirit of the Seven Sacred Mountains. He has been visiting our homes in order to learn about us and our ways, to make sure we will uphold the values of the Buddha Master, since he is no longer among us. Tuan Quan has accepted our presence on his mountain, and he will protect us along with all the other creatures."

Pretty soon everyone in Xa Ba Chuc knew about the old traveler.

A few weeks later, a different old traveler showed up at another house. This man was short and stout. The couple invited him to stay the night. They didn't even think about the tiger spirit.

That night a full moon shone in the windows and woke the couple. Out of curiosity, the husband crept into the room where the traveler was sleeping. The husband was confused by what he saw through the mosquito net, in the soft moonlight. He thought he was seeing an enormous tiger asleep on the bed. He heard the power of the tiger's breathing, and he smelled his musk.

He and his wife remembered what the *ong ganh* had said about Tuan Quan. They didn't run away, but they couldn't go back to sleep, either. They stayed up all night praying.

The next morning, they collected the tiger hair and showed it to Bon Su and to the settlers. That is why everyone in my religion believes in Tuan Quan, our guardian spirit.

29

TWO BEANS

t was June 1967; I was almost seventeen. I was looking forward to the end-of-the-year party in Ong Muoi's class because I was planning to perform some of the illusions taught to me by the magician in Saigon. I had performed other tricks at previous school parties. I prepared my props the day before.

On the morning of the party I hid my props in my pocket. I went into the kitchen to borrow some cookware and utensils to bring to school for my team to use for the cooking contest.

Our team made coconut crepes with shredded crab, hot and sour noodle soup with shrimp and mushrooms, and fried plantains with sweet and spicy lemongrass dipping sauce. Ong Muoi chose a panel of parents to judge the food. My team won, which meant that we were going on a trip to Sam Mountain to visit the oldest temple in the Seven Mountains.

We all ate the food for lunch, and then afterward Ong Muoi asked if anyone wanted to sing a song or recite a poem or do a magic trick. Ong Muoi surprised us all by doing two of his own magic tricks. For the first trick, he held his hands in boiling water for several minutes and solicited many gasps from the audience. When he removed his hands from the water, they weren't even red. I have no idea how he did that trick. His second trick was even more gruesome. He opened up his mouth to show us how few teeth he had, three molars and three incisors. Then he took the glass sleeve off his kerosene lamp and begin chewing it up into tiny pieces. He spit them onto a piece of paper for everyone to see. We were speechless. He chewed up half the glass.

A boy in the class named Ngo stood up to recite some poetry. We all cheered; everyone in Vietnam loves poetry. That is because to be a poet, you must be able to compose your own verse right on the spot when someone gives you a topic. The lines must rhyme and the intonations must match. I would have liked very much to be a poet, but whenever I tried, I got a headache.

I performed two sleight of hand tricks at the party. In the first trick I created the illusion that I could turn paper money into regular paper. I warned people in advance that I wouldn't be able to change the paper back into money again. For the other illusion, I tricked a volunteer into believing he had turned water into blood by uttering a magic word while stirring the water with a chopstick. Both tricks required props. In the second trick I had prepared a blend of oyster shell ashes and the ashes of a particular tree and secretly wiped it on the chopstick, but it wasn't visible. This powdered mixture turns blood-red when it gets wet. Nobody guessed how I did those illusions.

In September 1967 South Vietnam elected its second president, President Thieu. Our first president, President Diem, was a Catholic, and he tried to turn South Vietnam into a Catholic country. Many Buddhist monks were arrested. Life was so difficult for them that some of them set themselves on fire in protest. They meditated in the street as fire consumed their bodies. Other monks scooped up the ashes and brought them back to the temple. I heard that in the ashes of the most advanced monk, they discovered four dark diamondlike stones. Monks say those diamonds appear in the ashes of someone who has practiced meditation for a long time.

When President Thieu took office, a lot more people started coming to Tam Buu Tu to visit, as many as two hundred visitors each day. The master of Tam Buu Tu told us he was expecting over one thousand visitors to come for the next big holiday. Ong Bay began calling community meetings about building a dormitory and expanding the community room and temple in order to accommodate all the guests.

I yearned to get away and walk along the top of Elephant Mountain. I liked to jump from boulder to boulder like a panther. Sometimes I would see helicopters lowering cannons and huge nets filled with guns and supplies. Sometimes I went to visit Ong Nam.

I didn't tell Ong Nam about my father until the fourth or fifth visit, but when I did, he shouted with laughter. He said he and my father were dear friends. He said they studied together with the master who built An Son Tu.

I felt bad that Ong Nam didn't have any students to help him build the temple. The next time I saw my father I told him I wanted to live at An Son Tu with Ong Nam. My father couldn't believe his ears. He was very happy.

"But," he said, "An Son Tu is too far away from your teachers."

A few days later he said, "Tam Buu Tu is going to be renovated. I think it is a good idea for you to live somewhere else for a while. Let's go and ask Ong Nam if he knows someone over there who can teach you acupuncture and herbal medicine."

We went the very next day to visit Ong Nam. During the next weeks, my father arranged for me to begin classes with a new teacher. I was to move to An Son Tu after the big holiday coming up on October 15.

Just a few days after the big October holiday, Ong Bay, the master of Tam Buu Tu, died. He wasn't even old or weak. He just caught a bad cold and died. My father didn't know anything was wrong until his wife, Ba Bay, came running into our room one night.

More than a thousand people came to Ong Bay's funeral. Ong Bay's eldest son, Chu Hai, took over his father's responsibilities, including supervising the renovation of Tam Buu Tu.

After the funeral, my father hired two Honda drivers to take us to An Son Tu. I was careful to hide my sorcery certificate from Tattoo inside my clothing. That certificate meant that I was an accomplished sorcerer and that my teacher had given me the authority to teach.

I followed my father to the back of the temple, where he knelt in front of the pagoda where his teacher was buried. I knelt and prayed with him. Then I went up mountain path to look for Ong Nam. I had only climbed a short way when I heard Ong Nam cry out, "Quang, stay where you are. Don't take a single step."

I waited until Ong Nam appeared with his shoulder pole and heavy rocks. He said the mountain had been mined. He had seen four places where the ground cover had been disturbed. "It's probably the soldiers trying to keep the

Viet Cong away from their new base," he said. Ong Nam knew the forest floor so well that he wasn't worried about setting off a land mine himself.

He and my father looked at one another for a moment.

"We'll be careful," Ong Nam told my father. "I won't let him go on the mountain without me."

We went into the temple and Ong Nam showed me to my room. The nuns lived in a separate area. I felt happy to see the nuns because I thought they would make the temple more lively and warm. These nuns had shaved their heads like monks, and wore yellow robes draped over one shoulder, over a yellow blouse.

While the nuns served us our lunch, I started chatting with them. My father told me afterward that I wasn't supposed to do that.

During lunch, my father explained that I could either be a monk or Ong Nam's servant. He said that if I became a monk, I would have to shave my head. If I became a servant, I would shave the top, back, and sides and leave the front long. My hair had grown long again in the two years since my head had first been shaved.

My father preferred that I become a servant to Ong Nam, because I would be able to spend more time with his friend.

I decided to become a servant. Ong Nam went to get a razor. I watched my hair falling to the ground a third time.

Before leaving, my father gave me a lot of money. He said, "Now the war is closer than ever. It doesn't matter where you go; it is dangerous everywhere. Listen to Ong Nam and keep this money on you at all times. I will be going to the forbidden mountain for a while, and then I will be going home to Cho Lach to check my patients. I may not see you for many months."

He gave me a long hug and squeezed the arm of his friend. I watched my father walking away. It was the first time I felt afraid to be away from my father. I worried that I might get killed in the war and never see him again.

I arrived at my new acupuncture teacher's house for my first lesson. His wife told me he would be back in a few hours, and in the meantime, she had some work for me to do. She wanted me to lay down stones for her patio. I worked for about an hour, and then she wanted me to give her a massage. She said she had strained her back carrying the heavy rocks.

I told her that I didn't know how to give a massage, but she said she would tell me what to do. I followed her to her bed and watched her lie down on her stomach and then take off her shirt. She said to get the liniment from the table and rub it on her back.

After I rubbed in the liniment, she gave me some money and told me to go to the market and buy myself a treat and come back in one hour, because her husband should be home.

When I arrived at the time she said, my new teacher was angry with me. He said I had arrived an hour late for my lesson. He hit me and told me to go home and try to come on time tomorrow.

I didn't go back. I decided to spend the mornings with Ong Nam and help him build the temple. He always went up alone to look for land mines and booby traps and then he would bring me with him to show me where they were. I could see the sandbags piled up at the edges of the elephant's head. Ong Nam pointed to cannon barrels sticking through the sandbags. He said the cannons were all pointing toward Long Mountain.

Ong Nam took time to teach me about meditation.

I tried to meditate every day, but the longest I could sit was about forty minutes, then I had to get up and move around. The head nun used to force me sit for two hours at a time. It was easier to sit for those hours, because I knew she wouldn't bother me as long as I was sitting. She was very picky.

Ong Nam taught me that everyone has a lotus flower growing in heaven. The lotus flower saves our place in heaven. Every time we do a good deed our lotus flower grows, but each time we do something bad our lotus flower wilts and shrinks. He said that a person can cause their lotus flower to wilt so badly that it shrivels up and dies, and then they lose their place in heaven. I asked him if the lotus can straighten up again after it has been wilted for a while and he said yes. I was happy to hear that because I was certain my lotus flower was at least halfway wilted.

One night, when I was asleep in my room, someone grabbed my neck in the dark and started squeezing my throat shut. He was very strong, and I had to use all my strength to pull his hands off. Then he pinched my nose shut and tried to cover my mouth. I pried him off me and leapt out of bed kicking and punching him with all my might. I didn't see anyone in the room. I stayed up the rest of the night, in case he came back.

The next morning after chanting and doing my chores, I went to take a nap under the banyan tree. While I was sleeping, he attacked me again in broad day-light. This time I saw that it wasn't a person at all; it was invisible. It couldn't have been a ghost or a monster, because those have no strength in the light of day. One of the nuns saw me thrashing around, and she came over to ask me what was wrong. I told her I was having a nightmare. I didn't dare say anything about it, because I thought it had to do with my involvement in sorcery.

I was frightened. The spirit came to kill me several times a week. I kept a knife under my pillow, and I would lie awake nights. It made no sound, so I couldn't hear it opening my door or walking toward me in the dark. I had to wait until it grabbed me.

One night I charged the evil spirit in my room with a long knife that I took into my room every night from the kitchen. I ran into the wooden door and the walls several times. Ong Nam flung the door open, and the spirit went away. He said, "What on earth are you doing in the middle of the night?"

"I was just practicing my sword form," I said.

The next time the spirit came for me, I tried not to hit the walls, but I couldn't help it because the room was so narrow.

Then next morning Ong Nam called me over to sit with him under a tree. He said, "I wake up every night to the sounds of you stomping around in your room. I went in there and saw wedges of wood hacked out of the bed and the door. Would you please explain this to me?"

I told Ong Nam the truth. He told me to stop fighting the spirit because that only makes it stronger, and I could never stop it from coming back. He said the only thing that will make a spirit stop is to pray more.

"You must say you are sorry for intruding into a world where you have no business. You must ask to be forgiven for any harm or suffering you have caused. You must pray to Buddha to send protection for you."

I prayed a lot. I stopped trying to hurt the spirit, and I just fought with my hands for self-defense. The spirit didn't come as often. By the time I left An Son Tu, seven months later, it had stopped entirely.

One of the services monks perform for the community is to advise people on things like marriage, business, and building a house. Vietnamese peo-ple believe that important events like these must be carefully planned. They should take place at the proper times to be in harmony with heaven and earth.

Ong Nam taught me how to calculate the energetic and karmic forces that influence a person's life. These include Chinese astrology, palmistry, and the theory of the five elements. Ong Nam used several old books written in *Han Viet* with charts and lists to use for making calculations about all these things. I copied the charts into a notebook, and I still use them.

Couples who wish to be married try to consult someone like Ong Nam in order to understand the strengths and weaknesses of their relationship, and to find the best time for the marriage to take place. Someone like Ong Nam will tell them the month, day, and hour the wedding vows should be exchanged. Sometimes couples have to be married at three or four o'clock in the morning.

Some years are considered lucky for these things to take place and some are considered unlucky, depending on the time, day, and year you were born. In terms of building a house, once you know your lucky year, you must also find out the month, day, and and hour to set the ridgepole. If you have nowhere to live while you are waiting for the right time to build your house, you can build the walls and put up a makeshift roof without a ridgepole.

Ong Nam had advised so many people that he was able to know many things about them just by looking at their hands. He was able to know things in the future. He taught me how to see these things, but I have forgotten this.

M any Cambodian families came to worship and to volunteer at An Son Tu because it was in a Cambodian neighborhood. Some Cambodians also came to Tam Buu Tu, but not as many.

The Cambodians were very friendly to me and invited me to visit them in their homes. Everyone knows that the Cambodians hate the Vietnamese for tricking them out of their land, but it was different on Elephant Mountain because of To Thay. Many of his followers were Cambodians. Since then, they have intermarried.

The Cambodians in the Cambodian neighborhood were poorer and stronger than the Vietnamese. When Cambodian women gave birth, they carried their babies into the jungle to wash them in a waterfall. After a few days, they went back to work in the fields with their babies tied onto their backs. In Vietnam, women are supposed to stay warm in bed for an entire month after childbirth, and they don't tie babies onto their backs.

Cambodian men usually go without a shirt or shoes; they just wear short pants. The women tie a long cloth over one shoulder like the monks and nuns do. The women are too poor to buy colorful cloth for their dresses, so they wear old dull cloth.

I think the Cambodian people are very beautiful. They have dark brown skin and their hair is softer and shinier than that of the Vietnamese. Many Cambodians have curly and wavy hair. All the men cut their hair short, and all the women wore it long. There was something enchanting about the way the Cambodian people smiled. I used to wonder what made their smiles so different.

Whenever I went to their houses, I could hardly stand to eat their food or drink their water. Sometimes if I was thirsty, I would go to their cistern and draw a cup of water to drink, but it would always be brown. They didn't have money to buy an alum stone to separate the mud out. They drank water like that all the time, but I just pretended to drink.

I didn't like their food, but I ate a little just to be polite. It smelled very strong, because they cooked a lot of snails and fish and never washed the leftovers out of their cooking pots; they just kept adding more the next day. They didn't mind when the food was covered with flies. Even though these people almost never got sick, I didn't have the courage to enjoy their food.

The Cambodians ate a lot of snails, insects, and lizards, more than the Vietnamese did. I learned how to eat crickets when I went to school in Cai Mon. I used to help the older kids catch crickets to bring home for food. When you find a cricket nest, you put your finger down the hole to see which direction their tunnel went. If you walk in that direction, you will find the back door. Someone has to wait at the back door while another person pours water through a banana-leaf funnel down the front door. The crickets will all come running out the back door. Crickets in Vietnam are about as big as your thumb. You can roast them on a stick in the fire until they turn golden, then you pull off the legs and head. They taste a little like shrimp.

The Cambodians didn't grow rice, so they needed to earn at least enough money to buy rice and matches and cloth. Most people sold bamboo shoots and vegetables at the market, and some sewed clothing and peddled it from door to door. If they came to your house and you said that you didn't have any money, they would often insist that you take the clothing and pay them later. Vietnamese people were afraid of the Cambodians, because they believed that if they couldn't make their payments, the Cambodian peddlers would put a curse on them.

A Vietnamese man named Chu Ba came to the Cambodian neighborhood looking for a sorcerer to help him. He was in his early thirties. His stomach was so swollen, he looked six months pregnant. Chu Ba had been living in Cambodia with his Cambodian wife and their children. He was in Xa Ba Chuc visiting his parents. Chu Ba worked as an importer of Cambodian jewelry, and five years earlier had fallen in love with a Cambodian woman. They chose to raise their family in Cambodia, away from the war.

Some months earlier Chu Ba told his wife that he missed his family and that he wanted to go back to Xa Ba Chuc to visit them. She asked him how long he would stay in Vietnam, and he said, "Not more than three months." She said, "Do you give me your word that you will back with us in three months time, and not a day later?" Chu Ba gave her his word.

When three months were up, Chu Ba was still in Xa Ba Chuc. He began feeling sharp, violent pains in his stomach, as if something was biting him from inside. His symptoms were so severe that he checked into the Chau Doc hospital for treatment. His X-rays came out normal. The doctors could not find anything wrong. They sent him home with painkillers and muscle relaxants.

Chu Ba only grew sicker. He was far too sick to travel to Cambodia. He remained at his family's home, waiting to recover, but each day he felt worse. It wasn't until his stomach began to swell that he suspected it was sorcery.

I went with Chu Ba to ask Tattoo for help. When Chu Ba lifted his shirt and showed us his stomach, I felt sick. His swollen belly was moving as if mice were creeping under his skin. Tattoo told Chu Ba, "Go back to Cambodia, and your wife will bring you to the same sorcerer who cast this spell. Only he can remove it." As sick as he was, Chu Ba followed Tattoo's advice.

The next time Chu Ba came to see his parents, he was fine. He told us that when his wife brought him to the sorcerer, all he did to break the spell was give him a glass of water to drink, which made him run to the toilet. He didn't think he was going to make it to the outhouse, so he squatted in the woods. He couldn't believe his eyes when he saw what was coming out of his body. It was a ball of writhing snakes and some large splinters of wood. I found out later from my Cambodian friends that sorcerers can put snakes, cockroaches, sharp splinters of wood, or hair that twists around and cuts into the intestines, into a person's body.

My Cambodian friends told me that monks in Cambodia use sorcery to protect the treasures inside their temples. Cambodian temples are filled with solid gold statues and ornaments. Our temples look very poor compared to theirs. In every temple there is a ten-foot pit where people drop gold offerings to Buddha. Every year the pit is emptied and new statues are forged from the gold. My friends said that if a person ever tried to take something valuable out of the temple, he would fall down and not be able to move his body until someone found him and removed the curse.

"Aha!" I thought, remembering the time the robbers were lying paralyzed on my father's floor.

I considered finding a Cambodian sorcery teacher, but in the end I decided not to go too often into the Cambodian neighborhood, because the girls were too pretty. I was afraid that if I liked one she might put a curse on me.

About two months after I started living at An Son Tu, Ong Nam took in four new apprentice monks just about my age. Ong Nam gave us all temple names with the name "Thien," which was the name of his lineage. One of the new monks was also the firstborn son, and he was older than me, so Ong Nam named him Thien Hai. He named me Thien Trung. The others were Thien Chi, Thien Tai, and Thien Minh.

Thien Chi was almost blind. His eyes were so bad that eyeglasses did nothing to help him see. That didn't stop him from doing everything we did.

Even though I was a servant, I had to follow the same schedule as the monks. We woke up at four o'clock and took a bath and got dressed. At five o'clock we chanted, and then went back to sleep by six o'clock. We woke up again at seven and worked around the temple until we had to chant at ten o'clock. Then we ate lunch. Sometimes we went out after lunch until four o'clock, when we had to bathe again and chant at five o'clock. We ate dinner and chanted again at eight o'clock.

The nuns weren't very pleased to have four more mouths to feed. They had very little food to begin with, mostly rice and whatever grew around the temple. For breakfast we ate rice soup with chunks of stir-fried green jackfruit seasoned with sugar and salt. Soy sauce was a luxury that we only used on special occasions, but we did have plenty of lemongrass dipping sauce. For lunch we ate vegetable soup, steamed soybeans, more stir-fried jackfruit, and greens. Dinner was usually the same as lunch. There were plenty of jackfruit trees near the temple, but jackfruit takes a long time to grow ripe, because it grows from avocado size to watermelon size. When a jackfruit is ripe, the pulp is very sweet, juicy, and refreshing. You can roast the seeds and eat them, too. The stem of the jackfruit has a very sticky sap that always gets on the knife or on your hands. You can't wash it off with soap and water; you have to use kerosene.

I used to take Chi, Hai, Minh, and Tai up the mountain to look for other kinds of fruit because we were always hungry. One time we climbed up a high boulder and threw stones on a spot where Ong Nam told me a land mine had been planted. We kept firing stones until we made a hit. From up on our boulder, we were out of harm's way, but we could feel the heat of the explosion. Ong Nam and a group of the neighborhood people came running up the mountain in a panic, thinking that someone had been blown up.

When we got back to the temple, Ong Nam let the head nun think of a punishment for us. She led us before the altar and gave us each a long stick of incense. The long ones burn for two full hours. She made us kneel down before the altar and hold the incense stick between our hands when they were in prayer position. She sat down in the corner to make sure we didn't move.

It was an ordeal. We were suffering, but luckily the head nun fell asleep. We all broke our incense sticks.

Chi and I got into trouble another time with the head nun when the other monks were away on an errand. There was one jackfruit on the tree that she had been waiting to ripen for many weeks. When it was finally ripe, she served half of it for lunch. It was so delicious that everyone begged for more, but she said she was saving it for dinner.

Later that afternoon, when she went into the kitchen to start preparing dinner, she discovered the jackfruit had been eaten, and all that was left were the skin and the seeds.

She marched right up to Chi and me while we were raking and sweeping the grounds, and she told us to come with her. We followed her into the kitchen and she showed us the missing jackfruit. She said she knew we had eaten it because the other monks had gone on an errand in Chau Doc City.

We didn't eat it, and we told her so, but she didn't believe us. She said she was going to prove that we had eaten the jackfruit. She went and filled up two big bowls of water and gave them to us and told us we had to drink until we threw up. Then she would catch us in our lie.

We drank and drank and drank and then we both vomited on the floor. There was only water, no jackfruit. She still didn't believe us. She went into the pantry and dragged out two large sacks of beans, mung beans and red beans. She opened them and dumped them together into a vat, saying, "Now take this outside and sort these beans into two bowls. You may not do anything until they are all sorted, even if you have to miss dinner."

Chi couldn't even see the beans, but he could feel them. The mung beans were small and round, and the red beans were kidney-shaped. At first it wasn't so bad. After two hours, my whole body ached. We weren't sure which was worse, kneeling with incense or sorting beans.

Then I had an idea. In the outhouse there was an old bamboo basket where we put old newspaper and paper packaging to use for toilet paper. I went and got it. The holes in the basket were the perfect size to strain out the mung beans. It took us only half an hour to separate the beans. We hid the sorted beans in the bushes, put the basket back in the outhouse, and then we went off to eat fruit on the mountain. When we came back, she said she had checked on us and we weren't there. We told her that we took the beans on the mountain to sort. She believed us when she saw the beans.

We got into trouble with the head nun many more times. One time she gave us the choice of kneeling for two long incense sticks, or sorting double the amount of beans. We chose the beans.

I ran to get the basket from the outhouse, but it wasn't there. I looked all over and saw it in the kitchen, but I couldn't go in because the nuns were there. We monks were not allowed in the kitchen when nuns are there.

Chi and I had to go looking in the neighborhood to borrow a basket with the right-size holes, but we found one.

30

INDIVIDUAL PARTS

E very morning at four o'clock, when I woke up, I never went all the way to the outhouse to pee; I went behind a certain tree. Each of us had our own tree. One morning in January, while I was peeing, I was startled by a voice at my back, telling me to get everyone out of the temple immediately and go to the rice fields, because there was going to be a battle. I turned to see the shadowy face and checkered scarf of a Viet Cong guerrilla. I realized he had been standing by my tree, waiting for me.

On my way through the courtyard, I saw the heads of many Viet Cong guerrillas sticking out of holes that they had dug all over the ground. They yelled at me to hurry, because they were going to attack the soldiers' base in just a few minutes.

I ran around looking for everyone in the kitchen, bathing stalls, outhouse, and kitchen. The nuns hurried to get the sacks of dehydrated rice and sea salt.

When we got out to the road, we saw the people from the neighborhood had been told the same. When the first shots sounded, everyone started running. About one hundred villagers came to the fields.

It was winter and the rice fields were dry except for a small water hole where the water buffalos soaked. Unfortunately, the water wasn't safe to drink because it was contaminated with manure. There was a river about a mile away, but it was surrounded by soldiers who told the people to stay away. Some people tried to go back to the village to look for stragglers, and to get things they had forgotten like sun hats and food, but the soldiers had already arrived, and the battle had begun. There was nowhere we could go for food, shade, or water.

When Ong Nam began chanting the five o'clock sutra, many people joined him. They prayed that the fighting would be over soon. We could not see the temple from the rice field, but we could see the head of Elephant Mountain clearly. The first round of bombing started as we chanted. The Viet Cong blasted the army base with missiles, and the army responded by raining bombs down on the temple. Through the trees we could see bright balls of fire and black smoke. We saw a helicopter taking off from the base and watched it spraying bullets into the jungle.

By late afternoon, everyone was very thirsty, and the children were crying, but the fighting was still heavy. By evening, a fleet of army planes dropped soldiers in parachutes over our field. They landed all about us and we could see that many of them were Americans. They left their parachutes on the ground and people ran to grab them. Tanks arrived in our field, too, and began firing missiles over our heads at the village and the temple. One of the missiles fell short and landed just five feet away from me.

I saw the missile hit the ground and braced myself to be blown to bits. In an instant I apologized to my father for giving him so much trouble. I said goodbye to my father and Aunt Gioi, and I realized that I was going to meet my real parents. I watched the bomb explode. The impact hurt and deafened my ears. The bomb had exploded in the direction it was heading. Luckily it didn't kill anyone, but it did injure some people. I thanked Buddha for protecting me.

When night came, the bombing was still heavy. Airplanes were dropping lights and bombs all night long. There were red bombs that streaked across the sky like shooting stars, and there were green and yellow bombs, too. We made it through the night without anyone getting hurt.

We were still trapped in the field for another day and night. Our only choice was to drink the dirty water, which gave a lot of people diarrhea. The fighting remained strong the whole time. By the third day, most people had eaten all their dried rice. Some parents decided to sneak back home to get some food and water, but not all of them made it back alive.

On the afternoon of the third day, soldiers came and told us we could go back. We were walking up the path toward the temple when some Viet Cong guerrillas met us and told us they were not finished fighting. They told us to go hide in the caves. They wouldn't let us go near the temple.

When we got to the caves, we saw that the villagers had been given the same instructions. A search party was formed to find the old people and help them up the mountain. We were afraid to make a fire, because the soldiers might think we were Viet Cong, so we only ate raw food from the forest. The bombing started again that night. From inside the cave, we could hear bombs squealing and exploding on the mountain peak and also down below.

Our chanting echoed inside the cave. It felt so cool in the cave after being under the sun for three days in the rice field. I finally slept. The next morning was quiet. We listened until afternoon to make sure the fighting had stopped.

I volunteered go back to make sure it was safe. I said I would get some food and water to bring up to the cave. Halfway down the mountain I saw a hand lying on the path. I stepped around it, and then I saw some blond hair and part of a face. Some VC guerrillas met me on the path and told me to go back to the cave.

The fighting lasted two more days. We were so hungry and thirsty that people left the cave to find food and water. We learned that one of the caves had been hit and five people had died. By the end of the fighting, eighteen of the hundred villagers had died.

We started down the path and didn't get far before some people started screaming. I ran ahead to see what was happening. An American head in a helmet was dangling sideways in a tree, the eyes staring down at us. The whole way down was strewn with limbs, heads, intestines, and other body parts. Many people were crying. Chi asked me to tell him what everyone was screaming about.

Ong Nam was very quiet as we made our way to the temple. The monks and nuns walked silently behind him. When we reached the temple grounds, Ong Nam walked straight to the eight-sided pagoda where his master was buried. He walked all around it. There was a handless arm caught on the roof and the blood had trickled down, but the pagoda itself hadn't been damaged.

We walked toward the temple. Some walls were still standing, but the bigger part of it was just a pile of stones. Many of the holes that the guerrillas had dug had dried blood on the bottom.

We could hear the wailing from down in the village. People were crying for days as they buried their dead and sorted through the rubble of their homes. They dug several pits and combed the forest for body parts that were already festering in the heat, covered in flies. They wheeled the body parts in carts and dragged them in the parachutes, parts of all different people mixed together, Americans and Vietnamese, white, black, yellow, and brown.

The Communists always took care of their own dead and wounded, but they left their blood everywhere.

We dumped out all thirty barrels of rainwater and drained our water tank, because we were afraid the water might have been poisoned or contaminated by blood and dead bodies. We had to wash it with soap. It was a lot of water to waste, especially since rainy season was six months away.

I had to scrub the blood off the rocks. It wasn't easy, especially because we had to go far to get water. We worked all day for two weeks until the blood was finally gone. Our rooms had been destroyed, so everyone found a place to sleep on a mat on the ground. I slept under a tree and tied my mosquito net to the branches.

The fighting was also at Tam Buu Tu, but it wasn't as bad. The temple and the community building were both badly damaged. About ten people were killed. People thought it was a miracle that To Thay's throne was not broken. Chu Hai, Ong Bay's son, decided it would be better to tear down the buildings and start over.

The monks and some of the neighbors helped Ong Nam begin to put the temple back together. First we had to move all the stones out of the way.

Nobody came to the temple to pray for a long time, because they knew it had been covered in blood. We chanted four times a day as usual.

About five months later, my father came to bring me home for my eighteenth birthday.

31

SILK PATCHWORK ROBE

spent July and August working with my father in his clinic in Cho Lach. He
was teaching me how to recognize the different qualities of the pulse and to
palpate each pulse at four depths. Putting all that information together into
a diagnosis truly gave me a headache.

He was living on a crowded dirt road. His house was wired for electricity,
but he didn't want to use it. The war was getting bad in Cho Lach. He didn't
want me to stay long.

I still had a lot of the money that my father had given to me so I decided to
buy myself a camera. I didn't tell my father, because he didn't like machines and
electricity. I went to a camera shop in Cho Lach and bought one that had a
timed shutter release. It had a viewfinder that popped open on the top. If you
looked down into the lens, you could see the people standing in front of you.
When I went home to Cai Mon for a visit, I took pictures of my Aunt Gioi and
my Uncle Quon and his wife.

I didn't have much free time at my father's house, except for when he went
out to buy medicine or make house calls. We worked long hours, seven days a
week. One day when he was out, I was looking for my shirt and I lifted up a pile
of blankets and recognized my father's wooden trunk. I hadn't seen it in years.
It wasn't locked, so I opened it. On the top was a large brown paper package

tied with twine. I took the package out of the trunk and noticed that the trunk was filled with books. Many of them were magic books. I opened a little brown book bound in leather. It had many termite holes, and the delicate brown pages were as thin as onionskin. I was afraid they would crumble in my hands.

I checked to see if the charms were the same as the ones Tattoo had taught me, but they were different. They were simpler, but I knew they were more powerful. I was afraid my father would be back soon, so I put them away carefully and went out to the store to buy a small pocket-sized notebook.

Whenever my father went out, I opened the trunk, took out the package, and looked in the magic books. I copied as many charms and incantations into my notebook as I could. I wrote them backward and upside down and sideways and in many different wrong ways to keep them a secret. I made up tiny symbols and wrote them in the corners of the pages to let me know which way to unscramble them.

One time, I reached all the way to the bottom of the trunk and was startled when my hand brushed against something that felt like a dead animal. I parted the books and saw some brownish-black hair, but it didn't look like an animal. I fished the hairy thing out of the trunk to get a closer look. It looked like a horse's tail, but the hair was too fine. It was a crop of human hair, about two feet long, dead and lusterless, bound at one end with black thread. I set it on the floor next to the paper package. It looked like a dead, evil thing, the last thing I would expect to see in my father's house.

Seeing the hair made me wonder what was inside the package. The string was tied in a knot, so it took me a long time to undo it. The paper was really an old cement bag. Inside was a dark red silk patchwork robe. The shapes of the patchwork were very small, smaller than Ong Nam's robe, smaller than any robe I had ever seen. As I started to unfold it, a gold ornament slipped out. It was a solid gold hook-and-ring clasp, the kind worn only by monks of the highest degree.

My father came home and caught me looking at his robe. I said, "Ba, is this robe yours?"

He said, "I don't think it is right for you to be looking through my things."

"I am sorry," I said, "It wasn't locked."

"My teacher gave me his robe before he died. My teacher at An Son Tu."

"You mean Ong Nam's teacher?" I asked.

"Yes," he said.

I knew that his teacher would not have given my father that robe if he wasn't qualified to wear it. I felt very proud of my father.

My father then said, "Quang, you must never touch that hair whip. It is dangerous. I have kept it hidden all these years. I should have gotten rid of it long ago. It was made by a sorcerer who was truly evil."

I told my father I would never touch it. The next time I looked inside the trunk, I saw that all the books were gone. Only the hair and the robe remained. My father walked into the room and caught me holding the hair whip. He didn't say a word. He held out his hand for me to give him the hair, and then he left the house. He was gone for two days. When he returned, he told me that he had been out searching for a tree that was hollow, but still alive. He said he dropped the whip inside the tree and that it would take three months for the evil spirits to leave the hair. Evil spirits do not like to stay around trees because they are afraid of lightning.

"Why didn't you just burn it?" I asked.

"These things are more complicated than you would think," my father said with a frown. He took me by the shoulders as if to shake me but he looked tired. He said, "It is possible that one day you will be ready to learn magic and not be susceptible to evil. I hope that day comes, but until it does, promise me you will stay away from sorcery."

I promised, but I was more sorry that the hair whip and all those magic books had been destroyed.

My father said I was old enough to travel back to Elephant Mountain by myself. He wanted me to go back to Tam Buu Tu to help with the construction of the new temple and to continue studying acupuncture and plant medicine. My father had spoken with my plant medicine teacher and my acupuncture teacher before coming to An Son Tu to bring me home for the summer. My acupuncture teacher told my father that I was ready to begin treating his patients with needles.

My father took me to the Vinh Long bus depot in the rain. It was September, the rainy season. I was glad for Ong Nam that his water tank was probably full again. My father gave me a lot of money.

I climbed onto a gangster bus with my money, my new camera, and my new book of secret spells, confident that the gangsters would never try to rob or harass me. I thought that I would use those spells one day. I traveled the same way my father did, leaving the bus at the ferry crossings, taking a small ferry, and then catching a new bus on the other side of the river. I treated myself to a lot of good food at the ferry stations, and I rested in the hammocks.

I reached Tam Buu Tu in time for dinner. They had already finished building the new community building. The temple and the new dormitory building for the visitors were almost done. The three buildings were made entirely out of concrete except for the roof. Even the interior walls were concrete. The community building and the dormitory had roofs made of corrugated aluminum. There was a large open space between the concrete walls and the roof to let the hot air out of the buildings. The temple had an expensive ceramic tile roof.

The new beds were made of smooth cement, so they could be used as bomb shelters. Everyone liked them because they were cool. I had a lightbulb in my room powered by our new gasoline generator, but it only worked for two hours before curfew. There weren't any windows other than opening between the cement wall and the aluminum roof.

One evening after the sutra when I came to join the old-timers at the corner table, I noticed an old man I had never seen before. The others seemed excited to see him. I liked him right away because he looked intelligent and kind. He wore a long strand of prayer beads around his neck, and when he smiled all his teeth were black with decay. Nobody looked too good under the new fluorescent lighting.

When the man left, I asked who he was. Ong Tu said, "You don't know Ong Chin? He's the one who is always praying with his beads. He doesn't come to the temple much, but he has been here as long as anyone . . . except the time he spent in prison."

Bald Ong Chin said, "He used to live here in the village with his wife, and he taught martial arts. But now he lives in the jungle like a hermit."

Ong Tu continued, "A long time ago he had a student who joined the French army. The student used to come back on his days off because he wanted Ong Chin to teach him more."

"Ong Chin didn't like the student and he refused to teach him anymore," Bald Ong Chin added.

"And do you know what that idiot did?" Ong Tu said. "He accused Ong Chin of plotting to overthrow the French, and they came and burned his house down."

"And they locked him up in prison for fifteen years," chimed in Ong Sau the weaver. "And while he was locked up his wife died."

"Where does he live now?" I asked.

"About halfway up Long Mountain, near the trail," said Ong Sau the weaver. "It's just a shelter, but he likes it."

．．．

was ready to study martial arts again. It had been more than a year since I stopped going to Tattoo, but I didn't want to go back because he would probably want to teach me more sorcery. I thought I would stay away from magic for a while, until I could figure out a way to do it safely, like my father did. I decided to find Ong Chin on Long Mountain.

The fighting was worse than ever on Long Mountain; it was on about half the time. I waited for three quiet nights in a row and then, after helping to wash the teacups and put up the mosquito nets, I said good night to everyone and went back to my room and locked the door.

When I thought everyone had fallen asleep, I put a chair on top of my bed and jumped up to catch hold of the cement wall. I pulled myself up and over and dropped quietly to the ground in the rear courtyard of the temple. I was afraid of losing my key, so I left it in my room. It was about eleven o'clock.

I wasn't concerned about stepping on a land mine on the lower half of Long Mountain, except for the side facing the forbidden mountain, because it was a land mine–free zone. The villagers depended on that land for farming and collecting firewood. Even though it was land mine–free, there was still fighting there. Soldiers patrolled the vegetable patches all night long waiting to kill any guerrillas who dared to sneak down to glean the fields.

I didn't want to walk on the village road, or anywhere I might be seen, so I went the long way to Long Mountain through the forest. I wasn't used to walking in the jungle at night, and was surprised by how well I could see. There were enough spaces in the canopy for the starlight to shine through. There were some wide-open spaces with grass and scrubby bushes. It wasn't likely that I would step on a snake or a scorpion at night. I wasn't sure if the tigers still respected people the way they used to when my grandfather lived here. No one had seen a tiger on Elephant Mountain for a long time. I could hear the sounds of the nocturnal animals all around me: leopard cats, deer, foxes, wolves, and porcupines.

I was mostly concerned about the centipedes. It had been raining the past few days, and now they were out. I was more afraid of them than of a poisonous snake. You can see centipedes at night because they are covered with a kind of fungus that glows in the dark. During the daytime they look brown and shiny, about three inches long with many legs. At night they glow green and you can't see their legs. They look like fat green worms. The fungus is so poisonous that if it gets on your skin the spot will blister and bleed and become infected.

I had to keep looking down so I could avoid stepping on them. Before I knew it, I had arrived at a fork in the trail. A tree in the middle of the fork was all lit up with blinking lights. I had never seen anything like that before. I went closer and saw that the tree was covered with fireflies from the base of the trunk all the way to the tips of its branches. It was so beautiful that it took my breath away. I stayed looking at the tree for a long time.

I didn't know which way to go, but I chose the right path. I hadn't gone far when I came to a spot that was just swarming with centipedes. I turned back.

I didn't hear the soldiers sneaking up behind me. There were six of them, all pointing their rifles at me. They said, "Don't move or you're dead."

One of them grabbed me around my neck and another frisked me and another tied my hands behind my back. They took me to the army compound that was in the valley between the two mountains. It was very dangerous to go inside the compound with the soldiers. Many people who were led through that barbed-wire fortress were never seen again. Armed guards opened the gate. The soldiers escorted me through layer after layer of barbed wire before we reached the courtyard. Two of them went into a building, and the four others waited with me outside. They said they were going to punish me for helping the Communists. When I tried to speak, they hit me with their guns very hard and said, "This is just the beginning of what we do to nice boys like you who spy for the Viet Cong."

They were just about to beat me when their commander came out and recognized me. He said, "Stop. Release him. That boy is the son of the temple doctor."

I was lucky because people accused of being spies were often beaten to death the first time. After that, the soldiers at that compound all knew me and left me alone.

I returned to the temple and walked quietly around to the rear courtyard. Since it was under construction there was a lot of lumber lying around. I leaned some boards underneath my window and climbed high enough to grab the top of the wall and hoist myself over and into my room.

Even though the temple and the dormitory building were not finished, there were more visitors coming to the temple than ever before. About five busloads of people came every day. Most of them went back on the bus after dinner, but a lot of the visitors stayed overnight. I was so busy that I hardly ever saw Kam or Lieu or my other friends. We were trying to get the construction finished for our big holiday on January 15. We expected two thousand people to come that day.

The visitors sometimes approached me and asked me what kind of work I did at the temple. I told them that I was learning Chinese medicine and studying divination. Some wanted to consult me about certain problems in their lives. I told them I was just a beginner, but they said I could practice on them. One woman wanted to know if it was a good year to start a business. It took me about thirty minutes to find the appropriate lists and charts and to write down information and make the calculations. "Not bad," I told her, "but next year would be better."

I waited for the weather to dry up before I tried to find Ong Chin's hut again. I had bought a rope and tied a large hook on the end. That night I used it to climb out of my room. Once I'd scaled the wall, I was able to flick the rope and shake the hook free. I caught it so it didn't make a sound, hid it in the bushes, and set off for the Long Mountain trail, hoping to see the firefly tree again.

When I reached the fork in the trail I was disappointed to find no fireflies on the tree, but I was relieved that there were very few centipedes. I took the left path this time. There didn't seem to be anything that looked like a shelter. I was afraid to go too far up the mountain, for fear of stepping on a land mine, so I turned back. I tried the right fork again but had no luck. I looked for a long time, until the roosters started crowing. That meant it was about three o'clock in the morning. I had to run back or someone would discover I was gone.

When I got back to the courtyard, I could hear people stirring inside the temple and knew that Ba Bay would be coming to my door any minute. I threw up my hook and climbed up and over the wall just in time to answer her knock.

The third night I went on the left path first and hadn't gone far when someone said, "Hey you." That startled me, and I turned around expecting to see a soldier or Viet Cong guerrilla, but it was Ong Chin.

He said, "I heard someone crashing through the jungle for three nights now, was it you?"

'Yes, sir," I bowed.

He asked, "Do you want to learn martial arts?"

Ong Chin drew his face close to mine so he could get a good look at me. "I've seen you before. You live at Tam Buu Tu."

"Yes, sir." I bowed again.

"Are you one of the scribes?"

"No, sir. I help my father in the clinic, and I am studying Chinese medicine."

"Oh, you are Ong Sau the barefoot doctor's son. Does he know you came here tonight?"

"My father is in Cho Lach now," I said.

"What is your name, son of Ong Sau the barefoot doctor?" he asked.

"Quang."

"Did you know that I haven't taught anyone for thirty years?"

"Yes, I know."

"I suppose you would like to see where I live, then," he said.

I followed him a bit farther up the path. He disappeared around a high ledge of rock on the right side of the path. His house was nothing but a lemongrass roof attached to four trees. One side of his house was against the rock wall, and the other sides were open. He lit a fire in a broken ceramic stove and invited me to sit on one of two stones. My feet started to itch and I scratched them.

"I think you must have stepped on a centipede," he said. He went into the brush and gave me some leaves. "Chew on them and put some where it itches."

As soon as I put the leaf mash on my feet, the itching stopped.

"Thank you, I didn't know about that remedy," I said.

We talked for a while, and then he said he would teach me martial arts. He didn't consult an oracle.

"Right now I don't have much free time during the day," I said. "I can only come at midnight."

"Midnight is fine," he said.

I went to study with Ong Chin whenever it was peaceful on Long Mountain, about twice a week. I managed to get away during the day sometimes, too. I brought him pork and alcohol the first night, but he said he was a vegetarian. After that, I brought him sea salt, soy sauce, tofu, cookies, and rice. He had one cooking pot that didn't have a handle and two cracked and chipped ceramic cups that looked as if he had dug them up somewhere. He didn't cook much; he mostly ate vegetables, fruit and nuts from the forest.

He was a meticulous teacher, stopping me in almost every position to give me a correction. Ong Chin may have looked old, but he was strong and muscular and moved like a cat. He told me he had aged a lot when he was in jail, because he was sick. After coming home and living in the jungle for ten years, he became healthy again.

Ong Chin didn't do any magic, but he did keep two blackbirds who warned him when the soldiers were coming to his house. He raised them as hatchlings. Whenever I went to his house during the daytime, I would see them flying around. They would land on his house and ask for food. He would give them each a bit of rice cake and a small red-hot chili pepper.

I only got two hours of sleep on the nights I went to study with Ong Chin, but I had never felt better in my life.

The way through the forest to Ong Chin's house had become so familiar that I could run like a nocturnal creature in the dark.

One night when I was bounding up the trail I slammed into a tree, and the next thing I knew I was lying on the ground in a different hut. I had a splitting headache, and a different old man with strange-looking hair was looking down at me.

32

PHOTOGRAPH

You are lucky that I have connected with your soul," the man with the strange hair said, "because I knew that you were in trouble, and I got there right away."

I felt a wet cloth on my forehead. I was dizzy and confused. This hut was also built against a rock wall.

"It's not very smart to lie unconscious on the jungle floor at night with blood trickling out of your head," he mocked.

The man's voice reminded me of a crow.

"Who are you? Where am I?"

A sooty oil lamp hung from the ceiling behind his head, highlighting the edges of his bushy, shoulder-length hair that stuck out in all directions. The walls were made of living leaves. He was a very small man.

He walked over to the corner of the hut, into the light. I could see his face. He asked, "Would you like some food, Quang?"

His hair had equal amounts of black and white. His skin was dark like a Cambodian's. What was most unique about him was the color of his lips. They looked almost gray.

"Would you like something warm to eat?"

I knew better than to accept food from a stranger.

"No? Well, how about some fruit, would you like an orange or a banana?"

Before I could answer, there was an orange and a banana lying on the floor next to me. At first I thought he had thrown them to me. Then I realized that if he had thrown them, the orange would have rolled.

"Where am I? Who are you?"

The strange man laughed. "I see *you* every night, and you don't even know me. Next time I am going to test you. You may think you have a strong mind, but I am not convinced."

I lifted the cloth and felt my forehead. There was a bump, but the bleeding had stopped.

I sat up and suddenly felt nauseated. "I've got to go," I said. "Thank you for helping me."

The small man put a glass of water on the ground. He said, "Have some water. It will make you feel better."

The glass slid by itself across the dirt floor and stopped in front of me. I looked at the glass but didn't comment. I said, "Thank you just the same. I am feeling much better already."

When I left his hut, I saw that a curtain of dense, leafy vines spilled over from the rock wall and covered his tiny house entirely. "No wonder I never saw it before," I thought.

He walked with me to the trail, which was just ten feet from his house. He was no taller than my shoulder.

"Ong Chin is up that way," he pointed.

I hurried on my way.

"I'll be testing you," he taunted.

I didn't feel like explaining to Ong Chin about the strange, small man who found me in the forest. I told him I was running and was looking for centipedes, and I hit my head on a crooked tree. He said that the tree must have knocked me unconscious and that I was lucky a pack of wolves didn't find me. He went to find some leaves to make a poultice. Before he had a chance to put it on my head, the roosters started crowing, which meant it was around three o'clock.

I ran back as fast as I could, but I was later than I had ever been before. There was only a slim chance that I could climb back into my room unnoticed. I hid behind a tree on the edge of the temple courtyard. Chu Hai was outside lighting the breakfast fires. I had to get into my room and change my clothes before anyone saw me, and the key was locked inside. I walked over to the tree I always peed on, hoping that Chu Hai wouldn't look away from his task and notice my forehead. I said, "Chu Hai, your mother was looking for you."

I waited until he walked back into the temple. Then I darted behind the bushes, found my rope with the hook, threw it up and scrambled in.

B a Bay didn't mind when I rested in her new sitting room. It was connected to her bedroom, and it had an extra bed. I preferred to take a nap in there because Ba Bay always had a lot of cookies that were given to her by the visitors. She said I could eat all I wanted because she was going to give it all away eventually.

Instead of going home that winter for Tet, I stayed at Tam Buu Tu to help get the temple ready for the biggest holiday of the year in my religion, which is January 15. To my relief, Ong Chin didn't expect me to come for my lessons during the holiday season. I kept thinking about that small, strange person in the shelter behind the bushes. I couldn't help thinking that he had charmed me into crashing into that tree.

The holiday came, and there were more than two thousand people to shelter and feed for two days.

I t had been one month since I went for a lesson with Ong Chin. I saw him during the holiday celebration, and we sat at the same table to eat. In the middle of the meal, he got up and said he had to leave.

About fifteen minutes later, soldiers came into the community building and began looking around. They came to our table to ask if we had seen Ong Chin. Someone responded that he was here but he had left. I didn't see his birds, but I was sure they had landed on the wall of the community building and warned him.

It still wasn't safe to walk along the ridge of Elephant Mountain as I used to. During the holiday, I hired a Honda driver to take me to An Son Tu to visit Ong Nam.

When I got there, I was surprised to see only Chi and Ong Nam and the three nuns. Tai, Hai, and Minh had gone to another temple in Chau Doc City, because their parents were afraid of the war. Ong Nam was very busy rebuilding the temple. Luckily he didn't have to climb the mountain anymore to find stones. I felt bad for Chi, because the head nun was still bothering him. Sometimes I took Chi out for a walk on a small mountain close by called *Nui Nuoc,*

Water Mountain. There was a small army base there, but there wasn't much fighting because the Viet Cong didn't go there.

I sometimes went alone to Water Mountain just to get away from people. It was the safest place I knew. I thought of taking a picture of myself to give to Aunt Gioi and my father. I set my camera down on a rock and looked through the viewfinder. Then I tried to stand in the right spot before the shutter snapped the picture. Before I knew it, I had come to the end of the film. Luckily, I had another roll in my pocket. I changed the roll.

All of a sudden I was surrounded by soldiers. They grabbed my camera and tied my hands behind my back and pointed a gun to my head. I followed them through the barbed-wire fences and into a prison cell. They locked me behind a steel door in an empty cell with no windows, just a tiny space under the door. It was very hot inside.

Later they took me out and started asking me questions. They asked me where I lived. I said I lived at Tam Buu Tu. They didn't believe I was from the *Hieu Nghia* religion because the back and sides of my hair were still short from when I was Ong Nam's servant. They thought I was a spy who didn't know that the monks at Tam Buu Tu never cut their hair.

They locked me back into the cell. I stayed in there for the rest of the day. Just as it was getting dark, they opened the door and I saw Chu Hai.

The soldiers gave me back my camera, but they had destroyed the film. They didn't know that I still had one roll in my pocket. The picture on the cover of this book is from that day.

The next time I went to Ong Chin's house, I watched the trees along the way very carefully so I wouldn't hit one again. I had to watch the ground, too, because the centipedes were out. I thought maybe I had taken the right fork by mistake, so I went back, but then I couldn't find the fork in the trail. I went all the way down the mountain again and started over, but the same thing happened. I was getting later and later for my lesson. I started running around looking for a familiar rock or marker and discovered that somehow I was running in circles. I sat down on a fallen tree to catch my breath, and I heard a voice next to me.

"I am not a bit happy with you, Quang. I'm afraid you've been running in circles again."

I looked in the direction of the voice and saw the small man with the wild plantlike hair sitting up on the root ball of the tree.

"I thought your mind was stronger than *that*," he said in his crowy voice.

"I am sorry I can't stay and talk with you. I am late for my martial arts lesson."

"Let me point you in the right direction," and he led me to the path.

I took off running, but in just a few moments I was lost again. "Oh," I thought, "he is testing me." I saw the rock wall, so I thought I was very close to Ong Chin's house, but I couldn't find it. I looked and looked for a long time.

The small man appeared again and crowed, "Go back now or you'll be late. Home is that way," he pointed.

I was furious with him, but I didn't say anything. The last thing I needed was having a crazy sorcerer mad at me.

The next time I went the long way around, hoping to avoid the small man altogether. It took me twice as long. I was worried that if I didn't show up for my lesson, Ong Chin would be angry with me. I knew where I was the whole time, and was relieved that I had managed to elude that crazy sorcerer.

Since I approached Ong Chin's hut from the other side, everything looked different. He was outside sitting on his rock next to the fire waiting for me as usual. I sat down on the ground by the fire.

"I am sorry, Ong Chin," I said. "I have been trying to get here, but I have been having a problem with a crazy sorcerer."

"Quang, you rush around like a chicken. You think you are so clever, but you don't even know where you're going. You are trying my patience!"

I couldn't believe he tricked me again.

I looked at the fire and tried to think of what to do.

I said politely, "I promised Ong Chin I'd come tonight. I don't want break my word."

When I looked up, he was gone. I waited for a few minutes, then stood up and ran up the path the rest of the way to Ong Chin's.

33

LEAD LIPS

Q uang, you are getting lazy," Ong Chin said disapprovingly.

"I am sorry I am late again, Ong Chin. There is a crazy sorcerer who keeps charming me and making me lose my way. Do you know him?"

"Well, there are several. What does he look like?"

"He is very short and his hair is black and white and very wild."

"Sounds like Lead Lips."

Ong Chin told me his name was Ong Ba, but people started calling him Ong Ba Chi, "chi" meaning lead. It wasn't just because of the color of his lips, it was also because of what kind of magic spells came out of those lips.

"He keeps bothering me every time I try to come to see you," I said. "What can I do to make him leave me alone?"

"I don't think there is any way to reason with him. Maybe we could meet somewhere else."

T he next day I left the temple during lunch and I went to meet Ong Chin at a sweet potato patch on Long Mountain. I arrived without a problem. He taught me in the shade of a tree at the edge of the patch. When we were finished, he took me to a waterfall to cool off. A cloud of iridescent butterflies took off as we approached the pool. They had been sitting on a tree, just as the fireflies had done.

I didn't walk Ong Chin home because I didn't want to go near the sorcerer. Instead I headed down the mountain. I ran into Lead Lips sitting on a log.

"Hello," I said. "How are you today, Ong Ba?"

"I am having trouble catching my chicken; I need someone who can run in circles without getting dizzy," he said.

"I am in a hurry, Ong Ba. I am late for my job at the temple."

He said, "I'm afraid you didn't pass the test, but I like you anyway, because you didn't ask me how I made the glass move."

"No sir," I said.

"Help me catch my chicken and I will tell you." He gave me a knowing look.

I was curious to know. He seemed to be a skilled sorcerer, but I didn't trust him.

"I am sorry, Ong Ba, maybe Ong Chin will help you."

I bowed politely and ran away through the forest.

Ong Chin and I met at a different place each time for three months, but it didn't really matter where I met Ong Chin, because I usually ran into Lead Lips every time.

One day Lead Lips told me, "You have finally passed the test. Congratulations! I have accepted you as my new student."

"Thank you, Ong Ba, but I am too busy."

That made him angry. "Too busy? Are you too busy to help me catch my chicken?"

"I guess not," I said, "just too busy to be your student."

I followed him to his overhanging bush. There were six or seven chickens pecking around in the brambles.

Lead Lips ordered, "Stand over there and I'll chase one of them out of the bushes toward you."

He swatted at the chicken with a stick, but it didn't run in a straight line. I circled around and around chasing the chicken until I was dizzy, but I finally caught it.

"Quang," he cackled, "you are good at that."

He walked over to a jungle bush that was growing next to his shelter.

"Now throw the chicken into this bush."

"Throw her in the bush?" I repeated, just to make sure I did the right thing.

"Some magic uses spirits and some uses souls, you know," he said.

I walked over to the bush. Its long, broad, dark-green leaves were as thin as paper.

"Just drop her into it," Lead Lips smiled, smacking his lips.

I held the squawking chicken over the leafy bush and dropped her. I was thinking, "He may do good magic, but he sure is crazy."

As soon as the chicken hit the bush, she stopped moving. She was screaming, but she seemed to be paralyzed.

"If I don't feed my black bush one chicken per week, it gets hungry and it can be dangerous."

"Why can't the chicken move?" I asked.

"You know," the sorcerer continued, "it took me ten years to get that bush to eat a big chicken like that."

I heard a strange sound like hissing coming from the bush. I looked into the bush and saw that its leaves were rippling and moving.

He said, "When you charm a black bush, it develops an animal soul and starts to crave meat. Otherwise it is just a normal, harmless bush in the jungle."

Right before my eyes, the bush was wrapping its leaves around the motionless chicken.

"By morning, there will be nothing left but feathers."

"What?" I was furious with him because he had just made me kill an animal. "How did you charm that bush?"

"It's easy, it just takes time. You find bush growing in the jungle and bring it home and plant it. Then you draw the magic charm over it and say the incantation once a month for a year. Then you charm it twice a month for another year, then once a week for the third year, then three times a week for the fourth year, then every night for the fifth year. Then you start giving it eggs. Little by little the leaves start moving toward the egg, until one day they wrap themselves around it and eat everything. You give it eggs the sixth year and chicks the seventh year. By the eighth year, it can eat a young chicken, and by the tenth year, it can eat a full-grown chicken. By then it is very powerful and can be used for many kinds of magic."

"Will it grab onto me if I touch it?" I asked.

"Not now, because it is a well-fed bush. But it would burn your flesh down to the bone on the spot where you touched it if it was hungry. You can't wash the poison off.

"Today I am going to use a black bush leaf to find ginseng."

I said, "I don't need a charmed bush to help me find ginseng."

Lead Lips knew better. "Did you know that when ginseng grows very old, over one hundred years old, it develops a soul, too? A ginseng soul is different from a charmed soul that craves meat. It is the natural soul of the ginseng. Once ginseng has a soul, it can make itself invisible. A charmed black bush leaf cancels the ginseng's spell."

"Oh," I said.

"Come tomorrow, and I'll tell you about how the glass moved."

"I can't learn magic," I said. "The last time I tried, some spirits came after me and tried to suffocate me. It took me months to make them stop."

Lead Lips didn't ask me with whom I had studied; sorcerers never interfere in one another's business. He took a few steps toward me. All of a sudden he looked like a gentle, sweet man. "That won't be a problem," he assured me, "I am more powerful than those spirits. They would never bother one of my students; they wouldn't dare."

I believed Lead Lips was a more powerful sorcerer than Tattoo. Tattoo couldn't make a glass move on its own. I thought, "Today is my lucky day. I have found a teacher who will not let anything bad happen."

Lieu was waiting for me at the temple. Sometimes she invited me to eat dinner at her house, but I always told her I didn't have time. It was really because I didn't feel comfortable around girls. This time she said she had something important to talk about.

We sat under a star tree in front of the temple by the parked buses. I noticed she was wearing a pink flower in the back of her hair and that her hair was neatly combed.

She said, "Anh Quang, I was wondering if you could check my hand to see if I would be a good wife for you."

I took her hand, but I was just pretending to look at it because I didn't know what to say. The birds were singing in the tree. I thought about the bird we call the sweetheart bird—in America it is called the mourning dove. Mourning doves mate for life. If one of them dies, the other will pine away for its mate until the end of its days. The female lays only two eggs every season, and a male and a female chick are always hatched. If a predator steals one of the eggs or if it kills one of the chicks, then the remaining chick will never take a mate. I was thinking I was like the mourning dove that grew up without his sister. I didn't think I would ever take a mate.

Lieu touched my forearm and I remembered the first time I saw her, the day she rolled up my wet sleeves. "Anh," she said, "I would never marry anyone but you."

I could barely speak.

"Lieu," I said.

She looked sad.

"If I wanted to get married, I would marry you, but I can't marry. I have to go where my father sends me for many more years, because I am going to be a doctor and carry responsibility for our people as he does. He can't have a wife, and neither can I."

Lieu's eyes filled with tears. She was beautiful, but foreign to me.

I felt very bad, so I held her hand. We sat for a long time while more buses came and the others left.

I went to the market to buy some pork and alcohol for Lead Lips and proceeded to his overhanging bush. As soon as I got there, he popped his head out the door and said, "Quang, hurry up. We are going out."

"I brought you some pork and rice liquor."

"No, thank you, I am a vegetarian."

Lead Lips never wore anything except a pair of brown shorts. We walked all the way around to the other side of the mountain. I was afraid, but he said he had exploded all the booby traps already. We came to a cliff. Down at the bottom was the river.

"Never walk along the riverbank down there because you will pass in front of the wild pig cave. If they think you know where they live, they will tear you to pieces."

Wild pigs have a bad temper. They will go on rampages. Sometimes a lone pig will hunt down people and gore them to death. Wild pigs are very difficult to understand.

"If any animals maul you, there are many kinds of leaves that you can chew and put on the wound. Then it won't get infected."

We followed the ridge for about one mile, and then Lead Lips started climbing down to the river. We waded across and entered the forest on the other side where we came to the round opening of a cave.

"Here it is," he said.

The stones around the opening shone like polished lead. The hole was about four feet in diameter.

"Are we going in?" I asked.

"No, stay here and don't move," he ordered.

Before I could say anything, he went bounding up the hill and disappeared over the top.

I stood there for about fifteen minutes wondering why he didn't tell me where he was going. I thought maybe he was going to the bathroom. I waited a few more minutes, and then I turned around.

Just then something rammed into the side of my leg with such force that it threw me. I couldn't believe my eyes. It was a *ho may* snake, the largest snake in the world, whizzing out of its cave like a train coming out of a tunnel. I could have reached out and touched it. Those snakes grow to between thirty and forty feet long and are from three to four feet wide. I was lucky it didn't break my bones. *Ho may* means "cloud snake," because when it is out sliding in the jungle, people can hear it all the way in the village, and it sounds just like rain.

The old men at Tam Buu Tu told me there were no more cloud snakes. They said an avalanche covered the last cloud snake's hole, so it couldn't get out. I guess they were wrong. Bald Ong Chin and Ong Tu told me about the time many years ago when a farmer in the village heard his cow screaming. When the farmer went to see what was the matter, he saw his cow being dragged up the mountain by a cloud snake.

Bald Ong Chin and Ong Tu and many neighbors followed the snake's tracks to its cave. They could hear the cow screaming from inside the cave. They decided to smoke out the snake and hack it to death.

They gathered brush and lit a fire, but the snake didn't come out. Nobody wanted to go in after the snake. Some days later, the rocks above the entrance to the cave fell down and sealed the snake inside. Everyone was grateful.

Lead Lips came bouncing down the hill cackling like a demon.

"Where did you go?" I demanded to know.

"To the back door of the monster's cave," he crowed.

I was very angry, and I yelled at him. I said, "Why didn't you warn me first?"

He taunted, "Why were you afraid? I thought you were an experienced martial artist?"

I told him, "I learned how to fight people, not snakes."

Lead lips squinted at me and said, "Can your martial arts teacher fight a monster?"

"No one can fight a monster, even if they could see one," I said.

"I am no one," cackled Lead Lips.

"You see monsters?" I asked.

He whispered into my ear, "I can tie them up with a string and make them cry."

After I had chopped a whole pile of firewood for Lead Lips, he told me to sit down by the fire. "Now I am going to tell you how I moved that glass," he said.

I sat down right away and waited for him to begin.

"First take out the twenty-four dong that is rolled up in your pants," he ordered.

I stood up and took out my money and counted it. It was twenty-four dong exactly. I was astounded.

"And tell me why you left some French butter cookies in your room and didn't bring them for me," he teased.

"I will bring them next time," I said confusedly.

"Now you will do whatever I say, because you think I know everything. I know that you were found in the street and don't even know the day you were born. How are you going to set your wedding and burial dates?"

I asked him how he knew about me. He grabbed my ear and pulled it to his lips and whispered, "I don't know a damned thing about you. How could I? We've just met."

"So how did you know those things?" I demanded.

"I just showed you, didn't I?" He pointed to his ear. "My helper whispers them into my head."

"Your helper?"

"Do you want some cow manure?" Lead Lips asked suddenly.

Before I could answer, a dry patty of dung appeared on my lap.

"Or would you prefer fruit?"

A mango appeared on top of the dung.

"So you didn't move the glass at all? It was a spirit?"

"Welcome to the family," Lead Lips grinned.

Lead Lips sent me home with a charm and an incantation that would get me a helper on the 110th day of tracing the charm and reciting the incantation. He said I would have to sit near a grave, because the energy of the dead would help my helper to find me. He also told me that if anything unusual happened I shouldn't be scared or stop chanting the spell, or it would be broken.

I figured out that I didn't have to go far away to find a dead body. Right at Tam Buu Tu there was usually a coffin in the rear of the temple building, waiting for the proper burial date. I didn't think anyone walked back there at midnight.

I snuck out of my room every night for one hundred nights, many times sitting in the rain. I sat on a big rock next to where the coffins were placed. Every time I went to visit Lead Lips, he asked me if anything unusual had happened yet. I told him no, nothing. He said as long as I didn't miss a night I should expect some very unusual things to start happening during the last ten days.

On the 101st night, the rock started moving like an animal waking up from a nap, but it stopped. On the 102nd night it started moving more and tried to shake me off, but I didn't move. On the 103rd night, I saw a huge hole next to the coffin, and the rock started tilting sideways to dump me in. I felt myself slipping. I looked into the hole and saw there was no bottom, and then I heard people screaming in agony down there. I started to fall, so I grabbed onto the rock. That broke the spell. I had wasted 103 days.

I started again. When I was only one month into it, Anh Muoi, the oldest scribe, came outside one night and saw me tracing the charm and chanting. He climbed up and yanked me down by my shirt, and then he shook me because he couldn't talk. I told him I wasn't doing anything bad, I just wanted to see how it worked.

After that night, I went all the way down the mountain to the rice fields and sat on the ground between two cement tombs where no one could possibly find me.

34

THE HUNDREDTH NIGHT

ust like the first time, unusual things started to happen on the hundredth night, as I sat in the rice field in between the tombs. First a bloody arm dropped in my lap like a slab of meat, but I didn't flinch. The next night it was a bloody hand and a foot.

For the next eight days many more body parts fell down, but I didn't close my eyes or pause in my chanting. On the 110th day, all the body parts started moving toward each other and joined together. I thought it would be a person, but it wasn't. A monster lifted his head and growled at me. He smelled foul, like rotten meat, and had long, matted hair that was caked with blood. His bloody fangs looked as if he ate people. He had slimy green mottled skin that was oozing with sores, and red eyes that were craving my blood.

I was terrified, but I kept my eyes open and didn't move a muscle. I kept chanting and tracing the symbol in the air. The monster didn't go away. It grabbed my leg with the strength of a lion and started to sink its teeth into it. It hurt a lot, but I didn't stop chanting and tracing. He tried to drag me away, but as long as I stayed relaxed I stayed in one piece. After what seemed to be half an hour, I watched the monster change into a regular person.

He looked like a villager, not too young and not too old, very ordinary. He said to me, "Please forgive me for scaring you. I won't do it again."

He didn't move his lips when he spoke, but I heard him talking in my ear as if he were tiny and sitting on my shoulder.

"If you want some food, I can get it for you right away. If you want to know something that has already happened, I can tell you. I can warn you of danger," the person said.

"Good," I said.

"Teacher, can you give me a name?" the person said.

"I will call you Met Pop." Those words stuck in my mind because they were part of the charm I had just been reciting, and they were also in one of the charms Tattoo had given me. I don't know if "met pop" means something in another language.

"Thank you, teacher," Met Pop said and he vanished.

I wanted to tell Lead Lips right then, but there was not enough time left before I had to return to my room. I was happy and proud of myself, because now I had someone to protect me.

I went to see Lead Lips the next day during lunch. He was busy setting food out on a cloth on the ground in front of his house, cooked pork, shrimp, hard-boiled eggs, boiled cassava, raw greens, rice wine, and cookies. He brought out some paper money, the kind you burn for your ancestors, and said, "This food and money are for Met Pop."

I wasn't that surprised that Lead Lips already knew I had gotten my helper.

He said, "You must reward him every two weeks with food and money to show your appreciation, or he will leave you."

"If he leaves, will he come back if I start chanting again for another hundred and ten nights?" I asked.

"No, once he leaves, you can never get him back," Lead Lips said. He reached down and handed me a wooden bowl.

"Help yourself. We will join Met Pop and my servants for lunch."

We sat down on the ground next to the food.

I asked, "Did Met Pop come to me as a way to get food?"

"I don't think so. He might leave you even if you give him lobster every time. He might decide to leave you if he feels you don't need his help. He wants to be useful."

"Why does he want to be useful to me?"

"It's because Met Pop can't do anything in our world. Even a ghost can interfere in the lives of humans, but Met Pop can't. He can only interact with our world if you give him a command."

"What kind of things can I tell him to do?"

Lead Lips had to chew things for a long time because he didn't have many teeth. I could see the cassava mash in his mouth as he spoke. "Met Pop can find out information that might be of help to you. You can impress people, win their trust. He can warn you of danger, and he is always ready to attack your enemies."

"Can he kill?" I asked as I took a bite of shrimp.

Lead Lips drank some wine from an empty glass jar and smacked his lips. "Oh, he can kill, all right, but it takes time. He can enter a person's mind and drive him mad over time. He can also make people sick until the sickness overcomes them. But only if it is your will."

"Oh," I said.

Lead Lips gave me a gentle shove and said with his mouth dripping with wine and mush, "What makes Met Pop happy is to defend you. The happier he is, the longer he will stay with you."

After lunch Lead Lips wanted me to feed his bush. I caught a chicken but gave it to him to drop in. When I came back the next day, I saw only feathers in the bush.

One stormy night during tea at Tam Buu Tu, I noticed that a lot of rainwater was pouring down in front of the anteroom door. I went outside to take a look because it meant I would have to climb up the next morning and clean the leaves out of the gutters so the rain would fall into the cisterns and not be wasted. The next day when I was up on the roof clearing out the leaves, I overheard my partners, the scribes, talking about me.

I heard Anh Thiep say, "Well, if it's true, let's ambush him and see how good he is at fighting."

Anh The said, "I heard he has been training ever since he got here. He's got to be good."

"Well, if there are three of us, I don't think we will get hurt," Anh Thiep said. "I really want to see what he can do."

I didn't know Anh Muoi was also in on the conversation until I climbed down and walked into the room and saw him sitting at the table, too. Anh Muoi carried a notebook around and wrote down what he wanted to say.

They hushed up as soon as I stepped into the anteroom.

The next day Met Pop warned me. He talked into my ear and said, "They will be waiting with sticks tomorrow night outside the door. They are planning to hit you when you bring the cups outside."

That night after tea, I carried the tray out through a different door and avoided them.

Met Pop warned me again a few days later. He said they had set a rope trap under the tree where I always went to pee before going to bed. They were planning to hide behind another tree and pull on the other end of the rope and leave me hanging by my feet.

That night at tea, I yawned and said, "I think I'll go to bed as soon as I take these cups outside."

I walked out to the kitchen with the tray. Then I returned to the building and saw that my friends had left the room. I went through the walkway into the temple and left by the rear temple door and peed on a different tree. I think they waited for me to come pee for a long time.

The next morning at breakfast, I overheard my friends arguing. Anh Thiep said I knew what they were planning, but Anh The disagreed. He said it was just a coincidence.

That night I was sitting with them at the table after the evening sutra. Ong Muoi was pouring the tea as usual. As soon as he poured my tea, Met Pop spoke in my ear. He said, "Don't drink the tea; they put something in it."

I pretended to be clumsy, and I dropped my cup on the ground. They all started laughing and asked, "How did you know?"

I said, "Know what?"

They said, "What do you mean, know what?"

I looked at them as if I had no idea what they were talking about. I saw them giving each other looks.

Another time Met Pop told me that Anh Thiep was going to wait on the roof just after the sutra was over and jump on top of me when I went outside to the dishwashing area to get the teacups.

That afternoon, I took a broom and brought it into my room and hung my shirt over it. When the evening sutra was over I went to get it. I knew Anh Thiep would be waiting on the roof over the doorway. I held the broom out the door for a second and brought it back inside. Anh Thiep jumped. I came out a few seconds later and stopped to say hello. I told Anh Thiep that I had seen a ghost around the temple last night. The following day, I heard him telling Anh The and Anh Muoi that there was a ghost around the temple.

Even if my friends knew that I was studying martial arts, and suspected I was learning sorcery, they would never have known that I had a servant. I had never heard the old men or anyone else speak about servants. Lead Lips was the first person to tell me.

About a month later, Anh Muoi told me what they had put into my cup. He wrote in his notebook, "Remember last month when you spilled your tea on the floor? We put some medicine in the cup that midwives give to women to bring on labor. You would have run outside like a wild goat, and we would have found you somewhere out there humping the first thing you saw."

Met Pop started telling me things about the visitors when they asked me to read their palms. I sat down with one woman. Before I started, Met Pop told me that her husband had just left her for another woman and that was why she came to the Seven Mountains, to pray for him to come back. As I spoke to the woman, I started saying things that Met Pop was telling me, only I didn't hear them first, I just said them. From time to time I had to stop and mentally ask for a clarification, and he whispered it.

I told her, "Don't worry, you don't have bad luck, but you must fix your altar. It is facing east in the direction of your outhouse. You must turn it to the west, and keep the dust off it, because now it is full of cobwebs. If you do all of this your husband might come back.

"Also, I see your house is very dirty. Since your daughters left, there is too much work for you to do and you feel lonely. Maybe one of them would come back with her family and live with you again. It will bring you more happiness."

The woman said, "How do you know everything about my life and my house? You didn't even look at my hand."

I said, "Just practice."

(Met Pop couldn't tell the future. I made up the part about her husband coming back, because I felt like she needed hope to start her on a new path.)

That woman told a lot of people about me, and soon many people were asking me to read their palms. It was very tiring and I didn't know how to get out of it until I thought of a way. When someone asked if I was the young monk who could read palms, I told them no. I told them it was Anh Thiep.

Soon, many people kept interrupting Anh Thiep while he was painting his calligraphy to ask him if he would read their palms. He told them no, so they went back to me. I told them I was too young to have studied that long. I told them that Anh Thiep was just too busy. I said, "Just ask him later during his free time." The visitors bothered him for days. I was glad I had Met Pop looking after me because I was sure Anh Thiep was going to think of a good prank to get me back.

I heard some people talking about a fourteen-year-old girl in the village who was possessed by a ghost. It was a very persistent ghost. The family had already spent a lot of money on three sorcerers who couldn't help. They had just hired the fourth.

I found out where the girl lived. When I got there, a crowd of people stood in the doorway. I squeezed my way inside the house until I was in the room with the girl and her family. She was lying on her bed laughing. The sorcerer was holding a strip of thin yellow paper over the flame of a candle. As soon as it caught on fire, he held it over the girl's body, but she kicked his arm.

The sorcerer went outside and came back with a live chicken. He held it upside down by the legs and ripped the legs apart right in front of the girl and let the blood of the dying chicken drip into a rice bowl. He drew another charm over the blood and then took a knife and stuck it through both of his cheeks. He also drove a long metal stick through his wrist from front to back and held the bowl of chicken blood in the same hand. He sprinkled it on the girl, saying, "Drink this blood and leave."

He lifted the girl's head toward the bowl and tried to open her mouth, but she hit the bowl out of his hands, spraying the blood all over the room. Then I heard the ghost's voice say, "No one is going to make me leave." The fourth sorcerer gave up and collected his fee.

About one week later, the girl's mother came looking for me at the temple. She had heard I was a student of Lead Lips, and she wanted me to get Lead Lips to help her. She had been to see him but he told her that he was too busy.

I didn't understand how this woman knew I studied with Lead Lips. She did not belong to my religion and I never had seen her at the temple, so I wasn't that worried. I explained to the woman that it would be waste of time trying to get Lead Lips to change his mind.

She asked me if I would try to help her daughter. I told her that I had only studied a short time, and that I didn't know very much. I gave her the name of another sorcerer, but she said she had already asked him. I said I would talk it over with my teacher and let her know in a few days.

· · ·

didn't tell anyone I am studying with you, but they know," I said angrily to Lead Lips.

He was looking around his cooking area for something to eat. "What's wrong with that? Aren't they coming to you for help?" Lead Lips jumped up. "When are you going to bring me some more coconut tapioca squares with chunks of banana?"

"I'll prove to everyone that I am not doing anything wrong by learning sorcery. I want to help the girl. How can I get the monster to leave?" I asked.

Lead Lips went over to his *chuoi ta qua* plantain tree and picked a yellow one. Vietnamese people never plant *chuoi ta qua* plantains close to the house unless they are a sorcerer, because this plant can make a moaning sound at night when a pregnant woman goes into labor. Usually people get scared when they hear the sound. "Can you climb up the mango tree and find some ripe ones? I'm famished."

I climbed up his tree and picked two ripe mangoes and climbed back down. "How do I make the monster listen to me?"

"You know enough charms already," he said with his mouth full of raw plantain.

"Which ones?" I asked.

"Try one, and if that doesn't work, try another," he said, taking the mangoes and putting them side by side on his chopping block. He took out his knife and threw it down between the mangoes. The blade sank deep into the wood. "Just don't kill the girl by mistake," he grinned.

He pulled out the knife, peeled a mango, and started cutting it into slices.

"Help yourself," he said.

Since the mother of the possessed girl didn't come back for several days, I figured she had already gotten someone to help her daughter. I felt relieved because after visiting Lead Lips, I was uncertain about what to do.

A few days later, she came back and told me that her daughter was worse. She said sometimes her daughter tried to go out of the house in the middle of the night and that it took the combined strength of her husband, her two sons, and her other daughter to keep her inside.

I told her for the second time that I was just learning, but she still wanted me to try. She wanted to know if I needed a pig's head or anything. I told her I needed some incense and a candle and nothing else.

A lot of people came to watch me try, which only made me more nervous. Before entering her house, I stood by a tree and chanted Met Pop's spell for about five minutes so I would be able to see the ghost. A sorcerer can't do anything if he cannot see the ghost.

The girl was lying on the bed again, but this time she was quiet. I said hello to her and waited for the charm to affect my sight. I don't really understand how it works, but I was able to see what a ghost sees.

When the charm took hold, I didn't see the girl anymore. I saw the ghost in the form of a crazed-looking man with a stubbly beard, a broken nose, and rotten teeth. His hair was long and matted, and he was wearing dirty clothes. He wasn't as scary-looking as Met Pop had been, but he looked like a powerful ghost.

I drew a charm on some yellow prayer paper that I had taken from the temple, and I placed it on the ghost's chest. He immediately tried to peel it off, but it hurt his hands to touch it.

I told him, "Now get out of this girl and go away."

He didn't laugh or yell, he just looked at me. I thought he might be a little scared.

I asked the parents to bring me the longest and sharpest knife they had. I thrust it again and again into the monster's rib cage. There were many holes and just a little dark blood came out, but the ghost did not care.

The parents were used to seeing their daughter getting stabbed like that. When the first sorcerer tried to do that, they attacked him, but by the time I got there they didn't mind.

I remembered Lead Lips telling me that as long as I was seeing the ghost and not the girl, I could try to kill it any way I wanted to. Everyone else in the room saw me stabbing the girl. Once the knife was pulled out, they saw no wounds on her.

The parents looked disappointed. They had seen this all before. I could tell they had no faith in my ability to cure their daughter.

I told the ghost, "If you do what I tell you, everything will be fine for you, but if you don't I will have to tie you to a tree."

Ghosts are afraid of staying outside all day long, because they can't stand the light. They are also terrified of lightning. We believe that lightning hunts for ghosts and tries to kill them. If a ghost is lucky, he can jump out of the way of the lightning bolt. If the lightning misses the ghost three times, the ghost becomes more powerful. He becomes a monster.

The ghost said, "I am in love with her. I won't leave unless she comes with me."

I said, "Now I have to get you. I warned you, so don't be angry with me."

I burned some incense, took a piece of red string from my pocket, and began tracing a charm over it. The ghost grabbed his head and started screaming for me to stop. I told him, I wouldn't stop until he left the girl's body.

I tied his hands together with the string and pulled him up to his feet. He struggled, but I was stronger. When I pulled him away from the bed, I saw the girl lying there. That meant her soul had come back into her body. I could see both the girl and the ghost. She looked dead.

Her mother screamed and rushed to her bedside. She yelled, "She's not breathing."

A minute later she started breathing faintly, and about ten minutes later the girl opened her eyes. She said, "What happened?"

Her parents were very happy. They wanted to pay me money, but I told them no thank you.

I went out into the night with my captive ghost. I thought about the time Aunt Gioi tried to get me to see the ghosts in the field, but I refused to look. Now I was dragging a ghost by the arm.

The ghost was begging me to let him go, but I said not until I was convinced that he would never bother that girl or anyone else again.

I took him all the way back to Tam Buu Tu and tied him to a mango tree in the back of the temple. I told him, "When you know what you did wrong and you are sorry, then I will let you go. If not, you will stay tied to this tree until the lightning finds you."

I left him there for a few days. Sometimes sorcerers who do a lot of exorcisms forget about all the ghosts they left tied to trees. After ten years the magic wears off and the ropes break and the ghost can escape.

After three days, I put a charm into a cup of water and brought it to the ghost. I told him, "This water will burn up your insides if you ever bother a person again. I will let you go as soon as you drink this."

I told him, "If you pray and become kind, you can turn into a spirit. Maybe if you develop compassion, you might find your way to heaven and have another chance at life."

The ghost drank the water, and I let him go.

News spread that I was good with ghosts. More people came to ask me to help them. I went back to Lead Lips, who taught me some other charms for getting rid of ghosts. It was exciting work. I don't know if anyone from the temple knew I was doing this work. If they did, they didn't say.

35

ON MY WAY TO HEAVEN

One evening Grenade, the most powerful sorcerer, came into Tam Buu Tu during the evening tea. Some of those who recognized him got nervous and left. He sat down at the table with the old men. I was sitting with the scribes. Before he left, Grenade walked over to my table and said, "Quang, if you have some time, please come and visit me."

I said, "Okay."

After Grenade walked out, my friends were horrified. They asked me why I wasn't afraid of him, and I said I didn't know.

They said, "Why did you say you would come? Now you have to visit him, or else it would be an insult." They couldn't believe how stupid I was.

I didn't go right away. During the next few days, I don't know why, but it seemed like everyone was mad at me. I went to Thay Hai's house for my plant medicine class, and he was so angry that he sent me home. At the temple, my friends were ignoring me. Then I remembered I had an invitation to Grenade's house.

I didn't know where he lived, but I knew it was somewhere on the other side of the Xa Ba Chuc market. I stopped at the market and bought a baguette and soy milk and sat down at my usual table to eat. Dunking the crusty bread into the warm, sweet soy milk was a way I had learned to comfort myself. As I ate, and wondered how I would find his house, I saw that he was sitting at one of the tables.

When I was finished, he nodded to the waiter and paid for me. We went together to his house.

It was a small thatched house, very clean. When we walked in the doorway, I noticed that he didn't have an altar for his ancestors. He had a lot of fruit and cake, and he gave me more to eat. He didn't talk much to me, he just told me to make myself at home. I didn't know what to do, so I lay down on a mat and slept for a few hours. When I woke up I went back to the temple to help out for dinner. I thought he was very nice.

I went back to see him a few more times. Each time, he gave me a lot of food and sat down to talk with me. We didn't talk about sorcery or ghosts; he was just like an uncle. He told me that I could come to his house anytime, and when I got up to leave he said, "Come back soon; I will miss you."

A few days later, my father arrived at the temple and told me he was taking me back to Cho Lach to study more. It was September 1969; I was nineteen years old. We left the next day.

The first thing I did when I got to his house was to hide my book of spells very well so he wouldn't find it. I put it at the bottom of one of the tall metal containers in which he stored his medicine. He kept the medicine inside a plastic bag that he took out and refilled. I didn't think he would look very closely at the bottom of the can.

On my second day in Cho Lach, I suddenly fell ill. My fever was dangerously high, and it seemed as if I were slipping in and out of a coma.

My father tried to take care of me, but his medicine wasn't working. He wasn't sure if I would live.

He decided to take me back to Tam Buu Tu to pray to the Buddha Master. He told me, "If you die, at least you will be close to your religion."

He rented a minivan and a driver to take me. A group of his students and patients wanted to come to help. The Tiger was among them.

They had to carry me, because I was unconscious. When we arrived at the temple, they made a place in the anteroom for me to lie down in front of the altar. My father went inside to talk with Ba Bay. The others sat down at the tables and ate some food.

While they were eating, Grenade walked in and knelt beside me. Some of my father's students were watching and listening to him. He put his hand on my face and took my hand and said, "I miss you. Come back and live with me." Then he left.

I sat up right away, and I felt a lot better. My father's students brought me some food, and I ate. My father was very surprised. He checked my pulses. He found they were normal. He asked the others if someone had come near me. His friends told him about what Grenade had said to me. My father realized that Grenade had put a curse on me, but he wasn't that concerned. He said, "Tomorrow we will visit Buu Minh Doung and An Son Tu, and then we will go home."

My father gave Ong Nam a lot of money to buy food and make a feast at An Son Tu to give thanks for my recovery. Many people from Tam Buu Tu came to pray for me.

We set out in the minivan for home later that afternoon, but my father was not well. He was getting the same sickness I had. I started getting sick again, too. My father's students didn't know what to do.

The decided to go to Sam Mountain to Tay An Tu temple, the oldest and most well-known temple in the Seven Sacred Mountains. It started as a shrine, in 1820, under the direction of a woman engineer named Ba Chau Thi. This woman had been sent by Emperor Minh Mang to oversee the digging of a canal that would connect the newly constructed fort in Chau Doc to the seaport at Ha Tien. The canal was to pass by the Seven Sacred Mountains.

Panthers, tigers, pythons, and wild pigs were relentlessly preying upon Ba Chau Thi's workers. Afraid they would all perish, she built a shrine on Sam Mountain and prayed for the safety of her crew.

Several years later, a blue stone statue, about four feet high, was found not far from the shrine. Twenty men tried to carry the statue down to their boat, but they could barely lift it. They managed to carry it just a few feet. After it dropped to the ground, they couldn't lift it again.

In 1838, a village girl who lived near Sam Mountain began to speak with a voice that wasn't her own. The voice claimed to be the spirit of the blue stone goddess. The goddess spoke to the girl's family, and called for nine maidens to carry the blue stone statue to Ba Chau Thi's shrine.

The nine girls lifted the statue easily and they brought it almost all the way to the shrine, but it dropped to the ground and they couldn't lift it anymore. The stone goddess was named Ba Chua Xu. The Temple of Western Peace, Tay An Tu, was built around the statue. Ba Chua Xu became the guardian spirit of Sam Mountain.

. . .

When we arrived at Tay An Tu, someone got out and asked if we could stay for the night, because two people were sick. The nuns didn't look too happy about it, but they said we could stay. My father and I were carried into the temple, but there were no mats for us to lie on.

My father's friends were very angry. They knew the temple had a lot of mats for people to use. The Tiger was trembling with anger. He told the others that if the nuns didn't give us mats, he was going to bust up the temple. He was trying his best to calm down. Finally they pooled all their money and gave it to the nuns, who then brought out mats and asked what kind of food would we like for dinner. The Tiger was so mad that he told the nuns we refused to eat their food. The others were unhappy that the Tiger had turned down the meal.

The next morning, my father and I were worse and everyone was worried. They drove all the way back to Cai Be, where most of the students were from, and brought us to the Chinese temple. My father tried to pray, and to put his power into a cup of water for us to drink, because he was too weak to make medicine. His students brought in a doctor who practiced Western medicine. The doctor gave us some medicine to take, but it didn't work.

Two of my father's students, Chu Buu and Sau Ve, stayed with us and took care of us. They fed us, bathed us, and brought us the chamberpot. They were both older men in their sixties. I thought they were very kind.

My father started getting a little better each day, but I was not. Soon my father was well enough to make medicine for me, but I did not improve.

Someone brought a woman medium to the temple to help us. The woman lay down and went to sleep and then a spirit called Earth Mother spoke through her. Earth Mother told my father that he had something inside him to protect him, but that I didn't. She said, "You have only two options to save your son. The first is to take him back to the sorcerer who put this curse on you both, and the second is for you to go to your teacher and get something from him to save your son."

Some of my father's students didn't believe the medium was real. They lit an incense stick and touched the woman's skin to see if it would hurt. The woman didn't wake up, but they still didn't believe her. They went to the kitchen and pretended to put some things in a bowl and went back and asked Mother Earth what they had just put into the bowl. She said, "Nothing." They believed her then.

My father followed the medium's advice and went to the forbidden mountain to ask his teacher in the cave for help. His teacher gave him a piece of a root that grew through the ceiling of the cave and told my father to put the root into a glass of water and trace a word over the glass. My father came back and did as his teacher said, and I opened my eyes.

I told my father that I had gone far away to a place where wooden chairs and benches moved by themselves like cars and buses, and everyone was happy. There were crowds of people in the streets taking a walk and visiting shops to buy food and cakes. I told my father I could go anywhere I wanted to be just by wishing.

My father said I was so close to death that my soul went out of my body. He said I was lucky, because his teacher's spirit friends brought me back. He told me that I went to the place where people go when they have just died. He said everyone I saw there had just turned their eyes up and stopped breathing. Suddenly they are free of their pain and suffering. Everyone there is happy. But after a few days, when they realize they are dead, they suffer a great shock.

My father said there are all kinds of places in the afterworld. People of like mind come for you and bring you to dwell with others like you. If you caused pain and suffering to others during your life, you will be brought to live with people who have done the same.

I began to recover very slowly. I wasn't able to walk for an entire month.

I will always remember Chu Buu and Sau Ve for never leaving my side. The Tiger was there the whole time, too, but he didn't do much. He just told people what to do.

My father and I went to my aunt's house, where I would feel more comfortable. She cooked a lot of food for us to eat. I was worried about Met Pop. I hadn't fed him since I became sick. I called his name in my mind and he answered, "Yes, teacher." His voice sounded quieter than usual.

"Met Pop, I am sorry I didn't give you food,"

I was too weak to go fishing for shrimp and I couldn't kill and cook one of my aunt's chickens without everyone knowing. I carried some rice and fish, vegetables and fruit, and some cookies from my aunt's store and laid it out for him in the orchard where no one would see.

I didn't know if I could still do spells, so I tried one out on my Uncle Quon. I traced the fighting charm at the table where Uncle Quon and his friends were about to sit down and have a drink. About ten minutes after they sat down, they started yelling at one another. Aunt Gioi told me later that she had never seen Uncle Quon that upset in his life.

That made me wonder if I was powerful enough to charm my father.

Grenade had been able to do it. That night I traced a charm on his pillow and waited for him to come to bed. I pretended to be asleep. One second after he lay down, he sat up and took the pillow and began dusting it off as if it had ants on it.

The next morning he woke me up and made me drink a glass of water. My father said he had erased all my charms. I called Met Pop again and again, but he didn't answer.

My father was furious with me for doing sorcery. He said that seven out of every ten people who do sorcery begin to do evil without realizing it. He said, "After a while, you begin to think like a ghost. I don't want to lose you to them."

I remembered Lead Lips telling me that the thing Met Pop loved to do most was to defend me. I never gave him the chance to make someone sick the way Grenade had made my father and me sick.

My father told me that in a few days he was going to bring me to the forbidden mountain to meet his teacher in the cave.

I went into my aunt's bedroom and lay down on the ebony bed and looked at the mural my father made for me when I was six. I hadn't studied it for years. I recognized the shape of the forbidden mountain as well as that of the mountains next to it, Long Mountain, Elephant Mountain, and Water Mountain. I looked again at my grandfather standing next to a tree that grew on an overhang of rock. The roots of the tree emerged from the underside of the rock and grew downward, in front of the cave's entrance. The teacher was sitting in the heart of the mountain. All at once it dawned on me how strange it was that I was finally going to meet him.

36

FOURTH UNCLE

I t was January 1970. My father and I stepped off the bus at the foot of the
forbidden mountain. You have to be respectful when you go to the forbidden mountain, because it is enchanted with ancient magic that protects the
privacy of the hermits who go there to meditate. Most people are too afraid to
go past the temple at the lower half of the mountain because they believe the
mountain is haunted.

The spirits of the mountain let my grandfather live there for a year before he
found his teacher. My father told me that my grandfather went looking for caves
every day, but he never found his teacher's cave. His teacher came out of the cave
and found my grandfather, and told him that he accepted him as his student.

They went into the cave together. When my grandfather started calling his
teacher "Master," the teacher said, "Call me Fourth Uncle, because I am the
fourth one to sit in this chamber." My father said I could call the teacher Fourth
Uncle, too, even though he was a very old man.

The jungle beyond the temple was primordial. Nobody had made so much
as a path. We walked for about three hours until we came to a waterfall with a
pool. Some of the clay around the rocks was bright pink and orange. I had never
seen earth that color, not even on Elephant Mountain.

"We'll stop here for a rest," my father said. We stayed for about half an hour, but we didn't talk much.

"It is still a two-hour walk to the cave. The stream does not go any closer to the cave than this. You will need to know other ways to quench your thirst."

"Are you leaving me here today?" I asked nervously.

"No. Today I am going to ask Fourth Uncle if he will accept you. If he does, we will go back to Tam Buu Tu for a while so you can say good-bye to your friends."

"Good-bye? What do you mean by good-bye?"

"You might not see them again for a long time."

"How long? I don't want to go away for long."

"It will be up to Fourth Uncle," my father said.

We continued up the mountain a short way. My father said, "See those vines? They grow all over the mountain. Let me show you how to drink from them."

He reached up and pulled down a vine that was hanging from the branches of a tree. It had many small green leaves and was covered with white flowers that smelled very good. My father took out his knife and cut the vine in two.

"Now put this in your mouth," he said.

He reached up and cut the vine again, producing a free section about three feet long. A slightly sweet and watery sap started rushing out. It was enough for three swallows.

We walked along the edge of a steep cliff, and I looked down. I felt like I was looking down from the clouds. We had to walk along the edge to the other side.

When we got to the other side, we sat down for a rest on the rocks. There was a pack of wolves sitting on the rocks not too far from us. I got up and walked closer, but they ran away.

No big trees grew at the top of the mountain, just small evergreens and bushes. My father said we were going to walk across the top of the mountain and start down the other side, over boulders and through a lot of thick bushes and brambles, in order to get to the cave.

There was no path through the brambles, but they didn't seem to snag my clothes or scratch my skin. There were some nice rocks to climb. At one point I looked up and recognized the tree that my father had painted on my mural. It was growing on an overhang of rock. Its roots had grown right through the rock and down about four feet and into the ground. The entrance to the cave was not visible because the roots were overgrown with vines.

My father got down on his hands and knees and crawled behind the roots. I went in after him. We sat under the overhang and lit the candles.

"What should I say to him?" I asked.

"Don't worry, he probably won't say anything to you. He doesn't like to talk."

I followed my father through the diagonal slit in the face of the mountain. Daylight disappeared abruptly as the tunnel veered to the left. I hopped from rock to rock like a frog while holding my candle. The cave was a warm reddish-brown color. The rocks felt damp and gritty, and some were covered with brown moss. Here and there strong, twisted roots protruded through the cave walls. I didn't understand where they came from, because I didn't see any trees outside the cave besides the one, only rocks and bushes.

My father had always told me I would like the cave, and he was right. My father moved through the tunnel quickly. When I caught up to him, he would be sitting in a small chamber waiting for me. The rocks would be all around us. I would think we had reached a dead end, but then he would disappear into a hole that I would never have noticed on my own. Later I found out that there was more than one hole in every chamber.

One time I was certain we had reached a dead end when my father leapt down a hole on the bottom of the chamber. I looked down and saw his face in the candlelight looking up at me from about six feet below. Soon, when I looked down for him, all I saw was a faint glow. That tunnel went straight down for a long time. I didn't like to think about how many rocks and boulders there were above me. I kept waiting for the air to get stale and musty, but it didn't. Currents of fresh air seemed to be coming in from the outside.

At the bottom of the hole was a chamber large enough to stand in. There was an underground spring that fed a series of small pools.

"You can swim here," my father smiled. "That one over there is deeper than it looks."

I felt the water. It was cool and smelled fresh, but I decided not to go in.

Our candles were burned down to stubs by then, so we lit two more.

I followed my father through a concealed opening in the wall of the chamber and we crawled through a level tunnel until we reached another, shorter downward hole.

Photograph that Quang took of his aunt Gioi in the summer of 1968.
She is 82 years old.

Quang, age 12, at the Chinese school in Cai Be,
after he cut his hair for the first time.

Thau Van Nguyen at the Chinese Temple in Cai Be, 1963.

Thau with the Tiger at the Chinese Temple in Cai Be, 1963.

Quang, age 18, at the zoo in Saigon.

Quang, age 25, abbot of Quoc Thoi Tu temple of
Xe Long Thoi village in Cho Lach, 1975.

Painted portrait of Ong Nam, Quang's teacher and friend, abbot of An Son Tu temple on Elephant Mountain.

Painted portrait of the former abbot of An Son Tu temple on Elephant Mountain. Thau and Ong Nam studied together with this man. This painting depicts the silk patchwork robe that was passed down to Thau.

Quang's nearly blind friend, Chi, in 2002. He is the present abbot of An Son Tu temple on Elephant Mountain.

Thau, age 84, with his friend Quoc, at Tay An Tu temple on Sam Mountain.
The shape of Thau's black stone Buddha is visible over his right hip.

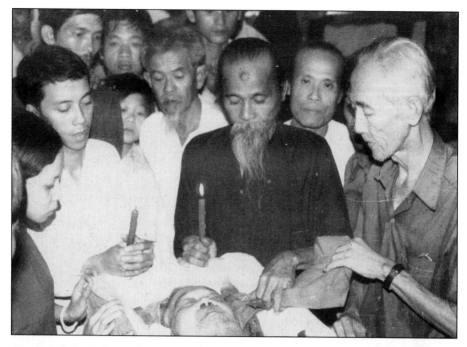

Quang's father's funeral service, December 1983. Quang's wife, Mai, stands to the left of the coffin. Quang and the Tiger hold candles. The bump on the Tiger's forehead is from hitting his head on the floor when he prayed to relieve his guilt.

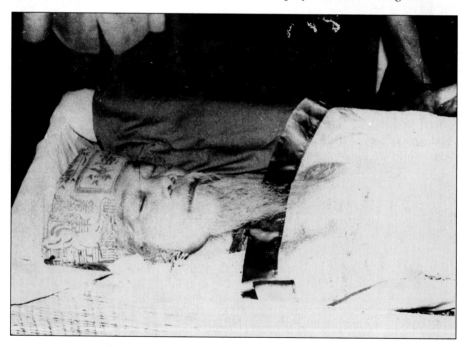

Thau Van Nguyen in his coffin, wearing a funeral headscarf painted with magical charms.

Funeral procession. The Tiger, dressed in white, helps lower the coffin. Mai, in white, kneels behind the coffin with her palms together in prayer position. Quang, also in white, can be seen behind the Tiger, bowing in prayer.

Quang, age 36, and Mai, visiting a seaside temple in Vung Tau, before he escapes from Vietnam. Mai doesn't know he is planning to escape.

Photograph that Mai sent to the refugee camp in Thailand, where Quang stayed from 1987 to 1989.

After that hole, my father led me into a crack between two rocks. We walked sideways for a while. I wondered how likely it would be for the two faces of rock to squeeze me to death.

At the end of the crack, my father started climbing up another hole. He was waiting for me at the top of the hole. He said the chamber where Fourth Uncle sat was just a short way from there.

My father blew out both candles before going into the chamber. He told me to follow him, but I couldn't see a thing. I tried to catch up to him and banged my knee very hard. I had to follow the sound of my father's breathing and the sounds he made as he moved over the rocks. The chamber was long and curved one way and then the other. After a few minutes, I heard my father talking softly in the darkness. I began to see the shapes of the rocks.

The chamber ceiling was high enough for me to stand. The floor was covered with big rocks, pebbles, and grit. It felt wet in some places. I followed the voices until I saw the shapes of two men sitting face to face on a long flat shelf of rock. I climbed up and sat next to my father. The air smelled like flowers.

I heard Fourth Uncle's voice. It sounded quiet but very clear, like a strong man.

My father said, "This is my son, Quang."

Fourth Uncle reached toward me and put his hand on my head and looked at me for about one second. His touch felt as sturdy as a tree. His fingernails were much longer than my father's.

He said, "All right, let him stay with me, and I will teach him."

Fourth Uncle shut his eyes and became as still as stone. We left without saying good-bye or thank you.

On the way back to Tam Buu Tu I tried to get my father to change his mind about sending me to live in the cave. I tried to convince him that I had learned my lesson and that I would never think about sorcery again. I told him that I would study medicine all day long, every day, and I would work nights and weekends for him in the clinic, just as long as he wouldn't send me to live in the cave.

When we got back to Tam Buu Tu my father gave me a lot of money to spend for fun during the next three weeks. He told me to go the shops and eat a lot.

I didn't see Grenade at all during those weeks, but I did go to visit Ong Chin and Lead Lips. My friends were sad that I had to go.

37

CAVE

Before leaving me in Fourth Uncle's chamber, my father took the things that he had brought for me out of his medicine bag and put them on a rock. We hadn't spoken much to one another most of the way up the mountain and through the cave. He knew I didn't want to be here, and I knew he wanted me to. He said he would be back in two months to visit.

At that moment I hated my father.

I sat on a rock and watched my father's dark shape fade into darkness. It would take him about an hour to get out of the cave. Later on, I realized that I should have followed him out, but by then it was too late.

He had prepared a special kind of food for me. He pan-roasted some dehydrated rice and some peanuts until they became golden, and then he ground it up and added sesame seeds and cane sugar. He said that if I ate two tablespoons of that meal and drank two cups of water with it, I would not feel hungry for a whole day.

Everything he brought for me was wrapped in a monk's tunic that was coarse and thick. I found a pair of pants, the pound sack of meal, another pound sack of dehydrated rice, and a small pouch of rock salt. My hands searched for his knife, but he didn't leave it for me. I found a kerosene lighter and a bundle of incense. That was all.

I sat on the rock for a long time. I didn't want to be there. I wished I had followed my father out of the cave and gone back to my friends. I didn't want to talk to the teacher. I just stayed on my rock.

When I got tired of sitting, I tried to lie down but I couldn't get comfortable, because the rock was too small and round. I tried curling up on my side so I wouldn't fall off the rock. I lay there clinging to the rock and thinking about my friends in Xa Ba Chuc, Anh Thiep, Anh The, and Anh Muoi, Lieu and Kam, Ong Nam and Chi, Ong Chin and Lead Lips, and the old men. My life had been taken away from me and my father had buried me alive inside a tomb of rocks.

My father didn't tell me where to pee. I rolled off my rock and began feeling my way around the chamber. I wondered if I would be stepping on the bones of the three other hermits who meditated in this chamber before Fourth Uncle.

Some of the rocks felt wet and others felt dry; it was the same with the floor. I peed in a dry place at the edge of the chamber as far away from Fourth Uncle as possible. Then I followed the wet spots on the floor until I found a pool of water. It tasted fresh and cool.

I started to stretch and work out. I hadn't practiced martial arts for about two months, since I was sick. Too bad I didn't have a stick to work on my stick form.

I looked at the ceiling for some kind of branch or piece of wood. The ceiling was just about a foot over my head and had a lot of twisted and tangled roots coming through, but none of them seemed to be growing straight.

I looked for a more comfortable rock. I tried a lot of them until I found one that was long and smooth and dry. I moved my belongings over to that rock, and then I lay down and went to sleep.

When I woke up, I didn't know how long I'd slept, or whether it was day or night. It occurred to me that day didn't exist now. It was going to be night all the time. I thought that my father was punishing me, because I had caused him so much trouble, practically getting us both killed by sorcery.

I made my way toward Fourth Uncle to ask him what he wanted me to do. His gray form seemed to hover like a cloud above the floor of the chamber, because he sat on a high platform of rock jutting out of the wall. There seemed to be more light around him than in any other place in the chamber.

I climbed up to his shelf and sat diagonally in front of him in the same spot I sat before. The flower smell was there again. He didn't open his eyes. He was at least as big as my father. He looked like the oldest man I ever saw, but his face wasn't weak, it was strong-looking, like his body. His cheeks were fleshy and pink. He had a thin white beard, and his hair was pinned up with a stick. Some of it had broken off and hung down the sides of his face. His grayish clothing was full of holes, and had unraveled up to his knees and elbows.

I placed my palms together in the prayer position and bowed my head. "I don't know what to do, Uncle," I said, trying to make my words as short as possible.

I waited for him to speak as he did with my father, but he didn't. Not one single hair on his beard moved. He was completely ignoring me, which made me confused and even more mad.

I wasn't hungry, but there was nothing to do, so I went back to my rock and looked for a spot that could hold water so I could soak some dehydrated rice.

I discovered that one of the rocks near my rock had several egg-sized holes in the surface. I put some rice into the holes and I went to get some water. It took several trips, since I had to walk so slowly; a lot of the water had dripped out of my hands before I reached the rice. I was angry at my father for not packing me a cup.

The rice had to soak for about twenty minutes. I decided to go swimming in the pool. I took off my clothes and slid silently into the still black water. The echoes of the water lapping against the rocks made a clear melodious sound. I swam in every direction to find out how large the pool was. It was shaped like a banana, about ten feet long and waist deep. The bottom was sandy.

When I went back to eat my rice, I couldn't find it. I searched the rocks all around my rock, but it was gone. I had to start all over again, but this time I stayed with my rice until it was soft, then I ate it.

I thought that Fourth Uncle had changed his mind about me. Maybe he didn't like me because I did sorcery. I went back and sat by him for a long time, but he treated me the same way, as if I didn't exist. I thought, "Even people who did bad, like Lead Lips and Grenade, treated me better than Fourth Uncle."

I was so frustrated that I went back to my rock and took out my lighter, some sticks of incense, and some food and began feeling for a way out of the chamber. I found more than one opening, but I tried to choose the one my father had used. Once I was away from Fourth Uncle, I lit a stick of incense and could finally see shapes and shadows.

My spirit felt happy, because I had decided to leave the cave and go back to Tam Buu Tu and be with my friends. I crawled and slid over the rocks for about twenty minutes hoping I would see the hole that went straight down, but I couldn't find it. I ended up in a chamber that was almost as large as Fourth Uncle's chamber. I was afraid there might be someone else meditating in there, so I left right away. I went back in search of that hole and realized that I must have taken a wrong turn, or maybe I had missed a turn. I had no idea where I was or how to get back to Fourth Uncle. After searching for hours, I ended up back in the chamber with Fourth Uncle by a different way. I was hungry and exhausted. I went to sleep on my rock.

I slept until I felt rested and I ate until I felt full. I went again to Fourth Uncle to ask him what I should do. Again he ignored me, so I tried to leave the cave a second time. This time I left stones behind to mark the places I had been. A single stone meant I could get back to the chamber that way, double stones meant come back later and explore, and three stones meant don't bother to go back this way.

The passageways were beginning to look familiar. I went back and forth climbing in and out of many holes and tunnels, but again, I couldn't find the hole I was looking for. It seemed that the longer I searched, the more openings I found. I searched until I was exhausted, and then I went back to my rock to sleep.

When I woke up the next time, I didn't even bother to go to Fourth Uncle. I went for a swim and ate some food and then I went back into the tunnels. I started to feel like a lizard and a frog and a rat, pulling myself over rocks on my belly, hopping from place to place, and poking my head into cracks.

Sometimes I came back to my rock to sleep and sometimes I slept wherever I was, hoping that I was almost outside the cave. I had found three places in the cave where I could get water. Sometimes I heard animals in the distance, but I never saw them. My incense didn't light anymore, because it was too damp, but I found that I could see well enough without it. I went over to Fourth Uncle from time to time, but he was never responsive.

I estimated the passage of time by how many long stretches of sleep I took. At the end of what I thought was two weeks, I was tired of looking for a way out of the cave, and I was sick of eating that peanut meal. I was so wound up that I went to Fourth Uncle and said, "Since you didn't accept me as your student, I want to go back to my temple today."

Then Fourth Uncle spoke. He didn't open his eyes, but he said, "Go ahead."

I said, "Could you please show me the way out?"

Without opening his eyes he said, "Just try to relax and then sit."

"But I need to go out. My food makes me feel sick." I said.

"Sit and you will find food," was all he said.

I didn't know what he meant, but at least he had spoken to me. I did what he said. I went back to my rock and sat down. Then I picked up my bag of rice. Something was wrong; the bag was empty. There was a hole at the bottom. I checked the bag of meal and found that it was the same. I was frantic. My father had given me enough food to last two months. Now, after just two weeks, it was gone.

I sat on my rock and waited for some food to appear. I thought he was going to make some by magic. I waited a long time and no food appeared.

I went back and told him, "Excuse me, Fourth Uncle, but I still have no food to eat."

He just said the same thing he had said before, "When you sit and relax, you will find food."

Then I realized what he meant. I went back to my rock and started to meditate. I meditated for about forty minutes. Then I got up and stretched and went swimming. I meditated again, but still no food appeared.

Just then I saw a mouse standing on my rock. It was shaking its head back and forth as if it was laughing at me. I picked up a rock and tried to kill it, but the rock bounced back and hit me in the forehead. That did it!

I just took off without any food. I crept through the tunnels, combing the rocks for the passageway that I hadn't seen before. I searched for many days without food until I ran out of strength. I dragged myself to my rock and drifted in and out of sleep. I felt cold. Eventually I couldn't move my arms or lift my legs. The mice were running over my body, looking inside my pockets and inside my clothes, but I didn't care. I didn't even care that I was dying, "Why should I?" I thought. "Nobody else does."

I must have fallen unconscious. The next thing I was aware of was swallowing some food. I opened my eyes and saw Fourth Uncle standing next to me. He reached up and took something off the ceiling. He said, "There was food around you all the time."

He put an oval root into my hand. It was no bigger than my big toe. I bit into it and found it to be crunchy and refreshing and just a little sweet. The energy started coming back into my body so fast that I wanted to sit up after just a few minutes. My mind felt clear.

Fourth Uncle said, "Now you can take better care of yourself."

I was so surprised at how quickly I had recovered my strength that I was speechless. I just looked at Fourth Uncle. He nodded.

He said, "Just relax and feel good. Imagine the warm energy from the sun streaming in through the crown of your head. Imagine the cool energy from the underground spring bubbling up through your perineum. These opposite forces will blend together in your body and balance your energy."

I knew he was talking about meditation.

"Do that for two weeks and then come to see me."

I folded my arms across my chest, bowed politely, and said, "Yes, Uncle."

I spent the next days swimming, relaxing, practicing martial arts, and practicing what Fourth Uncle told me. I sat cross-legged as he did and held my hands facing upward in my lap, thumbs touching together. I imagined the light of heaven bright inside my body and the cool water bubbling up from the rocks, quenching a deep thirst and protecting my body. I didn't think about leaving the cave anymore. I stopped craving food and found that all I needed to eat was one of those egg-shaped roots every two or three days.

After meditating and relaxing in the cave for about a week, I felt like visiting Fourth Uncle. I climbed up to his rock and said, "Uncle, I have been enjoying my time in the cave." I thought he would be happy with me, but he didn't move. I looked at him for a long time. He didn't look right; he looked stiff. I tapped his shoulder. It felt as if I was knocking on a wooden door. I tried lifting his arm, but it was as rigid as a corpse. I wasn't sure if he was dead. The idea made me scared, because I was afraid of ghosts and I didn't think he liked me very much. If he were dead, I wouldn't be able to get out of the cave until my father came back for me. If my father died, too, I would be stuck inside there forever.

38

FRIENDS ON THE MOUNTAIN

climbed down from Fourth Uncle's shelf and went back to my rock. I was too nervous to meditate, but I remembered something my father had told me. He said that when someone has meditated as long as Fourth Uncle has, his physical body changes. He becomes strong like a tree, and his soul can go in and out. He said that someone like Fourth Uncle can climb into a cave or into a hollow tree and leave his body there for a long time and then come back. His body will not rot.

I went back and put my hand under Fourth Uncle's nose and felt some warm air moving.

I returned to my routine of meditating, exploring the cave, swimming, and relaxing. I kept going back to his rock to check to see if he was back. When he finally opened his eyes, he said, "Quang, I told you two weeks. Do not come and ask me anything before then. You must let me practice." He was looking straight ahead.

I bowed and told him I was sorry.

He asked, "How is it going?

"Very well, Uncle," I said. "I have experience with meditation. When I lived in the temple I meditated a lot."

"Did you think about something?"

"I prayed to Buddha that I am sorry for all the bad things I did before, and I asked him to heal me and make me strong."

Fourth Uncle said, "That is no good."

He turned his head in my direction and looked at me. "From now on, you must not pray or chant when you meditate. Praying and chanting is grasping for something you want."

I was thinking that Ong Nam had taught me different.

Fourth Uncle said, "From now on, you must follow what I say. Keep everything quiet inside. Close the doors in every direction and do not let any thoughts come in."

Fourth Uncle stopped talking, but he was still looking at me. I nodded that I understood. He tapped the middle of his brow and said, "Focus your attention here, on your third eye, and continue as I told you before. Draw the yin and yang energies into your body."

"Yes, Uncle." I bowed.

"If you want to go outside and eat some food and make friends in the forest, you may go anytime you wish. If you are in trouble, your friends will help you. Go and have some fun with them, but don't talk with them. Just stay quiet inside."

"Please, Uncle, I don't know how to go out."

He pointed to one of the openings that I had been through many times. "Go that way."

"But teacher," I said, "I have been that way many times."

"Just go and you will find the way," he said. "Come back and talk to me in one month."

"How will I know when one month is up?"

"I will let you know," he said, then added, "You can know the weather outside by feeling the rocks. When the rocks feel wet and warm, it means it is a rainy day. When they are dry and cool, that means it is a clear day."

I touched the rocks, but I wasn't sure.

"They are dry and cool," Fourth Uncle said.

I climbed through the opening Fourth Uncle had indicated. I knew it well; I had been through it between twenty and thirty times, but this time I chose the wrong turn only once. I reached the jungle in forty-five minutes.

After that, I went out every day. I climbed a lot of trees and picked some fruit to eat, but I found that I wasn't able to eat more than a few bites.

That disappointed me, because the fruit tasted so good that I wanted to eat a lot more.

I found a lot of monkeys sitting in a tamarind tree. I climbed up their tree to play, but they moved to the next tree. When I climbed the next tree, they moved back to the tamarind tree.

I threw a ripe guava I had in my pocket for them to catch and eat, but I hit one of them by mistake. They got mad and started throwing tamarinds at me. I forgot not to talk, and I yelled at them.

The wolves were the first animals to approach me. I was sitting on a pile of stones not knowing I was near their den. They went in and out, observing me for a few days, before coming over to sit with me. I tried to pet them, but they always stayed about three feet away.

I found the leopard cats' den, too. They let me pet them and play with their kittens.

Close by, there was a bat cave where I saw thousands of bats hanging upside down from the roots of the ceiling. I don't know why, but they all hung in the center of the cavern over a crevasse that was so deep that I could not see the bottom. I think they could go out of the cave by flying down the hole. Since they all slept over the hole, the floor of the cavern was clean, and I could sit and watch them. They were as small as mice. I liked to see them wake up in the evening and fly out of the cave, covering the sky in a soft, dark blanket. Large bats also lived on the mountain, but I never found their cave.

Sometimes when I was in the forest after dark, I heard voices. I heard them so often that I felt like I knew them, a young girl, a woman, and an old man. They talked and laughed a lot together. I couldn't make out their exact words, but I could hear that they were speaking in Vietnamese. They told funny stories and made up poems. The girl liked to sing, and the woman and old man applauded. I tried many times to sneak up and get a look at them, but their voices always stayed the same distance away from me, about twenty feet.

I wasn't afraid of them because I knew they weren't ghosts. Ghosts can also speak in a pleasant voice but their energy is always heavy and unsettling. I felt happy around these people. I once asked Fourth Uncle how I could see them, but he said I wouldn't be able to, because they were too far away. When I asked how far, he said farther than I could imagine.

Every night I went back my cave to sleep on my rock.

One day I thought about going back to Tam Buu Tu to visit my friends. I left the next morning at sunrise.

. . .

It took a lot longer than I had expected, five hours to walk straight down the mountain and four hours to walk around Long Mountain to Elephant Mountain and up to Tam Buu Tu. I arrived in the middle of the afternoon.

My friends were very happy to see me. They asked me what I was doing, so I told them my father had sent me to a school on the forbidden mountain. They said they had never heard of a school there. I explained that it was just one teacher, a meditation teacher. They asked why I couldn't stay with them and learn meditation in Xa Ba Chuc. I said my father made me go.

At dinner, Anh Thiep served me a big plate of rice, shrimp, and vegetables. I forced myself to eat most of it. Kam and Lieu joined us at our table in the anteroom. I stayed talking with my friends until the scribes were called away to the temple for the evening sutra. I went in, too, and prayed a lot. I prayed to be a good student with my new teacher, and I prayed that my father would be proud of me. I prayed to my grandfather to thank him for finding Fourth Uncle.

During tea, I sat with the old men. They were very surprised to hear that I was living on the forbidden mountain. They told me to be careful, because that mountain has a very strong spirit.

"You could get into trouble there," Ong Tu said.

Bald Ong Chin said, "You might see an enchanted cave. Many people have seen them. If you go inside one, you will never be able to speak again. There was a woman once who came here with her bus tour after they went to the forbidden mountain. She had lost her voice completely."

Ong Tu said, "She wrote that when she was walking up the trail on the forbidden mountain with her group, she saw a golden gate. She pointed it out to her group, but they didn't see anything but bushes. She walked over and stood beside it so they would see better. When she was near it, they couldn't see or hear her anymore. Then she went inside."

"Now that woman is a healer," Ong Sau the weaver said. "She went back a few times to try to find the cave again."

"But no one has ever seen it twice," Ong Tu said.

Bald Ong Chin warned, "Be careful. There are spirits on the forbidden mountain that can make you follow them to another world and then you can never come back."

"And Cambodians from Ta Lon hunt there. Some of them would like nothing more than to put your head on a stake," Ong Tu said.

"Or dig a hole and bury you up to your neck and gag you so you cannot cry out for help," Bald Ong Chin said.

"The good thing is that there is no war there," Ong Sau the weaver said. "No one can fire their guns on the forbidden mountain. They just don't go off."

"Powerful magic," they all agreed.

Curfew sounded. I watched the others set up the mosquito nets for the visitors. After everyone went to bed, I went behind To Thay's throne and took a nap for about two hours, then started back to the cave. I arrived at dawn. My stomach had been hurting me all the way up the mountain. When I got near the cave, I emptied my bowels and then felt better. My body wasn't used to digesting food anymore.

Some days I didn't go outside at all, I just meditated and stretched and swam and slept. Sometimes I practiced martial arts in the cave.

I snuck up on Fourth Uncle many times. I wanted to catch him sleeping or eating or stretching, but every time I saw him he was sitting like a statue of Buddha. I remembered my father telling me that people who leave their bodies for a long time do not need to breathe with their lungs. They can absorb energy through the crown of the head.

I reached over and pinched Fourth Uncle's nose shut. I was waiting to see him open his mouth to take in air, but he didn't. I held his nose shut for a long time, so long that I had to change positions. He never parted his lips. Then I knew that the last time I had checked his breathing, he had started breathing normally only because he knew I was afraid he was dead.

39

TIGER SPIRIT

The day before my father came, my friends, the mice and squirrels and fire lizards in the cave, seemed more playful than usual. Later on, that was the way I knew when my father was coming. The fire lizards never opened their gills inside the cave, but outside when their gills were open, they looked as if bright orange flames were shooting out on either side of their heads.

My father found me inside the cave. He gave me a hug and then he squeezed the center of my palm with his thumb. I knew he was checking the eighth point of the pericardium meridian, but I don't know what he was checking for. He might have been finding out how much I had been meditating.

"How is it going?" he asked.

"Good," I said. "I didn't like it at first, but now I do."

"That is good; just keep trying. Do you ever go outside?"

"Yes," I said. "A lot."

"What do you do?"

"I exercise, climb trees, eat food, stay with my friends," I said.

"Did you ever go back to Tam Buu Tu to visit?"

I didn't answer right away, I was considering if I should tell him. "Yes, one time," I said.

"Did you walk or take the bus?"

"I walked."

"How was that?"

"Long," I said.

"How often does Fourth Uncle teach you?"

"Not a lot. First he said two weeks, now he said to come back in one month."

"That is good," my father said.

My father brought me some cookies, sweet rice cakes, more dehydrated rice and peanut mixture, fruit, and rock salt. I took the food, but I said I didn't need it now. I would give it to my friends. My father was happy. He said it was better not to eat anything except the roots in the cave; otherwise, he said, I would have to leave the cave just to poop.

My father went to another part of the chamber and took a rest while I meditated.

He told me he wanted to show me something outside. He took me out another way. We walked about two hours from the cave to a place where it was very rocky and there were many cliffs. He took a banana-leaf package out of his medicine bag and unwrapped it. Inside was a slab of meat.

My father put the meat down on a big rock and called out, "Tuan Quan, come and eat." Then we hid in some bushes about twenty feet from the rock. We sat there quietly for about ten minutes. A huge tiger came and carried the meat away.

"Tuan Quan will let you know when you must hide from the hunters. He will go to a small cave and made a deep sound three times that you can hear almost anywhere on the mountain. You will see the deer, pigs, and wolves running for cover, and you must do the same. The Cambodian hunters who come here do not like us. They wouldn't dare to hurt us when we are together, but if they saw you here alone, they might do something very bad."

Hearing that from my father worried me and made me believe the old men in the temple were not exaggerating.

Before leaving, my father wanted to give me money. He took a stack of bills out of his bag.

He said, "Here, I brought this for you. It's five hundred dong, in case you need to buy anything."

I knew he was just testing me. I laughed at my father and said, "If I take it, what will I do with it here?"

"You can go to Chau Doc City and buy something," he said.

"I don't need money," I said, knowing that I had passed all of his tests.

I walked with my father partway to the temple, where he was going to visit his friends. We hugged and parted ways. He said he'd be back in a few months.

About ten days later Fourth Uncle opened his eyes and said, "How's it going?"

"Good, Uncle," I bowed.

"Did anything happen?"

"Yes. My third eye felt itchy and then I saw a bright light start shining like a star."

He said, "That star will come and go. Don't let it distract you. What else did you see?"

I said confidently, "Heavenly colors. And there was a presence like an angel to my left side, like a warm yellow glow. It made me feel very peaceful and happy. I tried to follow it to find Buddha. And then I met some people who were carrying a big lotus. They laid it at my feet. They told me to sit down, and it would take me to heaven."

He said, "No, no, that's not good. Go back and try again. Don't care about what you see. Just shut the door on it."

Ong Nam had taught me that if I see the color yellow I should follow it, because it will lead me to Buddha. He said that if I should see a lot of monks sitting around a master, I should join them and learn. Fourth Uncle taught me just the opposite: Anything you see while meditating is not good because as long as we cling to our world, the next world cannot come in.

Fourth Uncle taught me how to circulate my breath by pulling the air slowly into my nose from a particular spot about three feet in front of me. He said to imagine the air was flowing in an upward arch into my nose. Then he said to think of the air going through my lungs to my navel and from there to my perineum, and then up my spine into the crown of my head. He said to leave my attention at the crown of my head while exhaling through my nose. He said to do that with every breath.

"Come back in one month," he said. "Remember, if you see something, don't see it. Close the door on it."

I meditated a lot after that, sometimes five times a day for two hours at a time. One time I had just started meditating about two minutes when a bright light appeared shining through my eyelids. I shielded my eyelids, and the light didn't change. Then I realized it was coming from inside my head.

I tried not to look at the shining star. I remembered Ong Nam telling me that if I started seeing a star, I should gaze at it. I did that just a little, because I was curious to see what Ong Nam had seen, and then saw a glimpse of a beautiful garden. I didn't let myself see more because Fourth Uncle didn't want me to.

I worked a lot on my meditation. Sometimes I didn't leave the cave for an entire week, but I did go to Tam Buu Tu see my friends again, two more times.

When Fourth Uncle opened his eyes again he said, "Where were you those two nights you didn't sleep in the cave?

I said, "I slept outside on the high cliff."

Fourth Uncle said, "Don't say things like that like or you will carry guilt."

I didn't say anything.

"It's okay," he said. "But next time tell me first."

"I will," I said.

"How is it going?"

"Good," I said.

I told Fourth Uncle that the star was still there sometimes, but that I didn't pay any attention to it. He was pleased. He said I was ready to stop thinking about circulating my breath and drawing the yin and yang energies into my body. He said it would happen on its own.

"Do you want to do well as my student?" he asked.

"Yes, very much," I answered.

"Why?" he asked.

A lot of thoughts came into my mind. I wanted to be powerful like my father and help many people. I wanted ghosts and monsters to fear and obey me. I wanted my father and my ancestors to be proud of me. I wanted to have a lot of students and patients who loved me. I wanted to have a motorcycle and a beautiful cement house.

"I want to do well for my father," I said.

"You've got to clean that up," Fourth Uncle said. "If you want to make your father happy, you will fail. If you need people to love and respect you, you are wasting your time. You must empty yourself of these desires, otherwise nothing new will be able to come in."

I was thinking that I didn't know if I could stop caring about love and respect.

"And remember," he said, "stay empty. Come and see me in three months."
When he finished speaking he turned back into a statue.

I stayed sitting on his rock for a long time.

Winter was cold on the mountain, damp, foggy and windy. When I went outside, the cool water would drip from my face, and my clothes stayed damp. In winter, the mist seeped into the cave and made all the rocks cold and wet. Fourth Uncle taught me some chi kung exercises to strengthen my body and keep me warm. The movements looked like tai chi chuan, slow movements that follow the breath. I did them in a cross-legged position.

You have to hold the inbreath and the outbreath a long time while you circle one arm and then the other while twisting at the waist. I was to do that for about half an hour each time. This practice warmed my body, increased my chi, or internal energy, and made the muscles of my arms and legs feel strong like a tree. I eventually learned how to sleep, meditate, and exercise while seated in a cross-legged position.

Fourth Uncle liked to teach me about the weather. He told me to meditate outside and feel the differences in the air. He said you can know a lot of things from feelings in the air, like danger.

Good weather was the most dangerous time on the mountain, because it was when the hunters came to the mountain. They didn't go very high up, but stayed on the lower part. They knew by experience that by the time they reached halfway up the mountain, all the animals knew they were there and had gone to hide.

Sometimes I ran with the pigs. When it was time for the pigs to move on, I always heard a very human-sounding voice call out, "ow . . . ow . . . ow . . ." I tried to see which one was the leader but I could never tell.

The pigs weren't afraid to let me touch them, and they touched me a lot. Sometimes when I laid down to rest after running for a long while with them, they would nudge me over with their snouts to look for food. They never hurt me with their tusks.

I watched the same herd for so long that I could recognize every pig, but I never once saw which one made that sound. I once asked my father about it and he said, "The master of the pigs is not a pig, it is a spirit."

I was with the wild pigs the first time I heard Tuan Quan's warning for everyone to hide. It sounded as if he had put his head into an echo chamber and made three long humming sounds. It was deep and penetrating, a feeling as well as a sound, like tremors in the earth.

When the pigs heard it they took off faster than ever. There was no way I could keep up with them. I hid inside some thick bushes. Fifteen minutes later I saw the hunters, carrying their bows and poison spears and arrows.

The Cambodians knew more than anyone about poison. They used snake poison to kill the animals and then used another kind of poison to neutralize the poison in the meat. I met some Cambodians at Tam Buu Tu who showed me how to make very good medicine to neutralize the poison from any kind of snake, scorpion, or insect.

In late summer during rainy season, there were so many centipedes and other poisonous caterpillars that I didn't go out much. One night, I came across a solid green-glowing carpet of poison a hundred feet across. I had to sleep out in the jungle that night, because there was no way to go around it.

I discovered that not all green-glowing carpets were poison centipedes. There is a kind of moss that glows in the dark and is safe to walk on, but it is difficult to know the difference at night.

Rainy season was my least favorite time on the mountain because of the insects and the scorpions. Back home in Cai Mon, scorpions were about the size of your finger, but here on the forbidden mountain they looked like black lobsters. During rainy season, they came out a lot. Even worse were the many different kinds of caterpillars. The caterpillars' fur was also covered with poison powder. They would come out of nowhere and crawl up your leg.

There were many interesting things to do on the other side of the mountain. I used to climb the highest cliffs so I could look out over the land. Those cliffs took five hours to reach.

Many old hermits meditated there. They sat on the rocks in the wind and rain. Sometimes they sat under a little shelf of rock. Some of them opened their eyes and nodded to me, but they never spoke. I never saw two of them together. They needed to be alone. Since they kept moving to different places, I never knew where or when I was going to run into one of them. Usually I saw them on the cliffs when I was climbing trees.

My father and Fourth Uncle told me to stay away from them, because I could cost them many months in their progress. They looked to be from different religions. Some shaved their heads and faces, and some had long white hair and beards. They all wore prayer beads around their necks, and orange or yellow monk's robes that were faded and torn to shreds.

There were some cracks in the face of the cliff that were so narrow that I couldn't put my arm in past my shoulder, but these hermits could go inside. If they knew I was coming, they would disappear into the cracks. I would see something like pale orange flame flying into crack, and I heard a sound like a gust of wind. I would go over and feel the place where they were sitting, and it would still be warm. It looked as if they knew how to turn into wind and fire. In my wanderings, I saw about twenty hermits, but there were probably many more.

One time after it had rained, I was going back to the cave from the cliffs when I noticed enormous tiger prints heading back the other way. That was when I realized that the tiger spirit, Tuan Quan, sometimes followed me when I went to where the hermits were. I think he wanted to protect them.

40

SOUL BABY

was having a difficult time meditating without concentrating on my breath. I didn't think the energy was circulating by itself, because I no longer felt the energy creeping up my spine like small ants. I sat on my rock and slammed the doors on all my thoughts, feelings, and visions, but it wasn't easy to have nothing on which to focus my attention. I found myself falling asleep.

I started having a recurring dream about a beautiful place where the people, animals, and plants were lovelier than in real life. The animals were tame and the people were very kind to me, especially the children, who took me around in a boat that glided along the water by magic. Everyone wore colorful silk clothing. There was a beautiful temple made of glistening gold and jewels. The gardens were abundant with fruit and flowers. I played a lot of games with the children and ate the most delicious food I had ever tasted. It was the perfect place for me. I thought, "Now I don't have to go outside the cave anymore to relax. I can meditate more often."

I thought Fourth Uncle would be happy.

When the three months were up, I told my teacher that now when I fell asleep during meditation, I relaxed in paradise and woke up feeling refreshed as if I had been outside.

He said, "You went very wrong. Now I will have to teach you again. If you keep dreaming like that, you will go away to that place and never come back."

He told me to start over and come to see him in three months. During the next three months my friends tried to keep me from falling asleep. They crawled up my arms and legs and tickled me when I meditated. They bit me sometimes, too.

I started going out of the cave again to go exploring. Even though it was a five-hour walk, I liked to go to other side of the mountain to the cliffs. I had so much energy, and felt so weightless, I could have run all the way there. I started jumping into trees by doing a high backward flip and hooking my feet around a branch and hoisting myself up.

I liked to climb trees that grew on top of the cliffs so that I could look down at the water and land spreading out in three directions. I could see farms, houses, roads, and tiny specks that were boats. People were barely big enough to see. I wasn't part of the world any longer. I was like a god looking down from a cloud.

It was on the other side of the mountain where I first tasted angel food, *dao tien*. Angel food grows on one of the tallest and broadest trees in the forest. There were no branches near the base of the trunk so it was impossible to climb, but I had discovered a tree growing at the bottom of a cliff. I could climb up the rocks and grab hold of a branch and pull myself into the tree. I wasn't able to eat the angel food in the tree, because it was inside a hard case like a coconut. I had to throw it down and hope that a pig didn't steal it. Angel food is their favorite food, too.

I split it open with a rock. You would think that for such a huge tree and such a huge shell there would be more to eat than three small creamy balls the size of eyeballs, but that's all you get. Angel food is very rare; the tree only produces fruit once every two or three years.

There was another tree I liked to sit in; it was a *cay me* tree. I would crave its delicious fruit, which is small and tastes sweet and sour. These kind of trees have thin branches, but they are very strong and do not snap even when they are dead. There was one *cay me* tree that was growing on top of a pinnacle of rock at the edge of a cliff. I knew this particular tree very well because it had the best view. Since a lot of the fruit was still green, I had to climb to the outermost branches to get the ripe fruit. I held on to the branch above me and walked along a limb to the fruit.

I don't know why, but the branch I was standing on bent suddenly downward. I lost my footing and hung onto the branch above. I lost my grip and fell straight down about thirty feet, landing on the side of my rib cage, pinned between the fork of two branches. It hurt too much to move or cry. It was painful enough just to breathe. All I could do was hang limply sideways by my rib cage. There was nothing beneath me but the forest canopy that looked like a carpet of moss. I was afraid to try to pry myself out from between the branches because if I fell, I would meet my death.

I stayed like that all day. I moved my chi through my torso to ease the pain and heal my injury as I had done many times before when I had banged my knee or sprained my ankle, but I didn't get much relief. I prayed a lot. By evening I lost consciousness.

When I woke up, I was back inside the cave with Fourth Uncle, inside a different chamber.

"How did I get here?"

"I got you here."

"How did you know?"

"I know."

"I could have died."

"Not really."

He gave me the same root food to eat.

He meditated next to me, and I slept for about two days. Then I could walk. My ribs still hurt, but not too bad.

Fourth Uncle told me that a soul egg had traveled up from my navel to the crown of my head. He said that it was gestating there. He explained that every time I circulated my breath to my crown, I was bathing the egg with the energy it needed to grow and mature. In a year or so, it would be fully developed, and then it would hatch from the top of my crown. (You can find your crown point by tracing a line straight up from the tips of your ears to the tender spot in the middle.)

About thirteen months later, the top of my head started feeling tingly and itchy. Once, when I was meditating, I felt a sensation like ants crawling up my back and neck. I heard a loud sound, like a bang. I felt the top of my head blow open and I felt the air going in and out. Then I felt myself standing up.

I turned around and saw myself sitting on my rock with my eyes closed. I was shocked to see how small and dirty and ugly I looked.

I told Fourth Uncle about it and he said, "Congratulations. You have given birth to your soul body. It is young and doesn't know what to do yet. You can let it out by concentrating on your crown. You can also keep it in, by focusing on your third eye. Don't let it out that much. Keep circulating the energy the same way as before."

I told him I still felt the air going in and out the top of my head. He said that was good and to come back in three months.

Fourth Uncle said he was going to show me some things on the mountain because I had worked a long time and had made good progress. I followed him and we were out of the cave in no time. I didn't understand how we got out so fast.

Walking with Fourth Uncle was just like walking with my father. When my father took a delegation of twenty monks and students to visit the temples in the Seven Mountains, you would always see the others straggling behind him on the mountain trails.

In the daylight, I could see Fourth Uncle much better. He looked like a robust ninety-year-old man with ruddy, plump cheeks. His frame was strong and muscular, and he moved lightly over the rocky terrain. His white hair was silky and beautiful, as if he took loving care of it. His clothing looked as if it had once been black. His shirt had faded to gray and his pants to purple. They were both so tattered and dusty and full of holes that I expected them to have a smell, but they didn't. I had spied on my teacher many times out of curiosity until I had tired myself out and had never seen him doing anything except sit like a statue in his spot. I never saw him eat, drink, sleep, lay down, bathe, or urinate.

I kept up with him for about an hour, until he stopped in front of some bushes and told me I could enter another cave behind them. He motioned for me to go in. I crawled through the opening into a spacious chamber. It looked as if someone had lived there long ago. There were old rush mats on the floor that were worn in many places from use. Some old pottery lay broken in a corner. I looked around for other rooms, but the passageways were too narrow. When I came out, I was dirty.

Fourth Uncle wasn't there waiting for me. I sat down and waited. I thought maybe he went into the bushes and would come back. I didn't know if it was all right to call him, but I did. I called out, "Uncle, where are you?"

I waited for him for about ten minutes, then I went looking for him. I didn't know if I should stay waiting for him or go back to the cave. In the meantime I found a really good mango tree and I climbed up to get some. From up in the tree, I saw Fourth Uncle sitting on top of a rock formation. There were no branches or roots or places in the rock where someone could climb up. I wanted to call to him from the tree, but it was too far away.

I climbed down and found my way to the rock formation. It was so high that I could not see all the way up to the top. I called up to him, "Uncle, how can I get up?" There was no answer. I went back and climbed the mango tree again to get a better look at where he was sitting. I tried again and walked all around the rock formation looking for a way to get up, but there was no place to step. I went back to the tree and watched and waited for him to climb down.

I waited in the tree for about an hour, and then I saw him stand up and do some of the exercises he had taught me. I raced down the tree and over to the rock formation and I called out again, "Uncle, how can I climb up?"

I heard him talk. It sounded as if he was standing in back of me. "If you want to climb this rock, you have to go back to the cave and practice more."

I turned around to look behind me, and I didn't see him. I pleaded, "Uncle, can you please help me to climb up there?"

He said, "No." Again, his voice came from behind me. I turned around and saw him there.

Fourth Uncle started taking me outside once every three months. The next time he asked me if I wanted to see a tiger's cave. I told him I did.

We walked about two hours to the edge of a cliff. He said that I would be able to climb down to the cave. I was nervous, because the tops of the trees were about fifty feet below the cliff. I wondered how the tigers could climb down such a steep place.

The cave wasn't very big. I couldn't imagine very many tigers could live in there. It was clean, and there was no smell. I didn't notice any tiger hair or animal bones. When I turned to go out, I saw Fourth Uncle standing at the entrance to the cave. He told me to go ahead and climb back up the rock wall. When I got back he was already at the top.

I asked him how he did that and he said, "It is easy. If you practice for a long time, you will also know how."

He showed me other caves. He always waited outside. One of them looked like a royal palace with four furnished rooms that were clean and bright. There were carpets and vases of fresh flowers and bowls of fruit, and several gold statues of Buddha. It smelled like freshly brewed coffee. There were incense sticks in the holders, but they weren't lit, and baskets of rice, corn, sea salt, and mung beans. There were chairs and tables inlaid with mother-of-pearl and a large bed with red silk pillows and curtains.

When I came out I asked, "Does someone live in there?"

"Yes."

"But I didn't see anybody."

"A lot of people live there, but they won't let you see them."

"Would it be okay if I took some food?"

"No. If you take something, you will not be able get out."

Fourth Uncle told me I must forget the cave and never describe exactly what I saw inside to anyone. That is why I didn't tell you everything I saw.

I don't know very much about that cave and who lived there, because I learned not to ask too many questions. When I did, Fourth Uncle would tell me that I was thinking too much and burning up my energy. He said it would set me back in my progress.

After a while my mind started quieting down. I just looked at the places he showed me and said, "Oh, very beautiful," or, "This makes me feel happy," and then I would try not to think about it anymore.

Once I found a cave on my own. There was a waterfall inside and a deep pool. I started going there often to swim and sit under the waterfall. I went exploring and found another room that had a large stone Buddha, larger than me, with a green, glowing stone in its third eye. The stone looked like a shrew stone, but it was very large and oval-shaped and smooth.

There were nice polished stones under the waterfall, and many kinds of stones all over the floor of that cave. I started taking stones out of that cave each time I went, and I put them in the drawstring bag my father had filled with peanut meal. I found quartz crystals, polished white and orange stones, green stones that looked like jade, gray stones as shiny as glass, and rough stones that were flecked with gold.

I tried to go back to the beautiful cave palace where people were living, but I could never find it on my own.

41

PRESIDENT THIEU'S WIFE

The top of my head stayed tingly for a few weeks. I let my soul body out once a day, but I had no control of where I went. Each time I felt as if I had been on a long journey, yet when I came back I thought only twenty minutes had passed, like a dream.

Once my soul body went to Tam Buu Tu, and I saw my friends inside the community building setting up the mosquito nets at curfew. I stepped on the nets, but they picked them up easily. I sat on the bed, but they didn't see me. I could hear what they were saying. I tried to talk to them, no words came out. The only sound I could make was a laugh, but they couldn't hear it. I felt like a dumb baby.

Some spirit people came for me and said, "Let's go." I went with them to a place that looked like paradise.

There were beautiful gardens, buildings, and temples where the people and animals were beautiful and friendly. Many children were playing team games, swimming, and climbing trees. I saw a procession of monks wearing yellow robes, and I joined them as they filed into a great hall of marble with many vases of flowers and incense that smelled like jasmine. I sat down on a plush carpet on a cushion and listened to their master's commentaries on the sutras. I didn't understand much of what the master was talking about.

The next time I saw Fourth Uncle, I told him about my soul traveling. He said, "You can go a little bit with the monks in the temple to hear them teach, but not every day. Don't go off with the kids to play and have fun, because you will lose energy and time."

Then he opened his eyes and turned to look at me. He said, "You need to practice more now, more than half a day every day, or else you will not have enough time to learn."

"Uncle, why do you say that? I live here, and I want to stay with you," I said.

"You will know later; you don't need to ask. Continue the same way. I am going to show you some more chi kung exercises to do."

These chi kung movements were done kneeling or standing. He demonstrated how to stand on my feet, so that only the balls and heels of my feet were touching the ground while I moved my torso and arms in various circular patterns that were designed to stimulate my inner organs. It hurt my feet to stand with the middle part off the ground. He told me to inhale and hold the breath until I felt a lot of heat and then exhale and hold until I had released all my intention. Besides nourishing and toning all the muscles and tendons of my body, these exercises were supposed to strengthen my heart, liver, spleen, lungs, and kidneys.

Fourth Uncle started teaching me magic charms to trace over water for people to drink. He didn't have a cup, so he traced the symbols over his hand for me to see. He said, "These charms are for healing. Another day I will show you the ones to trace over a person's body to protect them from danger." My heart leapt for joy. I had been waiting all my life to learn the charms my father used.

"Come back in two months."

"Two?" I asked.

He didn't answer. During those months, I tried not to think about what he meant about me not having enough time to learn.

I kept my attention on my third eye and didn't let my soul baby go out very often. I wanted to keep all my energy inside myself and not spread it too thin. I tried not to react to my thoughts and visions, no matter how real or appealing.

One time while meditating, I smelled the aroma of freshly brewed coffee, just like what I had smelled at the palace cave. I opened my eyes to take a peek. To my surprise, there was a table standing next to my rock, with a chair and tablecloth and platters of rice and vegetables and cake and sliced fruit and coffee. I thought it was a hallucination. I reached over to touch a slice of watermelon. It was solid and wet.

I picked up a piece of cake and took a bite. The flavor and texture flooded my senses. My mouth started watering and my stomach growled, but I remembered what Fourth Uncle told me, not to desire anything, not to pay attention to anything.

I took a few small bites, put the food down, and went back to my meditating. Every now and then, I cracked open my eyes to see if the table was still there, and it was. I tried not to think about it but my curiosity was very strong. I wanted to understand what made it come and whether it would go away.

When I finished meditating, the table of food was still there. I did some stretching and went for a swim. I didn't eat any more food. I took a nap, and when I woke up, it was gone.

The table and chair appeared again with a different food the next time I meditated. Again, I had a difficult time keeping it out of my mind. On the one hand, I was trying to keep my mind empty of thought, but on the other hand I wanted to learn how to control it.

The table of food sometimes appeared when I was out in the forest. I didn't eat any. I was satisfied with keeping my stomach empty and eating only one cave root every other day. I believed the table of food was there to test my willpower. I thought back on all the different kinds of distractions that Fourth Uncle told me to ignore. First it was my thoughts, then it was the star and the lotus flower, then I had visions of paradise, then I had lucid dreams of paradise, and then my soul traveled out of my body and went to paradise. Fourth Uncle wanted me to ignore those experiences. Now food was materializing and I had the willpower to resist it. I had passed the test. Now I could do magic like my father, magic without using an evil spirit helper.

When two months were up, I told Fourth Uncle about the table of food, about how I learned to make it appear or disappear.

"Did you eat much?" Fourth Uncle asked.

"No, I only tasted it once to see if it was real," I said.

"Good," he said. "Now you can enjoy some every now and then, but not too much."

I asked Fourth Uncle when I would learn to disappear like the monks on the cliffs.

"That comes after years and years. There are many stages in between," he said.

. . .

n the winter of 1972, my father came to the cave and told me he wanted me to come with him to Tam Buu Tu.

"Something wonderful is going to happen," he said excitedly. "I don't want you to miss it."

He explained the whole story on the way down the mountain to the road. He said, "A few weeks ago three army helicopters appeared in the sky, and they seemed to be heading straight for the temple. Everyone in the temple panicked and ran around in every direction, shouting out the names of their children. The helicopters landed right in the parking lot in front of the temple."

"What happened?" I couldn't understand why my father looked so happy.

"Soldiers came out of the helicopters. They didn't go anywhere. They just stood holding their rifles at attention."

I had to walk really fast to keep up with my father, because I didn't want to miss a word.

"It was President Thieu," my father said, "and his wife."

"The president came to Tam Buu Tu?" I said. "Did he come to pray?"

"No," my father said. "His wife wanted to tell Ba Bay about a dream she was having."

"What dream?" I asked.

"She dreamt she was all alone in the Gia Long Palace and was looking for something." My father explained, "The Gia Long Palace is a museum in Saigon."

"Oh," I said.

"Night after night, she dreamt she was walking down the marble corridors, past the wall hangings and vases and statues and display cases filled with jewels, but she never stopped to look at anything, because she needed to find something."

"Did Ba Bay know what it was?" I asked.

"Well," my father continued, "she finally found it. When she woke up, she told her husband that she wanted to go to the Gia Long Palace to see if it was really there. And it was."

"Ba, what was it? What did she find?"

"Don't you know?" he laughed.

I couldn't think of anything.

"It is something that belongs to Tam Buu Tu," my father hinted.

"I don't know, tell me," I begged.

"You will see today when it is returned," my father said.

When we reached the road I was surprised to see so many buses filled with people heading toward Elephant Mountain. We didn't have to wait more than a few minutes before a bus stopped to pick us up.

Xa Ba Chuc marketplace was crowded with people heading up the village road to the temple. My father started weaving between people, because he walks faster than anyone. I lost him in the crowd. I made my way up the road and saw that a large crowd had formed in front of the temple. Everyone was looking up at the sky.

I asked a man what was going on and he told me, "We are waiting to see President Thieu. He is coming in his helicopter."

"Why is he coming?" I asked.

The man looked at me as though I was crazy. "Don't you know the president's wife is bringing To Thay's throne back to Tam Buu Tu?"

"The throne!" I exclaimed. No wonder my father was so excited.

There must have been two thousand people there. I was surprised that so many people knew about To Thay's throne.

Ba Bay was happy to see me. She hugged me and then asked me to help serve the dinner. She seemed a little nervous. The president and his wife were going to be eating dinner in the anteroom with the village council members and other officials from Chau Doc City.

Three helicopters appeared in the sky like tiny flying ants. People started cheering. The helicopters landed in the parking lot, and the soldiers escorted the president and his wife to the front doors of Tam Buu Tu. On their way past the star trees, the president and his wife waved to the people. The crowd never stopped cheering. The soldiers escorted them to the front door of the temple to shake hands with Ba Bay and her son Chu Hai.

I watched as the soldiers removed To Thay's throne from one of the helicopters. People cheered even louder. The original looked just like the replica. As it was being carried toward the temple door, one of the red silk curtains came untied. I imagined that To Thay was sitting inside and had closed it himself for a little privacy.

Once the original throne had been installed and the replica put away to the side, the president and his wife were led into the temple with Ba Bay and Chu Hai. Not everyone could fit inside the new cement temple to worship with the president and his wife. I was needed in the kitchen. Anh Thiep, Anh The, and Anh Muoi attended the service.

At dinner, the scribes and I were asked to carry platters of food and set them down in the anteroom. President Thieu and his wife were sitting next to Chu Hai and Ba Bay. I didn't see my father anywhere. Later, I saw him eating outside by himself. I knew he didn't feel like talking with everyone.

The soldiers were dressed in a new style of uniform. It was green camouflage with an arm patch on the shoulder of a tiger's face. The tiger had a threatening face. The people in my village didn't approve. For us, the tiger stood for peace and not for war. For us, the tiger was our guardian spirit. It was Tuan Quan.

I returned to the cave the following day, and my father went back to Cho Lach, where he was living.

Since living on the forbidden mountain, I had heard Trung Quan's warning more than a dozen times, and every time I ran with the animals to hide in the bushes, or sometimes in a cave or high up in a tree. I saw the hunters a few times and grew to recognize them. There were usually five or six of them hunting together.

One afternoon I heard Tuan Quan's warning when I was looking in the bushes for a kind of vine that has a yellow berry inside a yellow pod. Since I didn't see or hear any animals running for cover, I didn't pay any attention. An owl landed on the bushes next to me in broad daylight. I said hello to her and she flew away. In Vietnam, we call owls catbirds, because we think their faces look like a cat.

The owl came back and sat right on the bush next to where I was standing and watched me. I didn't know why. About ten minutes later, the hunters walked right up to me and tied my hands in front of me and pushed me in front of them with their spears. I was afraid they might cut me and then I would be poisoned. They had four big rabbits that were dead, and a wounded pig. The pig was being led with a rope tied around its neck.

The hunters were talking and laughing a lot. I wished I understood Cambodian because they were probably discussing what to do with me. Two of them looked nice, but three of them had mean-looking faces.

We stopped near a stream. They tied the pig and me to separate trees. With my back against the trunk, they stretched my arms backward around the tree and lashed my wrists together very tightly. It hurt a lot. I couldn't slide down to sit. I had to stand for hours like that.

I watched them cook the rabbits. They cut away the flesh in the area where the poison arrows had entered the rabbits and put the powdered antidote to the poison on the flesh. They didn't skin or gut the rabbits, they just threw them upon the coals to cook.

The hunters seemed to be enjoying their hunting trip. They talked animatedly, told stories, laughed, and then feasted on the rabbits. They didn't talk to me or offer me any water. Every now and then, they all turned around and looked at me and made comments and burst out laughing. I pretended not to see or hear. I prayed for my friends to help me. I was afraid that after their dinner the hunters were going to cut off my head.

They talked for so long it grew dark, and then they got ready to go to sleep. I couldn't rest because my arms were stretched so tightly around the tree. Soon all was quiet except for their breathing. It was a moonless, cloudy night.

It must have been midnight when something started picking at my rope. I felt it tickling my wrists. I heard the sound of gnawing. I tried to look behind the tree, but I couldn't see anything. In just five minutes, the rope fell away. I was afraid to take a step. If they heard me moving, I was sure they would spear me with their poison-tipped weapons.

I moved very slowly toward the pig. She didn't make a sound as I untied the knot in the rope. I didn't think she would live. We walked very slowly about forty feet, then I heard footsteps on either side of us. I was afraid it was the hunters. I tried to listen carefully, but all I could hear was my heart pounding. I heard enough to know the footsteps were not human, they were animals, my friends. When I had snuck a safe distance away from the hunters I took off running. I didn't stop running until I had reached the top of the mountain. I climbed up a big rock and fell asleep for the night.

The army soldiers came to the mountain while I was living there and started building an base and a road. I didn't let them see me. I hid behind the bushes and listened to them talk. They were saying that they were spooked and wanted to leave. They had been hearing things like spirits yelling at them to go away. The insects were biting them all night long. Sometimes they woke up in the morning covered with ticks. Many came down with fever.

Americans started arriving and then the power of the mountain diminished.

I didn't hear anyone complain much after that. There was never any fighting on the mountain, because the Viet Cong would not come there.

In June 1973, just before my twenty-third birthday, my father came to the cave and told me he was taking me home to live with him because a famous doctor of Chinese medicine had moved to Cho Lach. He said the doctor had agreed to teach me. I was crushed.

I understood that it was an honor for such a well-known doctor to accept me as his student. I thanked my father for arranging this opportunity for me, but I told him that I didn't want to go. I begged Fourth Uncle to tell my father to let me stay. Instead, he told me, "No. Your time with me is over. Now you must study more and help your father."

My heart was wrenching. Tears stung my eyes and overflowed. I looked at Fourth Uncle and then at my father. It was clear the conversation was over. I struggled to follow my father out of the cave. I thought I deserved an explanation, but my father didn't seem to think so.

42

THE HOLE

had been living in the cave for more than three years and wasn't ready to come back to the world. All I brought from the mountain was my draw-string bag of stones. When we arrived in his new house, I tossed the bag of stones under my father's medicine table and forgot about them.

My internship with the famous doctor would begin in three days. All I wanted to do was go back to the cave and Fourth Uncle and continue to learn about the possibilities of human consciousness. I had come so far already; I wanted to go further. I sat outside under a tree and tried to meditate, but my father needed me to work in the clinic.

His patients kept staring at me. They said to my father, "Why does your son look so white? He looks like a girl."

Vietnamese women like to cover their faces with a scarf when they work out-doors under the sun, because they like to keep their complexions pale and soft. Men usually don't care about their skin. It is very unusual to see a man who has kept his face out of the sun.

On the day I was to begin studying with the doctor, war broke out in Cho Lach. The Communists had started an offensive to attack the army compounds in my province. The Communists stampeded the barbed-wire fences and threw their bodies on top of the wire as shields to protect their comrades as they climbed through. Then they launched shoulder-fired missiles into the barracks. The soldiers would chase the Communists into the neighborhoods, where there would be a battle with guns and grenades. The army would call for support, and then helicopters, tanks, and American gunships would arrive. The helicopters dropped bombs on our neighborhoods, and the tanks fired missiles through our streets. The Americans sped over the rivers and canals making such big wakes that if you were carrying something heavy in your boat it would tip over. Many people lost their boats.

The fighting went on for months. My father's patients tried to come early, before the fighting started, but sometimes we had to hurry into the bomb shelter. The top of our bunker was covered with sandbags. It protected us from gunfire, but if a missile had landed within twenty feet of our shelter, we would have been killed. A lot of people in our neighborhood came out of their shelters with blood coming out of their ears and noses. This happened mostly to children from the air pressure of the bombs. Many lost some or all of their hearing.

When we were inside the bomb shelter, my father would tell us not to be scared, but to pray instead. I spent more time with my father in the hole than in the clinic. When it was just the two of us, I tried my best to pray and meditate to demonstrate how much I had changed. I chanted sutras for world peace and for people to have compassion for one another and for all living things. I prayed for all people to be healthy and to have a way to earn a living. I prayed that no living soul would suffer from hunger. I prayed for the souls of all people who died before their time, to find their way to heaven, and I prayed for them to be able to have another chance at life. When my father joined me in prayer, it was as if I was hearing him for the first time. He sang the prayers with a depth of feeling that I had not found in myself. His sound filled the emptiness of the bomb shelter. His resonant voice filled my stomach and my bones.

Our songs of prayer continued for hours at a time as we lay against each other in the pitch blackness in our burrow under the ground. We listened to the sounds of helicopters and missiles, and the thuds of explosions. My father and I blended our voices to make a sound barrier of hope.

Not a day passed that I didn't ask my father to please take me back to the cave to study more with Fourth Uncle. I told him that I wanted to learn more, like he did. I pleaded and cried, but it was no use. I thought there must something that he wasn't telling me.

My father usually preferred to stay quiet, but we had many conversations while we were in the hole. I told my father everything about Tattoo and Lead

Lips and Met Pop. I told him about the times I had hauled ghosts out of people's bodies and houses.

He asked me if I had learned how to shrink a ghost and stuff him inside a ceramic pot. I told him that I had done that a few times.

"That is evil." My father's voice echoed in the darkness. "I hope you let the ghost out."

I was afraid he wouldn't believe me.

"I let them all out," I said. "I only kept them in the pot for about a week until they promised they would leave people alone."

"Did you know," my father said, "that sorcerers like Lead Lips continue to imprison souls inside jars? Sorcerers have been doing this for thousands of years. They trap ghosts inside pots, seal them with cement, and then bury them or throw then into the Mekong River where they are carried out to sea. Souls have become trapped like this for thousands of years."

"But those souls are bad," I reminded my father. "They hurt people and make them sick and insane. They take away their victim's life force little by little."

My father said, "It is evil to entrap a soul. Every soul, no matter how destructive, can change and become good again. Every soul must have its freedom. This is what we pray for."

In Vietnam, people were always burying their valuables. People often sealed their gold jewelry inside ceramic pots and buried them. People are always on the lookout for buried treasures from the past.

"What would happen if someone opened a pot and released a ghost that had been imprisoned for one thousand years?"

"Old people know about that. If they find an old jar sealed with cement, they would hope it was gold, but would never open it carelessly. They would try to break it from far away by throwing it against a rock."

"What would the ghost do when it came out?" I asked.

"Usually they will take revenge on the first person they see. But I have also heard that a ghost will sometimes show his gratitude to the person who let him out by protecting and helping that person."

"Then that means a ghost can become good on its own, without any help," I said.

"Maybe they are getting help from us when we sing sutras and pray for them," my father said.

I thought about my conversations with the ghosts I'd caught. They were afraid of me, and I had felt compassion for them.

"Quang," my father interrupted my thoughts, "when I was your age I made the same mistake you made, only I wandered farther into the world of evil than you did."

"You did?" I was genuinely surprised. "Did you have a servant like Met Pop?"

"I had several. I didn't realize what I was doing. That's the danger, you see. You think you are fighting evil, but what you are really doing is creating more evil in the world. You begin to think like them."

We were laying back to back. I became aware of the warmth of my father's body beside me. If I concentrated hard enough, I could feel his heartbeat on my back.

"Before I went to the cave, before my fiancée died, I studied sorcery in Cai Mon. I learned to see ghosts and I performed exorcisms. There was one sorcerer who liked me very much. He is the one who gave me the hair whip."

My father told me how the sorcerer had made the hair whip. When Vietnamese people move, they often dig up the remains of their loved ones, burn the bones, and take the ashes with them, so the spirits of their ancestors will be able to find them in their new home.

My father told me that the sorcerer who made the hair whip went to the grave of an adolescent girl whose body was being exhumed. He stole her long hair. It had already become detached from the skull. He bound it with thread, washed and combed it out, and then he rubbed coconut oil into it. He recited a magic charm over it every day for ten years until it had become a torturous and deadly weapon.

"That whip was so powerful it made ghosts and monsters howl with pain. I never encountered a monster that could bear it. It could kill the living. I almost killed someone, Quang."

I thought, "That is horrible. How could he do that?" I rolled over onto my other side so that I was facing my father's back. In my mind I saw his long gray hair lying on the bare earth and his shirt that needed more mending. For a split second I felt a dizzying sensation, as if the world had turned upside down. I became aware of an expansive sensation inside my rib cage, as if my chest were a ceramic jar where my spirit had been locked away but was now breaking free. A feeling of well-being flooded me. I felt compassion for my father's weakness, for his guilt and his suffering.

"What happened?" I asked.

"The whip wanted to destroy and to cause suffering through me. It started to interfere with my thinking."

His voice tapered off. I waited, wondering if he was going to tell me more. We rolled onto our backs, entombed in blackness, and we paused to listen through the packed earth for the sounds of gunfire.

"All I had to do to kill someone was to say his name and age and then crack the whip. The victim had to be within one hundred feet. I attacked a Vietnamese landowner who was beating his workers. I hid behind his house and cracked the whip. I heard him scream in agony. They brought him to my father's clinic the next morning. He was semiparalyzed. He never fully recovered. I didn't kill him, but I caused him a great deal of suffering."

"Did he stop beating his workers?"

"I suppose so," my father said.

Gunfire erupted, and we automatically stopped talking to listen for grenades and bombs. My father started praying and I joined him. The fighting stayed close to our house for about an hour before the sounds retreated in the distance. My father slept for a while. When he woke up he told me more.

"The next time I went to the sorcerer's house, I saw some very evil things. I saw five souls chained together, young men and women who had rings through their Achilles tendons and a chain running through. The sorcerer told me he had kidnapped these people's souls. On the night of their funerals he went to their graves and chanted a magic charm. He returned to their graves every night for four months until the flesh had fallen away from their bones. Then he opened the graves and took their skulls. He showed me the skulls.

"My spirit woke up and my head became clear again. I never went back to see him. He was furious with me, but he never attacked me. I think it was because I had the hair. He was afraid of the hair whip.

"After my fiancée died, I guarded her grave every night. I moved her body several times to make sure the sorcerer could never find her."

That was when my father shaved his head and became a monk. Four years later, he had the idea that he wanted to become a doctor to save people's lives. He went to Elephant Mountain to study medicine. Three years later, he went to the cave and stayed sixteen years with his teacher. My father explained that the spirits from the forbidden mountain helped him do magic to protect and heal people. The kind of magic he does now is a world apart from sorcery.

After my father told me his story, I stopped thinking I could never be like him. I thought I was like him already.

. . .

We spent one afternoon in the bomb shelter talking about river spirits. In South Vietnam, everyone knows that if you drop an article of clothing or jewelry in the river, a river spirit can come looking for you. If you are a woman, the river king will come, and if you are a man it will be the river queen. They come to you in your dreams, and you can't help falling in love with them. They don't come often at first, maybe once every three or four months, so you think it is just a dream. After a year, they start coming once or twice a month, and then once a week. After a few years, they come every night.

You know when someone in your family is possessed by a river spirit, because you can hear them making love at night. Ghosts who come at night to make love are called *mong tinh*.

My father explained, "You should send them away the first time they come, because once you have made love with them, it is very difficult to resist them. They fulfill your romantic and sexual desires the way no human can."

"What is so bad about that?" I said jokingly. I knew that possession by a ghost or spirit will drain the life out of anyone. It usually takes about seven years of growing weaker and weaker until you go insane and die.

"By the time the family has found out about the river spirit, the person will not want it to go away. They would rather stay with the spirit, even if it means losing their life in a matter of years," my father told me.

"How do you make the river spirit leave?" I asked.

"You can't let the person know that you are planning to drive away their spirit lover. You have to sneak into the house at night when the person is sleeping, and wait until you hear them making love. Most sorcerers go over to the bed and stab the spirit while the two are making love."

"That sounds terrible," I said.

"It is terrible. The person will see their lover slain in their arms. It is very real to them. They go mad with agony. Sometimes they try to kill themselves to follow their lover to the spirit world."

"Do you help people with that kind of ghost problem?" I asked.

"I don't do that anymore," he said, "Once was enough. There are others who can do that job."

One time I was delivering some medicine to my father's friend Chu Buu, the one who took care of me when I almost died. Sau Ve was there as well, and they invited me to have tea with them. While I was there, the bombing started, and all three of us went down into the shelter. While we were in there, they told me about a time when my father used magic to hide them and other people at his house.

Chu Buu said, "Your father was celebrating *Cung Binh*. About twenty people were there."

Cung Binh is a holiday to honor the soldiers who died in the war. My father made a *Cung Binh* ceremony once a month. He prayed for the Vietnamese army soldiers as well as the Communists. Many people who had lost their children in the war came to my father's house to pray for the souls of their loved ones to find peace.

"Your father's neighbors ran into the house and started yelling that the French soldiers were coming up the street, looking inside all the houses," Chu Buu said.

"There was a curfew then," explained Sau Ve. "You weren't allowed to have more then one or two guests in your house."

"It was a very dangerous time," said Chu Buu. "If we had been caught in there, we might have been killed."

"So what did you do?" I asked.

"Your father told us not to worry," Chu Buu said.

"He drew some symbols in the four corners of the room and then he sat right down and started meditating," said Sau Ve.

"About twenty soldiers passed right in front of the house," Chu Buu said. "We were worried, because we knew they were looking for your father back then," he added.

"Yes, I know," I said.

"Well, those soldiers walked right past all twenty of us sitting there like pigs in a pen."

43

LOST

The war dragged on for months, and many people started running out of food. They had no choice but to go asking the neighbors. Everyone tried to protect his food because nobody had enough.

Neighbors picked their neighbors' gardens bare, looking for a scrap of food to keep their families alive. They started eating the young banana trees, which have a white core that can be steamed until it is tender.

My father had enough food, so we didn't have to go out looking. We had dried rice, dried fish, and fermented soybeans. Sometimes my father went to Cai Mon to bring Aunt Gioi some food, but he didn't let me travel with him.

It had been three months since I came home from the cave. The Chinese medicine teacher had moved away, because of the endless fighting. My father brought me back to Elephant Mountain so I could continue studying acupuncture and plant medicine with my former teachers. I told him that I wanted to live with Ong Nam at An Son Tu, and he said it was all right. Chi was still there, and there were three new monks. We found out that Ong Tam, the village chief of my religion and the master of Buu Minh Doung, the temple where I lived when I was eleven, had died from his cancer. His son couldn't become the next *ong ganh* because he couldn't talk.

. . .

My father asked me if I wanted to shave my head this time like my friend Chi or to serve Ong Nam again as his servant. I chose to be Ong Nam's servant because I didn't want to shave all of my hair off. I would also have more time to talk with Ong Nam. My father didn't stay long, because he wanted to go back to Cho Lach for his patients.

I studied hard with my teachers and worked in their clinics attending patients. It took me two hours to walk from An Son Tu to the neighborhood around Tam Buu Tu. When I was over there, I didn't go to see Lead Lips or Ong Chin. The only thing in my mind was to go back to the cave and live with Fourth Uncle again.

I was happy to see Chi and the three new monks, but I didn't go out with them much. On the days that I didn't go to my teachers' clinics, I went outside to sit under a tree and continue my meditation practice.

I asked Ong Nam to show me where all the caves were, and he took me up the mountain. We looked inside them all. They were dirty with bat droppings. I wanted to talk with Ong Nam about how Fourth Uncle taught me to meditate, but he wasn't interested or impressed. He said, "Different teachers, different ways."

Ong Nam meditated twice a day. The first time was after dinner from six o'clock until seven, and the second was at midnight for one hour. He sat in a cross-legged position and placed his palms together and prayed for a minute to Buddha to help him have more power in his body. Then he brought his hands down on his lap, one hand cupping the back of the other. He inhaled the air to his navel and then exhaled the same way. He let the air make a sound in the back of his throat.

Ong Nam knew about the soul body hatching out of a person's crown. He said that when the soul first hatches it is just a baby. It doesn't know what to do. He said there are spirits who come to watch over the baby soul, and bring it somewhere for an education. Ong Nam said that when your soul child is born it must go to school in the spirit world for many years.

"Fourth Uncle told me not to let my soul body go out much," I told Ong Nam.

"I don't understand," Ong Nam said. "How is your baby soul supposed to learn how to travel in time and let people see and hear him?"

I told Ong Nam that people did come to show me around in the spirit world. They brought me to gardens and buildings and temples. I told him I sat in a great hall with fifty other monks, and listened to their master discuss the sutras and other things that I could not understand.

"That is what I mean," Ong Nam said. "I don't know why your teacher didn't let your soul go to school more often, That's what I would encourage you to do."

Ong Nam never gave birth to a soul body, because he didn't think it was important. He said, "A lot of work for what? I don't need my soul to travel, I just want to finish building this temple."

My friends at Tam Buu Tu didn't seem to like me as much as they used to. They said I wasn't any fun to be with anymore. I wasn't used to talking to people much. I had spent over three years trying not to speak. I wasn't really interested in talking much with people.

My friends thought I was putting on airs. Anh The was particularly mad at me. When he saw me, he usually made cutting remarks and called me "Your Heavenly Eminence."

I felt as if I didn't belong with my friends anymore. I didn't know where I belonged. I decided to go back to tell Fourth Uncle that I wasn't able to study with the Chinese medicine teacher because of the war. I would ask him please to accept me back as his student, because I didn't feel comfortable out in the world anymore.

I took an early bus to the forbidden mountain. It was raining very hard, and the bus got stuck in the mud. I didn't want to wait for someone to come pull it out. I got out and walked the rest of the way. I didn't get to the mountain until late afternoon.

I was very happy to be back on the mountain, but my friends weren't around; they were keeping out of the rain. The centipedes were out, but I didn't care. I bounded around them up to the cave.

I went past the wolves' den, and they came out to say hello. I was very happy to see them again. I ducked into Fourth Uncle's cave and strode over the rocks and boulders like a spider. Sometimes I would stop and snuggle into a familiar resting place, remembering the spaces between the stones. I rested in one spot and then another. I remembered past feelings of being hopelessly lost, of being hungry, of hating my father, of waiting for death to take me.

I made my way to Fourth Uncle's chamber. I stopped at my rock. I reached above my head and broke off some root food and tasted it once more. It didn't taste like much, crunchy and slightly sweet. That familiar feeling of satisfaction came over me. I sat and meditated on my rock for a long time.

. . .

I walked silently toward the shadowy statue of Fourth Uncle sitting on his shelf. I climbed up and watched his lifeless form. I remembered how I'd pinched his nostrils shut and waited for him to part his lips to take in air, and how I tickled him and prodded him. He never scolded. He was gentle with me.

I sat diagonally in front of him, and I felt peaceful. I felt love and devotion. He opened his eyes, but he didn't look at me. He said, "Our time together is over, Quang. You must live in the world of people now and study more medicine, so you can help."

Fourth Uncle closed his eyes and became quiet again. His words of rejection cut through my heart like knife. I couldn't control myself. I cried and sobbed. I went back to my rock and wanted to stay there forever. I stayed there until I fell asleep.

When I woke up, I tried to meditate, but I couldn't compose myself. I felt itchy and squirmy. I went exploring the cave and didn't see any of my cave friends. The cave had a different feeling. I felt all alone. I went back to Fourth Uncle. He wasn't on his shelf.

I looked in the other chambers, but he wasn't there either. I tried to go other places in the cave, but they were closed off. It looked like a different cave.

I slept there for a few days, but I felt so lonely that I left.

I spent two miserable months back at An Son Tu with Ong Nam and Chi. I didn't like living on the outside. I wasn't good with people. People are so petty and difficult. They are always making problems out of nothing.

My mind was fixated on returning to the cave and continuing my studies with Fourth Uncle. I wondered how I could appeal to Fourth Uncle to accept me back. I remembered the story of how my grandfather went to the forbidden mountain and prayed and didn't leave until he was accepted. I became hopeful, thinking that that was something I could do.

I went back to the cave but I couldn't get past the first tunnel. I went outside and around to the other entrances, but couldn't find them. I sat outside the cave and prayed for Fourth Uncle to show me the way in. I prayed and searched for four days, and then to my surprise I found my way into the cave.

I went as far as my rock, but could go no farther. Beyond my rock was a wall that wasn't there before. I sat on my rock and cried.

44

A CHILD AMONG GRANDFATHERS

In my culture, we commemorate the dates of our parents' death every year for the rest of our lives. Aunt Gioi and Uncle Quon did this for my grandparents every year. My father sometimes went to Cai Mon to attend it, but often he was too busy. Instead, he lit candles and prayed for his parents at his house. It is customary to pray for two days. The first day is to remember them in life, and the second to pray for their soul in the afterlife.

My father brought me home from An Son Tu in December 1973 to attend the anniversary of my grandmother's death on December 4 and 5 at my uncle's house. My father wanted me to stay home until the anniversary of my grandfather's death on February 24 and 25. I stayed most of the time at my father's house in Cho Lach, working with him in his clinic. I chanted the sutras with him four times a day, and I meditated at midnight with him.

One morning while my father was out at the market, someone from three villages away came to speak to me. He had heard that I had just returned from the Seven Sacred Mountains, and he wanted to know if I would consider the position of abbot at the Quoc Thoi Tu temple in Xa Long Thoi village.

I told the monk that I needed to speak with my father about it.

When my father came home, I told him about the offer and asked him if he thought it was a good idea. He said he didn't know.

I waited for him to explain. He sat down and stroked his beard. He said, "It is good, because people will bring you food and money, you will always have something to eat. It's bad because you will feel guilty for being comfortable when others are poor and hungry."

"I don't care about money," I said.

"If people give you money, you need to clear it. You must write down everything people ask of you, and you must pray for them and find ways to help them."

I felt proud for having been offered this position, but I knew that it was because of my father's reputation that people were interested in me. I realized that this position would serve as a test of my skill and my commitment to help people.

My father warned me, "The war is still heavy. You will have to conduct many funerals. You will witness pain and suffering on a daily basis."

"I am not afraid of that," I said.

"You will be watched closely by spies on both sides of the war, because you will be a person of authority in the community. Don't become involved with politics. Stay inside your religion," my father warned.

When the monk returned, I told him that I accepted the position.

"Would you be ready to start one month from now?"

"One month is fine."

I enjoyed working in the clinic with my father, because I knew I wouldn't be seeing him very often once I moved to Quoc Thoi Tu. One morning, when my father was out at the market, a new patient came to the house looking for my father. I assumed my father would be back any minute, and I invited the man inside to wait. He was about fifty years old. He was flushed with fever.

The man asked me who I was, and I answered, "I am Ong Sau's son, Quang."

The man asked me why I looked so pale, and I told him I had been living in a cave in the forbidden mountain.

He asked me how I could live in a cave, what I ate, and what I did all day.

I told him I meditated a lot and didn't eat much.

The man had been waiting more than two hours for my father, which was unusual. No other patients had come to the house. He was growing impatient, because he lived far away and would have to leave soon. He asked me if my father was teaching me medicine. I responded, "Yes, a little."

He said, "I hear your father is a very good doctor. People say that he doesn't need to give medicine, he can just trace a charm in the air with a pencil and blow it over the person's body and he is healed."

"He knows many ways," I said.

The man lifted up his shirt and showed me his stomach. His skin looked very infected. It was red and swollen, with lesions and pus. His skin smelled very bad.

I remembered Fourth Uncle telling me that I could treat any sickness with water. He said to take a cup of water, and close my eyes and see the water with my third eye for a few seconds. He said not to think about anything, just see the water. I wanted to try it out.

I went to get a cup of water. I closed my eyes and pictured it in my mind. Then I gave it to the man and told him to drink half. I took cup back, then lifted his shirt and threw the rest of the water on his stomach. He became angry and left.

That man came back a few days later and told my father I was a good doctor. He said, "That night, after your son threw water on me, I slept well. I had no fever. The next day my skin was dry and the bumps and swelling were reduced. The skin is no longer painful. It keeps getting better each day."

My father was pleased.

A t the end of February 1974, my father took me on a forty-minute bus ride to Quoc Thoi Tu, World Peace Temple in Xe Long Thoi village. A party was planned in my honor. I wore a three-piece suit, made by a tailor who specialized in making temple clothing. It was blue and had drawstring pants and a long-sleeved, blousy shirt with wide sleeves. Over that, I wore a floor-length formal jacket with pleats on the sides that opened and closed when I walked. It took a long time to fasten that jacket, because it had about thirty knotted Chinese buttons that ran down the front. My father told me that whenever I went out in public, I needed to wear those clothes. I was also wearing a pair of banana-twine shoes my father had made for me. We didn't wear them in the rain, because they would get soggy. On rainy days my father wore plastic sandals. I wore leather ones.

My father prepared several packages of root vegetables, cabbages and squash, rice and sea salt, red candles, and several different kinds and sizes of incense sticks to bring to the temple. I had two informal suits of clothing to wear inside the temple, one black and the other dark red. The black suit looked like clothing from my religion, and the dark red one fastened diagonally across my chest. All the shirts had a pocket that was on the inside of the front panel. I had also brought a yellow monk's robe with me.

We lugged our packages through the gates of the temple. There were several musicians seated on chairs on the lawn playing drums, a symbol, a bamboo flute, and a few reed horns.

The courtyard looked nice enough, but the temple building looked run-down. It was pockmarked in places where pieces of cement had fallen away. The roof had many broken tiles with vines growing under them.

"This place looks good compared to the way the Chinese temple looked when I first got there," my father said.

There were about ten distinguished guests seated at the tables under the shade of a large banyan tree. I wasn't used to associating with people like that, and it made me nervous. I turned to my father, but he just gave me a look as if to say, "Never mind about them."

Kim, the monk who had sponsored me, came to meet us, saying he would like to introduce us to the guests. My father said he couldn't stay. He gave me a pat on the back and disappeared through the gate.

Kim led me to a table and introduced me to the village chief and to some of the village council members, who were dressed in their street clothes. The spirit house was next door to the temple.

The other special guests were five high-ranking monks from other temples in Cho Lach. They were all sitting together at one table in their robes of various gradations of orange, signifying rank. I met the former master of Quoc Thoi Tu and his wife. They told me they were living in the house between the temple building and the temple orchard.

Some of the monks seemed to be confused about who I was. When Kim explained that I was the new abbot of Quoc Thoi Tu, they were noticeably surprised. I didn't look like a monk, because my hair was cut like a temple servant's, and I wasn't wearing an orange robe. The main reason they felt uncomfortable was because I was so young. I was twenty-three but looked much younger.

For someone my age to sit at the same table with such distinguished elders was unheard of. I looked like a child among grandfathers. Four out of the five monks at my table shifted a lot in their chairs and wouldn't make eye contact with me.

Dai Duc was the highest-ranking monk there. The color of his robe was just a shade lighter and the patchwork slightly larger than that of my father's robe.

He didn't seem to be bothered by my age. He was the only person at the table who spoke to me and tried to make me feel comfortable.

I didn't stay seated at the table for long. I ate only a little, and then I got up to look around the temple grounds. I noticed Kim had joined the musicians and was playing the *don co*, a two-stringed bowed instrument that is held on the lap. There weren't many people at my welcoming party besides the monks and the musicians.

I t didn't look so bad inside the temple. The two adjoining rooms were fairly small, and there was another separate room for the kitchen.

The community room had two long tables in the center of the room and four altars. One entire wall was covered in a lengthy mural of the ten regions of hell. I went to get a closer look. There were green-faced demons with pointed ears, goat horns, and long fangs that grew straight out of their mouths. There were also yellow demons with fur on their legs and blood dripping from their mouths. The green-faced ones were sawing people into pieces and throwing their heads into a vat of water. The heads floated on top of the water with their eyes popping open.

The yellow demons had a table with swords sticking out of the top, and they were pushing a woman down and the blades were cutting through her. The demons also used a machine to crush your bones and squeeze all the blood out of you. It was squirting all over the picture.

There was a long bench against that wall, underneath the mural. Kim had set up a small portable bed and mosquito net on the opposite wall.

The chapel was smaller than the community room and had a large stagelike altar in the center with many colorful statues of gods and goddesses, legendary creatures, and people. I didn't know who many of them were. Smaller altars stood against the walls and in the corners, fifteen altars in all.

The chapel opened to a patio, and beyond the patio, a wild, abandoned garden bordered the Cai Ga branch of the Mekong River. Peeking out from behind an overgrown hedge in the center of the back yard was a tall white statue of Quan An, the goddess of forgiveness.

I broke through the entwined branches that blocked the path and made my way to the river. The two gates leading to the water had rusted shut.

There was only one monk living in the temple besides me. He preferred to sleep outside on a hammock under an awning. Kim didn't live at the temple because he had a wife and three children. A full-time rice farmer, he only volunteered at the temple.

Kim said the temple and the grounds were run-down because the former master had been pocketing all the money from the temple's orchard business. The funds from selling the bananas, mangos, and coconuts were supposed to be used to hire workers to tend the grounds. Other donations to the temple were given to the village chief, who was responsible for maintaining the building.

Kim said the neighborhood people had been complaining that the former abbot was just pretending to be a monk. They didn't think he was really praying for them, because he kept jumping up every ten minutes to look outside at his trees to make sure nobody was stealing any fruit.

The former abbot told me not to worry about taking care of the orchard. He said that he was still going to do that job. He said that I could help myself to all the bananas, mangos, and coconuts I wanted.

For the first few months I didn't do much except light the incense, chant, meditate, and try to fix the place up. Not many people came to pray at my temple.

I kept the altars clean, and I arranged them with fruit and fresh flowers. I put on the yellow robe when I chanted.

Once a month, my father brought me two big sacks of potatoes, onions, carrots, squash, and cabbage, and money for rice and incense. His students helped him carry it from the boat.

About four months after I arrived, the war got very bad. I could hear the villagers crying and wailing day and night. There were bodies of dead Viet Cong soldiers lying in the street almost every morning. Their comrades dragged them home in the middle of the night so they wouldn't be seen. When their parents arrived, they were overcome with unbearable pain at the sight of their beloved children and husbands, bloated and blue, covered in flies like offal reeking in the gutter.

The Vietnamese National Army was drafting boys as young as fifteen if they looked big enough to fit into a uniform. These boys only trained for one month before they were sent to the front. These young teenagers didn't stand a chance of coming home alive. Parents started bringing their sons to

Quoc Thoi Tu to become apprentice monks. I could take only ten apprentices, because my temple was so small. Any more would arouse suspicion. The boys only stayed with me for a few months until there was room for them in Dai Duc's temple, Phuoc Lam Tu, Happy Forest Temple, in Hoa Nghia village. Dai Duc had room for fifty monks. Sometimes he sent them to temples in Saigon. They were safer at Dai Duc's temple than they were at mine. Dai Duc had significant political power. He was also able to feed his monks better than I could.

I was still able to make the table of food appear and disappear, which meant that I hadn't lost much of my power since leaving the cave. I could have amazed my apprentices by handing them platters of food out of thin air. Then people would say that I was enlightened, and many would come to follow me. However, I knew that if I ever wanted to use my power in this way, it would be taken away from me.

When the boys arrived, I shaved their heads and gave them each a temple name. I had to name all my monks with the first name Hue, because it meant they were from Quoc Thoi Tu. There wasn't much room for them to sleep, so they slept on the tables and on the long bench under the mural.

The next thing I did was go to Dai Duc to get identity papers for the new monks.

The new monks couldn't set foot outside the temple gates until their paperwork was ready. If they were caught on the streets without their identity papers, they would be drafted on the spot, and taken to army headquarters in Cho Lach.

Sometimes they got themselves into trouble. They couldn't resist going home to see their families again and eating more food. They weren't used to eating just rice and vegetables and sea salt. They would wait until they thought there were no soldiers around, and then they would sneak back home. The soldiers knew this, and sometimes they hid and tricked them.

I always knew when one of my apprentices got caught, because someone from the village would come running to tell me. They knew that the boy was being taken to his death. I had the authority to take the boy back, as long as I could find his papers and get to army headquarters in time.

There were times when I arrived at the Cho Lach army headquarters too late, and they had already taken my apprentices in a jeep to My Tho. From My Tho they took them to Saigon, and from Saigon they went to a training camp in central Vietnam. The army tried to process the boys' papers as quickly as possible, because they knew I was on my way with their papers to get them back. It took forty minutes for a Honda driver to get me to the headquarters in My Tho. If I missed them at My Tho, it would be too late. Luckily that never happened.

The monks at other nearby temples weren't able to accommodate all the funerals, so people started coming to ask me.

As soon as the body arrives at the house, you need to be there to chant for the soul while they wash and dress the body. The bodies of the Viet Cong looked and smelled worse, because they took longer to get home. Their bodies and heads would swell to more than double their normal size.

Dead soldiers were kept in an army morgue in Saigon. An army jeep would show up at the family's house to notify them, and to bring them to the morgue. When people saw jeeps entering their neighborhoods, they would drop to their knees and pray. Sadly, jeeps came often.

If a soldier was killed in central Vietnam or somewhere far away, the medics would remove the intestines so the body would swell less. All the bodies were put in crude wooden boxes that leaked body fluids. The soldiers in the jeep were willing to take you to a coffin maker so you could buy a better coffin to bring your loved one home in.

I tried to be in the home when the family members arrived back from Saigon in an army truck. I began chanting right away, even before they opened the box, so good spirits would come to find this dead soul and care for it. I could never get used to the smell and the sight of pink fluid oozing from the seams in the coffin.

After the body was cleaned and put into a new coffin, I had to sit with the family and write down all their birthdays and other information to determine the best burial date and time, and the best location and direction for the body to lie. I used the notes that I copied from Ong Nam's book. These calculations often took hours to complete. Sometimes the family wanted to bury the body right away, and they just wanted to know the best time of day.

I had to build a spirit house to bring to the house on the day of the funeral. I usually made it with incense wrappers like my father did. If people wanted a big house with furniture and a lot of clothes, they had to pay for the paper. Most people didn't have money, so I made them a small house and two sets of paper clothes. The clothes took a long time to make because they had to be two feet tall. I also cut out a long banner with five colors of paper glued together and I folded it and cut designs into it.

I had to prepare a certificate with the person's name, date of birth, and date of death in calligraphy on a large piece of yellow prayer paper, which is as thin as cigarette paper. During the ceremony I would burn all the paper items along with special paper money. Burning things is one way to send them to the other world, where the dead person's soul can receive them.

Once someone has died, the family has to put food on the altar every day for the soul. They are supposed to leave a full bowl of rice with two chopsticks for the spirit of the person who died. They also leave two partially filled bowls of rice with only one chopstick for the spirits helping the person who has just died. We give the helping spirits only one chopstick, so that they can't finish their rice in time to eat the rice left for the loved one.

One year after the funeral, the family must make a big celebration for their loved one. After that, they can leave food for them on the altar or on the table anytime they like.

We believe that if you take the funeral veil from the face of the dead person and keep it, you can look through it and see the spirit of your loved one eating the food at the altar. I have tried to figure out exactly what a ghost is, because everyone has one. I think a ghost is the crudest part of a person's soul that is too heavy to leave the earth. Most people don't keep the veil, because it isn't very pleasant to see your loved one as a primitive ghost with a hungry green face.

On the day of the funeral, I arrived at the house with five or six volunteer musicians from the community. A lot of them were young women about my age. The music and chanting are supposed to go on all night, to make sure the dead person's soul is in good company.

In Vietnam, we sing at funerals the same way we chant poetry—we make it up on the spot. It is appropriate at a funeral to sing of the tragedy of the situation and to describe in detail the grief and suffering of the whole family. If a woman has been widowed, for example, we sing about her destitute situation, how she and her children will continue to suffer from hunger. Sometimes the poetry is so moving that no one can hold back their tears. This is not convenient, because we believe that it is not good for the family members of the deceased to cry or show their pain. That only makes it harder for the spirit of their loved one to let go and find their way to heaven. If the spirit stays behind too long, the evil spirits will come and try to trick it into following them.

Kim had a good friend named Ut Chuan who was a very good poet and singer. He usually did the singing, but when he could not come, I had to do it. I did the best I could, but had little talent for that.

I played two instruments, a small brass cymbal and a three-foot-wide drum that I hit with sticks. There was also a hand drum that was played on both ends. The player must put a wad of chewed-up rice in the middle of the drumheads before he strikes it. There were also reed horns, bamboo flutes, and the bowed instrument that Kim played.

My father told me not to eat any food at a funeral, even though I had to chant all night long. He said to just drink water and maybe nibble on a cookie. He told me to lie down every two or three hours on a hammock and try to sleep for an hour outside in the fresh air. He told me to never accept money.

The last part of the funeral is when we move the body to its final resting place. Sometimes we had to walk several miles to the burial site. I would play the cymbal along the way.

If the family's house was small, sometimes I would accidentally bump against the dead body. The smell would stay on my skin no matter how many times I washed. I tried everything, soap, lemon, alcohol, ashes, but nothing worked. Then I figured out that the smell was coming from inside my own body, and it wouldn't leave until the next morning when I urinated. I thought that the smelly oils on the skin of the corpse had soaked into my skin and had circulated through my system.

The war was getting steadily worse. There were months when I had to conduct twenty funerals or more.

45

BAREFOOT DOCTOR

E ventually the old master of Quoc Thoi Tu was too tired to take care of
the temple orchard, and asked me to take over.

I did things differently. I let people come and pick their own fruit
and leave some money in a box. I never checked to see if they had cheated. I let
people who didn't have any money take fruit for free.

I also bought about twenty sacks of polished rice for the people in the community to borrow when they ran out of food. I called it borrowing, but I knew
that most times, people would not be able to pay the temple back.

Little by little, people started coming back to Quoc Thoi Tu.

As I got to know the villagers, I saw they had health problems. I started
doing medicine, too. I read their pulses and performed acupressure massage
because I didn't have medicine or needles. I also gave them water the way
Fourth Uncle taught me to do. More people started coming to the temple for
treatment, and they started making donations. I finally had money to take to
the village chief. The temple was repaired and painted, and it looked nice
again. We also had enough money from fruit sales to hire a part-time
groundskeeper.

.   .   .

One day, when my father came bring me food and money, he saw that I was helping people who were sick. He was very pleased. He told me that next time he would bring medicine for them. He told me, "Congratulations, now you are a doctor."

People say that monks who come from the Seven Sacred Mountains can touch a piece of grass and it will turn into powerful medicine. With that in mind, I just put in three or four ingredients into the formulas instead of ten to fifteen, because I didn't have very much medicine. It didn't seem to matter. I thought people were getting well just as fast. More and more sick people started coming to me for help. I was so busy with funerals that I didn't have time to see them all.

When I ran out of medicine, I had to use other things for treatments. My father taught me to treat some kinds of skin conditions with *co mut*, ink grass, mixed with saliva. We call it ink grass, because when you rub it in your hands, it leaves a black mark. Ink grass works like an antibiotic. My father just chewed up the black ink grass and spit it out on people's skin. He told me that if the person seems uncomfortable with that, then go into another room and chew up the herbs without letting him see. The ink grass doesn't work nearly as well without the saliva.

A fifty-year-old man came in with acute swelling in his lungs, which was so painful he could barely breathe. He thought he might have inhaled some kind of poison that was in the air from the war. He had so much pressure against his heart that I was afraid he could have a heart attack. I went out into the neighborhood and asked one of the children to pee in a cup. When the little boy asked me why, I said I wanted to check to see if he was healthy. I put some tiger balm on the rim of the cup and gave the boy's urine to the man to drink. In just a few minutes, he was able to breathe much better. He said I made very good medicine.

Sometimes when the body suffers from a trauma, the nerves and the circulation lock. Urine is an anti-inflammatory. It soothes the nerves and restores circulation in the organs and tissues.

I used urine in another emergency, when a woman who was six months pregnant fell and hurt her ribs. The swelling around her rib cage was triggering uterine contractions. Blood started trickling out of her vagina, and she was afraid she would lose her baby. I ran out into the neighborhood, found the children, and asked them for more urine. I waited until one of them could go in the cup. I brought it back and put tiger balm on the lip of the cup. The woman drank the urine. Within minutes her contractions subsided and she felt better.

While she was resting, the children walked into the temple and said, "Do you want some more pee?"

The woman was upset when she realized what I had given her to drink, but I told her it wasn't dirty, and that it might have saved her baby's life.

Children's urine is the purest, although it is also good to drink your own urine sometimes if you are very sick. Your urine has something in it from your sickness. When you drink it, it helps your immune system fight the sickness. The first urine of the morning is best. You shouldn't talk until you have collected it, or it won't be as strong. Take it from the middle of the flow and just drink a quarter of a cup. It is not a pleasant thing to do, but it can be helpful.

A twelve-year-old girl came down with appendicitis. Her parents didn't have money to take her to the hospital. They carried her to the temple. She was in a lot of pain, and she couldn't walk.

I hurried and made a fire. I had a piece of metal that I bought from a car junkyard. It was part of a long flat piece of metal from the bottom of a truck.

I asked her parents to lay her down on a mat by the fire. I put the metal onto the coals until it turned red. I took the metal out of the fire, and put it on the ground. I dipped my foot in a mixture of rice alcohol and vinegar and stepped on the red-hot metal. It made a loud sizzling sound. Right away, I put my foot on the girl's abdomen and pressed down and massaged her intestines. It was not comfortable for the girl, she cried and squirmed around, but after that, she got up and walked home.

In Vietnam, we have very large leeches. Sometimes, when people work in the water a long time, they don't notice they have a leech until they come ashore. Vietnamese leeches have a mouth at either end. When a leech is engorged on a person's body, it looks like a gray handle, one foot long and three inches wide. It is not a good idea to pull them off because a lot of flesh will come off, too. I used a mixture of lime ash and honey that I applied to both ends of the leech, and it would come off right away. If a leech is on the person for more than an hour, it can transmit a disease to the person. For that, we use glass cups or segments of bamboo to suction the poison out.

You have to prick the wound a bit to make it bleed more. Then you dip the end of a bean-sized ball of dried mugwort in alcohol and place it onto the skin, dry side down. You light it and quickly place a cup over it. The fire burns all the oxygen out and the flesh will be sucked up into the cup by the vacuum. Blood and fluid will trickle out of the wound. It is good to get about a tablespoon of fluid out of each wound. If you don't suck out the germs, the person could get very sick.

You can also use cupping to treat arthritis. First you have to prick the skin in the area of the problem with a special needle that leaves a tiny hole. You must make many holes about one inch apart. For the hands and feet, it is convenient to use narrow segments of bamboo that are like slim cups. I boil them fifteen minutes in a mixture of water, mugwort leaves, and ginger. I take them out with chopsticks and put them quickly on the skin. The heat will create a vacuum. Bloody fluid will come out and help the joints to clear up, but that is not the whole treatment. The rest is dietary. I tell the person to eat only one bowl of rice soup with vegetables and fish for nine days. They must not eat any shellfish or nuts. I tell them they have to be hungry for nine days. When the body is hungry like that it starts eliminating waste that has accumulated in the tissues. Once the body is cleansed of waste, the joints will have a chance to return to normal.

When people have a cold with fever and chills, I tell them to go home and make a rice soup with egg, onion, sea salt, and a lot of black pepper, about half a teaspoon of black pepper for one bowl of soup. After the eating the soup, they need to cover themselves in a blanket to promote sweating. They will sweat out the sickness and get better much faster.

People with a cold but no fever can rub tiger balm on their upper back, neck, and chest. Then take a coin and rub the skin very hard until the skin gets very red and pimply. That helps to eliminate the cold through the skin. It will trigger the cold symptoms to stop, and the congestion will clear up faster.

Clay is good for drawing germs out of wounds. In Vietnam, when someone gets bitten by a dog, the first thing people do is put a thick slab of clay on the bite. If the dog is infected with rabies, they need to go to a doctor, because clay is not enough.

One time a rabid dog came into the village and bit three people. All three of them came to me for help, because they didn't have any money to pay the hospital. There is an effective treatment for rabies in Vietnamese traditional medicine. You need to scrape the soot off the cooking pots and use it to thicken a mixture of herbal medicine. You apply some of the black salve to the wound, and you dilute some of the salve with another medicine to drink. It works very well.

Powdered herbs are very good to make for people who need Chinese herbs but can't afford them. The powder contains the same substances as the packets of medicine, but in higher concentrations, so you can use less. I taught my apprentices how to grind the powder, because I didn't have time. You grind the parts of the plant in which the medicine is most concentrated. It could be the seed kernel, the bark, the root, or the leaf; it is different with every plant. You grind the plant material into a fine powder using a kind of millstone that you roll back and forth with your feet, using all the weight of your body. You have to hold onto a branch so you don't fall.

There are many kinds of medicinal plants that we use to prevent febrile seizures. If a baby wakes up in the night with a high fever and his eyes start to roll back into his head, there is no time to run for a doctor. The parents can catch a house lizard and chew it up, or grind it with their spit and put it in the baby's mouth. It can save the baby's life.

I went to my father's house about once every two weeks to ask him questions about sickness and treatments. I was afraid to tell my father that some strange things were happening to me. I thought it was probably the same bad spirits that had been trying to kill me the first time I went to live at An Son Tu. I thought they were using me to give people bad luck.

One day, Kim told me he was going to Saigon and he would be back the next day. I said, "Oh, you will never get back by tomorrow. I probably won't see you for three days."

Kim came back in three days and told me that the war started up and he had to stay in his friend's bomb shelter.

Another person told me he was going to Vinh Long and I told him, "Be careful and try not to have an accident."

I found out later that the person had been run over by a motorcycle in Vinh Long and he had broken his leg.

Another time was at a funeral. The family offered me some mung bean soup with coconut milk, and I said, "No, thank you. I don't think that soup will agree with my stomach." After I left, everyone who ate that soup came down with diarrhea for twenty-four hours. They thought I had put a bad charm on their soup.

Sometimes I went to Cai Mon to visit Aunt Gioi and Uncle Quon. Once when I was there, some relatives stopped by to visit. They were on their way to Saigon in their boat to sell their fruit to the truckers at the docks. They grew chom choms, oranges, lemons, and coconuts. They also bought longans and mangos from their neighbors to sell for a profit.

I looked at the fruit in their boat and I said, "Why are you bringing so much fruit to sell? What if you can't sell it all? It will go bad."

My relatives came back to complain about me to my aunt. It was the first time they didn't sell one single piece of fruit. They told my aunt that I must have put a curse on them.

I prayed a lot, as I had done the first time the bad spirits were bothering me, but it didn't work. Finally I decided to talk to my father about it. I told him, "Ba, something very strange is happening to me. It seems that whatever I say to people comes true."

My father said, "When you come back from the mountain, it is better not to talk much."

"Do you think bad spirits are bothering me?"

"I don't think so," he said. "Just try to keep your thoughts to yourself."

My father told me, "Some strange things are happening to me, too. Every morning when I go into the clinic, I see stones on the floor. I pick them up and throw them out the window, but there are always more the next day."

I didn't know what to say.

"You didn't bring any stones home from the mountain, did you?" he asked.

I had forgotten entirely. "No," I said.

My father said, "I think someone is throwing the rocks in my window as a prank. Maybe kids."

After that, I stopped expressing my concern that something bad was going to happen, but bad things kept happening that made me look responsible.

The river in front of the temple started doing strange things. Sampans, canoes, and grain boats were making a much higher wake than normal. This wasn't good, because if another canoe or sampan was carrying a heavy cargo and was riding low in the water behind the wake, it would rock and take in water. These high wakes only happened in front of Quoc Thoi Tu. People tried slowing their boats down when they came to my temple, but the wake would stay big. People couldn't blame it on the American boats, because they didn't go on that river.

Fishermen complained, too. One man said he pulled in a good catch, but when he got home there was nothing but driftwood in the net. Another man went fishing off the back of his canoe, and all of a sudden his boat started moving as if it were being towed through the water.

Rumors started spreading about me. Some people said I was like Buddha, and I was very powerful; others said I was a sorcerer, and they were afraid of me. I told my father about it, and he said to stop talking altogether. Just listen.

"How can I do that?" I asked.

He told me, "Chew on a stick."

46

SON OF A GUN

O ne day when my father's patient was sitting at the pulse-reading table waiting for his medicine, he saw one of the rocks that my father had missed, and he picked it up. When my father came back, he said, "Ong Sau, I found gold in your clinic. Do you know where it came from?"

My father said, "Someone has been throwing rocks in here. I've been throwing them out the window into those bushes."

The patient went outside and looked for the rocks and brought them back inside. About four of them were gold. He told my father, "Take these to the jeweler. They are worth half a million dong."

"I'm too busy. You can have them," my father told his patient.

The next time I went to my father's house, he asked me again whether I had brought any rocks home from the forbidden mountain. This time I remembered my rock collection. I searched under the medicine table and found the drawstring bag. There were just a few rocks left.

My father became angry. He said, "You must never take anything off the mountain. Now you will have to return those to where you found them. Go outside and look for the rest. If I had known they were from the mountain, I would never have let my patient take the gold ones."

"What do you mean?" I asked.

"Some of them were gold," my father said.

We guessed it was the water rats that were taking the rocks out of the sack.

M y father lived in a part of town that was wired for electricity, but he was still using candles and an oil lamp. I told him I was going to ask the electric company to turn on his current. He said he only wanted electric lights for the backyard. I put two lightbulbs inside the house anyway. I thought he might get used to them.

My father wasn't getting enough rainwater from his roof to drink, so he hired four people to draw water from the river. I saw him pay them twice the amount I paid my workers at the temple. The next time I came to visit him I hauled the water for him so he wouldn't have to spend so much money. He told me, "These people have no job. They need the money. I want to pay them."

I told my apprentice monks that I was going to the Seven Mountains. They all wanted to go with me, but they knew it was too risky. If they lost their papers, they were as good as dead. I told them whatever happened not to walk out of the temple gate while I was away. If they were taken to the army headquarters, I was the only person who had the authority to ask for their release.

I felt both happy and sad to be back on the forbidden mountain. At least the animals still knew me. I climbed a tree to pick some tamarinds, and the monkeys jumped onto my tree to say hello. I stayed up there with them for a long time. They didn't let me pet them, but they sat close to me.

I headed next for Fourth Uncle's cave, but I couldn't get very far inside. I was angry at myself for even trying.

I went back to the cave where I had seen the big stone Buddha with the glowing stone on its forehead, to return the rocks. I put the some of them in the water and some on the ground. I stayed in the cave for a while and swam and relaxed. I was curious about the gold rocks, so I collected some more rocks and brought them out of the cave into the light. I rubbed one of the jagged stones and it shone like gold. I went back inside and found one more gold nugget. I thought, "These stones can save some lives if I use them to buy a motorcycle. My father is wrong. The spirits wouldn't mind if I used this gold for something important." I put them in my pocket and took them away.

On the way back, I stopped at Long Xuyen and asked around for a jeweler's shop. I found one that was owned by a Chinese couple. The jeweler took one of the nuggets and put it into a stone bowl. Then he lit a blowtorch and held the flame on the stone. I watched it melt into a golden puddle in just a few minutes.

The man said it was real gold. He paid me about a hundred thousand dong for the two nuggets. It wasn't as much as you might think, because the dong had devalued. I took the money and went straight to a Honda dealer, bought a new motorcycle, and drove it back to Cho Lach. It overheated once. I was angry with myself for only taking two nuggets from the cave. If I had taken one more I could have bought the Honda Dam, which had a better engine and a rain guard.

The Honda made it easier to visit my father, so I went to see him more often. He asked me where I got the motorcycle, and I told him I borrowed it from a friend. He didn't want me to ride on a motorcycle, because he didn't trust them. He thought they were much too dangerous. He kept insisting that I take the bus, but I didn't listen to him. Things were changing and he was too old-fashioned.

One time when I was at my father's house, I went down the street visit a neighbor and when came back, my Honda was gone. I thought someone must have stolen it. I walked all over the neighborhood asking people if they saw someone driving a brand-new blue Honda and someone told me they saw my father dump it off the bridge into the river.

I saved my own money to buy a used motorcycle and I never let my father know. I had to use it several times to get my apprentices back. I didn't always make it to Cho Lach headquarters in time, but I always got to My Tho before my monks were shipped to Saigon. I would have never beat the jeep to Saigon.

I taught my apprentices how to make a powerful kind of rice that would make them feel very good. It would give them a lot of energy even when there wasn't much food. It takes one hundred days to make. I used to make it with my father. I called it "flagpole rice."

You take two pounds of sweet rice grain and soak it in salt water for an hour. Then steam it for another hour. You spread it onto a mosquito net and tie all the corners together so the rice can't fall out. Then you hoist it up a pole and leave it up there for twenty-four hours. It doesn't matter what the weather is doing.

Every day for one hundred days you have to take the rice down, steam it again for an hour, and then hoist it back up again. You can't miss a single day, otherwise the rice will go bad. At the end of one hundred days you will only have one bowl of rice left, the color of rice hulls. You pinch it into pills and leave them out in the sun to dry. When you feel hungry you can chew two pills and you will have a lot of energy all day.

I also taught my apprentices how to cut paper into clothing and flags for funerals. They took turns coming with me and chanting at funerals.

Not one of my apprentices was taken to the army.

April 15 is Buddha's birthday. There was to be a big celebration at the Dai Duc's temple.

All the volunteers and my apprentices went to Phuoc Lam Tu together on the bus. I rode my Honda and got there before them. Dai Duc's servants didn't believe I was the master of Quoc Thoi Tu. I was twenty-four and looked about seventeen, and I wore my hair like a servant. I didn't mind sitting with the servants and monks.

There must have been about 150 monks in the hall. Later in the evening, Dai Duc noticed me and told his servants to apologize and to invite me to sit at his table.

He respected me, because he knew my father, and heard that I had lived on the forbidden mountain.

His monks performed an opera with musical accompaniment. I had never heard of monks performing opera before.

When the show was over, one of the guests from the neighborhood got up and announced that his kung fu and tae kwan do school and another school were going to hold a tournament here at the temple. He said any monks who knew martial arts were welcome to compete. He asked the audience if any of the monks knew marital arts. The monks looked around at one another. Some of them said they knew a little, but they weren't good enough. I didn't say anything. The announcement continued, "The tournament will take place in three weeks. If you are interested in competing, please sign your name on the list that will be posted on the front door of the temple."

A week later, I went to visit Dai Duc. While I was there he asked me to check his pulse. I told him that I would send medicine for him. He invited me to join him for lunch. Dai Duc ate meals at his own private table, because of his status. Ong Nam never behaved as if he had a higher status than any of his monks or nuns.

On my way out of the temple, when no one was looking, I signed my name on the tournament list.

About one week later, two monks from Dai Duc's temple came to visit me. They bowed respectfully and told me that someone had signed my name on the martial arts tournament list as a prank.

"It wasn't a prank," I said. "I signed myself up."

They looked at one another.

"Do you know martial arts?" the shorter one asked incredulously.

"Yes," I said. "A little."

"This is going to be a real fight. You could get hurt," said the taller.

"The neighborhood people might laugh at you," said the shorter monk.

"I'm not worried about that," I said.

The monks explained that the fighting schedule was going to be arranged at the end of the week. They wanted me to let them know as soon as possible if I changed my mind.

On the day of the tournament, Dai Duc's servants met me outside the temple door. They had orders to take me to their master's room. I bowed to their master and went inside. Dai Duc invited me to sit at his table and have some tea. After a monk served us, the master said, "These are professional fighters. They will kick you across the floor. The public will laugh at you. You will make all of us monks look foolish."

I told Dai Duc that I understood his concerns, and I assured him that I would not lose. He looked me up and down as if he were trying to find the martial artist in me. I bowed and left the room before he could find it.

My apprentices and the volunteers of my temple had no idea that I was going to fight in the tournament. When my name was announced, they looked stunned. I heard them say, "He looks like a girl, how can he fight?" and "They'll injure him for sure." They looked very worried about me. I cast a glance at Dai Duc, who was sitting with the abbots of the other temples, and saw the pained look on his face.

The audience hushed when they saw me stand up. I unbuttoned my long blue tunic and went up to the front in my blue drawstring pants and blousy shirt. My opponent was wearing a white gi and a black belt. We chose to fight with sticks.

As soon as we started fighting, I could hear the monks in the hall cheering for me. The match lasted about ten minutes, and I won gracefully. Dai Duc was so happy, he invited me to his table and congratulated me.

When my father found out I had fought in the match, he was surprised. He never knew I had also learned marital arts.

He didn't say anything about it when I came home. I think he was waiting for me to tell him. I didn't, so he asked, "Did you go to the martial arts tournament at Phuoc Lam Tu?"

I said, "Yes, it was very nice."

My father just laughed and said, "You son of a gun."

47

I GO WITH THE TIGER

When the news came to Xa Long Thoi that the war was over, all my apprentice monks left for home. It was 1975. I was twenty-five years old. I was surprised to see four of my monks patrolling the streets with guns, wearing Communist police uniforms. I realized they had been sent by the Viet Cong to spy on me.

Twenty out of fifty monks at Dai Duc's temple turned out to be Communist spies, too. They hauled him off to prison for being an important figure and having too many connections in the former government. He died in prison seven years later.

The Communist police also arrested the village chief of Xa Long Thoi along with the members of the village council. They were all replaced by Communist party members. I never saw those men again.

The Communist Party ordered the police to shoot all the dogs. It didn't matter if they had homes or not. Some people hid their dogs and gave them a medicine to stop them from barking. You take some roots from the *chum rot* tree and put them inside a monkfish and roast it in the fire. The juices from the roots go into the fish. When the dog eats the fish, the medicine makes its tongue contract. It becomes shorter and thicker and it chokes off their bark. I went to my uncle's house to make some *chum rot* medicine for Lucky, but the police got to him first.

The number of funerals decreased, but we were still busy because the anniversaries of all those deaths were coming up. I went with my volunteers to many houses to chant. A lot of young women started volunteering to come with me. They started coming to the temple to help out. People were starting to make comments about all the beautiful, young, female assistants I had.

There was a well-known doctor of traditional medicine in Cho Lach who was a friend of my father's. He and his wife went to introduce their youngest daughter to my father as a possible wife for me. The brought her to the temple to meet me. The next time I went to see my father, the girl and the mother were there. My father said they came to his house often, hoping I'd be there.

My father asked me if I was interested in their daughter, but I said I wasn't.

During the next two years, I had no apprentice monks anymore, but I had many beautiful women who cooked for me and washed my clothes and fussed over me. Two of them invited me to their homes for private martial arts lessons. Their parents treated me like a king.

People started gossiping that I had many girlfriends, and that put ideas into my mind. I was feeling a little worried that I might be tempted to go in that direction, and I wondered what to do about that.

Chu Buu and Sau Ve came to the temple several times to talk to me about going home to take care of my father. They said he was not eating well, because he had no one at home to go to the market for him and cook.

I knew it was my duty as his only child to take care of him in his old age.

I left my position at Quoc Thoi Tu in December 1977 and went to help my father prepare the New Year celebration.

The Tiger came to visit my father one day, and when he saw me there he began asking me questions about Fourth Uncle and the cave. I noticed there was a bump on his forehead just above his third eye. I asked him, "What happened to your forehead?"

"It's how I pray," he said. "I pray like that."

"What do you mean?" I said.

"When I chant I hit my head on the floor, to relieve my guilt," the Tiger said. I didn't know what to say.

"Things are very bad for me." The Tiger's face flashed with anger, and then he looked like he was going to cry.

"The Communists keep bothering me. They tortured me in prison twice. They are always watching me because of my past. A lot of people try to get me in trouble. I sat in front of the temple one day and poured gasoline on myself and set myself on fire, but my wife poured water over me. I want to go away from here. I want to live in the cave with the teacher and never come back."

After the Tiger left, I told my father about our conversation.

"I know," my father said. "He begged me to bring him to the cave so many times that I could no longer tell him no."

"You brought him?"

"Yes, twice."

My father said that both times he watched the Tiger give away all his possessions, his car, his money, his motorcycle, his clothing, and his coffeemaker. Both times my father watched him cry and kiss his wife and children good-bye.

"He is addicted to coffee and cigarettes, he couldn't even make it to the cave."

"Then why did you take him back a second time when you knew he would never make it?" I asked.

My father explained, "I thought at least it would motivate him to quit smoking. Besides, who are we to judge another's path to realization? Do you know the story of Milarepa? He was a Tibetan who lived one thousand years ago. He had a terrible temper, killed thirty people, but later in his life he attained Buddhahood."

I said, "He begged me to bring him to the cave. Could I please go?"

I could tell by the look on my father's face that he didn't want me to go, but he didn't say anything.

took an early bus to Cai Be the following morning. The basketball hoops were gone and the wooden fence had been removed. Otherwise it looked just the same.

The Tiger was finishing up a huge plate of rice, noodles, tofu, fish, potatoes, sweet potatoes, greens, salad, tapioca, cookies, and a large glass of coffee with sugar. His wife offered me some, and I ate a little. The Tiger smoked his last cigarette. He smoked 555's, a brand of cigarettes that cost three times as much as regular cigarettes.

We got ready to leave. The Tiger cried as he kissed his wife and children good-bye for the third time.

W̶e rode on the bus for free, because the same gangsters worked on the buses as before the Communist revolution. We climbed up the forbidden mountain as far as the temple and spent the night. We started out early the next morning. We had only been on the mountain thirty minutes when the spirits started making coffee.

The Tiger stopped and sniffed. "I smell coffee," he said. "It smells like someone left some right around here." I told him he'd never find it, but he insisted on trying. I sat down and watched him looking behind trees and crawling through bushes.

We started out again, but by this time he had tired himself out looking for the coffee. He was walking very slowly, dragging his feet. Finally he sat down and said, "I am so tired. If I could only have a cup of coffee I'd feel fine."

I had an idea. I told him to wait there and I would be right back. I walked for about five minutes to a spot where he couldn't see me and I wished for a cup of coffee to give to my friend.

The table appeared, with a cup of coffee. I took the coffee back to the Tiger.

"Where did you get that? Is there a house back there?"

I didn't explain. He looked into the cup and complained, "But it's only half full."

He tasted the coffee and said, "All my life I have been drinking the best coffee, but I never tasted coffee like this."

I said, "Now you will feel better."

He finished the coffee and said, "I want to give them back their cup."

I told him to leave it on the rock.

Fourth Uncle told me not to give anyone anything from the spirits for the purpose of impressing them. I wasn't trying to impress the Tiger. He already knew a lot about the magic on the mountain. I was just trying to help him make it to the cave, and it worked.

We lit the candles and crawled through the opening to the cave. We made it through the first tunnel all the way to the downward hole.

I told him to wait a minute before climbing into the hole after me because I didn't want him to step on my fingers. I went all the way down to the bottom and I waited for him. It was taking him a long time. I called up to him not to be afraid, but he didn't answer.

I waited a few more minutes and called to him again, but he didn't answer again.

I climbed back up the hole and I didn't see him. I went all the way back outside, but he wasn't there. I thought he might have started back down the mountain to get some more coffee. I didn't know what to do, so I just sat down and waited about thirty minutes.

He didn't show up, so I went back inside the cave to look for him some more. I went down the hole and there he was.

He was furious with me. He said I had gone ahead to see the master and left him behind. I explained that I was looking for him the whole time, but he didn't believe me.

We went just a little further and arrived at a dead end. "I guess it's not a good time," I said.

The Tiger wanted to try again the next day, but I told him it was a waste of time. He didn't believe me, so I took him to Elephant Mountain to talk with Ong Nam about it.

Ong Nam looked at the Tiger and said, "Do you still eat?"

The Tiger said, "Yes."

Ong Nam said, "When you live in the cave with the teacher, you barely eat anything."

Ong Nam invited the Tiger to stay for a while at An Son Tu so he could practice meditating in a cave. The Tiger said he would like to try.

After breakfast the next morning, we brought him to one of the caves and left him there alone to meditate. We returned for him noon. He almost fainted on the way down to the temple. We gave him more food to eat the next morning, but it wasn't enough. He was weak when we fetched him the second day. By the third day he was ready to go home.

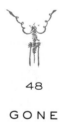

48

GONE

My father didn't want me to stay home with him. He wanted me to study more. In mid-March 1978 he told me that he was taking me back to Elephant Mountain, to arrange for Thay Hai, my plant medicine teacher, and Thay Hai, my acupuncture teacher, to continue with my training.

On the morning we were to leave, a man came to the house who was having a medical emergency. His jaw was pulled to one side, and he couldn't talk or eat. His hands and arms were clenched, and he couldn't walk. My father put liniment on his skin and massaged his muscles. He gave him acupuncture and medicine to drink. He helped that man all day until his jaw released and he was able to control his muscles again.

We were getting ready to leave the next morning when some other people came to the house with a very sick child. It was unusual for people to come when my father wasn't supposed to be home.

This continued for three days. On the fourth day, we heard a rumor that the Khmer Rouge, Cambodia's Communist army under Pol Pot, had crossed the border to Elephant Mountain, and was attacking the villages.

That afternoon, a police officer came to visit my father. He was someone who liked my father very much and sometimes stopped by for a visit. My father didn't usually stop work to take tea with anyone, but since he was a Communist official, he thought it was a good thing to do. This policeman told my father the rumors were true.

My father didn't want to go until we had word that the fighting had stopped. We finally left during the second week in May 1978.

As our bus drew closer to Xa Ba Chuc, we saw signs of war and devastation: bomb craters, houses blown to bits, no people. The bus let us out into a deserted Xa Ba Chuc marketplace, just a few people here and there, and a lot of police. I looked at my father, but he didn't look at me. There was such a heavy feeling in the air that I felt ill. We climbed down from the minivan. My father shook his prayer beads down into his hand and started praying.

He was praying while we walked. We made our way up the village road to Tam Buu Tu. We had to walk around a large crater about six feet deep. We passed black charred remains of houses. It was eerie; even the birds were gone. There were no children playing in the street, no people in the yards preparing the evening meal, no smell of food cooking over a fire, no flickering orange flames.

We reached Tam Buu Tu. All of the star trees were gone. The ground around the temple was charred and bare, no more flowering bushes and lawn. The outer side wall of the temple was a pile of rubble. Then I noticed three long mounds of earth. We stopped were we were. My father sank to his knees and prayed. I mimicked my father, but I couldn't concentrate on my prayers.

He got up and walked closer to the mounds of earth, where an altar had been set up. I followed him. There were many incense stubs and some bunches of bananas, but not much.

About twenty people walked out of the temple toward us. I recognized Anh The's aunt and uncle among them.

"Chu Chin," I said, "where is Anh The? Where is everyone?"

"Come inside the temple," another man said.

My father and I followed the villagers into the ruins of the temple. Tho Thay's altar was a pile of broken wood, porcelain, and bits of silk. His sandalwood throne had been hacked to pieces.

"We are leaving these ruins here like this. We are afraid the Khmer Rouge could come back at any time. We don't want them to know they destroyed the replica. To Thay's throne is safe. Chu Hai switched them."

Other people were scrubbing the blood off the walls. Lead Lips was among them. He turned around and looked at me, but he didn't come over.

W e went outside with Chu Chin and two men from the village. Everyone else went back to work in the temple. The five of us sat down on a bench in the shade.

Chu Chin said, "We still don't know who the survivors are. They are still coming back. Only the ones who managed to escape before the Khmer Rouge surrounded the village survived. We were the lucky ones."

They told us the story.

"They started bombing us on April first. They launched a thousand missiles a day for seven days. Many people died. On April seventh, a missile hit the wall of the temple during the evening sutra. Forty-five people were killed and forty-six were wounded. On April eleventh, more missiles hit the temple and forty more died and twenty were wounded."

My father said, "The army didn't come here to defend you?"

"No," they said.

"Well, they certainly knew about it," my father told the villagers. "A policeman in Cho Lach told me about it on April fifth."

Cho Lach is all the way on the opposite side of Vietnam. Everyone was stunned.

Chu Chin continued, "On April fourteenth, the Khmer Rouge surrounded the village. Eight hundred people went to Tam Buu Tu for safety, two hundred went to Phi Lai, and one hundred went to An Son Tu. The soldiers took everyone out of the temples and brought them into the fields. They separated the men from the women. They raped and tortured many of the women and they shot everyone.

"They threw grenades under the altars where people were hiding. There were only two survivors, women who lay among the dead bodies in the field for seven days. They crawled to the stream every night to get a sip of water, and then went back to lay the same spot.

"Some people went to hide in the caves and others hid in trees, in holes, in bushes, anywhere they could think of. These people were hunted down with dogs and beaten to death and hacked to pieces.

"It was horrible. People heard their friends and neighbors begging for their lives. They heard people screaming from being tortured. The soldiers swung the children by the legs and smashed their heads against the trees. They stabbed the girls and women through the vagina until they were dead.

"Their dogs found all the caves except one. They threw grenades in and killed everyone.

"Chu Tam the sugar maker and his wife were hiding in the last cave with forty people. Their babies were all crying because they hadn't eaten for days. The others told them their babies were going to give away their hiding place. They told them they had to sacrifice their children to save the others. Chu Tam and Co Tu smothered their four children just thirty minutes before the soldiers came to rescue them.

Anh The's uncle said, "By the time the survivors came back here, the bodies were so decomposed, it was impossible to tell who was who. That is why we put everyone together in a mass grave."

"We dragged everyone out of the cave and down the mountain," one man said, "We thought we should bury everyone together.

"There is another mass grave over at An Son Tu," the man said. "They even killed the Cambodians. They killed everyone, Chinese, Cambodian, Vietnamese," said the other, "Over three thousand all together."

"We have trouble sleeping at night. The air is foul with nightmares and ghosts. We are all afraid the Khmer Rouge are going to come back to kill the rest of us."

Nobody could understand how the soldiers in the Khmer Rouge could commit such atrocities.

I didn't sleep much at all that night. In the morning, my father and I set out for An Son Tu on foot. My father strode along with his black stone Buddha bumping against his hip. I kept up, but my feet kept stumbling as if I didn't know where the ground was. We didn't know if Ong Nam was still alive.

Once more I couldn't believe my eyes. Ong Nam and Chi were standing in front of the temple. Ong Nam looked up and exclaimed, but Chi didn't know it was me. I bounded up to him and squeezed both of his arms. In my culture we don't hug our friends.

On the bus ride back, my father chanted and meditated. I didn't. I was feeling haunted by the heavy ethers of Elephant Mountain.

The horror followed us home. The day after we arrived, I went to get some water from the river and I saw a skull bobbling at the edge of the river. The neighbors told me that a lot of bodies had washed up. They said the Khmer Rouge were dumping bodies into the Mekong River.

Hundreds of bodies came floating down the river during the next weeks. Whole villages had been dumped at a time. That is how we Vietnamese people came to know that a dead man always floats face down, while a dead women floats face up. We also know that a dead body left out in the sun bloats up so huge that you can hardly recognize the face, while a dead body that has been soaking in the river only bloats from the neck down. You can see the face clearly enough.

We dragged the bodies up the bank and buried them. We were getting accustomed to seeing death in our river. The children started hanging the skulls in the trees for a prank.

My father and I went back to Elephant Mountain two months later, so we could find out if anyone else had come back alive.

Ba Bay's eldest son, Chu Hai, his wife, and their three children were among those who came back. Tattoo and his family were also alive.

Lead Lips disappeared after the temple was cleaned up. People thought he went to live in a cave in Long Mountain.

Everyone else had been killed, Ba Bay, Kam, Lieu, Anh The, Anh Thiep, Anh Muoi, the old men, my plant medicine teacher and his family, my acupuncture teacher and his family, even Ong Chin and Grenade were killed.

Vietnamese Red Cross workers were there, building an ossuary memorial to remember the massacre. They were in the process of pulling the bodies out of the mass graves and cleaning and sorting the bones. Three months underground was enough time for the meat to come off easily. The eyes and brains were no longer inside the skulls.

The skulls and bones were drying in the sun. The workers were dipping the bones in wax and placing them inside the hexagonal glass case. The skulls were sorted into categories, babies, teenagers, mothers, fathers, grandmothers, and grandfathers.

After one year, the skulls all turned yellow. Volunteers had to take them all out and dry them in the sun again, and treat them with a chemical.

I saw the monument when it was finished. Of the 3,155 people killed in the massacre, 1,159 of them are inside the memorial. Their skulls are looking out of the glass case.

49

M A I

The Communist party didn't send me to serve in the army because I was the only child of my aged father. In Vietnam, the most important obligation we have is to care for our parents when they are old and to pray for them after they die. Even the Vietnamese National Army thought twice before drafting the eldest son of an aging parent.

The Communist party ordered me to work in the Cho Lach hospital. I wanted to work at home with my father, but they threatened not to allow him to work at all if I didn't follow their orders.

I worked in the outpatient clinic with two other doctors who knew Vietnamese herbal medicine. Thay Hai was in his fifties, and Anh Hai was just three years older than I. All three of us were "Hai," the first born, otherwise we wouldn't have been trained as doctors. We would have been drafted long ago.

Anh Hai had also been a monk and had studied acupuncture. Thay Hai didn't do acupuncture, but he knew a lot about Vietnamese plant medicine. We didn't have many Chinese herbs in our clinic, because they were too expensive. We were expected to go outside and collect local plants.

The hospital assigned us ten assistants. These were teenage boys and girls as young as fourteen. After training them to identify the plants we needed, we often sent them out on their own while we stayed in the clinic to treat the patients.

After I'd worked there for about one year, I was transferred to a jungle outpost in Cu Chi, west of Saigon, to look for medicinal plants and ship them to the hospital. In particular, they wanted me to find *do trang* bark, *hong huyet* and *mot thong* vines, and the tuberous root of the *hoa son*. These are considered to be Chinese medicinal plants, because they are sold in the Chinese herbal store. Linh, one of the teenage boys, was selected to go with me.

I didn't want to go. I told my supervisor that my father was ninety-two years old, but he didn't care. He said I would only have to be there for three years. He repeated that if I didn't agree to go, they would prevent my father from working.

I lived at a Communist base camp with twenty soldiers. The base was not very comfortable. We had to walk half an hour to bathe in a small stream and carry water back to our camp in bamboo tubes that we strapped to our backs. By the time we got back we were all hot and sweaty again.

We took turns walking four miles to market to buy food for the week. There wasn't enough money to buy much, just some tiny pinky-sized dried fish, rice, sea salt, oranges, guava, and watermelon. We had all the vegetables, bananas, and plantains we could eat in the jungle.

Linh and I spent every day walking around in the jungle. We made a bamboo rack to dry the plants in the sun. The soldiers liked me because I brought back mushrooms, roots, nuts, and leaves from the jungle to cook for dinner. I also made medicine for them when they were sick.

I was able to see my father one day a month, when I delivered a shipment of medicine to the hospital. It was about a six-hour drive from the base camp to Cho Lach.

There was an abandoned American army base about one mile from our camp. The soldiers often went there to look for useful things, like tools and machine parts. All the weapons had been taken out already. Someone had the idea to plant a vegetable garden out there on the cleared land between the buildings. It was overgrown with tall grass and bushes.

We brought shovels and hoes and started to turn over the soil. Somebody's shovel set off a land mine.

woke up in the Cu Chi hospital. Both my legs were covered in bandages. I felt a lot of pain. The nurse told me that one person died, two lost their legs, and one lost his hand. She said I was the luckiest of the injured. I was just full of shrapnel.

She began dabbing a liquid to soften the dried blood before she changed my bandages. Then she started pulling them off before the liquid was on long enough. It hurt a lot. Blood squirted up like a fountain from a wound on the right side of my groin. I had lost chunks of flesh on both sides of my groin, out of my calves, and on the tops of my feet. My doctor said the wounds went down to the tendons and the bone. I knew I would never have the strength to jump into trees anymore.

My father came all the way to Cu Chi once a week to bring me food. I had to stay in the hospital for two months, then I went back to live with my father. One month later, the shrapnel that was still between my tendons and my bones caused an infection, and I had to go to the hospital in My Tho for surgery.

The Communist Party gave me one month to recover at home. After two weeks, when I felt better, I started working with my father again.

When my leave of absence was over, I tried to convince the hospital administration that I needed to stay home with my father. They told me it was out of the question.

I was assigned to the pharmacy building to create formulas for different kinds of pills: painkillers, decongestants, sleeping pills, muscle relaxants, and antiparasite medication. This medicine was to be used at Cho Lach Hospital, and to be sold to other hospitals.

My partner was a young man, just back from Saigon, where he was trained to operate the tablet- and capsule-making machines.

Each day, I had to cook big vats of herbs. In each vat, I boiled fifteen gallons of water down to two gallons of medicine. Then I mixed the liquid medicine with powdered medicine that I ground from the strongest parts of the plants, using the foot-powered grinding wheel. The hospital eventually gave me five assistants to grind the medicine and stir the vats. The medicine came out very good.

Once my partner and I had trained our assistants well, we felt justified to cover for each other. Both of us took days off from work. Our salaries were so low that we both wanted to do some other work on the side. We arranged our schedules so that we worked in tandem. I worked part-time in the hospital and part-time with my father for about two years.

It was 1980; I was thirty-years old. People started bringing their daughters to our house to meet me. They would talk to my father in private, and then my father would ask me if I was interested in her. One woman brought her twin daughters. They were the kind of twins that had shared the same placenta. Those girls had to stay together, which means they had to marry the same man. They were very beautiful and kind, but I told my father I wasn't interested. My heart was longing to go back to the cave with Fourth Uncle.

It was around that time that I started hearing my father tell his patients, "Take this medicine every day and get well, because later you will go looking for me everywhere and you won't find me."

One day my father told me he was going to the forbidden mountain. I was surprised that he invited me to come along. I asked if he was going to ask Fourth Uncle to accept me as his student again. He said that I should ask him myself.

I was both happy and nervous to be going back. We climbed the mountain together, and I followed my father into the cave.

We arrived at Fourth Uncle's chamber. I saw the shape of his head, shoulders, and torso sitting still on his shelf. We both climbed up. Fourth Uncle smiled at my father. I had never seen him smile like that. Fourth Uncle said to my father, "My friend, how long are you staying?"

My father told him, "Three days." Then they started speaking in a language I didn't understand. I wanted to know what they were saying, so I listened carefully. I didn't recognize a single word. It didn't sound like Chinese or Khmer.

I climbed down the ledge and went over to lie down on my rock. My father and Fourth Uncle spoke together for a long time. Fourth Uncle was different with my father. He was happy. With me, he was always serious.

I climbed back up and sat down next to my father. I worked up the courage to ask. I said, "Uncle, I wanted to ask you if I could stay here and learn more with you."

Fourth Uncle answered, "No, Quang, you must live outside now. Your father is old now, you must stay with him."

I felt so sad. I thought I might never see my teacher again once my father died.

Fourth Uncle spoke to my father in Vietnamese. He asked, "My dear friend, when will you be going home?"

My father said, "Maybe a few more years. I want to finish everything before I go."

Before we left, my father collected some medicine for his patients.

On the bus ride home, my father told me that he had asked Fourth Uncle if he could leave his body in the cave, and go in and out of it like Fourth Uncle does. Fourth Uncle told him that it wouldn't work, because my father had been eating food for so long. It would take many years to be clean enough. He said my father's body would decompose.

first met Mai (pronounced My) in the spring of 1981. She had come to my father's house with her neighbor, Ba Tam, a long-time patient of my father. I had come home from the hospital for lunch and met Mai briefly.

Ba Tam had never married, and didn't have children of her own. When she was a young woman, she moved in with her older sister after her sister's husband died and helped raise her nieces and nephews. Ba Tam and Ba Nam had a nice house in Cai Be, next to the river. I knew them for many years. Ba Tam loved Mai and treated her like a daughter.

In the fall, I was on my way to Saigon to buy medicine and spent the night at Ba Tam's house so I could catch the bus out of Cai Be the next morning. As soon as I arrived at Ba Tam's house to ask her if I could spend the night, she went right over to Mai's house and invited her for dinner. That evening the three of us ate dinner together. That was the second time I saw Mai.

A few months later, Mai came with Ba Tam to my father's house to get some medicine. I went into the kitchen to get the teapot to make some medicine for one of my patients, and I saw her standing over the cooking fire stirring some soup.

I said hello to her and took a teapot down from where the pots and pans were hanging, then I went back to my patient.

At the end of the day, my father looked at my face and started laughing.

"What?" I asked.

He pointed to the side of my face. It was smudged with soot from the pots and pans. He said, "Maybe the kitchen spirits are trying to tell you something."

Mai and Ba Tam spent that night at our house. After dinner we were sitting outside by the fire drinking tea and eating cookies. Mai said she heard I could read palms very well. She asked me to read hers.

She wanted to know when she should get married. She was twenty years old, and very pretty. She already had two proposals of marriage. I told her that judging by her palm, she should wait until she was twenty-four.

The next morning, Mai asked my father to read her palm again. My father looked at her palm, but didn't say anything more than, "Oh, very good." Mai and Ba Tam left after lunch.

The next day when I came home from work, I found my father resting outside in his hammock. He asked me, "How do you like that girl Mai?"

"She seems nice," I said.

"Of all the girls you know, which one do you like the best?"

"Mai," I said.

Ba Tam had told my father some things about Mai. She said that Mai's father was killed when a bomb struck his rice field in 1973. She said that Mai's mother raised her three younger children alone, and sent them all to school, and that she never remarried. My father thought that Mai came from parents who truly loved each other.

Ba Tam also told my father that when Mai was nine years old, she wanted to go to temple to pray. She said they would often walk together, and that is how they became good friends.

My father's friends had been pressuring me to get married so my father could know his grandchildren before he died. I started thinking about Mai. One day I told my father I was ready to marry.

I went with Ba Tam to Mai's house to meet her mother and grandparents. Ba Tam asked Mai if she wanted to marry me. She said, "Didn't he tell me not to get married until I was twenty-four?"

Ba Tam said, "Well, he's changed his mind."

Mai said she would think about it.

A week later, Mai told Ba Tam she would marry me. Ba Tam brought my father to Mai's house to meet her family. My father checked Mai's birthday and he figured out what day would be good for our wedding. It would be on April 19, 1982.

My father gave Ba Tam money for Mai's dress, and he and I went to buy a pair of gold earrings and a gold chain necklace with a golden Buddha on it for the ceremony.

My father told Mai's mother not to bother roasting a pig. Mai explained to her mother that her future father-in-law didn't like to kill animals. We had a simple wedding at Mai's mother's house. My father gave us money as a wedding present.

Three days after the wedding, I took Mai to Elephant Mountain to Tam Buu Tu and An Son Tu. It was still a ghost town. I was sorry she couldn't have seen it when it was green and lush and full of people.

We didn't stay long. It is not a pleasant place to be. On the way back, I took her to Tay An Tu on Sam Mountain to see the ancient statue. We arrived during a holiday and had to sleep on mats on the ground in a sea of people.

I didn't go back to work after Mai and I were married. I told my supervisor that my father was old, and I needed to stay home and take care of him. My supervisor told me the same thing he always said, that if I didn't work at the hospital, my father would not be allowed to work. I said that is okay, because my father is too old to work.

50

MY FATHER GOES HOME

My father started going away every week to check up on his patients. That way the police wouldn't know that he was still working as a doctor. He would buy medicine in Cai Be, Cay Lay, or My Tho, and then he would prepare about fifty packets and take them on the bus to his patients in many places, as far away as Chau Doc City and Elephant Mountain. His patients stopped coming to the house. I asked my father why there weren't any more people coming to see him, and he said that he prayed for the spirits to let all his patients know not to come to the house. I think if the police had known he was still treating patients, they would have put my father in jail.

It was also dangerous for me to work privately as a doctor, so I started traveling to different villages and cities, too. My wife stayed home and used some of the money my father had given us to buy wholesale gold jewelry in Saigon and sell it at a small market in Phu An, near Cay Lay.

My father had some patients who were sick with cancer. I don't know if it was because of the chemicals from the war. Almost all of them had been to the hospital for radiation and chemotherapy and had been told they had just months to live. They had skin cancer, lung cancer, breast and uterine cancer, and liver cancer.

My father never knew if they would be strong enough to get well because they had been sick for a long time, and were weak from the treatment at the hospital. He would first give them some medicine from the Seven Mountains, a kind of long, thin root we call *ong mot*. He told them to cut a few slices and to put them in a cup of hot water to soak and then drink. If their pain lessened and their appetite came back, he would give them medicine to clean out their bowels. The medicine would make them move their bowels ten times in one day. Those patients would say that their waste was very foul, but afterward they felt light and had more energy. Then he would give them regular packets of medicine. He had several patients who had been told they had two or three months to live, but their cancer was in remission for many years.

Ong mot root is very good medicine. My father also used *ong mot* to help old people who were stooped over to stand up straight again. He would give them acupuncture down their back and then apply the juice of the *ong mot* on their skin, and also give them some to drink. You have to repeat the treatment once a day for seven days. It works very well.

My father told me he was sad that he hadn't learned this treatment until after his mother had died.

In September 1983, my father decided to give his house away to the government. It was a large house, full of furniture that people had given him. Before he signed the papers, he told his neighbors and friends they could take anything they wanted, furniture, blankets and pots and pans and tools, everything. The only things he didn't give away were his medicine, his candles and incense, his books, and his black stone Buddha.

I had to sign a paper that said I was Thau Van Nguyen's only heir, and that I understood that he was transferring ownership of his house to the government. My father's friends didn't understand why he wasn't leaving the house to me. Chu Buu said, "How can you leave your son with nothing?"

My father answered his friend so I could hear, too. He said, "I have given Quang his skill. That is all he needs to lead a simple life. If he works with his heart, he will have food and a place to live all of his days, but if he has too much he will get lazy and he will stop trying to help."

My father turned to me and put his hands on my shoulders and said, "This is the life of a barefoot doctor, do you understand?"

I told him I did.

My wife and I helped my father move his things to Ba Tam's house. It took us two trips on a taxi boat to bring all my father's belongings from Cho Lach to Cai Be.

I don't think my father realized that the police would be watching us more closely at Ba Tam's house than they had at our own house. Only three people were registered to live in that house, Ba Nam, Ba Tam, and Ba Nam's youngest son. All her other children had moved away to Saigon and to the United States. Mai didn't have to worry, because she practically grew up in that house, so the officials were used to seeing here there.

My father and I had to go back to Cho Lach, to the police station, to get a visitor's permit. Then we had to have it stamped at the police station in Cai Be. The visitor's pass was expensive, and the longest we could stay was two weeks. My father and I went through all that trouble and expense just once. After that, we made sure the police didn't catch us there without a permit. If they had, we could have been sent to prison.

For that reason, my father and I traveled more than before, visiting the homes of our patients from the South China Sea to the Cambodian border. We didn't always travel together because there were too many patients to care for. Mai stayed with her mother and with Ba Tam. I didn't get to see her very much.

My father started telling his patients not to throw away their herbs after they were used. He told them to dry the boiled herbs in the sun and then put them in a jar to use again in case anyone in the house got sick. He told them to keep each packet of used herbs separate, and to cook them with an inch of ginger, sliced up, and in less water. He told them they could reuse the herbs indefinitely until they disappeared. He said to do that because he was going away.

One time when we were riding the bus home from Chau Doc City, he told me, "In the future, if you go far away from here, remember the things I taught you. Remember the way we live. You don't need to make more money than you would use to live a simple life. If you get too busy, just slow down so you can have time to pray and meditate. You will be more healthy, and you will feel better. Always remember the spirits who help us. Even if you live somewhere else, try to do the same."

. . .

It was dangerous for us. We had to hide our medicine in Ba Tam's house. The two sisters helped us because they believed in what we were doing. The Communist Party was in the process of standardizing health care in Vietnam. All doctors were sent to work in government-run hospitals and clinics, and they were told how to work. My country was phasing out people like my father, who practiced medicine in a traditional way that involved spirituality.

Soon the Chinese herbal stores in Cai Be, Cay Lay, and My Tho were shut down. The only place we could still buy medicine was in Saigon. We had to be careful because we were working illegally. If the police caught us carrying a lot of medicine, or if they saw a lot of medicine in our house, they would assume we were practicing medicine illegally and we would be sent to a labor camp or to prison.

Once when we were visiting the Tiger, my father told him he didn't have much time left. The Tiger wanted my father to come back to live in the Chinese temple with him, but my father didn't want to. He said he wanted to die in peace, with just his family and close friends around him. I assumed the Tiger wanted to have my father stay with him so that the people would treat him better.

Even though Ba Tam's house was not far from the Chinese temple, the Tiger didn't like to go there. The house had a fenced-in yard, and he didn't feel comfortable waiting at the gate to be let in, so he didn't come often.

My father kept telling his patients to come to get more medicine, because he was going away. They would ask him where he was going. He always told people he was going home. I don't think they understood what he was talking about.

In December 1983, my father went to say good-bye to Fourth Uncle. When he came back to Cai Be, his clothes were all wet from the rain and he had caught cold. My father would sometimes get a light cold when the seasons changed. He would be slightly sick for two or three days but never enough to stop working.

One day, at Ba Tam's house, my father began looking through the bags where we stored his belongings. He took out some books and told me, "These are no good. I want you to burn them."

They were books of magic spells. I did as he asked.

Then he asked Ba Nam and Ba Tam to give him some land to lie down. They understood that he was referring to his grave and told him, "Of course. Don't worry."

My father told Ba Nam and Ba Tam that in the future their orchard would be more productive, and they would have enough money to live the rest of their lives in comfort.

We wondered why he was thinking so much about death. He looked and acted as healthy as ever.

On December 15, he asked Ba Tam and me to get him a plain, simple coffin. We went to the coffin maker to order one. By chance, he had one sitting in front of his shop all ready. I asked the neighbors to help me carry it home.

On December 16, he asked us to dig a hole in the ground for him.

When my father awoke very early on the morning of December 17, he went over to his belongings and took two red candles out of one of the bags, four inches wide and three feet high. He put those at the foot of his wooden bed. He took out a new white shirt and white pants, and the head scarf that Ong Tam of Buu Minh Doung temple had made for him.

Next to the candles, clothes, and head scarf, my father put the small wooden box of ashes he had asked me put inside his coffin with him.

After arranging his things, my father went over to the next bed, where Mai and I were sleeping, and sat down. I woke up and sat on the edge of the bed with him. He looked into my eyes and said, "Try. You can do it."

I could tell he was worried that I might be angry with him, because he gave away everything to other people and not to me. Truly, I didn't care about that. I reassured him that it was the right thing to do, I said, "It's our way. I want always to live our way."

Ba Nam brought my father some soup for breakfast. He held the bowl up in one hand and said, "This is the last one." We felt sad, but we didn't believe he was dying. He did not look like a dying man.

During that day, my father stayed in the house. He didn't go to the fish pond toilet. He asked me to help him with the chamber pot. I don't know how he did it, because he didn't take any medicine, but my father cleaned out his bowels. He filled the chamber pot seven times that day. After that, he was weak, and he stayed lying down.

On December 18, my father told me to pick eight different kinds of flowers and to boil them in water. He said to take a cloth and help him bathe with that water. I asked Ba Tam's neighbor to help me hold my father up so he wouldn't fall. The neighbor was reluctant to get his hand wet because he had just cut it badly and was afraid of infection. I told him not to worry.

The neighbor helped me carry the pot of flower water outside to the bathing stall and then he held onto one of my father's arms and I held onto the other. We brought him outside to the stall. I washed my father's long hair and his body, dried him, and dressed him in his white clothes. Then we led him back to his bed.

That evening my father said to us, "At three o'clock I go."

There was a big windup clock on the bureau. At one o'clock, he started to meditate as always. He sat cross-legged on the bed. Everyone was sleeping. I woke up, sat on my bed, and mediated with him. I didn't think he was going to die that night.

At two o'clock, he opened his eyes and told me to light the candles and the incense. I woke Mai, Ba Tam, and Ba Nam.

At five minutes before three o'clock, my father sat on the edge of his bed. Mai and I went over and sat on his bed next to him. He hugged me and told me, "Quang . . . It is time for me to go."

He tied the head scarf around his head and put his hands together and prayed, "My father and my mother, please help me go."

He laid back down just as the clock struck three and he closed his eyes as if he were going to sleep.

We stayed up all night praying for my father. The next morning Ba Tam went to the Chinese temple to tell the Tiger my father was dead. He came later that morning with a lot of people from the Chinese community who were dressed in their traditional mourning clothes.

My father had said that he wanted to be buried right away. He didn't want the news of his death to spread very far because then hundreds of people would come to the house and give us a lot of work to do. About eighty people came.

We set my father's coffin on two chairs. Everyone who came to the funeral knelt and prayed beside my father's coffin, and when they stood up Mai and I bowed to them.

By three o'clock in the afternoon, my father's body was in the ground.

After he was buried and everyone went home, I sat next to my father's grave and tried not to cry. I patted and smoothed the earth with my hand as if I was straightening out my father's patched shirt. I wondered where he was now.

I wondered if I would ever find him in heaven. I thought he might not go to heaven at all; he might just stay on the forbidden mountain with his teacher.

My heart was broken. I felt I had no connection to anyone, not even to my wife. I had no one to advise or teach me.

I couldn't help myself. I cried a little bit.

A large brown and yellow butterfly appeared on the mound of earth. I followed it toward the house. It flew in through the doorway and lighted on the altar where my father's candles and incense were still burning. It stayed on the altar for five minutes, and then it flew out the window. I followed it back to my father's grave, and it disappeared.

51

ESCAPE

continued working the way my father and I had done before, smuggling
Chinese medicine around the countryside and sleeping in a different house
every night. I didn't want to go back to making pills in the hospital, because
then I wouldn't be living in the way my father had taught me.

My wife understood why I was working that way. She loved my father. She
respected me for wanting to live as he did, even if it meant that we rarely saw
each other.

It was getting more difficult to travel to Saigon. There were never enough
buses. Long lines of people were turned away and had to try again the next day.
Sometimes friends of the Tiger would see me standing in line and would put me
on the bus ahead of all the other people. I didn't feel comfortable doing that, so
I stopped taking the bus entirely and went by boat, which took much longer.

The boat drivers started doing the same because they knew and loved my
father. I borrowed my friend's motorcycle to go to Saigon and was almost
searched at a checkpoint. After that, I always went to Saigon on the back roads,
which took five hours instead of three. I stayed overnight at a relative's house
where my father had been seeing patients for many years. Now they were my
patients.

. . .

After going from door to door every night for a year, I became very tired. I told my wife that I needed to go back to the cave to get my physical and spiritual strength back. I told her that if Fourth Uncle accepted me into the cave, I might not come home for several years. My wife knew that my father spent close to twenty years in the cave, though not all at the same time. Before we were married, I told her that I would like to do the same. She said she understood.

I climbed up the forbidden mountain and sat outside the cave for about thirty minutes praying for Fourth Uncle to take me back as his student. I entered the cave and was able to go farther than the other times. I felt hopeful. I reached a small chamber and was surprised to see Fourth Uncle sitting there as if he were waiting for me.

"Hello, Quang," he said, "I am sorry that your father had to leave you."

"Uncle, I have come back to ask you to let me stay with you and study more. Outside is very difficult. Everything has changed. The new government doesn't let me work the way my father taught me. I have to work in secret. I am very tired. I think I cannot help people, because my body and my spirit are so tired."

"That may be, but you have to stay outside now. Don't worry, just go home and try. Soon you will be going far away."

"I don't want to go far away, I want to come here from time to time, as my father did. That is all I need to help people."

"Your time with me is over. You belong somewhere else. Don't come back again. You will just be wasting your time."

I tried not to cry. I put my hands together and bowed my head and prayed for my teacher. I said, "I pray that you stay healthy and that your skill reaches the highest level. I wish in the future I will be back and that I will see you again."

I looked up and saw that I was alone.

I didn't want to listen to him. I wanted to stay in the Seven Mountains in a cave with a teacher. I decided to find another teacher who was like Fourth Uncle.

I went to Long Mountain and went into several caves, but they were dirty with bats. I discovered a cave that I couldn't get into, because it was a deep black hole without any bottom that I could see.

I went to the market and bought a long rope to lower myself into the cave. I tied one end of the rope to a tree and dropped the rope down into the dark. I climbed down with a lighted candle in one hand, but I was nervous. I could be intruding on a cloud snake, a tiger, a herd of pigs, or even a pocket of ghosts. I lowered myself into the darkness, paying close attention to any scent that wafted upward that might give me a clue of what was down there.

I reached the floor and found nothing. The cavern was high and wide. I knelt and prayed to the spirit of the mountain to help me find a teacher. I stood up, chose a direction, and went exploring. There were many tunnels. At one point I found another hole that went up to the surface. I saw that the sides of the hole were covered with big fruit bats. I found another hole where the sun was streaming down. I lay down and looked up at the trees high above me. I ate some peanut-sesame meal from my medicine bag and fell asleep. When I woke up I ran to where I had climbed down, afraid that if someone had taken my rope I would have no way of getting out. Luckily it was still there.

I went to another mountain called Nui Ba Doi Ong, Old Lady's Hat Mountain. People had told me it was full of caves, but the animals there attacked people. I decided to try there anyway. On my way up the mountain, I saw a lot of Cambodians gathering food and chopping firewood in the forest. I didn't see any Vietnamese, which frightened me. I passed some people on the path. When I was past their line of sight, I ran into the jungle. I prayed for the spirits to protect me and lead me to a new teacher. The jungle was so dense that I lost my bearings and wandered around lost for three days before finding the road.

I went to visit Ong Nam for a few days. I told him how tired I was and how much I wanted to find a new teacher and stay in a cave.

He listened and then he said, "I have never heard of anyone except your grandfather who had the good fortune of finding a teacher like Fourth Uncle. Luck like that doesn't come to many of us."

I tried one more time to find a teacher in a cave. I went to Sam Mountain. There are men and women in the forest there who live in little shacks and pray for people. I thought one of them might know of a cave on Sam Mountain.

It was a long walk to get to the first hut. By the time I got there, I was very thirsty. The woman inside the first hut prayed for me and gave me a cup of water. I drank it down and waited while she prayed some more. Before I had a chance to ask her about a cave, I felt drowsy. I couldn't resist lying down for a little nap. When I woke up, the woman was gone and so was my money.

On the bus back to Cai Be, I thought about what Fourth Uncle had told me about going away. The only places I could think of were Da Nang and Hanoi, but I didn't think things would be any different in Central and North Vietnam.

My aunt died a year later, in the winter of 1985. She left me five gold rings. One year after that, Tam, a friend of my father's, came to see me when I was spending the night at my patient's house in Vinh Long. He said he wanted to talk to me privately about something. When I was finished with my patients, we went for a walk. He kept looking around to make sure we were alone.

Tam told me that he was planning to escape to Thailand. He said the Communist Party had taken away his bakery business and his house as part of their policy of redistributing the wealth and punishing those who were loyal to the other side. Tam said he had no reason to stay in Vietnam. Most of his family had been killed. He wanted to live with his relatives in Canada. He said once he was living in Canada, he could send for his wife. It would be much safer that way.

Tam stopped and looked around to make sure no one was listening. "I am looking for more people," he said. "It takes a lot of money. You have to pay a lot of people along the way."

The thought of leaving Vietnam had never occurred to me. I told Tam I would think about it.

I had promised my father that I would continue to practice medicine the way he taught me, but I was tired of living in hiding. I wanted to be able to live with my wife in a house where I could work and pray and meditate. Maybe that would only be possible outside Vietnam. Maybe my father and Fourth Uncle were telling me that I would go overseas to a free country.

It was dangerous to try to escape. People who were caught were sent to a labor camp or prison. They said that life in prison was much worse under the Communists than it had ever been under the former government, or even the French.

People were telling stories about Vietnamese people who make a business out of helping people escape. These people are really pirates. They collect the money, take the people out to sea, shoot them, dump them overboard, wash out the boat, and then come back for more people. If they don't want to get their boat dirty, they bring the people to one of the islands and tell them they can get some food and water. When the people climb out of the boat and start wading toward the shore, they all get swallowed up in quicksand.

Even if you go in your own boat, it is easy for a storm to blow you off course. If you drift too far south, it is likely that you will die of dehydration before reaching Malaysia. If you are lost at sea, your only chance of survival is to be rescued by a passing ship. There are also plenty of sea pirates looking for Vietnamese boat people to rob and kill.

In spite of the danger, it became clear to me that I had to leave Vietnam and go to a free country. I gave Tam two gold rings to pay for my forged paperwork. I decided to leave Mai behind and to send for her later. I thought it would be too risky to tell Mai about my plan. She would tell her mother, her sisters, and Ba Tam, and someone might overhear them. There were informants in every village. Even longtime neighbors and friends had become wary of one another.

In February 1987, Tam said he had enough people to make it work. Everyone had to chip in four gold rings or the equivalent amount of gold to pay for paperwork, for people to hide us in their boats and homes, and finally for buying a fishing boat and outboard motor.

We were five men, two women, and one eight-year-old boy. One of the women was a high-ranking Communist official in her late twenties. We met at eight o'clock at the Vinh Long market on March 17, 1987. It was a good time to leave, because during February and March the winds blow westward toward Thailand.

Our group gathered in front of a noodle shop. We sat at a large table and ate breakfast together and introduced ourselves. Everyone was nervous.

I brought only a few things that could be carried in my pocket: some money, three gold rings, my father's prayer beads, and two of his medicine books in which I wrote some of magic charms used for blessings and protection.

Tam showed us our work permits, which certified that we had been hired to work at a Vietnamese-owned furniture factory on the island of Ko Kung in Cambodia. One of the factory owners, a young man named Thanh, was going to escape with us. Thanh knew people on the island and was waiting for our gold to trade for a fishing boat and an outboard motor. Tam told us that we were only going to use our work permits as a last resort, because they weren't perfect.

We left the market in a ferryboat with about one hundred other people. Only twenty of the hundred passengers were planning to escape. This boat sailed up the Mekong River all the way into Cambodia. Tam had paid the captain of the boat to let us off the boat before all four checkpoints. We had to walk in the forest past each checkpoint and hurry to the next village, where the boat would be waiting for us. Sometimes the captain waited up to an hour for us to get there. I didn't hear any of the passengers complain about it. I am grateful to them for that.

It wasn't easy to find the next village because we were walking in the jungle, and the river did not run in a straight line. Sometimes we had to roll up our pants and wade through a swamp or go through some dense brush. We took turns holding the boy on our backs. People were afraid of stepping on a poisonous snake. One time some Cambodian soldiers heard us and knew we were escaping. We feared the worst, but instead they helped us and showed us the way to the next village. We gave them cigarettes for their help.

At the end of the ferry ride, we found ourselves in a small city in Cambodia. A Vietnamese man met us at the ferry station, identified himself to us, and took us to his house. We hid there for five days until we could catch a bus to the port town of Ruong Mui, where we would be taking the ferry to Ko Kung Island.

Both Cambodian and Vietnamese music was coming from the neighbors' houses. We hadn't heard popular music in twelve years, since the Communists took over the government in 1975. I was in hiding, but I felt good because I could hear the sound of freedom just outside the door.

During the bus trip to Ruong Mui, we had to show our paperwork at a checkpoint. Everyone was nervous, but we made it through. That was a relief, but we still had to pass through the territory of a notorious gang of renegade Khmer Rouge soldiers who launched missiles at buses from behind the trees. Luckily, there were no missiles.

The ferryman had been paid to hide us on his ship. There were so many Vietnamese people escaping through Ruong Mui that the police searched every ship. He hid us under sacks of rice. We had to lie there for two hours. I heard the police searching the boat. I don't know why they didn't find us.

Once we reached Ko Kung Island, we were taken to another house where we met Thanh and gave him our gold.

After three days, rumors were going around that Thanh was planning an escape. The person who was hiding us felt nervous. Thanh had to spend more time and money to find another house for us to hide in. Tam had become so afraid that he had changed his mind and wanted to go back to Vietnam. He didn't want to leave us behind because if we were caught and sent to prison, it would be his fault.

Thanh brought us to a house that stood on stilts over the harbor. He was happy about the location because he said it would be easier for us to escape. We could look down through the floorboards and see garbage floating in the water. Half-eaten cookies and rolls, tangles of noodles, and candy wrappers were riding on the waves. It looked as if people had enough to eat. It felt like freedom. I was so happy to feel freedom all around me that I wanted more. I wasn't thinking of turning back. Tam felt differently. He wanted to go home.

We talked together during most of the night. Tam was the only one who felt strongly about turning back. The rest of us didn't know what to do. In the end, Tam was the only one who had a change of heart.

I walked with Tam to the ferry. We didn't see any police. We walked through a market, and I bought a new shirt and put it on. Then I put some things inside my old shirt and tied it into a bundle.

"Will you take this to my wife?" I asked Tam.

He said he would.

In Vietnam, men call their wives *em*, which means "little sister." I had written a note for Mai. It said, "*Em,* I went to the mountain, and then I escaped to Thailand. I was in a hurry and didn't have enough time to let you know. Please forgive me. When I get to a free country I will send for you. Don't worry. Quang." I also put some other things inside the shirt—my watch, my last gold ring, and a new plastic zipper that I had found lying in the street. I knew Mai liked to sew.

52

WOMAN IN THE WAVES

We didn't know what was happening with Thanh, because he hadn't come to see us in two days. The last time we saw him, he told us he was waiting for the outboard motor to arrive on the ferry.

We were starting to get worried that he had been arrested, but he showed up late the next night. Thanh rowed our fishing boat up to the house. He tied it to the poles and climbed up the ladder to wake us up. Thanh was wearing the kind of dirty old clothes that fishermen wear. Hong, one of the men in our group, a university professor from Vinh Long, volunteered to be the other fisherman, and he put on the other set of fisherman's clothes.

We climbed as quietly as possible down the ladder and stepped into the boat. It was about twenty feet long and five feet wide. A massive fishing net took up most of the space inside the boat. The rest of us hid under the damp, smelly net.

Thanh told us the police had been looking for him. He had wanted to buy a gun and get more food and water, but he didn't dare to go out. Instead of waiting one or two more days, he decided to leave as soon as he got the motor. We only had one gallon of water and a few packages of cookies and crackers.

Hong and Thanh each took an oar, rowed our boat out into the bay, and started the motor for the first time. We all felt happy that it worked. Other fishing boats were in the harbor, so we didn't stand out.

It takes ten hours to get to Thailand by boat if you go in one straight line between the islands, where the pirates waited. We couldn't afford to sail that close to shore because of the pirates and the patrol boats, so we headed farther out to sea. We thought it would take us about twenty-four hours to reach Thailand.

We had to pass through one checkpoint in the harbor between two patrol boats. Six of us were lying underneath the nets. Thanh nodded to the crews of both coast guard ships. I prayed that the guards didn't ask him any questions. Thanh spoke a little Cambodian, but probably not enough to fool the guards. The guards clicked their spotlights on and aimed them at our fishing net. They let us pass.

Once we were out at sea, Thanh told us to come out and look at the beautiful night sky. There were some dark clouds, but we could see enough stars to know which direction was west.

We had only been sailing for three hours when our motor started shaking. We saw that one of the bolts that was holding the motor to the boat had come off. Then another bolt came off. Hong took the wire from around a handheld fishing net and tried to secure the motor, but it didn't work. Hong and Thanh held the motor and tried to keep it steady, but the crankshaft hit against the boat so many times that it cracked, and the propeller stopped moving. Now we were at the mercy of the currents and the wind. We were worried that we were still close enough to Ko Kung Island for the tide to push us back.

We took turns rowing with the oars while the rest of us leaned over and used our hands to paddle. Just as we had feared, the current carried us inland. We were heading toward the great hulking shape of a mountain standing up in the sea.

We had to work very hard for our boat not to be drawn ashore, but we made it. We paddled by two more islands before getting our boat back out of sight, on the open sea. We were thankful for not running into any pirates, but we were exhausted from staying up all night. We had used up all our food and had managed to save a little water.

We paddled all the next day under the hot sun and had finished the water. We were more hopeful that evening when the wind came up, because it would push the boat toward Thailand.

We rested for an hour, and then started raining. There were two soldiers' helmets onboard. (That was what fishermen used to bail water out of their boats.) We set them out to collect some rainwater to drink. Before we could take even one sip, black and purple storm clouds covered the sky. It was if they were at war with one another, sending bolts of lightning that crashed in our ears. The waves grew so high around us that they were breaking over our boat. Thanh and Hong grabbed the helmets and began bailing out the water. The rest of us used our hands.

Our boat rode waves that were so steep and high that it seemed at times that our boat was standing on end. The rain was so heavy that it was difficult to see what was happening. We tried not to fall out of the boat while we were bailing out the water.

At one point during the storm I looked over the boat and saw a woman standing in the water, as if the ocean were only chest deep. She was bare-breasted and had long wet hair. She motioned with her hand for me to come with her.

I thought for sure that we were going to die, because she must have been a spirit coming to help our souls find our way to heaven.

I pointed to the woman in the ocean and asked some other people in the boat if they could see her. They said they couldn't. Then I thought that I was going to be tossed out of the boat alone.

Slowly, the storm subsided. All we knew was that we were still alive and that we were somewhere out at sea. We knew which way was west, but we had no way of knowing how far we were from Thailand.

We fell asleep for the rest of the night, our second night on the ocean. We were weak from exertion and dehydration.

By early dawn, we woke up and saw a boat in the distance. We were both happy and frightened, because it could be a patrol boat or a pirate ship. We needed water so desperately that we had no choice but to wave our shirts and call attention to ourselves.

Fishermen usually carry guns in case of pirates, but Thanh hadn't had time to buy one. We prayed as the boat drew nearer. It looked like a Thai fishing trawler, but it could have been pirates who had stolen a trawler. Of the five men standing on deck, two aimed machine guns at us.

We held out our helmets and pantomimed that we were thirsty. We heard stories that pirates first give you food and water to throw you off your guard, and then they kill the men and take the women.

We waited like that, holding out our helmets, wondering what they were going to do.

One of them took a jug and held it over one of the helmets and started pouring water into it. We passed it around while he filled the other helmet. They pointed in the direction they had come from. They engaged their motor and left us. We were very relieved.

The wind was strong that morning, and it helped us as we paddled our boat. By late afternoon, we saw an island that we presumed was in Thailand. We all prayed to thank Buddha that we hadn't been blown off course by the storm.

As we drew closer, we passed two empty fishing boats. By sundown we landed on the Thai island of Cotsan. People there welcomed us. They were Thai, but some of them knew a little Vietnamese. They took us to a community building that was just a thatched roof supported on logs. We sat on mats, and they brought us food and water. While we were eating, they kept saying, "You are lucky, very lucky."

A man told us, "Yesterday, the Thailand police would have killed you. For many months, the coast guard police have been taking Vietnamese boat people out to sea and shooting them."

We didn't understand.

A woman tried to explain more. "Starting today they will bring you to the refugee camp. Don't worry. You are safe now, and very lucky."

We remembered the empty boats drifting on the water. We wondered what would have happened if our motor hadn't broken down. We felt lucky but also very sad for the ones who came before.

As we expected, we were taken to the Chambouri Refugee Camp in Pannatnikhom City on mainland Thailand.

We were happy to see that it was very crowded with Vietnamese people. When we talked to them, we found out that most of them had been in the camp from three to seven years. No new refugees had come to the camp in many months. We told them what the Thai islanders had told us. Everyone was shocked.

I lived in the camp for more than two years. There were eighteen thousand refugees when I arrived and thirty thousand by the time I was transferred to another camp in the Philippines. Most of the refugees were Vietnamese, but there were also many Cambodians, Laotians, and Chinese.

This camp was dirty, and there was very little food to eat. The toilet was a long open trench of human waste that was always overflowing. Rats and mice climbed in and out of the trench and ran over us at night, sometimes biting us. Many people became ill with dysentery, fevers, and infections.

At first I was assigned to pumping the waste out of the trenches and cleaning the bathroom. After four months, they let me work in the health clinic, doing wound care. I worked in the mornings cleaning children's wounds and applying antibiotic ointment and bandages.

Many people had money in the camp. Ba Tam's son who lived in California wired me one hundred dollars through the American Embassy. In the afternoon, I started seeing patients at my bed area. I read their pulses and prescribed medicine for them to cook. People gave me money for medicine, and I gave it to one of the women who came to sell things at the market. She went to a Chinese herbal store in Bangkok to purchase my order. I paid her for this service.

I had many patients in the refugee camp.

I was able to write to Mai and receive mail from her. She told me that she had tried to escape a few months after I did, but her group was caught at the Cambodian border. The border police confiscated all their belongings and detained them for three days before allowing only the women to go home. The men were sent to prison.

Mai wrote that the border police gave her back her money and her gold, but they kept my father's black stone Buddha. She also let me know that the Tiger had taken the three gold Buddhas from the house in Cay Lay for safekeeping. He tried to keep them safe, but shortly afterward they were stolen.

I was transferred to Morong Bataan refugee camp in the Philippines on June 26, 1989. Two weeks after I arrived, I was called for an interview with a Canadian woman who worked at the Canadian Embassy. She asked me questions through an interpreter. I wasn't accepted into Canada.

One month later, I was called for an interview with someone from the American Embassy. I didn't understand why they called my name, because I was never a soldier. At the end of my interview, the interpreter told me that the immigration officer was impressed that I knew how to write *Han Viet*. He said that I had passed the interview and that I had been accepted to immigrate to America.

Nobody in the camp believed that I had been accepted by the United States because they only accepted soldiers. Two months later, my name appeared on the list that was posted on the bulletin board. Then people believed me.

In November, I boarded an airplane to California with fifty other refugees from my camp. Of the fifty of us, I was the only one who had a connecting flight to Concord, New Hampshire.

COAUTHOR'S NOTE:
THE MAKING OF THIS BOOK

f I had crossed paths with Quang in a public place, I doubt I would have noticed him at all. It could be the slightness of his stature or his shyness, but I think it's probably because he is the most humble person I ever met. His type of humility makes him practically invisible.

Quang was delivered into my life in a blue Volvo sedan, when my husband's best friend, Jared, brought him to our house to go on a ginseng walk. This was in August 1992, just weeks before I discovered that my nine-year-old son, Jovi, was ill.

Jared met Quang through his friend Jade Ngoc Hunyh, a Vietnamese refugee who was a student at the same college where Jared taught music lessons. Jade was working in Concord, New Hampshire, as a housing coordinator for other Vietnamese refugees. He was assigned to find housing for Quang, and after meeting him asked his American wife if Quang could live in their home in Vermont.

Shortly after Quang moved in, he started building birdhouses with whatever materials he could find. Before long, Jade's yard was a watering hole for birds. One evening, when Jared stayed for dinner, Quang went outside and dug up a jar that he had buried in the backyard. It was wine infused with strengthening herbs. Quang commented that it would be stronger if it was left underground for many years, but he wanted to share it with his first American friend. Jared looked out at the yard and wondered what else was buried out there.

Jared made plans to take Quang to his land to show him the native medicinal plants. He was looking forward to comparing notes about herbal medicine.

A few days later, my husband received a call from Jared.

"Derrik, I have met the most amazing person. He knows more about herbal medicine than all my books put together. He told me all this amazing stuff, though it is really hard to understand him. He works as an orderly in the old age home, but he sounds like some kind of spiritual master or shaman. My friend Jade told me his father was a highly respected monk in South Vietnam."

I winced as Jared's heavy old car banged and rattled over the washboard section of our driveway. Jared got out of the car first, followed by Jade, who started right in breaking the ice, chatting comfortably in English. I realized that I had never listened to a Vietnamese accent before. Normally, I would have been thrilled to speak with such an interesting, handsome, and charming man, but my attention kept wandering. I could hardly restrain myself from getting a look at the person who was still sitting in the backseat.

I watched as Quang climbed out of the car and stood awkwardly in the driveway. I left the others and walked around to the other side of the car to meet him. He was very slight of build and, apart from his Adam's apple, looked more like a boy than a man. His shiny black hair was combed very neatly to the side. He was wearing a pressed yellow shirt that was buttoned at the collar and tucked into black trousers. I had never seen an adult whose eyes were as clear and tender as a child's. His face had that same quality. As soon as I perceived Quang's shyness, I made a conscious effort not to probe.

During our meal, Jade told us about his good fortune. He was going to graduate from an American college, his wife was expecting their first child, and he had just finished writing his autobiography, *South Wind Changing*.

It started to rain, so we decided to postpone the walk. The three friends left after lunch. Quang didn't say a word the whole time.

. . .

Jared brought Quang back to our house the following week. During our outing in the woods, Quang stopped to see, smell, and taste many plants. He walked along the path like a sprite and approached the plants with tenderness and respect.

You had to be practically telepathic to understand Quang's attempt at speaking English. He told me that he was a doctor in Vietnam and that he practiced herbal medicine and acupuncture.

He showed me which plants were good for medicine. He was eager to see the plants growing on top of the mountain because, he explained, plants that can withstand low temperatures are more powerful. I was surprised when he said that 70 percent of the plants he has seen in Vermont grow also in Vietnam.

My husband dug out a large and beautiful ginseng root and presented it to Quang. Then Quang took out of his pocket a red cloth bundle and carefully unwrapped it. Inside were three ginseng roots. They were dried and preserved, but they were not wrinkled and did not appear to be dehydrated. He took out a pocketknife and cut a few slices for us to try. The roots had a translucent quality and tasted fresh even though they were bone dry.

Then something happened in which all at once I understood Jared's excitement about meeting Quang. We were on top of the mountain and Quang started talking about tigers. It was strange to start talking about tigers in Vermont. Perhaps he thought we might come across a tiger. I struggled to understand what he was trying to say. I thought he was saying, "If you ever see a tiger, the first thing you have to do is to take off your shirt while facing him. Then take three steps backward. Never turn your back on a tiger." Jared gave me a "Now do you see what I mean?" look.

Three weeks later, our son Jovi was not well. A pain that he had been complaining about in his right hip had now become excruciating. I took him to every kind of doctor in my area, but none were successful in diagnosing or treating him. I decided to take him to Quang.

As soon as we entered the house, I recognized the musky smell of Chinese medicinal herbs. The house was clean, tidy, and sparsely furnished. Quang took our coats and then sat down behind a card table and waited for my son to sit opposite him. On the table was what appeared to be a paperback book covered up in a little red cloth pillowcase. Quang placed Jovi's hand, palm up, on the cloth-covered book. He then traced an invisible line on his skin before placing his own three fingers on my son's upturned wrist.

Quang began to read my son's pulses. Something made me avert my eyes from Quang's face. He was concentrating so hard on what he was doing that he had abandoned his self-consciousness and was vulnerable to my scrutiny. To this day I never look at Quang's face when he is reading pulses.

Afterward he drew a few Chinese characters in a spiral notebook. "Ma-jy . . . sorry," he said. "Your son is very sick. He has an infection." He went on speaking. I understood him to mean that germs had entered my son's body by mouth and then went into his bloodstream. They became trapped in his hip area, because he had a bad bruise there. Quang drew a picture of the femoral artery at the front of the hip. He also drew a picture of the inside of the hip joint and indicated that the germs had spread from the artery into the joint capsule and had damaged and infected the cartilage. He said natural medicine was not strong enough. He told me to go to the hospital and get "pharmacy medicine."

We took my son to New York's Mount Sinai Hospital. After an MRI and a CAT scan we were told my son had a seven-inch-long tumor in his femur.

The doctor scheduled a biopsy and a bone transplant to take place in two days. During surgery, they opened his femur and to their surprise, there was no sign of a tumor. The bone transplant was not performed. The surgeon did see degeneration of the cartilage and took a sample for a biopsy.

The biopsy did not indicate an infection was present. My son's doctor transferred the case to the department of joint diseases. The head of the department diagnosed my son as having a type of degenerative autoimmune arthritis. The doctor explained, "Your son's joints will continue to deteriorate as he grows older. The only thing we can do for him is to give him cortisone and other steroids to diminish the pain and swelling."

I was suspicious of this diagnosis, not only because of Quang's explanation, but because I was given a checklist of the symptoms associated with this disease. I checked off very few of the associated symptoms. I told the doctors that the profile did not seem to fit my son's symptoms, but they didn't consider this observation to be relevant. I refused to give my son the prescribed drugs.

I was convinced that our doctors at Mount Sinai had misdiagnosed my son. I had no evidence they were wrong except Quang's evaluation. A few tense days went by. Jovi was still in the hospital recovering from the exploratory surgery.

Meanwhile, in Rio de Janeiro, Jovi's Uncle Henrique heard of the standoff at Mount Sinai. His partner at work had a son with a similar-sounding problem.

Henrique arranged for the doctor of the Brazilian boy to send a case history to our doctors in New York.

My son's case was then transferred again, to the infectious disease department, to Dr. Vicky. After running the tests that were recommended by the Brazilian doctor, Dr. Vicky discovered that my son had tuberculosis of the bone. His was the only case ever reported in the United States.

Tuberculosis is treatable with very strong antibiotics, taken without missing a day for one or two years, providing it is not a drug-resistant strain.

I have learned recently that bone tuberculosis is not uncommon among children of developing nations. In Russia there is a bone TB ward in every major city. I am sorry to say that many of these infected children live at the hospital for years until they die. What makes this disease so serious is that if it is not caught in its early stages, the germs will penetrate deep into the bone, where the antibiotics are not able to stop them.

If I had accepted my doctors' diagnosis at the hospital and had treated my son with painkillers and anti-inflammatory drugs, the tuberculosis infection would have become untreatable.

Out of respect and gratitude to Quang for the role he played in my son's full recovery, I decided to help him bring his wife to this country from Vietnam. He had filed papers for her as soon as he immigrated to the United States. Four years had gone by and she was still on a waiting list. He was doubtful she would ever obtain permission to leave Vietnam. After all, he left illegally, as a boat person. During those four years of waiting and working as an orderly at an old age home, he had been sending her money to pay certain "fees" that the Vietnamese immigration officials required. For this reason, Quang believed the officers in her district had a strong incentive to keep her in Vietnam.

It took four years of unrelenting persistence and the help of Congressman Bernie Sanders and Senator James Jeffords of Vermont to get Mai out of Vietnam and into the United States. After nine years of separation, Mai and Quang were finally reunited.

Never before had I invested so much time and effort to help a friend as during those four years of making phone calls and writing letters to Vietnamese emigration officials. Quang had almost given up hope of having his wife join him in America.

At first I didn't know whether to believe some of the things he told me, that his grandfather discovered an old monk inside a cave in the late 1860s, who was the same monk Quang lived with in the cave in 1970, and last visited in 1986. Assuming the old monk was fifty years old in 1868, that would make him 168 years old in 1986. Quang also told me that he became the abbot of a Buddhist temple when he was only twenty-three years old.

As the years went by, I noticed that Quang spoke of these things only to those he considered his closest friends. Quang won my trust and respect through his extraordinary skill as a diagnostician and healer. There were others whose trust he won. Paul Scott and his wife, Joan Fish, made it possible for Quang's dream to come true, to live with his wife in their own house. They also helped Quang establish himself as a certified acupuncturist and doctor of herbal medicine in the state of Vermont.

All of Quang's new patients found him through word of mouth. Many of them were among those whose medical problems could not be resolved through the American health care system. Quang has been able to help many of these people become well again.

One day I asked him if I could record his story for a book. I was truly surprised that he agreed. I wanted to verify his story and to understand it as much as possible. I began reading many books on Vietnamese culture and history.

In my research, I was fortunate to find an out-of-print a book written by the current head of Harvard University's South East Asian Department, Professor Hue-Tam Ho Tai. Reading her book was like opening the window onto Quang's life. I learned more about the fabled Seven Sacred Mountains, the history of Quang's religion, To Thay, the Buddha Master of Western Peace, the enchanted forbidden mountain, and Vietnamese popular beliefs about spirits and magic. It wasn't until I read Ho Tai's book that I understood the significance of Quang's story as the documentation of a bygone culture.

I am grateful to Quang for sharing his story. By choice, he leads a very quiet life practicing traditional herbal medicine in his modest home in Vermont and relaxing with his wife on weekends. He would say he has had enough excitement for this lifetime. Now he craves peace and simplicity. He left Vietnam so that he could practice medicine according to his spiritual beliefs in the tradition of his father and grandfather.

I believe the medical and spiritual achievements of the old Vietnamese culture must be documented, just as the civil liberties of my own culture should be remembered, to serve as testaments to our human potential.

Quang cherishes his newly found peace and freedom in the United States. He always tells me that I don't know how lucky I am to know peace all my life.

One last thing—of course I asked Quang to show me some sorcery. He said he gave that up long ago, and besides, it would cause bad karma for me as well as for him. I have heard from Quang's patients and friends that the magic is still happening in quieter ways.

七山玄妖

院々虔